INTERNATIONAL TURNAROUND MANAGEMENT

International Turnaround Management

From Crisis to Revival and Long-term Profitability

Bo Arpi

with

Per Wejke

MACMILLAN
Business

First published 1999 by
MACMILLAN PRESS LTD
Houndmills, Basingstoke, Hampshire RG21 6XS
and London
Companies and representatives
throughout the world

ISBN 0–333–79425–7 hardcover

A catalogue record for this book is available
from the British Library.

This book is printed on paper suitable for recycling and
made from fully managed and sustained forest sources.

10 9 8 7 6 5 4 3 2 1
08 07 06 05 04 03 02 01 00 99

Editing and origination by
Aardvark Editorial, Mendham, Suffolk

Printed and bound in Great Britain by
Creative Print & Design (Wales), Ebbw Vale

This book is dedicated to the memory of Professor Ulf af Trolle
...esteemed teacher, tough boss, inimitable example and admired turnaround artist

Contents

Preface   viii

Acknowledgements   xii

Part I
On the Driving Range: Principles and Techniques

1 International turnaround management: definition, purpose, symptoms and trends   3

  1.1   What is 'turnaround management'?   3

  1.2   Turnaround-like activities triggered by acquisitions, mergers and privatizations   6

  1.3   Domestic turnarounds versus international turnarounds   7

  1.4   Main thrust and boundaries of this book   14

  1.5   The book's primary target groups   15

  1.6   Painting the turnaround stage: 22 common symptoms   16

  1.7   Preventive medicine, radical surgery or voluntary death   21

  1.8   Desirable changes indicated by the listed symptoms   23

  1.9   The disposition: two main parts, fourteen chapters of which six represent in-depth cases   27

2 Different kinds of turnaround situation   32

  2.1   Purpose of chapter   32

  2.2   The immediate cash crisis ('10 days from sudden death')   34

     2.2.1   If the climate allows, do your homework first!   34

     2.2.2   When there is simply no time for extensive homework   34

     2.2.3   Asset disposal to raise cash   36

     2.2.4   Summary as to urgency   37

  2.3   The unprofitable subsidiary (with headquarters functioning as the rather friendly and patient banker)   38

     Summary   40

  2.4   Cost cutting and downsizing versus volume-improving or margin-improving marketing solutions   40

     2.4.1   Cost cutting is not the only way to improved profits   40

2.4.2	A volume-increasing solution	41
2.4.3	'One Step Up' – a new profit improvement method	41
2.4.4	Where to place the emphasis	44
2.5	**The leadership difference**	**45**
2.6	**The importance of the country in which the turnaround takes place**	**49**

3 Overview of the different steps involved in most turnarounds **54**

3.1	**Purpose of chapter**	**54**
3.2	**Discussions before accepting the turnaround assignment**	**55**
3.3	**'Homework' before arriving on company premises**	**57**
3.4	**Establishing numerical benchmarks**	**60**
3.5	**Four types of cash-flow calculation**	**60**
3.6	**Taking charge and confronting the troops while sending symbolic signals**	**62**
3.7	**Establishing a tighter set of cost and payment controls**	**65**
3.8	**Liquidifying the balance sheet, also by asset sales**	**67**
3.9	**Learning by systematically following a cross-functional trail**	**68**
3.10	**Defining the Business Mission and the Blueprint for the Future Company**	**68**
3.11	**Gaining acceptance and formal approval of the turnaround plan**	**70**
3.12	**Implementing the plan with ruthless determination**	**71**
3.13	**Chronology of actions and the overall time-frame**	**73**
3.14	**Chapter summary and the links to subsequent chapters**	**76**

4 'When Cash is King': squeezing the balance sheet for cash **79**

4.1	**Top priority: cash, manpower reduction or profit improvement?**	**79**
4.2	**Selling different kinds of assets on a fire sale basis**	**82**
4.3	**The selling of a complete SBU**	**84**
4.4	**Five examples of activities spun off in major turnaround situations**	**88**
4.5	**The 'selling' of Société Générale de Belgique, Belgium's largest industrial holding**	**90**
4.6	**Freeing up cash tied up in receivables overdue**	**93**
4.7	**Freeing up cash tied up in inventories**	**96**
	4.7.1 Cash tied up in purchased goods or WIP	96

4.7.2 Cash through improved inventory turns of finished goods 97
4.7.3 Other positive spin-offs from bringing down inventory levels 98

4.8 Stretching vendor credits, whenever possible 99

4.9 Freeing up cash by renegotiation of loans and repayment schemes 100

4.10 Quantifying the cash needs and the urgency 101

4.11 Creditors watching the debt ratio and coverage ratio 106

5 The Blueprint for the Future Company, quantitative benchmarks and choice of strategy 108

5.1 Purpose, contents and structure of this chapter 108

5.2 Meaning and function of the Blueprint for the Future Company 109

5.3 Blueprint compared to Business Mission, and other terms and concepts 111

5.4 Current status, key trends and benchmarked goals 115

5.5 Four more aspects of the Blueprint, needing a reality check 118

5.6 Productivity benchmarking and value benchmarking 121
5.6.1 The relation between productivity and value 121
5.6.2 Productivity benchmarking 123
5.6.3 Examples of profitability benchmarks for selected industries 126
5.6.4 Value benchmarking: two real-life examples 130

5.7 Cross-border 'value' benchmarking to aid the choice of strategy 131

5.8 'Distinctiveness', seen as an alternative to ruthless cost-cutting or lower unit costs through acquisition of more critical mass 133

5.9 More on 'cost leadership' versus 'superior value' companies 135

5.10 How to avoid being a 'me-too', 'stuck-in-the-middle' company 137

5.11 Company size and strategic emphasis 139

5.12 Implementation planning, including the allocation of responsibilities 141

6 Rebuilding the new management team and creating a new team spirit 143

6.1 Purpose of chapter 143

6.2 'Movers and shakers', 'empty sacks' and 'snails gaining speed' 145

6.3	**Who to fire early on, why and how**	**146**
6.4	**Early actions with high 'symbolic value'**	**148**
6.5	**Building the new management team: what is meant by 'new'?**	**150**
6.6	**Motivating the new management team**	**153**
6.7	**Evaluating the interim management team**	**156**
6.8	**Motivational problems after a merger, perhaps over country borders and involving several cultures**	**158**
	Six pieces of post-merger advice	**158**
6.9	**Advice to a turnaround manager running a recently acquired company**	**161**
6.10	**Enjoy the turnaround, but leave when the job is concluded!**	**165**
7	Where to get plan input data	**167**
7.1	**Purpose and contents of this chapter**	**167**
7.2	**The most obvious in-house sources**	**169**
7.2.1	Internal accounting data	170
7.2.2	The controller: a reliable source, or part of the problem?	172
7.2.3	The business plan and other strategic documents	174
7.2.4	Acting as cross-functional trail-blazer and detective	176
7.3	**Employees as key sources**	**177**
7.3.1	One-on-one interviews	177
7.3.2	Group discussions	181
7.3.3	The individual assignment	184
7.3.4	The group assignment	185
7.3.5	Individuals not working for the troubled company	186
7.3.6	Learning from 'management by walking around'	186
7.4	**External information sources: an introduction**	**187**
7.4.1	Tailor-made market research and competitive studies	189
7.4.2	Purchase of existing market research studies	189
7.4.3	Using charge-free Internet information versus more professional databases	198
7.4.4	Market and competitive information available on CD-ROM	202
7.5	**Other data-gathering sources and techniques**	**205**
8	'Penetrating the fog': activity-based costing (ABC) in three turnaround situations	**211**
8.1	**'Capacity demands' put on the company**	**211**
8.2	**A definition of activity-based costing**	**212**

8.3   **A more complex analytical model accommodating many product/market segments and multiple profit contribution levels**   213

8.4   **Advantages of 'bottom up' costing instead of 'top down' costing**   220

8.5   **ABC techniques applied to a national warehouse operator for metal products**   222

8.6   **Using ABC analysis to evaluate managerial performance in a turnaround**   225

8.7   **Application of ABC-based simulation techniques to the automotive aftermarket**   227
    8.7.1   Piecing together an excessively fragmented cost/revenue puzzle   228
    8.7.2   Pinpointing and measuring 'organizational tension' within a distribution chain   229

8.8   **Complete computer simulation of a troubled company, all its distribution channels and product lines**   233

8.9   **A marine satellite communication case**   235

8.10 **Summary of the practical usefulness of ABC-related techniques**   237

8.11 **Are ABC analyses worthwhile in a typical turnaround situation?**   238

8.12 **Do the time pressures allow ABC studies?**   240

8.13 **Living happily without consultants and advanced analytical techniques?**   241

Part II
'Taking it to the Course': Six Complete Turnaround Cases

9   The Allgon Case Study   **246**

List of Contents   **246**

Introduction   **247**

9.1   **The company's development up to 1990**   **248**

9.2   **The troublesome situation in 1991**   **249**
    9.2.1   The Orbitel debacle   249
    9.2.2   The US subsidiary debacle   250
    9.2.3   Friction with the part-owners of a jointly owned German sales company   250
    9.2.4   The 1991 situation: a summary   251

9.3	**Functional analysis of Allgon's problems**	**252**
	9.3.1 An old company faced with a young company's problems	252
	9.3.2 Management and organization	252
	9.3.3 Foreign sales and production companies	253
	9.3.4 Market contacts and market know-how	253
	9.3.5 Product programme evaluation	254
	9.3.6 Administrative procedures and information flow	255
9.4	**Problem awareness within the organization itself**	**255**
	9.4.1 The old president's viewpoint	255
	9.4.2 Attitudes among headquarters' staff	256
	9.4.3 The board's view	256
9.5	**Management change and the first strategic moves**	**257**
	9.5.1 Profile of the new president	257
	9.5.2 Priority 1: cleaning up after the Orbitel disaster	257
	9.5.3 Appointing a new head of the systems division	257
	9.5.4 The new group management team	258
9.6	**Changes in the organizational structure**	**258**
	9.6.1 Clarification of responsibilities and performance evaluation criteria	258
	9.6.2 New reporting relationships for the foreign sales companies	259
	9.6.3 Analysis and paralysis versus decisive actions	259
9.7	**Marketing and customer contacts**	**260**
9.8	**Improving the product programmes of the two divisions**	**261**
9.9	**More rapid decision-making**	**261**
9.10	**Performance diagrams showing this turnaround's impact on sales, profits, and so on**	**262**
	Notes	**263**
10	The ESAB Group restructuring the European welding industry	**265**
	List of Contents	**265**
	Background	**267**
10.1	**Industry-wide overcapacity in a not particularly price-sensitive market**	**268**
10.2	**The four phases of the turnaround, using Igor Ansoff's growth matrix**	**269**
10.3	**Overview of the 12-step strategy used**	**271**
	10.3.1 Step 1: 'Kill all lingering hopes'	271

10.3.2 Step 2: 'Cleaning up ESAB's own act': radical changes in ESAB's production structure 272

10.3.3 Step 3: 'The industrial clean-up statement' 273

10.3.4 Step 4: ESAB's systematic elimination of industrial overcapacity 274

10.3.5 Step 5: Rationalization of product ranges without disturbing markets 275

10.3.6 Step 6: Establishing a short-term brand strategy 276

10.3.7 Step 7: Establishing a medium- and long-term brand portfolio strategy 277

10.3.8 Step 8: Revising the pricing strategy 279

10.3.9 Step 9: Introducing a 'parallel' sales force strategy 280

10.3.10 Step 10: Matching the countries, brands, product portfolios and strategies 281

10.3.11 Step 11: Organizing for change 282

10.3.12 Step 12: Heavier customer orientation and a new distribution structure 284

10.4 Looking closer at two of the cells in Igor Ansoff's 'growth matrix' **285**

10.4.1 Introducing old products in new markets (1986–88) 286

10.4.2 Expansion mainly based on new products sold in new markets, or new market segments (1986–90) 287

10.5 On management style and the importance of the ESAB board **288**

Score Cards: **Performance charts for this turnaround** **290**

Notes **293**

11 Atlas Copco Tools **295**

List of Contents **295**

Introduction to the Atlas Copco Tools case **296**

11.1 The Atlas Copco group and its tools division **297**

11.2 The situation before the turnaround interventions **297**

11.2.1 The board's perception of the tools division's general viability 297

11.2.2 The very costly international sales organization 298

11.2.3 Divisional morale and motivation 298

11.2.4 A blurred divisional business concept 299

11.2.5 Excessive cost levels 299

11.2.6 Summary as to the root causes 300

11.3 Actions taken to address the situation **301**

11.3.1 Appointment of a new president 301

11.3.2   Evaluating the competence of the divisional
         management team   302
11.3.3   Clarification of the future business concept   302
11.3.4   Improving the cost efficiency of the sales organization 305
11.3.5   Production structure and production overcapacity   306
11.3.6   Production planning and factory layouts   307
11.3.7   Product development finally guided by
         profitability criteria   307
11.3.8   Summary with performance graphs   308

Score Cards: Performance charts for this turnaround   **309**

12   Atlas Copco Mining and Construction   **313**
List of Contents   **313**
Introduction   **314**
12.1 Situation before the turnaround intervention   **315**
12.1.1   The company, the MCT division and its products   315
12.1.2   The managerial situation in 1984   315
12.1.3   Studies to pinpoint the root causes   316
12.1.4   Two specific projects, two major problems   316
12.2 Actions taken   **317**
12.2.1   Creating a new management team and a new team spirit   317
12.2.2   Profitability measurements and allocation principles
         for common costs   317
12.2.3   Speeding up and cost reducing the robot rig project   319
12.2.4   Closing down the Cleveland (tunnel boring) unit   320
12.2.5   Strategic customer satisfaction research kills misconceptions 321
12.2.6   Summary: key actions and key results   323
Note   **323**
Score Cards: Performance charts for this turnaround   **324**

13   Almex   **327**
List of Contents   **327**
Introduction   **328**
         The company, its key products and target groups   328
13.1 Excellent products, but unsatisfactory profits   **328**
13.1.1   An under-dimensioned central sales organization   329
13.1.2   More on Almex cost levels, prices and profitability   329
13.2 Key elements of the new action plan   **330**
13.2.1   Reinforcing the sales organization   330
13.2.2   The new pricing policy   331

13.3 Results achieved during this turnaround 332

***Score Cards:* Performance charts for this turnaround** 332

14 The Tarkett Case 335

List of Contents 335

Introduction 336

14.1 Key stepping stones in Tarkett's development from 1900 to 1987 337

14.2 Main reasons for the substantial Pegulan acquisition in 1987 340

14.3 The introduction of badly adapted organizational and strategic concepts 340

14.4 The turbulent 1987 to 1989 years, including ownership change 343

14.5 1990: The urgent need to once again find a new owner while restructuring 344

14.6 1991 to 1993: An even sharper strategic focus and further divestments radically improve profits 345

14.7 1994: The first of two more ownership changes 347

14.8 1997: The merger with Sommer introduces a French owner 347

14.9 Strategic keys to success: core business concentration, internationalization, and two-way cross-border learning 351

14.10 Simple top management principles might be the most useful ones 352

14.11 Cross-border cultural shock sets in and the CEO leaves 354

Notes 359

***Score Cards:* Performance charts for this turnaround** 360

Index 363

List of figures

1.1 Some forces boosting the need for international turnaround management 12

1.2 Domestic versus international turnarounds: the latter often preceded by acquisitions and mergers 13

1.3 Contents and general structure of the book 28

2.1 How the One Step Up™ system works 43

3.1 Elements in the overall turnaround process 56

3.2 The gradual change of emphasis (selected examples) 75

3.3 How the turnaround time varies with the task in hand 76

4.1 Different emphases: cash vs profit concerns, and 'just saving' the company vs also 'transforming' it 94

5.1 Approximate relationship between four terms discussed in this chapter 111

5.2 The truly performance-driven company 121

5.3 The performance-driven company's 'performance vector' 124

5.4 Productivity benchmarks: 6 companies in 4 countries 125

5.5 Profit margin (%) and return on capital for selected UK industries 128

5.6 Tarkett-Sommer benchmarking against its competitors through industrial field research 131

5.7 The U-Curve illustrating alternative strategies 134

6.1 Overview of Chapter 6 contents 144

7.1 Examples of automotive reports and monthly newsletters published by just one source, *Financial Times* 193

7.2 On-line search to identify valid research reports, and buy them on-line (chapter by chapter) 195

7.3 Form for self-administered frequency study in an insurance company 209

8.1 Capacity demands made on the troubled company: the basic concept 214

8.2 The troubled company (its different functions and the costs generated within each function) 216

8.3   Example of cost formulas used during an actual turnaround of a metal wholesale operation to establish net profits (or net losses) for each product/market segment served   217

8.4   Car parts – comparison of resulting net profits for the car manufacturer and for his authorized dealers, when activity-based costs have been allocated to 11 different distribution channels   231

8.5   The performance-driven company   244

8.6   The performance-driven company seen from a turnaround perspective   244

9.1   Allgon: invoiced sales 1989–96   249

9.2   Allgon: dividend per share 1992–96   263

9.3   Allgon: operating income and net income 1989–96   264

10.1 Growth vector components   269

10.2 Product portfolio versus market share matrix   281

10.3 The ESAB case: RBA and share price developments   290

10.4 The ESAB case: return on capital employed and on equity   291

10.5 The ESAB case: growth in turnover   292

11.1 Atlas Copco Tools: sales development 1979–84   309

11.2 Atlas Copco Tools: capacity utilization 1979–86   310

11.3 Atlas Copco Tools: development of earnings and return on capital employed   311

12.1 Perceived relative importance of different MTC features within MCT HQ, within foreign sales companies and among end-users   322

12.2 Atlas Copco MCT: operating income and return on capital 1981–87   324

12.3 The Atlas Copco MCT case: sales value and sales per employee   325

13.1 Almex – annual results before extraordinary items 1973–79   332

13.2 The Almex case: sales and income   333

14.1 The Tarkett history   338

14.2 Major forces at work in the Tarkett case   349

14.3 Some of the profit improving actions taken   350

14.4 Key traits of 'The Scandinavian Management Style'   355

14.5 Tarkett case: annual sales values   360

14.6 Tarkett case: sales value (in thousand DM) per employee and volume (in thousand m^2) per employee   361

14.7 Development of EBIT   362

List of Tables

4.1   Some key ratios used as benchmarks   102

7.1   Information sources discussed in Chapter 7   169

8.1   Example of computer output showing how the original gross profit in a particular product/market is 'wiped out' step-by-step by different kinds of cost   219

8.2   ABC computer output for two different product/market segments in the same industry   225

Preface

This book has been long in the making, close to a decade. In the meantime, its subject has grown in importance. The creation of the European Common Market and later the European Union, has dramatically increased the number of cross-border acquisitions and subsequent turnarounds implemented in a multi-cultural setting. The recent introduction of a common European currency (the 'Euro') has made international performance comparisons much easier. This transparency has resulted in a further momentum for cross-border mergers and acquisitions, not least in industries providing financial services.

Parallel to intensified cross-border activities in Europe, one sees a 'globalization' of many industries, from communication and entertainment to vehicle components. A prerequisite for globalization is cross-border, even intercontinental, acquisitions and mergers. These are regularly accompanied by very substantial turnaround activities, in order to produce really cost-effective global players having maximum market impact, while simultaneously providing maximum shareholder value. These developments make this book more pertinent today than when the project was started.

A description of this publishing project and of the two authors might be of some interest.

In 1977, Arpi International, a Brussels-based top management consultancy, was founded. Its original business mission was to help Scandinavian multinationals adapt their strategic plans to the new realities of the gradually emerging European Common Market. While client headquarters were typically located in Scandinavia, the clients' problems were usually found elsewhere, in quite another cultural setting, manifesting themselves in different value systems, commercial habits, languages, and sometimes even different legal systems.

By 1985, most multinationals believed that they knew well how to create a strategic plan. As a result, Arpi International was increasingly often asked not to help shape strategic plans, but to find out why the carefully planned Blueprint for the Future had miserably failed to materialize. Had the strategic plan itself been wrong, the underlying assumptions erroneous, or the plan implementation less than professional? If the latter, perhaps a new country manager or a new president for a major foreign entity was required?

Increasingly, Arpi International's senior consultants found themselves engaged in *ex post facto* evaluation of failed strategic plans and of the quality of the plan implementation. How did a senior consultant evaluate the management team responsible for the plan's implementation, and what should be done about the present mess?

Could the management consulting company possibly provide an experienced, multilingual senior consultant on a 'manager-for-hire' basis, prepared either to be responsible for the full turnaround exercise, or at least to get it rapidly started? Such assignments included the merging of three companies in France, splitting up a major company in Spain, and the closing of a substantial factory in the UK. Often, a redefinition of the client's Business Mission and of his future core business was also called for.

To systematize the experience gained (that is, principles, methods, tools, techniques and results achieved), Dr Bo Arpi started debriefing consultants and gathering the body of collective knowledge in the form of a tentative turnaround manuscript. A senior partner became responsible for the latter part of the book, and planned to cover half a dozen detailed case studies of his own choice.

This plan was never realized as originally perceived. The partner in question left the company, took one of the best senior consultants along, and started his own consultancy. As a result, this publishing project was put on ice for a few years. However, in 1997 it was suddenly revived for two major reasons:

- The subject of international turnarounds had become increasingly 'hot'.
- Bo Arpi met Per Wejke, a highly experienced and respected turnaround manager, who could easily provide at least four of the six detailed case studies envisaged for the book. Many of his results were quite spectacular.

After having turned around Almex (a company providing ticket-issuing equipment for public transport), Per Wejke turned around Atlas Copco Tools, followed by Atlas Copco Mining & Construction. He then took a troubled company called Allgon (which produced radio wave propagation equipment, including vehicle-mounted antennae for mobile phones), on a quite spectacular turnaround exercise and an exceptional growth journey. During a three-year period, Allgon's shareholder value increased 30-fold. Allgon became the darling of the Stockholm Stock Exchange. The Scandinavian financial press declared the company 'Winner of the Year', and Per Wejke became one of the most celebrated Scandinavian turnaround experts. Not only is he responsible for four of the six in-depth case studies in the second part of this book, but he also acted as a tough but constructive devil's advocate when Bo Arpi set out to rewrite the text, and added two in-depth case studies of his own, namely the ESAB and Tarkett cases.

When a weak company is acquired, it is rapidly subjected to *turnaround management*. Also when a sound and profitable company has been purchased, it is nowadays often subjected to some form of turnaround management, to 'realize the synergies', to increase profits and shareholder value, but partly also to generate the cash needed to ease the substantial debt burden often assumed in connection with a major acquisition. Peripheral 'non-core activities' are normally rapidly sold. Part of the resulting income might be used to achieve a further concentration on the company's redefined future 'core business', and increase the company's market share.

Cross-border acquisitions, mergers and turnarounds have become increasingly common during the 1990s. 'Merger mania' is an often-seen cover story in the business press, although 70 per cent still fail to meet pre-merger expectations. Hostile takeovers, which a few years ago were regarded as 'completely unacceptable behaviour' in many European continental markets, not least in Germany, have suddenly started to happen.

As a result, multilingual senior managers with a good track record from normal line management, increasingly often find themselves appointed *turnaround managers*. As such they strive for a combination of maximum speed, a minimum of mistakes, and fast results. Many desperately grope for a coherent framework, useful checklists, concrete advice, and success stories which provide valuable ideas with regard to what to do, and what not to do. In spite of the rapidly increasing number of turnarounds – today often in a multi-cultural setting – it is still quite difficult to find professional books which systematically, extensively and in a generalized fashion cover most aspects of international turnaround management.

Newly appointed turnaround managers constitute one of the four primary target groups for this book. A second target group consists of managers who have always been fascinated by the mystique surrounding turnarounds, but who have never found a coherent presentation of what is really involved. A third target group are MBAs and business people engaged in continuing education, either at university level or at international business management schools. A fourth group consists of experts (attorneys, accountants, bankers, venture capitalists and so on) who, from their specialist platforms, occasionally interact with under-performing businesses.

The contents of this book are highly practical, its structure perhaps slightly academic. As to style, the authors have tried to live up to standards which provide more than 'an easy read', that is, more than entertainment value. The six in-depth case studies in Part II, as well as some 40 mini case studies throughout the book, demonstrate the nuts-and-bolts reality of a turnaround manager and the applicability of our principles in real life.

Together, the two authors represent half a century of turnaround experience from a number of different industries, countries and language areas. This has broadened the scope of this book, and hopefully also its practical application in a wide range of turnaround situations.

Bo ARPI (main author) and
PER WEJKE (contributing co-author)
Brussels and Stockholm, 31 March 1999

Acknowledgements

Both authors have dealt with turnarounds, although from entirely different vantage points. Bo Arpi gained an early experience of turnarounds when for three years he worked as a young assistant to Professor Ulf af Trolle, probably Scandinavia's most respected turnaround manager after the Second World War. By dedicating this book to his memory, we also pay tribute to his achievements.

Under the legendary Harold S. Geneen, ITT continuously acquired and systematically turned around companies, until a worldwide conglomerate employing 440,000 individuals had been created. Bo Arpi worked as a marketing director for ITT Business Systems, responsible for the sale of telephone switching equipment and data terminals to organizations throughout Europe, as well as teleprinters and message switching equipment to countries as far apart as South America and the Soviet Union. This provided valuable insight into mergers and acquisitions and subsequent turnarounds. It also presented many opportunities to reflect on cultural differences and their importance in a commercial context. Today, little remains of Harold S. Geneen's conglomerate, but the lessons learned remain vivid among former ITT executives.

Over the years, senior consultants from Arpi International have repeatedly been sent to different troubled companies to address serious and highly interesting turnaround situations. This is the place to thank senior consultants of Arpi International for interesting turnaround assignments successfully completed during the last 20 years and the experience subsequently shared.

On several occasions, Bo Arpi has been invited to move in on company premises in parallel with a recently appointed CEO, to speed up the turnaround process. Although not occupying the 'hot seat' himself, the issues dealt with were almost identical: rapidly identify 'bleeders' and underlying causes, help create a more reliable fact base, redefine the Business Mission and the future core business, help establish new goals and plans, facilitate communication to maximize the understanding and the active involvement of employees, lead in-house meetings, document the conclusions arrived at and so on. Bo Arpi wants to thank the CEOs in these companies, both for their trust and for pleasant cooperation.

In a similar fashion, Per Wejke would like to thank the board members of Atlas Copco Tools, Almex, Atlas Copco Mining & Construction, and Allgon, for their confidence in his abilities and for their constant encouragement. He would also like to thank members of the management teams who valiantly and successfully worked together with him to 'conquer' four of the six turnaround cases documented in great detail in Part II.

The universal applicability of the principles advanced in this book has been thoroughly demonstrated, by inserting into the book a large number of 'text frames', each containing a mini case. Together these provide a wide selection of examples, including some from well-known corporations in the US and on the European continent. Although the corresponding text has usually been substantially abbreviated, rearranged and rewritten for the purposes of this book, the original source has more often than not been one or more articles from *Business Week*. To the extent that this has not been explicitly indicated already in the text box itself, it is hereby gratefully acknowledged. For the rest, every effort has been made to trace all the copyright holders but if any have been inadvertently overlooked the publishers will be pleased to make the necessary arrangements at the first opportunity.

The manuscript preceding this book has been retyped five times. The responsibility for typing, retyping, keeping track of diagrams, correspondence and so on has rested with Bea Praet, Bo Arpi's secretary for 13 years. Only through her determined and sustained efforts has this project now come to a successful completion.

Finally, the two authors want to thank Stephen Rutt of the publisher, who early on saw 'the gap in the business book market', appreciated our manuscript and helped turn it into an attractive book.

BO ARPI and PER WEJKE

Part I

On the Driving Range: Principles and Techniques

Chapter

1   International turnaround management: definition, purpose, symptoms and trends   3

2   Different kinds of turnaround situation   32

3   Overview of the different steps involved in most turnarounds   54

4   'When Cash is King': squeezing the balance sheet for cash   79

5   The Blueprint for the Future Company, quantitative benchmarks and choice of strategy   108

6   Rebuilding the new management team and creating a new team spirit   143

7   Where to get plan input data   167

8   'Penetrating the fog': activity-based costing (ABC) in three turnaround situations   211

1 International turnaround management: definition, purpose, symptoms and trends

1.1 What is 'turnaround management'?

The term *turnaround* is nowadays often confused with 'downsizing' or 'restructuring'. Although downsizing might be *part* of a turnaround plan, it does certainly not constitute a turnaround in itself. Even drastic downsizing cannot guarantee that a troubled company will survive and prosper. That requires – among other things – the company to develop a clear-cut competitive edge, sustainable over time, and a corporate strategy which is valid well beyond the acute turnaround period. Therefore one can seldom judge the ultimate success of a turnaround until three to five years later. (This is also the minimum time period used for the performance diagrams accompanying the six detailed turnaround cases in Part II.)

However, let us for a moment leave aside the long-term aspects and just focus on what characterizes a company in urgent need of a turnaround.

The term 'turnaround management' primarily refers to companies or other organisations in distress. Such organisations are usually 'sick' when measured on different criteria. Often they show life-threatening symptoms. They urgently need to be restored to health, even if this should call for radical surgery or – minimally – a whole battery of somewhat softer interventions. From this, one might derive a first useful – although somewhat limited – definition.

Turnaround management is the systematic and rapid implementation of a range of measures to correct a seriously unprofitable situation. It might include dealing with a financial disaster or measures to avoid the highly likely occurrence of such a disaster.

Let us now turn our attention to the hero of this book, that is, *the turnaround manager* and his (or her) crucial role.[1]

If the company – or other organisational entity – in need of turnaround treatment can be compared to a troubled patient, the work of the turnaround manager can be compared to that of a 'company doctor'. His function is to rapidly identify symptoms, draw conclusions as to the likely underlying causes (that is, diagnosing the disease), but above all to propose and also implement remedies, that is, corrective measures.

The latter aspect is worth repeating for added emphasis: detached analysis and good advice are not sufficient in a turnaround situation. The turnaround expert also has to *take the full responsibility for the actual implementation of all the necessary actions*. This might be compared to having an incapacitated patient in an intensive-care unit, or perhaps even undergoing radical surgery. However, during a subsequent 'recovery phase', the patient himself must become much more active and personally assume the responsibility for much of his continuing improvement. In a turnaround situation this corresponds to *reanimating* a passive management team and *jump-starting* a sluggish organisation, sometimes by shock therapy.

If part of the old management team does not respond favourably and rapidly to the proposed cure, 'transplants from foreign bodies' (that is, executives hired from other organisations) might be the answer.

So what causes a company to end up being a 'turnaround case'?

The typical turnaround situation is not characterized by *force majeure* or the sudden impact of a completely uncontrollable outside force. Normally, the undesirable situation has gradually developed over a number of years. As demonstrated by the six case studies detailed in the second half of this book, the need for a turnaround is usually the result of a complex web of unfortunate strategic decisions and pure mismanagement as well as inadequate responses to important changes in the company's market position and competitive situation. It is hardly ever the result of one external, unavoidable event.

Renee Fellman (the Turnaround Management Association's annual award winner in 1977) shares this opinion. She stated: 'Only one sign all by itself does not mean major trouble. It is a set of *multiple problems* that bring companies to the brink of disaster.'

Turnaround management includes an element of *crisis management*. In the medical literature, the term 'crisis' often indicates that a turning point has been reached. A company needing turnaround management has usually also reached a highly crucial and decisive moment in its life. Such a turning point can either be for better or for worse. The turnaround manager is simply there to make sure that the turning point is for the better, and not the beginning of the end.[2]

The characteristic *symptoms* of a company (or other troubled organisation) being an unmistakable candidate for a major turnaround management effort are listed in Section 1.6 of this chapter.

So when is a turnaround mission completed? Expert opinions differ. In the minds of the authors of this book, the turnaround is *not* completed just because a bankruptcy has been avoided, or because the most acute crisis is over. First class turnaround managers worry equally as much about the long-term health prospects of the recently 'saved' patient.

As repeatedly shown throughout this book, this means that capable turnaround managers early on critically review – and usually radically revise – the company's *Business Mission Statement*. Thus they make sure that the goals and broad directions contained therein represent a valid, desirable and attainable *Blueprint for the Future Company*, as discussed in Chapter 5.

In our opinion, it is the turnaround manager's obvious responsibility to make sure that the company can indeed prosper and also, if and when the turnaround manager in question has left the scene, perhaps to assume other turnaround challenges. Why take the trouble to save a company, just to leave it tottering on the verge of a pending new catastrophe?

However, there are two other more immediate and highly compelling reasons why the company's future Business Mission must be defined early on:

■ The turnaround manager cannot just shoot from the hip. He needs a *target picture*.

■ Employees need a *marching song* reflecting a belief in the future of the company, encouraging their efforts and sacrifices to help the company survive and prosper.

The turnaround manager might early on have to *sell off* certain business activities (business units, factories) to generate cash. He might like to sell off or close down others because they are unprofitable and/or require too much management attention, which distracts from the more important tasks. To know what to sell or close down, but also what to focus on more strongly (and perhaps even invest in), he needs to define and cleverly communicate the company's new Business Mission. If he fails to do so, he is a cowboy shooting from the hip, and the troubled company still lacks a common marching song. Retrenchment without a vision is dangerous.

Thus, the ideal turnaround expert must be equipped with a Janus face, with one side focusing quite sharply on immediate cash and profit improvements, while the other side is turned solidly towards the future.[3] This is certainly not easy, but nevertheless quite a fascinating task.

Our original definition of 'turnaround management' can thus be broadened to include also the longer-term ambition:

To also provide the troubled company with excellent chances to survive and prosper in the longer term – although it will then most likely be operating within the confines of a radically redefined Business Mission.

1.2 Turnaround-like activities triggered by acquisitions, mergers and privatizations

Turnaround activities can be triggered by many other factors than just mismanagement. For instance, turnaround activities are today quite commonly initiated:

■ when a smaller company has just been *acquired*,
■ when two major companies in the same industry are being *merged*,
■ when a state-owned company with a bloated bureaucracy has just been *privatized*.

In such situations, the term 'turnaround' is not necessarily used. Instead one might hear terms like:

- restructuring,
- downsizing,
- avoiding duplication of efforts,
- realizing the very substantial synergies,
- reducing existing overcapacity in the industry.

Whatever the terms used, most of the actions taken are pretty close to those in a typical turnaround case, as discussed in quite some depth in this book.

If a loss-making company has been acquired, turnaround management is called for by the new owner. If the shares of a successful company have instead been acquired, then the price paid might exceed the normal stock value by 50 per cent. Turnaround management activities are then usually called for to 'realize the substantial synergies identified'. These activities might include the divestment of the acquired company's non-core businesses, partly to be able to repay the loans taken on to finance the transaction itself. Leveraged management buyouts (MBOs) often trigger similar responses as shown for example by the rather spectacular Beatrice Food and J. R. Nabisco cases.

1.3 Domestic turnarounds versus international turnarounds

Most English-language books on turnaround management have been written by US authors. The turnaround experience reported by them has primarily been based on the turnaround of:

- US companies,
- meeting relatively few language and cultural barriers,
- with US accounting and reporting standards,
- with most of their sales in their huge domestic market,
- with relatively few reported turnaround problems directly related to cross-border acquisitions.

The present book is different. It is called *International Turnaround Management*. The six case studies at the end of the book all relate to companies with more than 70 per cent of their sales in *foreign countries* at the start of the turnaround effort and often 90 per cent at the end. The turnaround managers – like the authors – have all been multilingual, sometimes fluent in as many as four to seven languages.

Furthermore, one of the six in-depth case studies describes how a company moves its headquarters out of its original home country and places it abroad, in an entirely new language area and with quite a different company culture. Two cases describe how companies on the verge of bankruptcy were not only saved, but also systematically and profitably grown through acquisitions to become No. 2 in the world in their respective areas.

In one case the owner was French, and the headquarters were located in Germany, while the manager was Scandinavian. How much more cross-border can one become? Interestingly enough, this case also deals with the dire consequences when 'cross-border cultural shock' sets in at the very top.

Obviously, the cross-border dimension substantially adds to the complexity of corresponding turnarounds, but also to the value of the lessons learned.

Three anecdotal examples follow, developed more fully later in the book.

(a) In one case, senior German managers of an acquired company were seen sitting in a meadow in a foreign country, where they certainly did not understand the local language. They sipped lukewarm champagne served in paper cups and listened to what the new owner in all his lonely wisdom had decided about their company's and their own fate after the acquisition. (A few years later, over 90 per cent of these – often quite capable managers – had left the company, sometimes creating difficult-to-fill empty slots.)

(b) In another case a desperate general manager of a recently acquired US subsidiary asked Dr Arpi, who had been called in as a senior consultant: 'Where does the buck stop, and when? To our minds no decisions have been taken, in spite of having been locked up in a retreat by the Scandinavians for all of two days.' While the Scandinavian owners congratulated themselves on 'the good atmosphere during our constructive common meeting', the US subsidiary manager, (no doubt used to more strong-headed, decisive and very outspoken US managers) complained bitterly about the Scandinavians 'now probably trying to introduce some kind of Management by Osmosis'.

(c) After the announcement of the Daimler/Chrysler merger, it was suggested that the US workers should one day celebrate the new inter-continental 'partnership' by eating typical German food (like sausages and sauerkraut), while their new-found German colleagues were supposed to simultaneously enjoy typical US food. Hamburgers were rejected. Instead, 'corn on the cob' was chosen at the suggestion of Chrysler executives. Unfortunately, in Germany, corn is widely regarded as animal food. The German workers dutifully chewed away. However, some workers wondered if there might possibly be a hidden message from their new-found American friends. Cultural glitches might somewhat diminish the positive impact of well-meaning, cross-border 'partnership enhancing' activities.

Stories of this nature could easily have passed as just pleasant anecdotes had it not been for the quite impressive, presently ongoing explosion in cross-border mergers and acquisitions and subsequent turnaround activities now increasingly taking place in a highly complex multinational setting. This trend is here to stay and can perhaps best be illustrated by:

1. The rapid growth in cross-border mergers within Europe, fuelled by the European Union, but also by the new Euro currency, the removal of previous acquisition obstacles (including French state-owned 'golden shares' and the gradual phasing out of shares with unequal voting rights).

2. The equally contagious boom in intercontinental mega-mergers like Daimler/Chrysler and Deutsche Bank/ Bankers Trust.

Comments and illustrations to each of these two strong trends are given below and followed by a comprehensive overview in Figure 1.1.

The consequences of the now rapidly implemented frontier free European Union must not be underestimated. From January 1999, the new Euro currency has provided a much enhanced cross-border transparency. For instance, company comparisons can now be made in the very same currency and acquisition prices can be established without concern for local currency variations and resulting currency exposures.

Further, there are now few remaining niches in which a European company can hide. The gradual removal of state-owned 'golden shares' and similar tricks used by European governments to block 'undesirable' cross-border company acquisitions also mean that cross-border acquisitions and subsequent turnarounds are now reaching peak levels throughout Europe.

A few recent (that is, 1998/99) examples are:

■ Hoechst (Germany) and Rhône-Poulenc (France)
■ Merita Bank (Finland) and Nordbanken (Sweden)
■ Astra (Sweden) and Britannica Zeneca (UK).

The strong cross-border trend in Europe is not only of interest to Europeans, but also to US and Japanese companies which want to increase their foothold in Europe, as part of the ongoing globalization of business. The six international turnaround cases provided in the second part of this book will hopefully provide not only European managers, but also US, Japanese and other managers as well with some thought-provoking and useful inputs.

The number of intercontinental mega-mergers, including one major European company, is also rapidly increasing. (A few examples are Daimler/Chrysler, Deutsche Bank/Bankers Trust and Alcatel/DSC Communications.)

Such mega-mergers are almost always accompanied by downsizing or restructuring and other turnaround-related activities. Indeed, downsizing and closures are nowadays almost *a prerequisite* for the deal itself. Expected manpower reduction and other major changes are today often announced simultaneously with the deal, partly to impress financial analysts and the stock market. For instance, when Deutsche Bank bought Bankers Trust it was announced that 5,500 jobs would be cut, leading to a 'cost saving of $1bn by 2001'.

Now back to somewhat more typical turnaround situations and to the main thrust of this book.

Many more cross-border mergers in the pipeline

During the second half of 1998, a flood of mega-mergers was announced. Investment banks were acquired and merged almost on a weekly basis. For example, Deutsche Bank bought Bankers Trust of the US.

However, major cross-border mergers were not limited to the financial sector. Hoechst merged with Rhône-Poulenc of France. In the oil business, British Petroleum (BP) merged with Amoco of the US, following the example set by Exxon, having acquired and merged with Mobile. In the consumer luxury goods industry, LVMH and Printemps Redoute (both of France) started a hostile bidding war over Gucci of Italy. In the car industry, Volkswagen and Ford both made offers for Volvo's car division, which was in 1999 sold to Ford for $6.5 billion.

There were several factors driving this trend towards the end of 1998. The drop in stock market prices a few months earlier forced many companies to put their acquisition plans on ice. Further, when the world economy weakened, many multinationals concluded that they could no longer primarily rely on 'organic growth'. A common solution was to merge with other substantial players, and this was accompanied by rationalizations and new organizational structures.

The gradual making of the borderless Europe, with 11 out of 15 countries adopting the common Euro currency on 1 January 1999, has increased transparency, the ease of making correct company and market comparisons over country borders, and a resulting desire to expand and consolidate over such borders.

In Scandinavia, a lot of attention has been paid to mergers (or expected mergers) among banks, insurance companies, brokerage houses and so on. While major industrial restructuring through mergers and acquisitions once was primarily implemented *within* a particular country, today most restructuring is on a *cross-border* basis. The merger between the Merita Bank of Finland and the Nordbanken of Sweden has recently taken place. It is generally expected that this will be followed by yet another acquisition of a Danish and/or Norwegian bank.

Other service companies like consulting companies (including those engaged in automotive engineering and in the construction industry) are also expected to be restructured during 1999, partly as a result of 'outsourcing' being increasingly used by, for example, automotive producers.

European mergers, cross-border and otherwise, were fuelled by US investment bankers and deal-makers, aggressively operating throughout Europe, suggesting both specific deals and financing packages. For the first time ever, hostile take-over attempts started to be regarded as 'acceptable business behavior' also on the European Continent. (More such attempts were actually seen during the first quarter of 1999, than during all of 1990–1998).

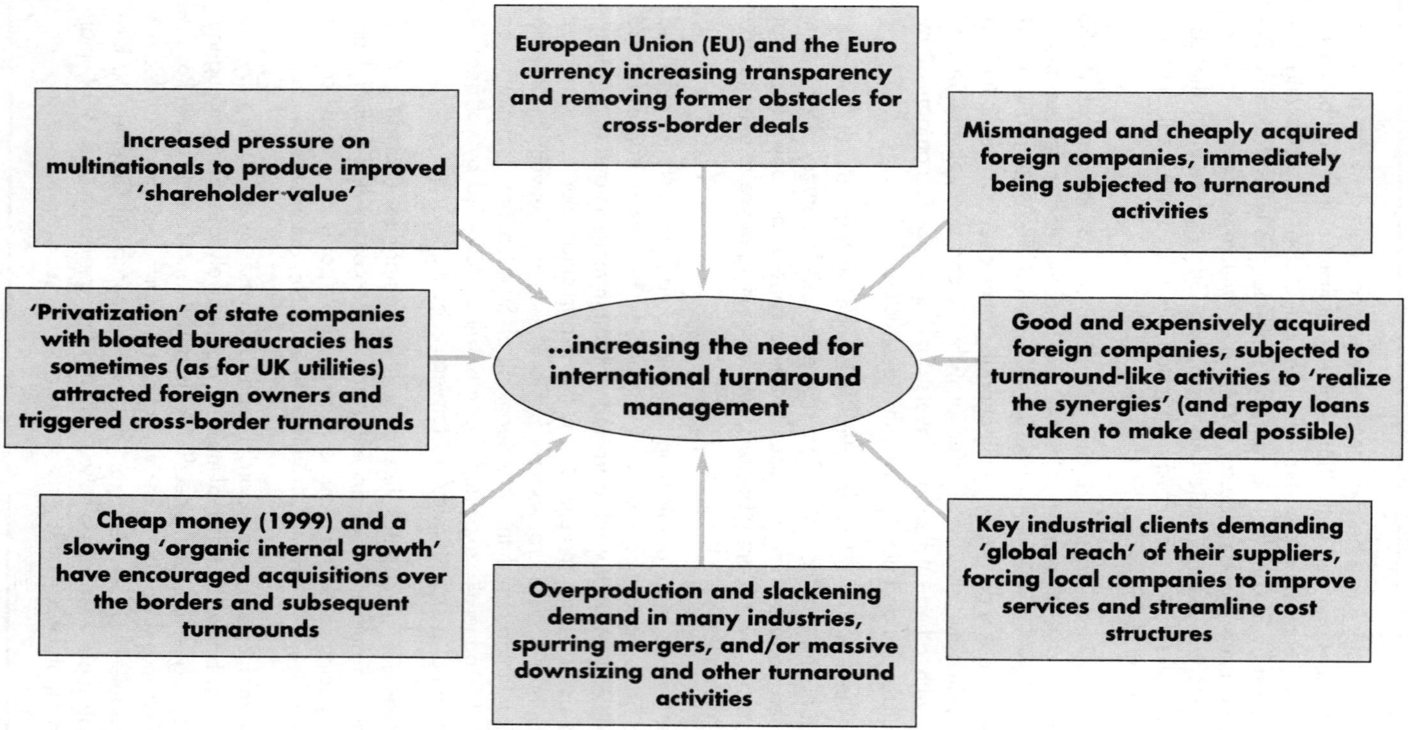

Mismanaged and cheaply acquired foreign companies, immediately being subjected to turnaround activities

Good and expensively acquired foreign companies, subjected to turnaround-like activities to 'realize the synergies' (and repay loans taken to make deal possible)

Key industrial clients demanding 'global reach' of their suppliers, forcing local companies to improve services and streamline cost structures

European Union (EU) and the Euro currency increasing transparency and removing former obstacles for cross-border deals

...increasing the need for international turnaround management

Overproduction and slackening demand in many industries, spurring mergers, and/or massive downsizing and other turnaround activities

Increased pressure on multinationals to produce improved 'shareholder-value'

'Privatization' of state companies with bloated bureaucracies has sometimes (as for UK utilities) attracted foreign owners and triggered cross-border turnarounds

Cheap money (1999) and a slowing 'organic internal growth' have encouraged acquisitions over the borders and subsequent turnarounds

Figure 1.1   Some forces boosting the need for international turnaround management

Geographic scope	Degree of difficulty	Growth trends	Key driving forces	Special problems	Notes	Reference to some well-known cases
ALL turnarounds (i.e. common traits)	*Difficult* (Good management under extreme pressure is always difficult)	*Up* (for all kinds)	(Different for domestic and international turnarounds, as shown below)	–		
DOMESTIC turnarounds	*Least complex* type (Regarded as a pretty 'normal' managerial activity)	*Slow growth* (Increasingly regarded as part of 'normal' management)	*Consolidation of the domestic industry structure* ('Cleaning up the present mess', and often creating national oligopolies)	*Relatively few* (However, if the affected companies have over 50% of their sales abroad, many of the problems below apply)	Estimated medium-term success rate: 80%	Chrysler Corp. (was actually turned around *twice*, first by Lee Iacocca, later by the co-pilots Robert Eaton and Robert Lutz)
CROSS-BORDER EUROPEAN mergers and turnarounds	*Rather complex* (For reasons explained under 'special problems')	*Explosive growth*	*European Union and the 'Euro' currency* (Obstacles to cross-border deals removed, increased transparency and comparability, similar 'rule books' applied throughout Europe. Hostile takeovers finally 'acceptable behavior'*)	*Language and cultural barriers* (Incl. different traditions, laws, tastes, preferences, and national pride/ lingering chauvinism. Different management principles)	Estimated medium-term success rate: 50%	The Tarkett & ESAB cases at the end of this book, Hoechst (Germany) with Rhône-Poulenc (France), Merita Bank (Finland) with Nordbanken (Sweden), Astra (Sweden) with Zeneca (UK), BMW's so far unsuccessful turnaround of Rover (UK)
INTER-CONTINENTAL mega-mergers and/or turnarounds	Often *highly complex*	*Growing* (Still relatively few, but spectacular 'mega-mergers' followed by turnarounds)	*Globalization* (for increased critical mass, global reach, and better service to multinational clients. US investment bankers and deal makers finance and speed up change)	*All of above+ sheer size* of subsequent turnaround & geographic distances to be covered	Estimated medium-term success rate: unknown (probably less than 50%)	Pharmacia/Upjohn, Daimler/Chrysler, BP/Amoco-Arco, Deutsche Bank/Bankers Trust, Ford/Volvo Cars and a host of others now in the pipeline

Figure 1.2   Domestic versus international turnarounds: the latter often preceded by acquisitions and mergers

* There were more hostile Continental takeover attempts first quarter 1999 that during all of 1990–1998

1.4   Main thrust and boundaries of this book

Where has the main emphasis of this book been placed, and what kind of turnaround situations have been given a more perfunctory treatment?

- This book deals primarily with *saveable* companies, not with liquidation cases.

- It deals only with the turnaround of *entire companies* or at least very substantial divisions of major multinationals.

- All six case studies in the second part of the book deal with companies whose sales mostly came from *outside their home market*.

- Although the main thrust is on European turnaround cases, most of the scrutinized companies also had US operations.

- The general principles discussed in the first part of the book are applicable in any country, and even to domestic US turnarounds. To prove this, about 40 'boxes' containing concrete and recent examples of direct interest to a US audience have been scattered throughout the book.

- All six major case studies (as well as three others discussed in Chapter 8) are based on the *inside experience* gained during the turnaround process itself.

- Isolated happenings of a crisis nature in otherwise sound companies are not dealt with. However, unpleasant happenings are certainly dealt with if and when constituting an integral part of a particular turnaround situation, for example in the Atlas Copco MCT and Allgon cases.

- Spectacular government bailouts have been left outside of this book. They tend to fall more within the framework of public policy, social concerns and vote-winning politics than within the scope of business administration itself.

- The turnaround of state-owned European companies has also been left out since the number of such companies is rapidly decreasing, and they are usually privatized before any real turnaround takes place. (By then the very same turnaround principles apply.)

■ As earlier explained, this book focuses just as much on the creation of *viable, long-term solutions and structures* as on temporary 'survival management', however spectacular such an effort might be at a certain point in time. The authors believe it is the turnaround manager's task to create a sound company which has excellent chances to continue to prosper for many more years.

What about the authors and their combined experience?

Of the two authors, Per Wejke, has usually been employed by the distressed company's board and has run the company as its CEO for several years. The other author, Bo Arpi, has considerable personal experience of operating as a turnaround consultant, usually working hand-in-hand with a newly arrived chief executive who wants to move much faster while relying on an experienced consultant.[4]

Further, as a principal in an international top management consulting company for 20 years, Dr Arpi has repeatedly sent out senior colleagues to function as temporary, full-time CEOs, usually for a period of six to nine months. (Obviously, not everything could be achieved during this time-span. However, a valid turnaround plan was developed and most actions put in motion, including the active search for a new – and this time permanent – CEO who could take over after the initial, often rather unpleasant, cleaning-up period was concluded.)

Thus, together, and from different but complementary vantage points, the authors have fifty years' experience in both turning around ailing companies in an international setting and in detecting underlying problems and their solutions.

1.5 The book's primary target groups

When writing this book, the authors had primarily four target groups in mind:

1. A *line manager* who, in the middle of his successful career, is suddenly given a turnaround assignment. He rapidly needs to find a valid frame of reference, some checklists, and concrete examples of how others have attacked similar problems and succeeded. To this group might be added temporary 'turnaround managers for hire', and senior consultants deeply involved in assisting a turnaround manager, often on a full-time basis.

2. Other *professionals*, who from their specialist platforms occasionally interact with seriously under-performing businesses. This group includes attorneys, accountants, bankers, investors, venture capitalists, board members, credit managers, executive search as well as outsourcing experts.

3. *MBA students*, as well as executives participating in continuing education activities, who need to get more closely acquainted with the turnaround discipline. This includes how to identify problems, deal with people problems, rapidly gather badly needed information, take the necessary decisions, and then swiftly move on to implement them to achieve the intended results.

4. Other individuals in business life for whom the term 'turnaround management' holds a fascinating but somewhat mysterious ring. This book lifts the veils by showing the tools and techniques used by experienced and highly successful turnaround managers.[5]

1.6 Painting the turnaround stage: 22 common symptoms

Listed below – without any order of priority – are 22 characteristics or 'symptoms' usually found in turnaround candidate companies.[6]

The first 14 are of a rather objective or technical nature. The last eight are more directly related to 'corporate culture' and 'managerial mentality':

1. Heavy accumulated losses for previous years, and continued heavy losses also for the present operating year, *with no obvious and credible relief in sight* (in spite of dutifully presented, rather optimistic budgets, which neither the board nor anyone else believes in any longer).

2. Although the losses shown on the company books might be limited, for example due to different kinds of non-operating/non-recurring income and 'creative accounting' in general, *the cash position of the company is usually weak* and rapidly deteriorating. (Lacking a well-meaning and financially strong parent company, this might mean that the troubled company cannot even meet its payment obligations one or two months down the road.)

3. *Company goals and strategies are usually unclear and inade-quate*, sometimes even non-existent (at least in the minds of most managers). If written company goals and strategies do exist, an experienced turnaround manager will usually find that they are either completely unrealistic, not known or believed in by most key managers, and/or that the strategies agreed on have not been implemented in a stringent fashion. Sometimes, 'blue skies strategies' were not even transformed into a concrete action programme, but just collected dust.

4. The present management team seems to have run out of alternatives as well as the energy to implement necessary actions. In spite of occasional bursts of tough talk, they lack the decisiveness to take radical actions to correct the situation.

5. The somewhat half-hearted measures which have indeed been implemented have not had the hoped-for *impact* on the company's market shares, costs and revenues. Standard financial ratios continue to deteriorate, but the management team does not draw the right kind of conclusions as to the underlying causes and suitable corrective management actions.

6. Easy *excuses* are found. Some finger-pointing takes place, sly remarks are made. ('Our future is in the marketplace, and certainly not among all our financial bean counters.')

7. During the last few years, the management team might have *oscillated* between different organizational concepts, fancy marketing philosophies, constantly revised product range strategies and so on with little apparent positive impact on profits. (Examples: decentralization versus centralization, product diversification versus 'sticking to the knitting', export efforts into entirely new markets versus concentration on main market areas.)

8. Nor have the last-ditch *miracle cures* – for instance the introduction of a new revolutionary product on a crash-course basis – lived up to the very high hopes attached to them, and to the high costs usually incurred. (For more concrete examples, the reader is referred to the 'Cleveland Tunnel Boring' and the 'Robot Rig' projects in the Atlas Copco MCT case at the end of this book, or to the 'Total Flooring Concept', not pre-tested and therefore failed, described in the Tarkett case.)

9. Top and middle management starts showing increasing signs of *defensive behaviour*. Everybody tries to protect their own position and own department while putting the blame on others. Cooperation over functional borders has deteriorated. A high turnover of employees – particularly among promising middle managers and other key employees – can be noticed. Part of the company's sales force might also have started to migrate elsewhere, sometimes to the competition.

10. Telling symptoms also come from the company's business environment: one or more *major clients* are lost. The company's *image* is tarnished. Sales relations might suffer. (Some clients also use the weakened position of the company to ensure extended credit terms or extra discounts, resulting in further deteriorating margins and accounts receivable.)

11. Apart from financial ratios, such as current ratio and net quick ratio, other ratios for the productive use of company resources keep deteriorating, for example inventory turnover, return on assets managed, gross margin generated per sales force hour, or the number of days outstanding for accounts receivable.

12. At existing cash-flow levels, it is likely that the company will not be able to meet its payment obligations – nor to continue desirable investments – without an infusion of new capital and/or other extraordinary efforts.

13. By now, the controller's department is usually under severe pressure. It is obviously tempting to show non-recurrent/non-operating profits (for example from asset sales) as operating income. In reports to the stockholders, further proof of 'creative accounting' might be called for. Good sounding, but fundamentally false, explanations for present problems appear. Given a 20-year time axis, today's problems might be presented as unimportant temporary 'blips'.

14. If the company's ailment has reached a highly advanced stage, the following additional symptoms might also appear: unplanned borrowing at very high interest rates, a drop in the company's credit rating, more overdrafts and perhaps unexplainable delays in the issuing of financial reports. (This is usually also the time when the last remaining respected member of the board chooses to leave his position!)

However, there are usually also a number of other symptoms related to corporate culture, managerial mentality and intellectual honesty, as discussed below (items 15–22).

As earlier discussed, a turnaround manager must have a 'Janus face', being able to attack the immediate problems while also trying to find a viable Blueprint for the Future Company. However, parallel to these two endeavours, he must also try to change the prevailing 'company atmosphere' and the 'managerial mentality', which has indeed made all previously committed mistakes possible. This section highlights some of the typical corporate culture traits found in turn-around situations.

By identifying these traits, the turnaround manager might better understand what *psychological and intellectual changes* it will take to re-create a sound company with a bright future.

Deficiencies reflected in financial numbers and key performance ratios are one thing. They could easily add 20 more items to our list. However, in the rest of this section we focus more on weaknesses in intellectual honesty, managerial qualities and the corporate culture at large. In a turnaround situation, the following signs are rather common:

15. Information used is often both *misleading* and *self-serving*. Substantial amounts of data are usually found scattered throughout the company. However, such data are seldom system-atically brought together and seldom organized in such a way that they objectively highlight the most pertinent management problems.

16. Existing problems and underlying causes are badly identified, badly analysed, and only partly understood. (Analyses are made, but they tend to be of a subjective 'storytelling' variety, and seldom of an objective, decision-orientated nature.)

17. Even after very substantial investments in IT-systems, some trou-bled companies still have information systems which are more geared to keeping track of transactions than to providing deci-sion-orientated top management information. Decision-making might also require quite other types of data than those contained in an accounting-orientated system. (Old cost accounting systems – often based on rather crude cost allocation keys – have increasingly become irrelevant for decision-making purposes. Examples and cures are provided in Chapter 8.)

18. If there is a lack of objective data, structured in an intelligent and understandable fashion, most employees are forced to base their opinions and actions more on *myths, traditions and rumours*, than on facts about the company and its relationship to its business environment.

Let us now change focus to *plans* and their implementation, or rather lack thereof:

19. There is usually an abundance of highly unrealistic sales forecasts, budgets and action plans. A 'post-audit' of plans and budgets (typically undertaken two years later) often shows that the troubled company has a consistent history of rather ambitious plans and budgets which have never been fully implemented. The troubled company might therefore never have achieved more than 80 per cent of budgeted volumes, or more than 50 per cent of budgeted operating results.

20. The formal organization (including the allocation of responsibilities, corresponding reporting lines and so on) is usually unclear. When a clear-cut organization plan exists, it seldom reflects the true needs and priorities of the distressed company. Real-life decision-making might also have rather little resemblance to what the formal organization suggests. More than half the cases in the second part of this book required a *radical revision*, not only of the troubled company's Business Mission, but also of the allocation of associated managerial *responsibilities*.

21. One often finds two or three quite capable managers discreetly tucked away in peripheral organisational 'boxes', for example marked 'special projects', or 'at the disposal of the CEO'. (This is often the case if the departed former CEO could not tolerate deviating opinions, which he regarded as 'opposition'.) Some of these individuals might simply have been impertinent enough to ask valid but unwelcome questions. As a result, the previous CEO found them troublesome, and removed them from centre

stage. (In the US, such sideways moves are more seldom seen than in Europe. In the US, 'difficult individuals' are more likely to have been fired, with reference to 'personality clashes', 'incompatible management philosophies', 'lack of chemistry' and so on.)

22. Morale is low. Sniping is common. Both the board and middle management have long since lost faith in the recently departed CEO. A pleasant consequence is that the arrival of the new turnaround manager is often actively welcomed as well as dreaded. ('Finally, somebody will actually *do* something about this mess'.)

In summary, among turnaround companies, it is exceptionally unusual to find a well-structured, smoothly operating organization with a clear idea about what the Business Mission is (or ought to be), and what the problems are and what should be done about them. One of the tasks of the turnaround manager is to change the existing mentality, improve the intellectual climate and increase the momentum, while making the whole company more focused, that is, goal-driven, and the managers change-orientated instead of being status quo defenders.

1.7 Preventive medicine, radical surgery or voluntary death

It is today commonly acknowledged that preventive health care is preferable to sick care. What then about the use of preventive soft medicine in a turnaround situation?

Unfortunately, when a turnaround manager is called in, the situation has usually deteriorated to a point where 'soft medicine' is no longer a valid option. Such medicine is not strong enough and the time available for the cure is too limited. Therefore more radical measures (often including organisational surgery) are usually called for.

Is a troubled company or major division always worth saving? Are there no situations when a company is simply better dead than terminally ill?

Of course, it does not make much sense to help a troubled company to reach a stage where it can totter around on the brink of bankruptcy for another ten years while absorbing even more capital and management attention better used elsewhere. Such help is of dubious value. Expressed differently, the company doctor does not want to create a permanent invalid, but a healthy person, even if this should first require radical surgery.

After accepting an assignment, the company doctor's first duty is normally to try to save the company (or at least viable parts of it). However, as just mentioned, there are also cases where bankruptcy or voluntary liquidation might indeed be preferable.

Bankruptcy is a legal term implying insolvency, that is, the company is simply unable to pay its debts. If so, assets are usually sold off at substantial discounts and under rather distressing conditions. Many interested parties are bound to lose from such bankruptcies, particularly suppliers, shareholders and workers, while banks and other credit institutions usually have managed to cover at least part of their exposure through collaterals.

As compared to bankruptcy, *voluntary liquidation* is usually preferable, particularly if assets and/or whole strategic business units (SBUs) can be sold off in an orderly fashion. (If so, they are likely to bring in more revenue than under fire sale conditions.)

In this book the authors will simply assume that the company doctor's first concern will be to try to *save the company including all its inherent parts*. If this is not possible, or economically viable, his second-line strategy must be to identify and delineate the company's *future core business(es)*. Subsequently, he will rapidly sell off what are primarily time- and money-consuming 'peripheral activities'. This will improve the company's cash position and future cash-flows, and also radically increase the amount of management time available for the core business, that is, for the intended backbone of the future organization. After such an operation, the patient might indeed have lost a limb, but can continue to live, perhaps even with very good prospects.

1.8   Desirable changes indicated by the listed symptoms

From the long symptom list previously presented, the reader can almost 'smell' the usual turnaround atmosphere at the outset of a typical turnaround. From the list he might also be able to deduct at least some of the actions typically called for, although here quite apart from more case-specific activities:

a. The management team in the distressed company must critically review and reformulate its *Business Mission* and develop a valid *corporate strategy*. The latter must also be operationally formulated so that it automatically guides real-life activities and decisions, instead of 'floating high above'. Further, it is not enough that a sound strategy is well documented; it must also be effectively communicated throughout the organization and professionally *implemented*. (Good-sounding general credos, for example describing how responsible the company is versus all its different stakeholders, will not help much. Such statements provide very little concrete operational guidance in most turnaround situations.)

b. Myths, rumours, storytelling and unquestioned traditions must be replaced by *objective and relevant facts*, however unpleasant. This might call for an improved information structure and information flow. (But stay with the basics: 'Who should get what data, structured how, in order to be able to do what?') The information is there to trigger adequate management responses. After improving greatly the access to pertinent information, the turnaround manager has the right to expect all managers to read, understand, reflect and also *act* on the information provided.[7]

c. In-house *preferences and traditions* have to be subordinated to transformations called for as a result of changes in markets and customer needs, in marketing conditions and competitive pressures. In companies ripe for a major turnaround, 'executive myopia' is common on the executive floor. (The outlook is inside-out, rather than outside-in, as will later be discussed.)

d. Initially, a company (or a major division) in a crisis will usually welcome an *enlightened dictator*. However, rather soon this management style must be replaced by a dedicated *leadership team* and sufficient middle-management depth. (One person – however good – cannot in the long run guarantee the proper functioning of the company. Therefore, a prolonged dictatorial leadership will sooner or later become counter-productive, although perhaps initially being necessary.)

e. The company must rapidly be equipped with a reasonable number of built-in controls, including stringent *cost controls* and *goal fulfilment checks*. Such controls can sometimes be supplemented by early warning signals (that is, alarm bells going off whenever a predetermined critical value has been reached, or when going-rate forecasts indicate that the company is most likely heading for lower than budgeted profit and sales values or other trouble). Again, the purpose here is to help make a phlegmatic organization more alert to threatening developments which call both for early management *attention* and early corrective management *action*.

f. Most internal reporting systems can be manipulated. It is therefore imperative that the turnaround manager makes sure that financial accounts, as well as managerial reports, are not one-sided or manipulated, but that they *reflect the true situation* and can serve as a basis for correct decisions. This is not only a technical problem. The root cause of such report manipulation might be scared managers trying to protect their turf and their jobs. If so, the psychological aspect must be dealt with as well.

---

g. An *enlightened dictatorship* might be necessary for the first few months of a turnaround to shake up a complacent organization, displaying inertia. However, gradually such a management style has to be replaced by more normal management methods. A systematic delegation of certain tasks can start being made on the first day on company premises. However, a more permanent and further-reaching delegation of responsibilities might have to await the existence of clear-cut goals, a clarification of each manager's responsibilities and authority, and decisions as to who shall have access to what information. Until then, an enlightened dictatorship might not only be accepted, but also necessary.

Thus, before the turnaround manager can adopt a more laid-back style, largely based on delegation, he first has to ensure that first-class managers are on board, and that stringent monitoring and control procedures are in place. Established targets should normally be reached and any substantial shortfalls rapidly reported. However, most likely it will take quite some time to get both good managers and systems in place. In the meantime, the enlightened dictator continues to rule, while he simultaneously tests the quality of the managerial material already available within the company.

h. A company in distress might have developed many defensive attitudes. In extreme cases, 'departmental myopia' might have set in. ('We work so hard, the problem must certainly be elsewhere'.) Often the employees' focus might be entirely on transactional efficiency rather than on the *relevance and profitability* of the transactions in question! To avoid such departmental myopia, it is imperative that the turnaround manager encourages cross-functional thinking and that cross-functional cooperation increases. If middle managers remain incapable of applying a broader managerial perspective, interdepartmental infighting (and resulting profit sub-optimization) will continue.

Just the fact that a major turnaround exercise is called for, implies three things:

■   *Early warning signals* were not properly monitored. At least they did not trigger adequate managerial actions.

■   While the crisis was probably obvious to most independent observers, including clients, the crisis was not correctly dealt with. Often it was only explained away. ('Just a temporary hiccup. Don't worry. We have seen similar problems before. They always go away by themselves.' – 'This is just a little blip on our long-range curve. Don't worry.') Such intellectual dishonesty tends to cost a company fortunes and must be attacked.

■   The management team in place was obviously incapable of correctly *analysing the true causes of the crisis, identifying corresponding remedies* and – above all – *taking strong, decisive actions* to correct the situation.

In section 1.6 we described typical *symptoms* in a turnaround situation. In the present section we have listed some obviously *desirable changes*. The idea is to give the reader a pretty good idea as to the problems and tasks awaiting him when arriving on company premises, quite apart from the case-specific problems and realities which always exist. (Many of the latter can be found in Part II, the book's case section.)

Techniques and some common tools used during different phases of the turnaround (such as problem analysis, revision of the Business Mission, creation and implementation of an action programme, as well as the tools for the close monitoring of the success of the ongoing turnaround process against goals, plans and critical milestones) are discussed at some length in Part I, without getting too technical. The cases in Part II add further depth and realism.

Admittedly, if the company situation has been allowed to deteriorate far enough, the turnaround manager might simply have to focus all his attention, for the first two months or so, on simply making the company *survive* in a very hostile environment, including jittery bankers threatening to pull the cord on the company. In such cases, the manager is then well advised to think about his task as consisting of three distinct phases:

a. an acute survival phase
b. a retrenchment and recovery phase
c. an implementation of the Blueprint for the Future phase.

The recovery phase normally provides time to think, plan and evaluate people more in depth, while enjoying the fruits of, for example, the initial cost-cutting exercises.

However, creating a viable company with a sustainable competitive advantage calls for much more than just cost-cutting, however deep. Requirements are:

1. A revised *Business Mission Statement* and/or *Blueprint for the Future Company.*
2. A *strategy* and some kind of *transformation plan* showing how to change the company and achieve the turnaround goals.
3. Actually *implementing the plan in real life* with rather ruthless determination.

This is essentially what this book covers through text and in-depth case studies, supplemented by approximately 40 boxes (framed mini cases) scattered throughout, the latter providing a range of concrete and very recent examples, including a substantial number from US corporations.[8]

1.9 The disposition: two main parts, fourteen chapters of which six represent in-depth cases

This book consists of two major parts. The first has been called 'On the Driving Range', the second 'Taking it to the Course'. Non-golfers might appreciate an explanation of this golf analogy. An experienced golfer knows:

■ that the swing can be photographed, broken down into its different minute components and analysed accordingly, that is, 'intellectualised'. However, when it comes to using the swing in real life, it must be just one smooth movement.
■ that you train on the driving range, but when you finally get out there on the course itself, you should be target-driven, not technique-driven.

The same is true in a turnaround situation. It is in reality one integrated – and often rather messy – process. Further, as in golf, the terrain for the turnaround exercise is often only partly known and the hazards you desperately tried to avoid, might end up blocking your intended way, forcing you to modify your strategy.

In Part I we discuss principles and techniques, admittedly based on a somewhat artificial division of the turnaround process into different main components or aspects. We call this part *'On the Driving Range'*.

In Part II, *'Taking it to the Course'*, we deal with the more complex reality, that is, when these principles are supposed to be applied, more or less simultaneously and under considerable time pressure, psychological tension and economic constraints. As in golf, the turnaround manager has a less than complete picture of the terrrain ahead. Still he has to choose a club, make his bets, pray to God and get at it. Thus, based on his experience and skills he 'takes it to the course'.

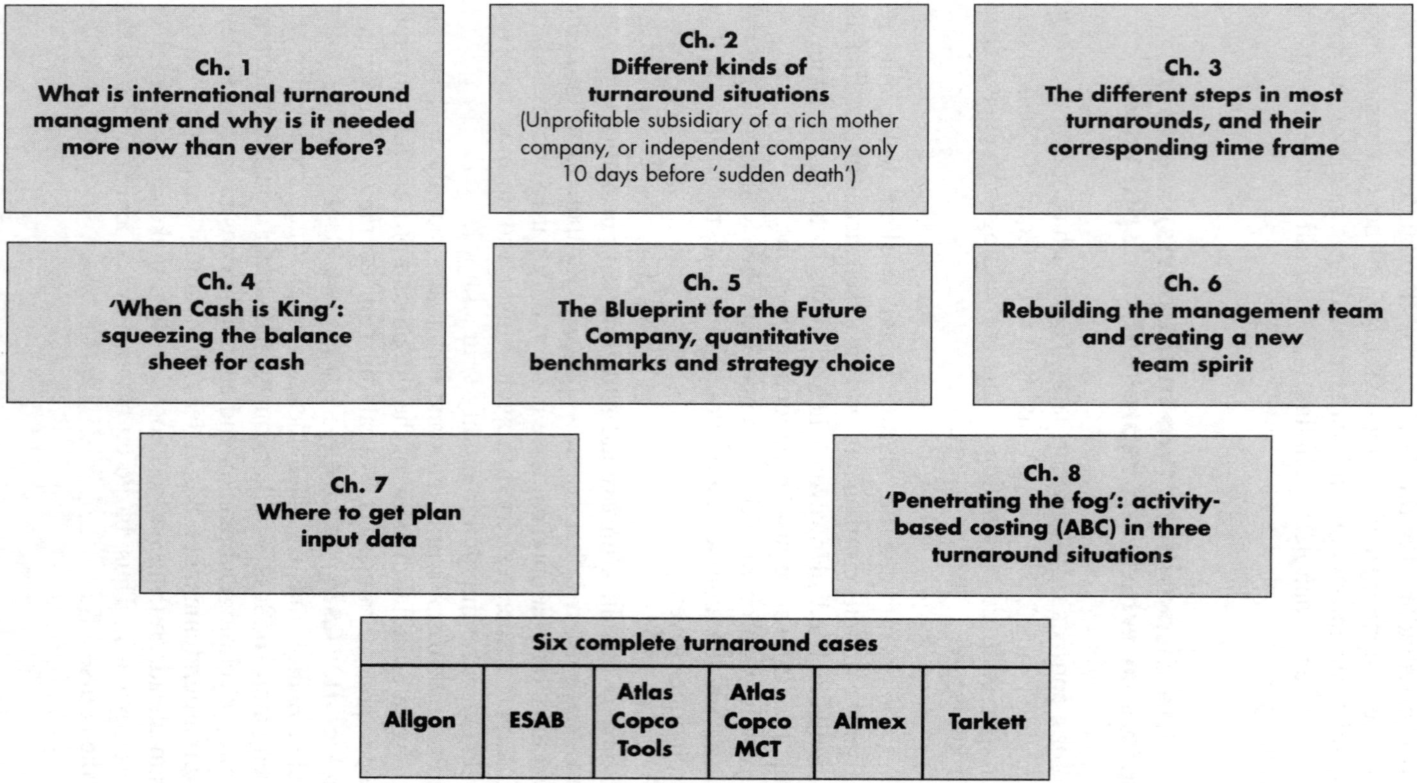

Ch. 1
What is international turnaround managment and why is it needed more now than ever before?

Ch. 2
Different kinds of turnaround situations
(Unprofitable subsidiary of a rich mother company, or independent company only 10 days before 'sudden death')

Ch. 3
The different steps in most turnarounds, and their corresponding time frame

Ch. 4
'When Cash is King': squeezing the balance sheet for cash

Ch. 5
The Blueprint for the Future Company, quantitative benchmarks and strategy choice

Ch. 6
Rebuilding the management team and creating a new team spirit

Ch. 7
Where to get plan input data

Ch. 8
'Penetrating the fog': activity-based costing (ABC) in three turnaround situations

Six complete turnaround cases					
Allgon	ESAB	Atlas Copco Tools	Atlas Copco MCT	Almex	Tarkett

Figure 1.3   Contents and general structure of the book

Part II of the book also deals with down-to-earth 'course manage-ment' by taking the reader through six tricky turnaround situations, successfully mastered. It is then possible to see how the principles and techniques (discussed in Part I) interact to generate quite outstanding results also *on the course*, as fully reflected in corre-sponding numerical performance graphs (that is, 'score cards') covering the full turnaround period. Sometimes the authors have even chosen to include a few years before and after the actual turnaround to bring this out in full relief.

Part I is universal, that is, not case-specific. Thus, it deals with 'Principles and Techniques' and covers common symptoms, problem definitions, useful tools and procedures, as well as critical conditions for success, including psychological and motivational aspects. The advice provided is firmly based on real-life experience gained from a large number of turnarounds. Part II, 'Taking it to the Course', contains six in-depth case studies.

To facilitate the reader's overview of the case contents, most cases have (in their middle) been provided with a 'Summary Sheet'. On its left side are listed the *identified key problems*. On its right hand side are listed *major corrective management actions* taken to correct the situation.

The said summary sheets are normally preceded by an in-depth discussion of the problems and their origins, and followed by an in-depth discussion of corresponding management actions.

Finally, the *results* achieved are shown in several *turnaround performance graphs*. These usually only cover the turnaround period itself, but sometimes they also include a few years leading up to the distress situation which had to be attacked.

The main thrust of each chapter is reflected in Figure 1.3.

In Chapter 2, different kinds of turnaround situations are discussed. The spectrum is broad. It covers 'sudden death cases', that is, companies threatened with running out of cash within the next ten days, to much more comfortable situations, for example when a turn-around manager is addressing the problems of an unprofitable daughter to a parent company with considerable financial resources and substantial patience.

Chapter 3 contains an overview of the different steps involved in most turnarounds. (Although all turnarounds are somewhat different and often have different key emphases and priorities, they also have many common features.)

Cash is sometimes more important than profits, to avoid sudden death. Thus, 'When Cash is King': liquidifying the balance sheet is the first concern. How to liquidify the balance sheet is discussed in Chapter 4.

Chapter 5 contains a further discussion of the crucial importance of establishing a Blueprint for the Future Company, and doing this early on. (It is certainly not enough to slash, burn and cut, there must also be a stimulating future worth fighting for.) Objective benchmarks against which to measure turnaround progress are discussed in the same chapter.

Chapter 6 deals with how to evaluate the existing management team and its members, as well as – when required – how to build a new management team, including the critical importance of creating quite another team spirit.

Contrary to a few other turnaround books, the authors here assume that the reader knows elementary economic terms (like fixed and variable costs), elementary economic calculations (like break-even analysis and cash-flow analysis), and that he or she can read a balance sheet or a P&L statement, understands normal financial key ratios, and also knows how to react to them. Also, although tempted, the authors do not attempt to list all the different techniques which might be helpful in a turnaround situation, from traditional market research and benchmarking to corporate re-engineering.

However, in Chapter 8 the authors make an exception. Here, they describe and illustrate the practical use of a few selected tools proven to be particularly useful in connection with several turnaround cases. Common to these cases was that the turnaround situation was not very clear, but rather fragmented and blurred, and thus in urgent need of objective illumination. (The tools discussed and illustrated in Chapter 8 are closely related to what is today often called activity-based costing or ABC. Their practical use and usefulness in turnaround situations are demonstrated with three cases, all from industries other than the six covered in the special case section at the very end of the book.)

The case studies in Part II, 'Taking it to the Course', vividly illustrate the validity and real-life application of the general turnaround principles and techniques discussed in Part I, 'On the Driving Range'. The six concluding in-depth case studies represent *six different industries*, all heavily dependent on *successful cross-border operations* and thus come under the title 'international turnarounds'. Two of the cases

(ESAB and Tarkett) deal with multinationals which were once close to liquidation but – taken on by aggressive and smart turnaround managers – were not only saved, but successfully grown until each became *No. 2 worldwide* in their respective industries. In a third case, Allgon, shareholder value grew thirty-fold over a three-year period. Performance graphs provided by the companies themselves accompany the presentations to objectively show the impact of the actions taken and corresponding time frame.

Notes

1. For the sake of simplicity, in this book the turnaround manager will normally be referred to as 'he', although the authors fully acknowledge and quote some female turnaround experts.
2. In the minds of many, the term 'crisis management' has primarily come to be associated with the handling of unexpected occurrences completely outside the control of the company, such as a factory burning to the ground, or terrorists kidnapping the chief executive. Although cases of this nature are certainly worthy of the name 'crisis', they obviously do not call for comprehensive company turnaround activities as described in this book.
3. Janus, an ancient Latin divinity was the 'spirit of the doorway', invoked on entrances and exits. Since the gates of Rome could open both ways, for example to let armies in or out, Janus is always depicted with two faces pointing in opposite directions. He is also the god of 'new beginnings', so dear to any turnaround manager.
4. In Section 8.13, called 'Living happily without consultants and advanced analytical tools?', the reader is faced with a contrasting view. However, as shown there, even 'Chainsaw Al' Dunlap – who likes to 'fire all the consultants' – actually uses senior consultants, although sparingly and selectively.
5. For turnaround management seminars to be run on the client's own premises, Arpi International SA has developed an integrated seminar package containing advanced learning tools, and further turnaround examples not included in the present book. (For information, please contact Arpi International SA, 42 Avenue de l'Espinette Centrale, B-1640 Rhode-St-Genèse/BELGIUM.
6. Priority issues will be discussed in Chapters 2 and 3.
7. Harold S. Geneen, the legendary ITT boss, used to say: 'The first responsibility of a manager is to MANAGE'. Another way to express the same idea is to insist on 'rapid, valid, corrective management response'. (This is quite different both from 'business as usual' and lingering 'paralysis through analysis'.)
8. Although often heavily rewritten, reorganised, abbreviated or combined (for the purposes of this book), more often than not, the starting point has been an article from *Business Week* and/or the *Financial Times*, which are hereby gratefully acknowledged.

2 Different kinds of turnaround situation

2.1 Purpose of chapter

In Chapter 3, we will discuss the different steps involved in most turn-around processes. Before discussing these steps and also the specific tools and techniques available, it might be useful to consider the rather broad spectrum of turnaround situations which might appear. The nature and urgency of the situation at hand influences the turnaround managers' priorities as well as the degree of freedom available to them.

Key parameters influencing the turnaround situation include the following:

- ■ The ownership structure of the troubled company.

- ■ The urgency of the crisis (as reflected in cash-flow projections, but also in the attitudes displayed by different stakeholders, including banks and key suppliers).

- ■ Whether the company must be radically cost-reduced, or if other valid and realistic alternatives exist.

- ■ The *management team* presently in place. (Its professional quality and attitudes to change. Its responsibility for the present crisis and its remaining degree of credibility – internally as well as externally.)

- ■ Whether the new turnaround manager is supposed to move in as a long-term CEO, or as a temporary CEO, for example during a 12–24 month turnaround period.

- ■ Whether he operates as a 'lone wolf' or is assisted, for example by a senior consultant with massive previous experience of turnarounds.

The above list is certainly not comprehensive. However, it contains a number of key variables with strong impact on:

- the degrees of freedom available to the turnaround manager
- the time available for contemplating and deciding on priorities and actions, as well as
- the methods and tools which are most suitable.

The knowledgeable reader might like to add a number of other factors, for example:

- whether it is a trading company, a service company or a producing company

- which particular industry the company represents

- whether the products are undifferentiated mature products, or young products still associated with the idea selling phase

- the size, market share and reputation of the company

- how clever and aggressive their key competitors are.

An extension of the discussion along these lines at this point would hardly serve any useful purpose. Instead, additional factors will be discussed in their logical context in later chapters.

Although this book illustrates a number of turnaround strategies for a great number of international companies, and pages 121–39 deal with key strategic choices (for example cost cutting versus added value creation), it is not meant to replace the standard texts on choice of a viable corporate strategy. For instance, strategies for 'mature undifferentiated industrial products' are discussed in the very substantial body of strategic planning literature available today. Professor Mike Porter deals with strategy choice problems in at least five of his books, including *Competitive Strategy: Techniques for Analyzing Industries and Competitors*[1], and *Competitive Advantage: Creating and Sustaining Superior Performance*.[2] Service management strategies are discussed by several authors, including Richard Norrman in his standard work *Service Management: Strategy and Leadership in Service Business*.[3]

2.2   The immediate cash crisis ('10 days from sudden death')

2.2.1   If the climate allows, do your homework first!

Many turnaround managers insist on spending at least three weeks studying the case before they actually appear on the premises of the troubled company. They study company reports and business data from the last 5–10 years (with the last three years often broken down on a monthly basis). They look at previous budgets and long-range plans, and then compare them to later known outcomes, that is, perform so called 'post audits'. They compile *key performance ratios* for the company and compare these with corresponding ratios for competing companies (or with benchmarks from respected companies in similar industries). They study annual reports of the last 5–10 accounting years, and protocols from board meetings during the last 3–5 years.

The two main purposes of such a homework phase are usually the following:

■ To learn as much as possible before visiting the company, thus acquiring a good and objective view early on.
■ To be well prepared on arrival and thus able to have maximum impact on the company and its personnel from Day 1.

Of course, there is usually a third reason for the homework period:

■ To find out if it is likely that the company *can be saved at all* and, if so, what kind of broad changes must be considered. Early approval for such drastic actions from the company board might be needed, even before the turnaround assignment is finally accepted. (If no road to safety can be found or the powers required to finish the job are not given to him, the potential turnaround manager should simply decline the assignment rather than engage in a lost cause.)

2.2.2   When there is simply no time for extensive homework

Sometimes the turnaround situation is such that there is simply not enough time available even for three weeks of homework.

The company might be running out of cash within the next 10 days. Rumours might be circulating concerning the almost certain 'sudden death' of the company. The bank (or other creditors) might be jittery and threaten to pull the cord on the company. The exposed situation encourages key suppliers to insist on being paid cash on delivery which does not help the cash-flow situation. (This situation is discussed in great depth in Chapter 4: 'When Cash is King'.)

Under such circumstances, the turnaround expert cannot usually afford the luxury of sitting at home, calmly studying documents or comparing key ratios. He[4] simply has to get to the scene and move into action. Now is not the right time to consider the most elegant future organizational arrangements. There will not *be* a future organization to worry about a few months later if he does not manage to solve the company's most urgent problems.

Given this kind of scenario, the turnaround manager usually only has the time to assure that he has *full backing* (usually by the board), *sufficient operational freedom,* and a formal *power base* from which to operate effectively. Then he moves onto company premises, putting most of his emphasis on two urgent things:

1. Producing cash (or at least delaying certain cash payments) in such a way that the company is not running out of cash, but can meet its most important payment obligations.
2. Calming the 'stakeholders', that is, the different interested parties having a stake in the company, including employees, clients, vendors, banks and shareholders.

He has to see to it that vendors continue to deliver, that key clients do not desert the company, that key managers and experts whose availability is crucial to the success of the company do not desert it and that the bank and other creditors are convinced that they have more to win from giving the company a last chance than seeing it go bankrupt.

Under these circumstances, the turnaround manager has to:

■ *move fast*

■ show that he is *firmly in charge*

- show that he has a *viable turnaround strategy* (although not yet a complete plan with all its details)

- start *making things happen* and happen FAST.

A substantial part of his first few days on company premises will focus on *cash-flow projections*, at least on a week-by-week basis. The first question to answer is simply: 'How quickly will we run out of cash if things proceed as presently?'

His second set of cash-flow projections will most likely be a 'worst case scenario', for example based on the assumption that some major suppliers will insist on COD payment, that some clients will try to use the company's predicament to get bigger cash discounts or force the company to accept longer payment terms. The bank might also refuse to renew certain kinds of credit which the company has always taken for granted.

Equipped with one set of going-rate and one set of worst-case cash flow projections, the turnaround manager will have a pretty good idea as to both the size and urgency of the problems at hand. He then has to act.

As well as trying to negotiate special deals with (often understanding) key suppliers and (most likely less understanding) banks, he might also have to consider some kind of 'fire sales', as discussed in Chapter 4, section 4.2.

2.2.3 Asset disposal to raise cash

The easiest way to release some cash is probably to sell the receivables (via factoring) and also part of the existing inventory, which is probably both too large and badly balanced, anyway.

The turnaround manager might also consider selling off some fixed assets. An alternative is to sell off buildings and then lease them back. In case these two options are closed or exhausted, the turnaround manager might have to consider even more drastic actions, including the selling off of one or more complete business units.

He might be able to raise cash by selling a loss-making and cash-thirsty strategic business unit (SBU). If this is not possible, he might instead be forced to sell off one or more profitable SBUs. Such a move can be justified, provided that he is not in the process selling off the company's intended future core business, which represents the best future chance for the company.

Classical US cases of selling whole SBUs include airline groups selling their hotel chains and other real estate (sometimes including their headquarters building), while (rightly or wrongly) keeping their loss-making airline operations, supposedly representing their future core business.

An interesting Scandinavian case is Nordstjernan, once the flagship of the Swedish Johnson Group. When this highly diversified group encountered big financial difficulties during the mid-1980s, a new CEO, Bert Magnusson, was appointed. Two years later, he had sold off a very substantial number of SBUs, including companies in many different industries, but he kept the company's construction arm.

In 1988, the downsized but cash-rich Johnson Group bought the ABV construction group to be merged with their own activities into JCC, (the Johnson Construction Company). Asked why, Magnusson answered:

> We badly needed to focus on one clear-cut future core business, and construction was probably the least weak of all the weak SBUs we had within Nordstjernan. By combining forces with ABV we hope to have created a viable core business also for the future. The cash generated by our earlier spin-offs has made this purchase possible.

In 1997 SIAB was also integrated with NCC which, by 1999 – with 22,000 employees and a turnover of 34 billion Swedish crowns – was the biggest construction and property company in the Nordic and Baltic Sea areas. Bert Magnusson's vision had been realised.

2.2.4 Summary as to urgency

If a company is likely to run out of cash only two weeks later, and its bank insists on seeing a well-founded turnaround plan on its desk within seven days, the turnaround manager will certainly not have the time to develop all the details normally contained in what we call the Blueprint for the Future Company, nor the corresponding implementation plan showing what changes are called for and when.

Under such 'close to sudden death' circumstances, the new manager has to put the main emphasis on only two things:

a. *Immediate cash position improvement,* and a radical improvement also in operating cash flows for the next four to twelve months. ('Going-rate' projections, 'worst case' projections and 'likely turnaround impact' projections are useful tools.)

b. *Convincing and calming key stakeholders,* by showing in clear-cut numerical terms that the company can achieve a fully viable future end state. Financial key ratios and benchmarking values from well-run companies in the same industry – or from well-run companies in industries with similar characteristics – are helpful tools. (Benchmarking techniques for such purposes are discussed in section 4.3.)

2.3   The unprofitable subsidiary (with headquarters functioning as the rather friendly and patient banker)

If the troubled company is a subsidiary of a well-known multinational group with strong finances, a radically different situation exists as compared to the '10 days from sudden death' scenario. Such a group does not stand or fall with the fate of a singular subsidiary. Although an embarrassment to group management, headquarters seldom consider letting a daughter company go bankrupt. As to the time-frame for the turnaround, the key consideration is seldom maximum speed. Rather, the focus is on sound actions taken in a systematic fashion, and without creating too much noise or disturbing corporate relations. In the meantime, headquarters might be grumbling, but are usually prepared to continue to supply needed capital through appropriate means. (Exceptions exist; the Swedish Match Group never guaranteed the debts of their loss-making German Kübel Group, but left it to its local managing director to negotiate with the German bankers.)

Given the friendly headquarters scenario – which radically differs from the 'ten days from sudden death' scenario – the turnaround manager can certainly organize his work and go about it in a much more structured fashion.

Most international headquarters – with the possible exception of some particularly trigger-happy US ones – are in reality prepared to give a knowledgeable turnaround expert up to one month to evaluate the overall situation and its root causes, and perhaps one to three months to prepare (and sell!) his proposed Blueprint for the Future Company. In the meantime, he operates primarily as a fire fighter, attacking miscellaneous smaller, but urgent calamities.

The Blueprint for the Future Company must contain a revised Business Mission Statement, but ideally also financial and volume targets, and a broad strategy statement which embraces the most important changes called for. (Document contents and terminology used in different companies are discussed at great length in the first two sections of Chapter 5.)

It may take five to six months before most pieces are in place, including:

- the Blueprint for the Future Company and associated documents describing strategic goals and key strategies
- an action programme (with time and cost frames and forecasted profit impact) approved by the board, or whatever other relevant party
- a revised top management team committed to new goals and the strategic changes needed to reach them.

It might take another 5–6 months until most of the proposed actions have not only been put in motion, but also started producing their expected impact on cost structures, sales volumes, margins and revenues. Admittedly, eight to ten months might seem to be an unreasonably long period. However, in an international group it is usually still acceptable to group headquarters for several reasons:

- They know that a new (or at least reinforced) management team is in place, increasing the likelihood that necessary changes will also be forcefully implemented.

- The new strategic goals and necessary changes have been carefully evaluated. They are therefore well founded and can be sold more easily to unions and other interested parties, as well as to the mass media. (This is something entirely different from letting a pretty wild 'turnaround cowboy' shoot from the hip, even before he is acquainted with the landscape and its inhabitants.)

- They know that the full management team has been actively involved in the creation of the Blueprint and the corresponding implementation plan. Therefore, team members can be expected to be both emotionally and professionally committed to the success of the plan.

However, there are also limits to the understanding and patience of HQ. The turnaround manager is certainly not expected to spend six months primarily on studying and planning. As a troubleshooter, he is expected to take charge[5] and also implement a number of short-term actions to improve operations and profitability while anchoring his grand design for the future company with the stakeholders. Areas for short-term managerial action include:

- Areas in urgent need of improvement, quite independent of the contents of the overall turnaround plan.

- New procedures, tools and systems – often of a surprisingly simple nature – needed to create a company environment in which necessary major changes can be implemented with a minimum of delay, and with maximum impact. This phase often includes the clarification of managerial responsibilities and the removal of other organizational obstacles.

Summary

While the '10 days from sudden death' scenario necessitates immediate action and also substantial risk taking (sometimes on the verge of gambling), the 'unprofitable division or subsidiary' scenario usually allows the turnaround manager sufficient time to analyse, plan and evaluate key managers, and to evaluate different products, markets, competitors, – key suppliers, – and in-house SBUs – before implementing major strategic changes that might have a tangible long-term impact.

2.4   Cost cutting and downsizing versus volume-improving or margin-improving marketing solutions

2.4.1   Cost cutting is not the only way to improved profits

In the public eye, turnaround experts are too often only perceived as 'shrinkers', 'headcount reducers', or 'cost cutters'. This may certainly be one of the functions of a turnaround expert (during an early phase of the turnaround), but not the only function, and perhaps not even the most important one.

Productivity can most simply be defined as 'sold output divided by corresponding use (that is, input) of company resources'. One of the key concerns in a turnaround situation is to *improve the overall productivity of the troubled company*. However, productivity can be improved in many different ways. One is to carry out the same amount of work with a smaller amount of resources. Another is to simply get rid of large chunks of the troubled company, that is, parts (products, markets, divisions and so on) associated with low productivity. A third way is to increase 'perceived customer value' and corresponding price levels and margins. All three of these means are illustrated in Part II of this book, and also briefly discussed below.

2.4.2 A volume-increasing solution

'Marketing-orientated solutions' increase sales volumes and/or margins without any matching increase in corresponding resource utilization.

John Whitney once used such a solution when turning around a US supermarket chain. Instead of cutting back on manpower, he very slightly *increased* the number of cash register operators. This made it possible to go from an opening time of 12 hours per day to 24 hours a day. The resulting 20 per cent volume increase saved the chain from bankruptcy. This is a good example of a marketing solution influencing revenues much more than costs.

2.4.3 'One Step Up' – a new profit improvement method

The 'One Step Up'™ margin and profit improvement system operates via a radical improvement in *the product mix actually sold*, and therefore also via the average sales price obtained per unit sold. This is done by convincing the average customer to buy a product just one price category higher ('One Step Up') than they would normally have chosen.

Thus, the One Step Up profit improvement system is exactly the *opposite* of all short-term promotional and discounting activities which over time tend to destroy profitability. One Step Up – and similar systems – can also safeguard a permanent profit increase, partly by fundamentally changing the interface between the salesperson and the end-users.

Finally, the system encourages independent dealers to become close partners in a common profit improvement effort – rather than to remain in a traditional negotiating counterpart relationship.

One Step Up has been successfully used in several industries and different turnaround situations, including the Tarkett case, recapitulated in great detail in Part II. The underlying principles and typical results achieved are documented in Figure 2.1.

Case Study

A GERMAN ONE STEP UP™ PRICE AND PROFIT IMPROVEMENT CASE

The Tarkett-Sommer Group is the largest flooring company in Europe and the second largest worldwide. Since 1990, it has been reshaping its structure to work more efficiently and profitably in the face of mounting global competition.

With its cost-cutting phase completed, group management focused its sights on defining and building a strong competitive advantage based on internal organizational efficiency coupled with high external market efficiency. Lars Wisén, then president of the Tarkett Group, explains: 'By using our customers' own perceptions and value systems as a benchmark, instead of our own subjective ideas, we were able to systematically create better customer value.'

Brussels-based consultants, Arpi International, were asked to lend their expertise to this effort. Using a technique originally developed for market and competition studies for Volvo Penta in six countries, consultants from Arpi International conducted face-to-face management interviews with flooring wholesalers and dealers in three of Tarkett's most important markets. These findings clearly showed Tarkett's competitive profile against that of its competitors, highlighting where improvement was needed.

This benchmarking study was followed by the implementation of the One Step Up™ Price Improvement Programme. The programme was first field tested for Tarkett during summer 1996, under closely-monitored conditions in three European test areas. At the end of every working day all 'impact' data – such as changes in customer floor traffic, sales, product mix improvements, and increases in average prices obtained – were fed directly from the test sites into a powerful database maintained at Arpi International in Brussels. Each week, performance improvement charts were relayed both to the Tarkett group management team and to participating dealers.

During spring 1997 this programme was broadened to cover no less than eight regions, *resulting in average price improvements of 30 per cent per square metre sold.*

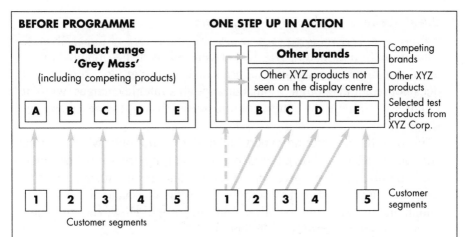

BEFORE PROGRAMME

Product range 'Grey Mass'
(including competing products)

| A | B | C | D | E |

| 1 | 2 | 3 | 4 | 5 |

Customer segments

ONE STEP UP IN ACTION

Other brands — Competing brands

Other XYZ products not seen on the display centre — Other XYZ products

| B | C | D | E | — Selected test products from XYZ Corp.

| 1 | 2 | 3 | 4 | 5 | Customer segments

Explanation: Products are ranked from A to E with increasing end-user price. Customer segments are ranked from 1 to 5, with 1= very price sensitive. Each segment tends to be associated with a given product price bracket, provided clients are not actively persuaded to take One Step Up.

Result: Most clients have indeed taken 'one step up' on the pricing scale. Selected test products have grown to represent over 50% of the total turnover with the dealers.

With One Step Up, everyone wins: the dealers are now making more money, so does the producer; and the end-user has also gained. He/she has purchased a better product which will also last longer.

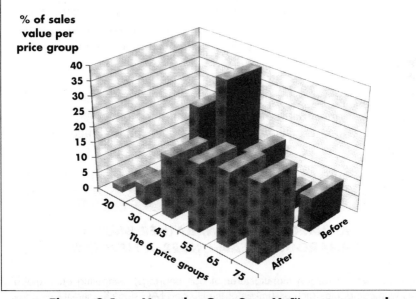

% of sales value per price group

40 35 30 25 20 15 10 5 0

20 30 45 55 65 75
The 6 price groups
After Before

Figure 2.1   How the One Step Up™ system works
(developed by Arpi International, Brussels. Documented in print in English and German.
Also available on the World Wide Web (www.arpi.com)

2.4.4 Where to place the emphasis

The old notion of cutting 10–15 per cent all over the organization is usually a rather unintelligent approach. In a turnaround situation, it does not result in enough savings or enough strategic changes, while it might still strangle the future core business, that is, the best hope for the future.

Instead, the turnaround expert has to decide not only what must be cut back (and/or sold off), but also which activity areas must be given *more* attention and resources in the future. There is no inherent contradiction between cost reduction policies on the one hand and revenue-enhancing marketing solutions on the other. However, they are usually applied in entirely different areas.[6]

A note on terminology might be warranted here, for example the term 'revenue-enhancing marketing solution' does not imply a lowering of margins. A margin squeeze is rather one of the main reasons why a company has ended up as a turnaround candidate. To then start buying more market share at the expense of lower margins usually leads to even more 'volume sickness'. In contrast, the strategic concept to 'gain a dominant position in selected market niches' is often associated with being able to get *higher prices and margins*. (The ESAB case study at the end of this book illustrates this magnificently.)

While the turnaround manager must identify early on areas which will constitute the core business of the future company, he must simultaneously attack:

- areas which represent 'money-thirsty distractions',[7] or
- just glamorous dreams with few factual underpinnings,[8] and
- expensive traditions in which the company can no longer afford to indulge.

Case Study

SKF IMPOSES A NEW, RATHER BRUTAL TURNAROUND PLAN UNDER A NEW CEO

SKF is the world's largest manufacturer of ball bearings, competing on a global basis with companies such as Timken of the US and FAG Kugelfischer of Germany.

Over-capacity and weakening demand (not least from the all-important automotive industry) had driven prices and margins down. Prices had fallen faster than costs, offsetting the favourable impact of earlier rationalizations.

SKF's new CEO, Mr Carlsson, said: 'Tinkering is not enough. More brutal treatment is now urgently required'. Before Mr Carlsson's arrival, thousands of employees had been fired by his predecessor, and the company restructured. Even so, the SKF share prices fell by 43% between December 1997 and December 1998, and the pretax loss for the first nine months of 1998 was SEK247 million. So what was the new set of 'corrective management actions' envisaged by Mr Carlsson?

The company announced that it would withdraw from certain non-core businesses, including textile machinery components. Another 5,000 jobs would be sacrificed, of which close to 2,000 before year-end 1998. Production and production systems would be more geared to customer demand. Most likely, some US factories would be closed, and some other loss-making operations either closed or sold off. Investments in capital equipment would be cut from SEK2,500 million to SEK1,500 million a year.

Both SKF and the Volvo Group have their headquarters in the Gothenburg area. Almost simultaneously with SKF's announcement of 5,000 redundancies, Volvo announced they were going to cut their manpower by a similar number.

However, SKF's 'Blueprint for the Future' also identified profitable growth areas. Corresponding plans included much more aggressive moves into the ball bearing aftersales market and the selling of certain services. (In these two areas, the margins are approximately 15%.)

Nobody expected SKF to show a profit during 1999. However, the new sound turnaround strategy, both clearly communicated and ruthlessly implemented, was expected to finally raise SKF's share prices from their historic low registered during the last quarter of 1998.

2.5 The leadership difference

The present (or recently departed) chief executive officer often constitutes an integral part of the troubled company's problems. He has in fact presided over the problems, failed to analyse them in time, or at least failed to attack them effectively early on. As a result, his credibility both within the company and elsewhere (among board members, clients, key shareholders, key suppliers, banks and so on) has usually been severely hurt or completely exhausted.

Therefore, the board of a company in distress usually decides either to replace such a chief executive officer by a permanent new CEO (intended to be the long-term solution), or to employ a temporary CEO (that is, a manager-for-hire) from the outside to 'clean up the worst mess', while the board keeps looking for a longer-term solution to the obvious leadership problem.

An experienced top management consultant can either function as turnaround expert in his own right, or work in parallel with a new CEO. Dr Arpi and other senior consultants of Arpi International have been successfully involved in a number of turnarounds, either as temporary CEOs (with an average full-time assignment lasting nine months), or by working as key advisors to a newly appointed CEO. The second author, Per Wejke, has normally operated as a CEO brought in by the troubled company's board, and he has been expected to stay on for at least 3–4 years, that is, until the full profit impact of his turnaround was visible, and the future company had largely been realized.

A permanent new CEO, a temporary CEO and a senior turnaround assistant/advisor face similar problems and look for similar solutions, but operate differently. The role of a permanent new CEO is quite clear and undisputed. Immediately upon arrival on company premises, he will be bogged down in all the details of day-to-day operating management. This is cumbersome, but it is also an excellent way to get to know the company, its key employees, value systems, traditions and operating procedures. Unfortunately, such day-to-day concerns can easily divert a lot of valuable time from more central issues concerning the company's future.

If a specialized turnaround consultant moves in to work *in parallel* with the new CEO, the former might be able to stay out of the immediate fire and be able to focus his undivided attention on:

- *problem analysis*, including rapid data gathering (internally, but also related to markets, customers, products, end-users and so on)

- the design of a desirable and also realistically attainable *Blueprint for the Future Company*

- description of corresponding *turnaround action plan*, and perhaps also an *implementation plan*, all later described in great detail

- at the CEO's request, assist in securing the understanding by and commitment from all key managers and crucial in-house experts who are supposed to make the plan become a reality. (The running of in-house workshops, intended to create better two-way communication, cross-functional and cross-border understanding, and a deeper employee involvement, might also be the responsibility of the turnaround consultant.) Example of verbatim discussions during such in-house seminars are found in Chapter 7, particularly in section 7.3.

Thus, a senior consultant might be operating as a temporary turnaround manager himself, or he can assist the new CEO. By adding his own weight and considerable analytical skills, he should be able to speed up the necessary change process while identifying and helping to limit associated risks. If 'manager for hire', the leadership quality and turnaround experience of the consultant is the critical issue. If assistant, his capability to efficiently run management seminars while providing heavy analytical and conceptual inputs becomes a more critical skill. (Needless to say, any turnaround consultant must also be able to work very closely and effectively with a new, permanent CEO. The latter is very likely a hands-on, hurried go-getter with rather strong opinions of his own. The two must be able to work as co-pilots, pulling powerfully in the same direction although each by different means.) The following case might illustrate such a cooperation.

Case Study

A major European distributor of semi-finished metal products and commodities started showing heavy losses. The CEO, who represented the ownership family, decided to leave the company. In September, a new managing director with a strong background in finance was brought in. In October, and with the board's blessing, Dr Arpi was brought in to add more expertise, particularly in the marketing and computer-based financial simulation area.

He rapidly detected that the hard-working, so-called regional managers were not analytically skilled, nor true decision-makers. Rather, they were 'branch shop superintendents' who never questioned either the assortment of products provided or the existing price levels. The over-extended product range was conveniently exonerated with reference to a statement by the previous CEO that the mission of this company was to be a 'full-service company'. Nor could price levels be touched, since 'this might start a relentless and damaging price war'.

The work allocation between the new CEO and the consultant was pretty obvious. While the new CEO focused on stakeholder relationships, evaluating employees, selling off unnecessary and expensive staff departments (including a data processing department containing 54 individuals), the external consultant could focus on making the branch superintendents more aware of the fact that they were themselves actually in charge of certain decision-making parameters and were indeed supposed to actively use them to the benefit of the company. This turned out to be a monumental educational task.

The consultant finally found that a highly useful educational tool was the creation of a huge computer-assisted market/product matrix containing more than 100 different market/product segments. The following values were indicated for each of these segments:

- turnover for the market/product segment
- gross margin for the same segment
- remaining profit contribution value (often called the segment's 'marketing contriution' value) after the deduction of segment-specific marketing costs
- as above, also after deduction of segment-specific order-handling costs
- and so on step-by-step for different types of function and activity and their associated costs.

All in all, ten different 'contribution levels' were identified in a similar fashion. To identify the size of the profit contribution at each level, costs of each type were identified and measured based on a combination of time studies, analysis of accounting data, discussions with key managers and so on. (The techniques used and findings arrived at are illustrated in Chapter 8.)

As a result, a quantitative, fact-based (and inescapable) picture could be presented for each product/market segment. The earlier passive 'shop superintendents' could now for the first time clearly see how different cost types were gradually reducing the revenues, resulting in a net loss in most of their product/market segments.

Helped by such company-specific analytical tools, it now became possible to turn 'superintendents' into 'managers' discussing the need for price increases, cost reductions, the complete abolishment of certain products, cheaper marketing procedures versus certain low-priority target groups, better ways to more effectively use existing equipment (including a substantial vehicle fleet and expensive loading equipment in the terminals).

Since the full product/market matrix was firmly linked to a computer programme containing all underlying key data and cost formulas, it was even possible to simulate the likely impact of contemplated management actions. In this particular turnaround case, the senior consultant worked in parallel with the CEO for about 12 months, gathering facts, building the descriptive computer model, running top management seminars, simulating the impact of different types of contemplated changes, highlighting the urgent need for others, and so on.

At the end of this 'educational process', regional managers and product line managers had *entirely changed their perception of their roles and responsibilities*. They had never been so well informed as to the cost and revenue structure of the company as a whole, and for their own particular area of responsibility. The figures themselves were a cry for management action, and the managers were now not only prepared to *welcome* changes, but to *lead* these changes themselves. However, throughout this whole process, there was never any doubt about who was the CEO of the company and who called the shots when it came to making fundamental decisions and making sure they stuck.

2.6   The importance of the country in which the turnaround takes place

Existing turnaround literature is scarce. Most of it comes from the US and it seldom deals with European turnarounds or cross-border turnarounds. This is a clear-cut drawback for European readers since turnaround conditions in Europe not only differ from those in the US, but also differ between various European countries. Although restrictions formally imposed by national laws or regulations are now gradually replaced by EU-wide laws, there still remain substantial differences as to culture, tradition and value systems which cannot be ignored in a cross-border turnaround.

Thus, the turnaround situation, and the means available to correct it, is often substantially different depending upon the country in which the troubled company's headquarters are situated, but also in what other countries problems (and potential solutions) reside.

Co-determination laws might be used as a concrete example. Although both Sweden and Germany have longstanding laws about participative management (*Mitbestimmung* in Germany, 'MBL' in Sweden), the actual implementation of these laws is very different in the two countries. As a result, some Swedish managers with a long domestic habit of consultations with representatives of the blue-collar workers as well as white-collar workers have, to their surprise, found themselves faced with substantial problems when trying to understand how Germany's *Mitbestimmung* works.

A Spanish Case Study

In Spain, an A.I. turnaround expert once tackled a troubled company traditionally having had a CEO and a controller of foreign extraction. This had created a confidence gap and several grave incidents. For example, the foreign controller had been savagely attacked only shortly before the arrival of Arpi International's turnaround expert, and sustained life-threatening knife wounds. By now sending in a turnaround expert who not only spoke Spanish fluently, but also had a great understanding of Spanish culture and mentality, the foreign mother company – to their great surprise – found that they suddenly had an exceptionally receptive and cooperative Spanish management team. When the union representative was asked if he was fully prepared to support the implementation of the turnaround plan, he answered with a very warm and personal speech, expressing his full support.

The result of the turnaround was a success within an 18-month period; losses in the order of 400 million Pts were turned into profits of about 425,000 Pts.

Senior partners of Arpi International have operated in a dozen major turnarounds in France, Sweden, Spain, Germany, the UK and the US. Per Wejke's four turnarounds, reflected in Part II, were all on behalf of Scandinavian-based multinational companies operating in a large number of countries. However, as reflected in the case studies, many of the key problems resided abroad, not where headquarters were located.

Two French Case Studies

France has provided several interesting turnaround cases of which two are touched on below. French laws and regulations made it virtually impossible for a foreigner to move in as CEO. In France, one does not easily achieve the status of PDG (President Directeur Général) or even of Administrateur Délégué (Managing Director).

In one French turnaround case, A.I.'s turnaround expert joined the board of the French company, and was given special written powers from the French company's chairman. The message was not lost on the organization. Excellent working conditions were created for his successful turnaround efforts which also included the merger of three companies.

In another French turnaround case, A.I.'s expert was formally only allowed to move in as Divisional Manager for the most important division (although this produced approximately 80 per cent of company turnover). However, he still had the formidable task to get the signature of the still lingering old PDG, who did not like seeing somebody else belatedly implement a series of successful and long overdue actions he had not been able or willing to implement himself.

To survive and succeed as an outside, full-time turnaround expert under these circumstances is a delicate task. The concept of a 'steering group' to which the turnaround expert could report was not readily understood in the French company environment, which tends to be much more formal and legalistic than in Scandinavia, where pragmatic arrangements, acceptable to all parties concerned, can usually be found. (For an Anglo-Saxon turnaround expert, it is also well worth remembering that the French legal system is based on Roman and Napoleonic law, which is very different from Common Law as applicable in the US and the UK).

Even *mergers* between two US companies (despite their common language, legal framework and similar body of professional thinking and literature) often lead to a collision between two different company cultures. The success rate is less than 50 per cent. Against this background, it is easy to imagine the much more substantial collision risks when a 'foreign' CEO or temporary turnaround expert-for-hire attacks a troubled company, perhaps with subsidiaries located in several different countries. US turnaround literature seldom covers the consequences of national, legal or cultural differences. The epilogue to the successful turnaround of the Tarkett Group, detailed in the latter part of this book, is revealing and partly disturbing. With a CEO of Swedish origin, German headquarters, and French owners, the situation became unmanageable and the CEO left. 'Cultural shock' was mentioned as a key reason.

Imagine a foreign turnaround expert faced with the delicate task of negotiating substantial manpower reductions (and/or frozen salaries) with representatives of a French Communist union. Obviously, the negotiations have to be carried out in the French language and within the confines of French law and French union traditions. Our experience is that, even if an oral agreement has indeed been reached, the union can still refuse to sign the written accord. An obvious consequence is that, in principle, strikes can break out again at very short notice, if the highly sensitive overall situation is not properly handled.

A similar situation is rather difficult to imagine in Scandinavia, where a handshake between the negotiating key players is usually enough to guarantee adherence to the deal, later formally documented in writing. However, the breakdown of the intended Renault–Volvo deal in 1993 had heavy ingredients of cultural shock. It was long known that Swedish engineers felt much closer to German engineers, to their design philosophy and quality commitment. Thus, a cooperation with Audi of Germany had been more natural to most Volvo engineers than a cooperation with French engineers at Régie Renault, who were often unable or unwilling to express themselves in any language other than French, a language of Latin origin having few words in common with Swedish, which is much closer to German.

Further, to approve the deal, the French state insisted on holding a 'golden share' in one of the intended new key companies. This share could be used by the French to effectively block Volvo from increasing its participation in one of the common key structures. Not only are such golden shares unheard of in Sweden but, if a minister tries to run (even a state-owned company) from his ministerial desk, he is breaking the law. In the French environment, such a state-directed *dirigisme* is common, and not unlawful. Hesitation among Swedish shareholders was also high as a result of the difficulty in evaluating what the shares in a *privatized* (future) Renault might be worth, and what the French state's golden share implied. (Since the old owners of Renault had cooperated with the Nazis during the Second World War, after the war Renault was turned into a state-owned 'Régie', with no shares traded on the French stock exchange, and therefore rather difficult to evaluate.)

The chairman of the Volvo Group, Pehr Gyllenhammer, stated that the golden share was just a formality, and that he had been given firm guarantees by representatives of the French government that the golden share would never be used against the interests of Volvo and its previous Swedish shareholders. When this interpretation was not officially confirmed by Paris, the deal unravelled. Gyllenhammer left Volvo after more than 20 years at its helm. Five years later, Mr Gyllenhammer is back, this time as the president of the largest British group of insurance companies. The Volvo Group has in the meantime sold off many of its non-core activities, and focused much more on its core business – *vehicles*. Volvo's return on capital has improved spectacularly during 1993–98, while Renault's profitability has been lacklustre in spite of the launch of many new car models. At the beginning of 1999 Ford made a 'friendly' SEK46.5 billion offer to acquire the passenger car activities of the Volvo Group, allowing the group to focus even more strongly on trucks and other heavy vehicles.

As shown by several of these examples, the countries affected by the turnaround, and the language capabilities of the turnaround manager (as well as his familiarity with local laws and traditions) are key elements which directly influence the likelihood of success, and the choice of suitable managerial tools, as well as the cooperation/confrontational atmosphere which is likely to characterize the necessary change process.

In the light of the gradual realization of the frontier-less European Union, some US readers might think that national differences within Europe have by now largely disappeared or at least diminished in importance. This is an erroneous assumption. Although some laws and regulations are indeed harmonized, basic cultural differences and differences as to language and management style remain. Therefore, in the future, a turnaround in West Germany will be very different to a turnaround in France, and a turnaround in Sweden will be very different to one in Spain.

Case

France was the host country for the football Worldcup of 1998. It ended with France winning the cup. However, it started with foreign spectators 'welcomed' by a French pilot strike and a French train strike. When the un-French Euro-Disney amusement park outside Paris was opened, not only did train strikes break out, but also work boycotts as an expression of negative feelings against the US owners and the dominating American themes, even though this theme park was located in Europe. The way American management methods and working conditions were imposed did not please the French unions either.

The arrival of any turnaround manager of foreign extraction can create equally strong negative (partly quite irrational, chauvinist) reactions and lead to severe obstruction of the turnaround efforts, if not anticipated early on and cleverly dealt with.

Notes

1. Free Press, second hardcover reprint edition, 1998.
2. Free Press, first edition, 1998.
3. John Wiley, second paperback edition, 1991.
4. For the sake of simplicity, the term 'he' will be used throughout this book, whether the turnaround manager is male or female.
5. What 'taking charge' means in real-life turnaround situations, and what it requires is discussed in Chapter 6: 'Rebuilding the Management Team...'.
6. For a more stringent discussion of 'value enhancing' solutions versus 'cost reducing' solutions, the reader is referred to Chapter 5, particularly section 5.7. This discussion is taken even further at the end of Chapter 8.
7. The Cleveland tunnel boring project as described in the Atlas Copco Mining and Construction case at the end of this book is one example.
8. The robot rig project (described in the same case study) with in-house developed computer hardware and software might fall in this category.

Overview of the different steps involved in most turnarounds

3.1 Purpose of chapter

This chapter provides a background to all subsequent chapters. It includes a discussion of the different elements and the chronological steps of a turnaround. When needed, concrete examples are provided. These often consist of snippets taken from the ensuing chapters. The typical length of different kinds of turnarounds is also discussed.

From the previous chapter it can be concluded that one particular turnaround situation might differ strongly from another, for example as to the underlying causes, existing time pressures, appropriate tools and techniques, and valid solutions. It is therefore difficult to present a comprehensive checklist pinpointing not only what to do, but also in what order to proceed.

In real life, the chronological order of steps taken varies, not only as a result of the characteristics of the turnaround situation, but as a result of the particular turnaround manager's personality, earlier experience and preferred working mode. Other influencing factors might be the strong preferences expressed by the person(s) having engaged him, usually the chairman of the board.

Although acknowledging the existence of such variations, from an educational viewpoint it is still desirable to provide an *overview of the analytical steps and key activities* characterizing most turnaround situations. That is the main purpose of this chapter.

The 29 listed items (Figure 3.1) are of a 'touchstone' nature. Taken together, they are representative, although they may not cover some highly special cases.

Since most items will be dealt with in more depth in later parts of the book, in the present chapter enough will be said only to make the overall meaning and relevance of each turnaround element obvious to the reader.

The relative importance and the chronological order between the different items vary considerably from one turnaround situation to the next, for reasons already touched on. However, Figure 3.2 in section 3.13 highlights how the emphasis typically changes during the course of most turnarounds.

Figure 3.1 (see next page) provides an overview. On it are listed actions to be taken *before* arriving on company premises, *on arrival*, but also *later on* during the turnaround process.

For example, certain cash-flow calculations and the establishing of many numerical benchmarks can be done before arrival on company premises, others only after. Taking charge, confronting the troops, and evaluating existing managers can obviously only be done after the turnaround manager's arrival on site. Creating a Blueprint for the Future Company and building the new management team are critical tasks which cannot be completed during the first few weeks on company premises, but will take longer. Even later follows the plan implementation.

3.2 Discussions before accepting the turnaround assignment

Whether formally employed by the company as its new CEO, or temporarily brought in as an outside 'manager for hire' – a turnaround manager never approaches the distressed company without first having been *briefed* by key members of the board, by a headquarters' representative (if the company belongs to a larger group of companies), or by the bank (as is sometimes the case in smaller, family-owned companies).

Opinions expressed during such briefings include what is perceived to be the main problem and its underlying causes and – as a result – what is expected can be achieved via the intervention of the turn-around expert.

Although useful, such an introductory description of the existing situation and its root causes is seldom even remotely complete. Sometimes the description might even be incorrect and self-serving. Even so, this brief is quite important. It provides the turnaround manager with a first set of assumptions as to what problems to look for,

1. Before arriving on company premises	2. Arrival on company premises	3. Improve cash position and cash-flow	4. Build Blueprint for the Future Company	5. Build the new management team
Ensure getting the necessary authority, freedom of action and a formal power base	Take charge! (Confront the troops)	Renegotiate deals (mainly with stakeholders)	Identify the future core business	Reinforce management team
Do your homework	Symbolic first actions	If needed: sell off inventory to rapidly generate cash, i.e. fire sales	Specify the target picture. (What? How big? When? In what markets?)	Test team members!
Contact knowledgeable industry sources	Cashflow projections (best and worst cases)	Sell off and lease back buildings and equipment	Develop strategy showing in broad terms how to get there	Replace prima donnas, reward friends
Establish benchmarks and other key reference points	Introduce first set of new cost and payment controls, including new spending limits and attestation controls	Sell off non-strategic assets, including loss-making SBUs	Identify human resource bottlenecks, manpower surplus, existing imbalances when realizing strategy	Improve team spirit and company culture
	Calm stakeholders!	If necessary: sell off even profitable SBUs, provided they are not the company's future core business	Detailed implementation plan with key data and 'Critical milestones'	Introduce helpful new tools and procedures
		Possibly: go for a revenue or margin improvement strategy (not only cost-cutting)		Communicate, educate, motivate!
				Involve also lower levels of employees
				Communicate success stories (internally and externally). Be proud!
				Make sure improvements stay and the 'new company' remains lean and mean

Figure 3.1   Elements in the overall turnaround process

perceived management weaknesses which must be overcome, the general urgency of the situation at hand, and what is being expected from him in more general terms.

Before even accepting a turnaround assignment, it is quite common that a turnaround manager requests two to three weeks to study the situation (including pertinent financial data and other documents) in more detail. Only then is he in a position to discuss what he believes can realistically be achieved, how fast, and what formal power base and degrees of freedom of action are required in order to succeed. These early findings might be so disheartening, or the ensuing discussions so full of conflict and diverging opinions, that the turnaround manager decides not to accept the assignment. Sometimes his findings will convince the board that a rescue operation is not worthwhile. The patient is then allowed to die.

3.3 'Homework' before arriving on company premises

If the distressed company is not in the middle of a life and death fight, a turnaround manager might afford the luxury of spending up to three weeks studying the company from the sidelines before actually moving in on company premises to take charge and start making things happen.

How will he typically use these homework weeks? First of all, he is likely to study carefully the annual reports for the last 5–10 years, analyse major trends reflected therein, perhaps even deconstruct the officially reported profit picture to arrive at a more telling picture, for example of true operating profits from different SBUs. (Special techniques to rapidly penetrate the dense fog are discussed in Chapter 8.)

He will try to detect creative accounting tricks used to hide unpleasant truths from jittery shareholders and/or members of the board. He will identify and put aside the impact of asset sales, temporary currency exchange gains, accounting changes, increases in the value of stocks (or other monetary instruments held), to allow a closer look at *authentic income* from the normally ongoing business operations, that is, operating income, unaffected by non-operating/non-recurrent items.

An experienced turnaround expert is likely to be 'sniffing' the pages, not only for small asterisks, indicating changes in the accounting principles used, but also to identify projects proudly announced in earlier annual reports, but suddenly conveniently forgotten in later reports. In general, any abrupt change in what has otherwise been the normal behaviour of the troubled company (or division) is worth a closer look.

As always, the study of just one isolated annual report is of limited value. A comparative study of all annual reports over a five-year period is much more revealing. Reported profits as well as the official story and explanations provided by the troubled management team must be regarded with considerable scepticism. What really interests the turnaround manager are the elementary truths, very often covered behind beautiful colour illustrations, smoothly flowing flowery language, manly declarations of noble purposes and intent, remarkable successes achieved, and the deep belief in the company's bright future.

Other documents normally studied by a turnaround manager during this homework phase include the following: *organization charts* and *manpower figures* for the last five years, *protocols* from board meetings, *business plans* and *budgets* (preferably accompanied by information about the real outcome as compared to plans and budgets. Such comparisons (or post audits) have much to tell about the company's culture and normal behaviour, for example in connection with planning and the later implementation of plans and achievement of established goals.

Articles and other published material on the company as well as on its competitors' markets and products might be highly useful. The bigger the troubled company and the more the public is fascinated by its industry and its products, the greater the chance that the industry, the company, its competitors, products, markets and so on will have been covered in depth by the commercial press (such as the *Financial Times, Business Week, Frankfurter Allgemeine, Trends,* and so on) or perhaps by more industry-specific publications. Such market and competitive information is today readily available on-line, through the search of computerized databases available from external sources. Access to these – or at least access to complete article texts – often requires the signing of a contract with a data service provider. (Examples: *Financial Times* 'FT Profile', Dialog, Infotrade, Eurodata, Knight Ridder, Dun & Bradstreet – and any combination thereof, one should add – since 'merger mania' and cross-service deals are extremely common among the major players in the commercial database field, just like for many other media.)[1]

Today there remains no good excuse for not scanning external databases for relevant information early on during a turnaround.[2] It is simple, fast and inexpensive – at least compared to the very substantial values at stake in a turnaround situation. Admittedly, the captured information is usually not ideally structured for its intended purpose, but is surprisingly rich. It can sometimes provide a quite new and valuable perspective on a particular industry, a perspective which is not necessarily even known within the troubled company itself.

Specialized information-search companies such as Dun & Bradstreet can provide detailed financial company and industry information (as will be demonstrated in section 4.10). Many other organizations (for example Stanford Research Institute, Business International, Frost and Sullivan) publish broader industry studies on an *ad hoc* basis, often providing added background. Many other sources and types of media, including *CD-based sources*, must today be added to this list. Their relevance in a turnaround situation largely depends on which countries and which industry are relevant in the specific turnaround situation. Sources available to the turnaround manager are discussed in depth in Chapter 7.

Apart from using printed sources, the turnaround manager is likely to use the informal contact network available to him, and discreetly contact a few managers with extensive experience of the industry and/or country in question. Some of these managers might work for the very same group of companies or at least in the same ownership sphere (in Scandinavia, the 'Wallenberg sphere' might be a good example).

In summary, the purpose of the homework period is to make the turnaround manager reasonably well acquainted with both the industry and the particular company in question. As a result, when he actually arrives on company premises he will – broadly speaking – *know what to look for*. Also he can distinguish more rapidly any self-serving storytellers from those capable managers more inclined to attack the real problems urgently.

3.4 Establishing numerical benchmarks

Studying actual financial ratios for the troubled company is one thing. The turnaround manager might also like to establish another set of values to serve as 'normative benchmarks' guiding his future efforts and behaviour. Such benchmarks might be based on the performance standards of well-run companies in the very same industry, or in industries with similar characteristics, markets, products and problems.

Benchmarking techniques are described in substantial detail with examples in Chapter 5, which also contains an in-depth discussion of 'cost and productivity benchmarking' in contrast to 'perceived value benchmarking'.

Such performance benchmarking can have many purposes and practical uses:

■ It allows comparisons between the troubled company's own past and present performance to that of the industry leaders. (The measurement of the troubled company's 'general performance gap' provides a first indication as to the size of the realistic improvement potential.)[3]

■ It makes it possible to determine more exactly the size of the required changes in different functional areas, for example in production costs, marketing costs, pricing structures, logistics and so on, and which competitors might be worth studying more closely in each respect in order to learn.

■ To assist in specifying key elements of the turnaround strategy and corresponding goals.

3.5 Four types of cash-flow calculation

In a drastic turnaround situation, *cash* is the first concern, not profits. This subject is discussed in great depth in Chapter 4, 'When Cash is King'.

In such a situation, the turnaround manager might need monthly cash-flow projections for at least the next 12 months and most likely also weekly projections for the next three months. Ten years ago, this was regarded as a formidable calculation task.[4]

Today, PC-based simulation models – usually spreadsheet-based – make cash-flow analysis quite easy. However, exceptions exist. For instance, in industries with expensive technically complex products, perhaps on average sold only four times per annum, the corresponding monthly or quarterly revenue and cash projections are still very much guesswork. (Tunnel-boring systems, later discussed in the Atlas Copco MCT case, are good examples.)

A turnaround manager might sometimes use up to four different sets of cash-flow projections.

---

1. The first set usually represents a surprise-free projection, that is, outlining what is likely to happen (on a 'going rate basis', but accounting for normal seasonal variations). Thus, a 'surprise-free projection' represents 'ongoing business as usual', that is, if nothing exceptional happens and no drastic management actions are taken in order to change the unsatisfactory income and expense patterns.

2. The second set of values might represent an even more scary 'worst case scenario'. Such a scenario shows what might happen if key suppliers start asking for cash on delivery, the sales force grants clients extra long payment terms, the bank simultaneously decides to terminate some types of credit arrangements and so on. Making 'worst case calculations' is always a sobering and useful exercise. Such calculations also highlight how much leeway the company still has. Thus, they demonstrate the necessity of dealing effectively and rapidly with different types of stakeholders and using the limited cash available in the most effective manner possible.

3. A third set of cash-flow projections can depict the 'desirable and achievable future situation', that is, it corresponds to an early version of the Blueprint for the Future Company to be discussed later on. The purpose of this exercise is to verify and demonstrate that the troubled company can indeed become a viable, self-supporting entity under certain clearly specified conditions. To verify that these conditions are realistic, comparisons are usually established with other, better managed companies. (The often used 'upper quartile' bench-marking concept is discussed in Chapter 5.)

4. A fourth type of cash-flow projection is more closely linked to changes (than on the likely end-states). Such calculations obviously start from the present situation, but have their main emphasis placed on the expected impact (on profits and cash-flow) of all strategic changes and corrective management actions to be implemented. (They also show the impact on volumes, revenues, margins, cost levels, product mix, market mix, account receivables, number of days outstanding, inventory turnover, and so on.) By clearly linking planned specific management actions to corresponding impact on inward and outward cash-flows, the need for the unwavering implementation of a radical action programme is further highlighted. The recommended 'bitter medicine' can then be perceived more easily as the road back to a healthy situation.

Of the four types of cash-flow projections discussed above, types 1 and 3 can usually be made (with quite acceptable accuracy) even *before* the turnaround manager arrives on company premises. In contrast, type 2, that is, 'worst case scenario projections', might have to wait until the turnaround manager has spent at least a week on company premises. Such projections require a more detailed knowledge of the company itself, of its supply and client structure, of invoicing and collection procedures, and so on. The availability of a first-class financial controller's department certainly facilitates the calculation task. (However, in some turnaround situations later described in this book, one of the very first, and absolutely necessary actions was to fire the incompetent or dishonest controller!)

Dynamic type 4 projections are often shown in connection with the presentation of the turnaround plan. Similar but rougher estimates are needed much earlier, since they highlight the approximate size of the improvements needed (and thus of the size of the action programme itself). They also highlight the limits of what the troubled company can indeed *afford* to do if only operating within its own existing financial constraints.

3.6 Taking charge and confronting the troops while sending symbolic signals

The arrival of a turnaround manager is associated with a mixture of hopes, fears and scepticism. His behaviour (including working habits, way of asking questions and insistance on well-founded answers) will be closely scrutinized, subjectively interpreted and widely commented on throughout the organization. Not only *what* the turnaround manager does is important, but also *how* he does it, that is, his management style.

Since a company in a turnaround situation is often a mismanaged company with disillusioned managers, it is important that the turnaround manager conveys on his arrival an impression of optimism, firmness and a strong decision-making capability. However, he must at the same time demonstrate a willingness to listen to opinions and carefully weigh them before moving ahead at full speed. ('Paralysis through analysis' must be avoided at all costs.)

'Signals with substantial symbolic value' are highly useful. They are discussed in greater depth in section 6.4. Such signals indicate that a new and more promising era has started. The following examples – most taken from the two authors' personal turnaround experience – should convey the general idea.

Let us assume that the previous CEO was fond of fringe benefits (for example company limousines, perhaps a plane mainly for his own use, a luxurious office with expensive Persian rugs, a separate top management dining room with food prepared by a special chef and so on). Items a, b and c of the following list of typical 'symbolic actions' should then be seriously considered:

a. *Move* from your predecessor's top corner office down to a less ostentatious room, perhaps even located in a factory building! *Sell* your predecessor's expensive Mercedes limousine and Persian rug under highly visible arrangements. (Use the company billboard, but also put an advertisement in the local press 'White Mercedes 600 for sale', accompanied by the company's name.) Whatever the text books say, at least initially, show deep disregard for 'established reporting patterns'. Do not hesitate to *bypass* the usual chain of command. If you follow strictly only normal procedures, you will tend to get isolated from the truth (which more often than not resides with the front-line people, not with headquarters' staff). Therefore, talk with workers, salesmen and employees several steps below what has been customary. In this book, this is simply part of 'Management by Walking Around', abbreviated to MBWA.

b. *Start eating in the employee canteen.* You will meet people you would never see on the executive floor, but who have known this company for many years. You will most likely learn a lot. Perhaps you will soon find that other executives have taken the cue and also started mingling. If you find that the environment or that the food in the canteen is unacceptable, do not revert to the executive dining room. Do something about it! (In France, *always* do something about it. There, to a large extent, employees evaluate their employer according to the quality of the food served!)

c. *Start making appointments* with individual executives as early as 7 am. Conferences with several participating executives might start no later than 8 am. Make people understand that it really *is* 'now or never' – they had better get on board fast, since you are not going to stop and wait for any foot-draggers. Do not be afraid of keeping tired top executives in a meeting until a consensus has been reached. Listening capacity and decision-making speed in meetings will soon improve and a badly needed consensus over functional borders will become increasingly common.

d. Some *austerity measures* with high symbolic value should be introduced immediately upon your arrival. These may include a hiring freeze, or lowered limits for spending without specific approval by yourself. At least for the first two months, consider signing all cheques yourself that are above a rather low threshold level. (You will learn a lot from it. You will also stop a lot of nuisance spending, teach some individuals to think before they spend, and others to think twice before they pay at an early date.)

e. In a company characterized by excessive product and model proliferation, you might insist on *approving every change order*, particularly if there is a risk that such orders might result in a completely new product or model.

f. *Speed up imperfect communication processes*. Find ways to penetrate the traditional 'communication filters' and remedy the impressive 'message distortion' so often at work whenever a message passes through several organizational layers. (Introducing fewer organizational levels also helps the communication process!) Consider introducing a very simple turnaround bulletin, but with the widest possible internal distribution.

g. Provided you are a decent speaker, you can consider gathering up to 600 employees at a time and *talking to them*. If the company auditorium is not big enough or not democratic enough for your taste, you may instead (like Gunnar Engellau, a previous Volvo CEO) simply choose to make your speech from the loading platform of a forklift truck in a factory hall. When the fork is raised, everybody in the chosen factory or yard can see and hear you quite well. (A bullhorn or other simple loudspeaker is helpful.) Employees will actually appreciate that you took the trouble to come to them. During his rather spectacular turnaround of SAS during the 1980s, its president and CEO, Jan Carlzon, became famous for running airplane hangar meetings in a similar fashion. He later shared his experience in a best-selling book called *Tear Down the Pyramids* in Swedish, and *Moments of Truth* in English. (HarperCollins, 1989.)

During such information gatherings, your messages must be pertinent, simply expressed and to the point. There is no time for academic speeches or rambling. People want to know who the turnaround manager is, what he looks like, and what he stands for. Employees must be able to make up their minds if they dare to believe in him, and if they are prepared to put in the added 'blood, sweat and tears' called for. (When in 1942 General Montgomery took over as a commander of the British 8th Army in North Africa, he made a brief, pertinent and highly memorable speech to his troops. Some turnaround experts have actually used this speech as an admirable example and many 'turnaround versions' exist today. Churchill's 'Blood, Sweat and Tears' speech has provided a model for others.)

If the turnaround manager is uncomfortable with such mass gatherings, or lacks the corresponding charisma, he is probably better off running a series of smaller meetings, each with 20–60 individuals. Of course, this will require more time, and provide a less spectacular setting. However, this arrangement also allows for more questions and answers, that is, two-way communication.

3.7 Establishing a tighter set of cost and payment controls

If the company is in a serious cash squeeze, the turnaround manager cannot allow executives (particularly those severely influencing investment, purchasing and payment decisions) to continue spending as if there were no crisis. Therefore, immediately upon arrival he is likely to introduce some austerity measures. These might include:

■ a moratorium on hiring
■ a freezing of already decided investments (or at least making them subject to critical review and re-evaluation)
■ the insistence on personally approving all new investment decisions (above a certain level), and
■ the signing of all cheques above a certain (usually rather insignificant) level.

Such austerity measures serve at least four purposes, discussed below:

1. *Symbolic signalling value:* They send important signals throughout the organization that a new era has started, a new person is

firmly in charge, and new rules already apply. In other words, the turnaround manager has arrived and means business!

2. *Cost-reduction and cash-flow impact:* The existence of austerity measures tends to reduce costs and improve cash-flow, primarily by abolishing, downsizing or delaying many projects as well as associated investments and purchases. Non-essential purchases can be dropped or at least trimmed back to a size appropriate to the serious situation at hand.

3. *Rapidly gaining insight and managerial control:* By critically reviewing all new investment requests (plus all earlier granted but not yet implemented investment decisions), and by personally signing a substantial number of cheques, the turnaround manager rapidly gains a surprisingly good insight into the company. He sees how investment and purchasing decisions have traditionally been made. He gets acquainted with the general spending behaviour of the company, associated employee attitudes, and (usually lax) routines.

    Equipped with this knowledge, he can start to improve existing investment, purchasing and expense patterns, and existing planning and control routines, but also – and most importantly – change existing attitudes.

4. *Forcing others to think more critically:* The implementation of strict new procedures and the systematic questioning of old habits, forces all managers to critically reconsider their own manpower and investment needs, and learn to manage well with less. Some will also in the future get the resources asked for. However, they will be forced to justify their requests in greater detail than they have been used to.

All this provides the turnaround manager with an excellent basis for getting to know all key managers, discussing their professional needs, while assessing their priorities and their depth of understanding (or lack of understanding) of their company's predicament.

The turnaround manager must make sure that the limited cash available is really actively managed in the best possible fashion. For instance, no cash purchases can be accepted when reasonable credit terms are available. No thoughtless early paying of bills will be permitted. (Surprisingly often – even in a deeply troubled company –

employees do not critically evaluate such factors, although they have a direct impact on the troubled company's cash situation.)

> In summary, the new set of controls, new approval procedures and new payment routines are put in place in order both to save cash and to force the organization to think along new paths, and change its behaviour.

So far, we have mainly discussed controls on *outgoing cash*. However, management actions can also to a great extent influence *incoming cash*. This is for instance true for account receivables (where better collection procedures might lead to a lowering of the number of days outstanding), and by an increase in inventory turns, that is, better use of the capital tied up in inventory. Factoring of receivables and the 'sale and lease back' of fixed assets must be considered standard procedures in most turnaround situations. (Associated matters are discussed more in depth in Chapter 4.)

3.8   Liquidifying the balance sheet, also by asset sales

As already mentioned, cash is sometimes much more important than profits. In some turnaround situations, the company will simply cease to exist if the cash position and cash-flow are not rapidly improved. Should the company run out of cash within the next 10–30 days, it will be unable to meet its payment obligations, including paying the next payroll and its key suppliers. The authors call this situation 'the sudden death scenario'; to be avoided by all available means.

> However, there is also a longer-term perspective on cash-absorbing activities and what to do about them. One obvious starting point is a critical review of the balance sheet and the question: 'Where is cash unnecessarily tied up?' – in an inflated inventory, accounts receivables long overdue, or in fixed assets which could be sold and leased back, or what? The second question is: 'How do we get a lot of this cash out of the balance sheet,' that is, how can we 'liquidify' the balance sheet?

The 'Squeezing of the Balance Sheet for Cash' is discussed at great length in Chapter 4. Improving the operating cash management (OCM) is discussed in sections 4.6 to 4.9. The selling of a complete strategic business unit (SBU) is discussed in section 4.3. Five concrete examples of the selling of major activities in connection with turnarounds are found in section 4.4.

3.9 Learning by systematically following a cross-functional trail

Substantial cost savings and efficiency improvements can usually be achieved within each and every functional department. However, even greater gains can usually be found in the border areas between two or more company functions.

There are several reasons for this. In a turnaround situation, most individuals tend to be defensive. Therefore, first they think about themselves and their position, then about their own department and closest working colleagues. In the process, the broader cross-functional overview and the identification with overriding corporate goals are easily lost. The turnaround manager must therefore constantly reintroduce and re-emphasize the importance of this broad perspective.

An excellent way for a turnaround manager to pinpoint cross-functional problems is to select one cross-functional process and follow it in great detail from beginning to end – like a bulldog – while continuously asking pertinent questions and insisting both on fast and reasonably correct answers.

Similar cross-functional approaches are used in 'business re-engineering', and in many other efforts to systematically shorten the order processing time as well as the products' 'time-to-market'. These concepts are discussed in Chapter 7. Related activity-based costing techniques (also called ABC) are discussed in great detail in Chapter 8 – with illuminating numerical examples – from three substantial turnaround cases, not covered elsewhere in the book.

3.10 Defining the Business Mission and the Blueprint for the Future Company

A turnaround manager is not primarily there to shoot from the hip at isolated problems he happens to come across. Rather, he is expected to *create, sell and implement* a comprehensive and consistent turnaround plan, which not only guarantees the company's immediate survival, but also its sound, long-term future. Several planning dimensions are needed, often resulting in more than one plan document.

Many different terms (such as Business Mission, Blueprint for the Future Company, Our New Marching Song, and so on) are used. The meaning of these expressions is discussed in Chapter 5. There, these concepts are also compared to the contents of a classic business plan.

The terminology used in a turnaround situation varies from company to company, and from one turnaround expert to the next. However, to the authors, a Blueprint for the Future Company exists if it contains:

■ a definition of the future core business(es)
■ one or more Business Mission statements
■ a more comprehensive target description (for example Our Company Year 2005)
■ a strategy document which, at least in broad terms, outlines what changes are required to obtain the strategic goal.

The Blueprint for the Future Company primarily describes a desirable and achievable *end state* reflecting the situation strived for, when the turnaround has been fully concluded, that is, when all actions taken have had their full impact, usually 2–3 years from when the turnaround started.

This Blueprint for the Future Company reflects the desired and expected combined consequences of all decisions and actions, for example which SBU's products, brands, factories, markets and market segments to keep, which to reshape, which to phase out. The sum of all these decisions will indeed determine the future company's size, scope, character and structure.

Thus, the Blueprint might be perceived primarily as a strategic target description, not as a detailed action programme with timetables and budgets. It normally contains a crisp Business Mission Statement which is operationally formulated to give maximum concrete operational guidance. But it can also outline the grand vision in much greater detail.

In contrast, the action plan focuses more on all the different activities needed in order to get 'from here to there'. If an implementation plan is attached, it lists all necessary key actions, but also corresponding timetables, responsibility allocation and resource requirements, as well as the expected (quantifiable) result of each listed activity. (ITT executives might think of such a document as an Action Assignment List. Other companies prefer to use other terms.)

Since the Blueprint contains a description of a set of highly desirable goals, it also helps considerably to energize employees and to coordinate their combined efforts, thus making sure they are pulling in the same direction. The implementation plan contains all major steps and activities necessary for the company to realize its grand vision, as reflected in the Blueprint. (Therefore, the former is usually a better tool for the stringent monitoring of subsequent progress than the Blueprint itself.)

The important thing is certainly not the name, but the quality and realism of the thinking which has gone into these documents, and the practical value and actual use of these documents for steering purposes, that is, to assist the change process, including the all-important motivational aspect.

The revenue and cost structure of the future company and resulting financing needs can be determined from the above documents. So can resulting financing needs. (Should the realization of the Blueprint require the acquisition of other companies, a provision must be made for such items. However, the exact place in time of such acquisitions will most likely be decided by future stock market prices as well as by the cash position of the purchasing company.)

3.11 Gaining acceptance and formal approval of the turnaround plan

Somewhere along the line, the turnaround manager has to convince not only his board and own troops, but also convince external stakeholders that his Blueprint is sound and that his strategy has a fair chance to be successfully implemented. (In many turnarounds, the turnaround expert must therefore also be able effectively to deal with the *mass media*, since these are key information channels to many stakeholder groups, including employees, clients, vendors, and shareholders.)[5]

Under the very best of circumstances, the turnaround manager can expect a certain degree of stakeholder understanding, cooperation and even sacrifices. By calming stakeholder nerves, a badly needed breathing space is created, which allows him to concentrate on his turnaround programme instead of being constantly engaged in both internal and external battles.

Lee Iacocca's famous – and well documented – turnaround of Chrysler Corporation,[6] primarily 1978–82, is an example where calming and convincing external stakeholders, including the US government, were at the very top of his priority list, and a prerequisite for success.

Admittedly, turnarounds of daughter companies belonging to a much larger and richer group, with no intention of letting any subsidiary go bankrupt, provide a somewhat cosier environment. Although internal 'selling' of the turnaround plan is still important, more draconian measures are not expected before a thorough analysis has been concluded and findings and recommendations have been reported.

In reality, selling the Blueprint and associated implementation plan is seldom a one-time event. Rather, the situation might be such that three (or more) different presentations have to be made. The limited purpose of the first meeting might be just to show that (one or more) viable alternatives do indeed exist. At a second meeting, the recommended alternative might be presented, backed by financial calculations. A third meeting might be for formal decision-making (or decision-confirmation). During this, the stakeholders present are supposed to agree and to support the plan. Should different stakeholders insist on having separate meetings, the number of meetings might easily mushroom, and become unreasonably time-consuming.

3.12 Implementing the plan with ruthless determination

Most readers have presumably seen thick and fancy-looking business plan documents, which unfortunately never became more than dust-gathering documents on the shelf – far removed from what later actually took place. A similar lack of systematic, coherent implementation of the planned activities, at the projected speed, in a turnaround situation might simply jeopardize the survival of the company. The turnaround expert has then also jeopardized his own professional future, since he has lost his most important asset, his own credibility.

The implementation phase normally should not meet any insurmountable problems, provided:

- that a capable CEO and a highly motivated (and reasonably good) management team is in place
- equipped with a well-designed Blueprint and some form of action implementation plan (listing the required actions as to contents, purpose, time, cost, responsibility and expected impact)
- and with the full approval, blessing and support by the board and/or other key stakeholders.

If the organization is sluggish, a ruthless determination on the part of the turnaround manager is needed, as well the ability to keep the pressure up both on the management team and on the rest of the organization.

Knowing how to *motivate* the organization is a key prerequisite. In Chapter 6, the reader will find 20 pieces of sound advice, all dealing with how to motivate people. A few of them are repeated in the following text frame.

Communication and positive feedback is of great importance throughout the implementation stage. (Hail and reward all the heroes! Hang out non-performers who are not on track! As to foot-draggers – insist on crash programmes to make up for lost time!) Do not forget to inform the whole organization about how much better the company is doing now compared to before, where the company stands in relation to the turnaround plan, and how much still remains to be done. Convey the message that the turnaround of the company is well under way, but that it still requires very substantial and sustained efforts from everybody involved.

Run internal *progress report seminars* where you restate critical elements of the plan, what actions have been taken so far and with what kind of results. Critical milestones reached in time and within agreed resource frameworks should be *celebrated as important achievements*. Also, let the participants reflect on what they have learned from the common experience so far – both from a general viewpoint and with regard to future needs of the company. The purpose is to let people fully enjoy the fruits of their own endeavours, but also to reinforce lessons learned in such a way that good managerial behaviour becomes a *habit* in the company.

To succeed, people will have to be *informed, actively involved*, and *identify strongly* with common corporate goals. To speed up the necessary changes and make sure that everybody pulls in the same direction, it is often necessary to clarify roles, responsibilities and the expected cooperation pattern. Any lingering departmental myopia must be removed, so that people effectively cooperate over functional borders to the benefit of the whole company.

The previous lack of focus and a common marching song might indeed have encouraged whole departments to grow complacent. A turnaround situation, correctly handled, is a tremendous opportunity to remove inertia, energize people and departments, and improve cross-functional understanding and cooperation.

3.13 Chronology of actions and the overall time-frame

As shown, the turnaround manager has an impressive number of tasks and issues to attend to. Is there a natural chronological order for his different actions? How long is the overall time-frame for the complete turnaround cycle? These two questions are discussed below.

Some activities (doing one's homework, confronting the troops, and a fire sale of inventories to generate badly needed cash), obviously come early in the process. Other activities (those aimed at consolidating a substantially enlarged core business) come much later. Activities like building and motivating the management team, providing feedback, and changing corporate culture, are *ongoing processes* throughout the full turnaround period.

The chronology between different actions is often situation-dependent. An opportunity to sell off a non-profitable major SBU, or perhaps even to swop SBUs with another company might suddenly appear quite early on. (The Finnish Valmet and Wertselä groups once decided to swop shipyards against forestry machine production, thus letting each become a more formidable and more specialized global player in their respective core businesses.)

For financial reasons, the turnaround manager might be forced to patiently sell off loss-making companies and/or divisions, close loss-making factories, leave certain markets and drop a few brands before the company's financial situation has improved to a point when he can even consider acquiring any substantial new entity to reinforce his future core business area.

Although the exact chronology is 'situation-dependent', there is a typical *change of emphasis* throughout the turnaround process as to management style, key sources, the nature of controls and so on. This change is reflected in Figure 3.2 (opposite). Underlying case-specific realities will repeatedly be illustrated by the six in-depth case studies presented in Part II.

What about the overall time-frame for a turnaround? A turnaround might last from nine months to eight years, although the most typical period is *two to four years*. What then are the main reasons for substantial variations in this time-frame?

If the turnaround concerns several countries, and is run in parallel with a very ambitious growth and internationalization plan, at least tripling the company's size, and with most of this impressive growth through acquisitions outside the company's home country, eight years is certainly a more typical figure than three years in order to experience the full benefits. This situation applies to the ESAB, Allgon and Tarkett case studies in Part II.

However, in cases with much more modest growth ambitions, with the operating problems more or less known from the outset, and with the financial resources and full authority available to the turnaround manager from Day 1, he might be able to leave within 9–12 months. By then, the necessary key actions have been set in motion, and a new man (the long-term CEO) has probably been identified to complete the task.

One might argue that such a limited mission does not really represent a complete turnaround assignment, but rather a *management-for-hire assignment*, since the problems analysis has already been completed before the turnaround manager arrives, and later he departs before the full impact of all the measures put into action are known. Figure 3.3 makes distinctions between such a time-limited assignment, the average turnaround assignment, and a complete

DEVELOPMENT OVER TIME

ASPECT	Survival	Change and build	Consolidate obtained positions
Critical mission:	Survival	Change and build	Consolidate obtained positions
Divestment acquisition purposes:	Improve cashflow / Create breathing space	Liquidify balance sheet / Get rid of non-core businesses	Enlarge, reinforce and entrench the new core business(es)
Change in CEO style:	'Enlightened dictator'	'Participative management' — 'Care-taker' (monitoring progress)	Discreetly phasing out
Handling of Management Team:	Test existing members	Replace weak members / Reinforce existing team	Empower team / Increase delegation
Motivational emphasis:	Provide hope! — Provide leadership!	Reward performance!	Enjoy positive feedback!
Purpose of controls:	Reduce spending and investments / Gain insight	Improve management processes and professionalism	Ensure that enough resources are directed into the realization of strategic goals
Data and SOURCES:	Those available — Cross-functional 'MBWA' — Interviews with key sources	Ad hoc studies — More substantial, systematic data gathering (MR etc.)	Regular data from improved information systems

Start of turnaround   (Time axis)   End of turnaround period

Figure 3.2   The gradual change of emphasis (selected examples)

turnaround also involving the realization of an ambitious international growth scenario.

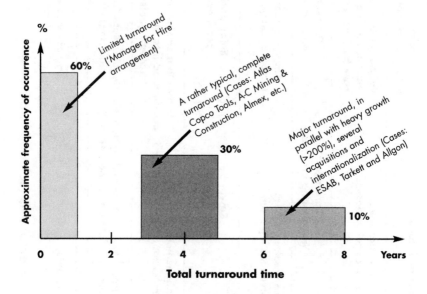

Figure 3.3   How the turnaround time varies with the task in hand

3.14 Chapter summary and the links to subsequent chapters

In the present chapter are listed the many items of importance during a turnaround process. An overview of these has been provided (Figure 3.1), while grouping the items into five main categories. Most of these aspects have been briefly commented on already in this chapter; other aspects will be dealt with in greater depth in subsequent chapters. Thus, this chapter is only meant to provide an *overview*. It is primarily an introduction and a background to the later chapters. What is then the main subject for each of the following five chapters?

Liquidifying the balance sheet is the subject of Chapter 4. The Blueprint of the Future Company is discussed in Chapter 5, as well as benchmarking to help establish realistic targets contained therein. Chapter 6 deals with how to create and motivate the new management team. Chapter 7 contains advice on sources to ensure pertinent plan data.

While common data sources are discussed in Chapter 7, some highly specialized analytical tools are presented in Chapter 8. These include the effective use of computer-assisted activity-based costing (ABC) in three different turnaround cases, 'where the fog was intense and clarity badly and urgently needed'. As shown there, this particular technique helped three loss-making major organizations in three different industries (and in two different countries) to rapidly decide which activities and products to *drop, replace, sell off, price differently, cost-reduce* or to simply handle in an entirely new fashion.

Part II contains half a dozen concrete and detailed turnaround studies. Each of these highlights the symptoms, underlying causes, managerial actions taken and the results *de facto* achieved. Combined, these cases illustrate the real-life, hands-on, down-to-earth application of the principles and techniques discussed in Part I. Performance-related diagrams, based on analysis of the official annual reports, have been included to show the actual achieved impact of all the turnaround-related activities described, for example on sales, capacity utilization, profitability and share prices.

Notes

1. The difference between 'free for all information' on the Internet and more powerful and more neutral professional databases with 'back data' for several years, is discussed in Chapter 7, section 7.4.
2. Readers primarily used to 'surfing the Internet' by looking at *website contents* should realise that website information is usually carefully selected, screened and 'massaged' by the website-owning company itself. In contrast, a broader search including commercial databases will normally also produce articles, *critical* of the company and/or the behaviour of industry. Such information can modify in-house information as well as website-derived information quite considerably.
3. The industry's 'upper quartile' values are often used as tentative target values. Similar techniques were also often used by the legendary Harold S. Geenen before his beloved ITT acquired a company. Thus, he calculated the 'realistic improvement potential' if the acquisition candidate was properly run. This largely determined the upper limit for the acquisition price.
4. In 1987, John O. Whitney (a CEO, but also a previous associate Dean of the Harvard Business School) wrote an excellent and quite early turnaround book: *Taking Charge*. In it, he is thrilled by the arrival of the first PC and the 'Lotus 1–2–3' spreadsheet, and spends close to ten pages describing corresponding cash-

flow calculations. In the present book, we have simply assumed that the turnaround manager can rely upon the troubled company's financial, control, and budgeting staff, all equipped with computer-based spreadsheets, suitable for the intended purpose.

5. The handling of the relationships to different stakeholder groups, particularly during the downsizing phase, is discussed by Cynthia Hardy in *Strategies for Retrenchment and Turnaround: The Politics of Survival*, de Gruyter, 1989.

6. Lee Iacocca with William Novak, *Iacocca – An Autobiography*, Bantam Books, 1984. Lee Iacocca, who ran the company from 1978 to 1992, saved it once, and then drove it right back into disaster 1988–92. The company therefore had to be saved a second time, this time by the two co-pilots, Robert Eaton and Robert Lutz. Thus, Iacocca's celebrated 'success' was substantial, but time-limited. Although Lee Iacocca's own book is still selling in paperback, perhaps its readers should also study Robert A. Lutz, *Guts – The 7 Laws of Business That Made Chrysler the World's Hottest Car Company*, John Wiley & Sons, 1998.

'When Cash is King': squeezing the balance sheet for cash

4.1 Top priority: cash, manpower reduction or profit improvement?

The authors undertook a small and no doubt highly unscientific poll. It contained only one question: *'In your opinion, what is the most urgent concern in a turnaround situation?'* Ninety per cent of the answers received fell into one of the following two categories:

Group 1 ('Deep Cuts'): Downsizing, cutting back, demassing, retrenching, streamlining, getting rid of bloated bureaucracies and other similar expressions, indicating the need to *rapidly slim down* a fat and often slow-responding ('lazy') organization.

Group 2 ('Whatever it takes, as long as it works'): Radically improving company profitability *by whatever means necessary*. To these respondents, the importance of the goal (that is, a successful turnaround) seems to justify almost all of the varied means available to a turnaround manager, provided they work and work fast.

The first group of answers might lead to the premature conclusion that a turnaround manager normally starts by firing people. Although a few unhelpful prima donnas might be fired for pedagogical purposes, massive firings are seldom part of the turnaround manager's first day on company premises. There are several valid reasons for this:

a. He must focus on what is most urgent, which might be *cash*, not rapid manpower reduction, or even profits. (This particular situation is the premise for the discussion in this chapter.)

79

b. He might like to spend some time developing *problem awareness*, but also *trust and understanding* before taking any really drastic action. (First, he might be required to deal astutely with labour unions, including their official representatives on the board, as required in some countries.)

c. Improving the *short-term cash position* is seldom done by firing, at least not in continental Europe (a lesson some trigger-happy US managers with temporary assignments in Europe have learnt the hard and expensive way), with impressive amounts of severance payments to fired, long-term employees.

d. To know *where, why, and how deep to cut*, the turnaround manager usually needs some time for customer contacts, market research, in-house studies (although often 'quick and dirty', rather than sophisticated), and calculations of the likely impact of contemplated changes.

e. Before even contemplating selling off or closing whole business areas or business units, he must also have a pretty good idea about the company's future Business Mission, including its future *core business*. The same goes for the abolition of product lines, the closing of markets, and so on. Only when knowing what to build can he confidently decide on what to cut back in size, or what could be sold as a coherent entity.

In some Western European states with an elaborate, protective welfare system, it must be remembered that the abrupt termination of employment may lead to very substantial *cash severance payments*. Such payments are probably the last thing needed by a company in the middle of a serious cash squeeze! The selling of a whole strategic business unit, lock, stock and barrel (or by encouraging a leveraged management buyout) might immediately stop the cash-drain from a loss-making (and perhaps overstaffed) unit. This will improve the remaining company's cash position. Provided the book values of the divested entity were low enough, it might even create a non-operating profit.

Certainly, solid profits from the company's core business areas are necessary to guarantee the medium- and long-term survival of the troubled company. On the other hand, if there is not enough cash available to allow the company to survive even the next few months, the turnaround manager hardly has any reason to worry about next year's profits!

Selling an SBU or encouraging a leveraged management buyout of an SBU is often a more elegant, profitable and human approach than just going for massive downsizing, often perceived as a ruthless 'burn and slash' policy by an insensitive new CEO.

SUMMARY

In many turnaround situations, the most urgent issue is not profits, nor manpower reduction, but *cash* in the near future. If so, a better answer to our unscientific poll question might be as follows:

Evaluate available cash, and forecast future cash-flows in substantial detail. Improve cost controls and other kinds of management control. Then find ways to improve short-term cash-flow so that the troubled company can meet its payment obligations. When this is done, start profit improvement activities.

Massive downsizing by firings is therefore *not* the first action which springs to mind, although it might be necessary later on. Therefore, the main thrust of this chapter is cash-improving solutions, either through sources within the company itself, or externally.

This chapter deals not only with how to get cash out of *fixed assets* and/or *inventories*, but also by better collection methods for *accounts receivables* and by stretching *vendor credits*. (Accounts payable is in this connection regarded as an important *asset*, although reported on the liability side of the balance sheet.)

Wringing more cash out of the balance sheet might also be called 'liquidifying the balance sheet'. (This term is not found in Webster's dictionary. However, the authors have avoided using the term 'liquidizing', which too easily leads to thoughts of the liquidation of the company, which is exactly what the turnaround manager is desperately trying to avoid!)

A concluding section is devoted to how to deal with the (usually quite) jittery banker, and the (admittedly small) possibility of *renegotiating loans*, repayment schemes, interest rates, and possibly *even forgiveness of part of the principal*. Our basic assumption is that most external sources (for example shareholders, the normal bank connection, and other credit institutes) are *not* prepared to extend further cash through credits, subscription to new share capital and so on. However, there are exceptions, for example if the company is as huge and nationally important as Chrysler Corporation was, and the name of the turnaround manager is Lee Iacocca. When major banks are on the verge of bankruptcy, they also tend to get special treatment. This was true when major US banks had seriously overextended their credits in South America, and when the (then) Swedish Nordbanken had engaged itself too deeply in badly secured property loans, just before the property prices unexpectedly started falling.

4.2   Selling different kinds of assets on a fire sale basis

Freeing up cash tied up in receivables overdue in inventories, in payables and so on is discussed at great length in sections 4.6 to 4.9. However, if the troubled company is only 10–30 days away from 'sudden death', that is, when it can no longer meet its payment obligations, the turnaround manager might be forced to *sell some fixed assets to rapidly generate cash*. The list below is by no means complete, but it contains a broad spectrum of actions typically worth considering in such a situation:

- Selling land and buildings presently not used for operating purposes.

- Selling and leasing back buildings actually used for company operations.

- Selling one or more fully owned component manufacturing units, and instead using external supply sources in the future. (This kind of 'facility outsourcing' has been common, for example in the automotive industry, over the last ten years.)

- Selling off whole SBUs which are of a rather peripheral interest in relation to the saved company's intended future core business.

- Encouraging a leveraged management buyout of non-essential companies or business areas, thus shedding manpower and costs without having to pay any associated severance payments.

Case

This was how Lackawanna (US leather manufacturers) and several other companies were spun off by Beatrice in 1984/85 to generate US$1.4 billion, making it possible to repay part of their enormous debt of US$5.1 billion created by their 'mega purchase' of Esmark Inc. (Esmark was itself at that time in the process of digesting Norton Simon, a conglomerate it had purchased in 1983. These divestments did not only bring in *cash*, but also generated a *profit* of US$220 million after tax, then corresponding to $2.20 per share.)

In this fashion, not only was the necessary cash raised, and the debt to equity ratio improved, but higher profits per share were shown at the same time! Beatrice could report earnings of $4.77 a share for the fiscal year ending in February 1985, instead of only $2.57 a share. Here we leave aside the rather tempting discussion of the difference between operating income and non-recurring/non-operating income and related 'creative accounting' tricks.

- Selling off and leasing back trucks and production equipment, computers and some other types of office equipment. (In one turn-around case engaging Dr Arpi, the whole computer department – including its 55 employees – was sold off, upon which only 60 per cent of the department's capacity was leased back at a much lower price than earlier annual costs. In the process, the service level provided increased substantially as well!)

- Fire sales of obsolete and/or slow moving stock of parts or finished goods in order to free otherwise tied-up capital. (However, be very careful not to help create new competitors who can undersell you for years to come! In the scaffolding rental industry, examples abound.)

- Assigning full ownership of the troubled company's field warehouse stock to a financing company (thus raising cash) while only receiving additional payments when and as goods are actually sold.

■ Selling receivables to a 'factoring' company which – although being an expensive solution – has the endearing feature of rapidly releasing cash.[1]

If the factoring company forces the troubled company to keep all problematic receivables, the latter still has to maintain a substantial staff dealing with credit approvals, collections, investigations of contested invoices, bad debt reporting and most other administrative overheads associated with an account receivables department. Thus, on top of carrying substantial factoring charges, the troubled company also is forced to retain most of their costs for the accounts receivables department!

In the medium-term perspective, the turnaround manager must certainly take all necessary actions to bring down the number of bad debts, contested invoices, and associated administrative costs, while considering turning from factoring to receivables financing at his bank, usually a much less expensive alternative than selling all receivables without recourse to a specialized factoring institute.

What is smart, necessary, possible and desirable when it comes to raising cash certainly varies from case to case. For an independent company in a dramatic crisis situation with few outside helping hands, the options available can be much more limited than the above list suggests.

4.3 The selling of a complete SBU

A key consideration is not only how much cash can be raised by a certain divestment, but also how long it will take. For instance, just the process of selling a company in Belgium takes on average three months. (This figure disregards the date for 'declarations of intent' by representatives of the two companies. The figure rather reflects the typical time from signing the agreement to the date when the selling company will experience a cash improvement from its divestment.)

Selling a whole strategic business unit lock, stock and barrel may take anything from one month to a year. Key factors influencing the speed are:

■ whether the unit is logical, well delineated
■ whether it makes profits

- whether it fits nicely into the organization and expansion plans of another group
- the amount of high level industry connections available to the turnaround manager, who is making discreet contacts to identify potential buyers.

Other important factors influencing the time horizon are:

- price expectations (for example expressed as a multiple of profits generated)
- whether the accounting books for the particular unit in question are clearly organized, transparent to the buyer and provides all the answers to the questions normally asked by a buyer
- whether the intended buyer is used to acquiring such companies and has the management resources and management experience for the subsequent 'house cleaning operations'.

The latter aspect is particularly important if the SBU up for sale is a badly run entity, with low or no profits.

The Electrolux Group is well-known for buying relatively weak companies and not waiting long before attacking the purchased company, bringing down costs, streamlining the product line, increasing prices and integrating the purchased unit with other already existing organizational entities. Only in connection with relatively few major acquisitions, like Zanussi or AEG, has Electrolux provided a longer period of grace.

Sometimes an SBU does not immediately find its final home or destination, but continues to move between different owners.

Case

The Swedish TV, radio, and computer manufacturer Luxor, was first sold to Ericsson (trying to integrate Luxor and Data Saab with other parts of the then fast-growing Ericsson Information Systems). When Ericsson scaled back its very ambitious but unprofitable venture into PCs and other types of computers, without any direct relationship to their core business, Luxor resided for a while with Electrolux, only to end up being sold to the Finnish Nokia Group. Luxor was 'in play', and continued to move between different companies, each seeing a different use for the organizational entity.

Although the turnaround manager will look for a logical buyer from the very start, that is, a buyer to whom this particular SBU makes sense, his own main concern is not to find a final home for the sold entity, but rather to raise cash quickly. This cash might also be needed to reinforce the remaining core business areas.

It is difficult to rank-order each type of asset with regard to how quickly it can normally be turned into cash. The factoring of accounts receivables and/or the fire sales of inventories are normally fast-working alternatives. However, both authors have seen examples of very substantial fixed assets changing hands within less than a week. (One reason: It is usually rather easy to correctly evaluate a good industrial property when its location, size and condition is known.)

Even *major competitors* have sometimes been acquired with amazing speed, or been subject to rather unexpected mergers.

Case

Most of the analysis and negotiations preceding Asea's merger with Brown Boveri (into what is now known as ABB) actually took place during the summer vacation of 1987. The decision-makers decided to openly accept remaining risks in order to use the momentum created, and before any serious obstacles appeared.

So far, US and Swedish executives have tended to move faster than continental European managers, partly because of different traditions and different mentalities. However, since the end of the 1980s, the European continent has experienced a number of startling exceptions. Around this time, raiders like Carlo de Benedetti (and half a dozen like him) started to move both faster and much more aggressively compared to what well-established European corporations were used to.

Case

Carlo de Benedetti's sudden public offer for the shares of Société Générale of Belgium at New Year 1988 sent shockwaves through the whole Belgian industrial establishment (see Section 4.5). It gave everybody a first taste of what the 'frontier-less Europe of 1992' was soon to bring in areas such as insurance, banking, media, food distribution and mechanical engineering industries.

In Europe, two types of company have been particularly vulnerable to cross-border takeover attempts:

a. *Mature electro-mechanical industries* with rather undifferentiated products, where low unit costs through long production runs have often been the key condition for survival and success. (Cars might be added to this group.)

b. *High-tech industries* with exceptionally high development costs for each new generation of products. Telecommunications, aerospace, pharmaceuticals, mainframe computers and chip manufacturing are some examples.

Nowadays, it often takes less time to sell fixed assets than to turn *current assets* into cash. Thus, the traditional distinction between 'fixed' and 'current' assets is gradually being blurred. Simultaneously, the traditional distinction between 'fixed' and 'variable' costs is becoming increasingly irrelevant for many managerial purposes, including product cost accounting. Manpower costs (traditionally treated as typical variable costs in macroeconomic literature) are nowadays sometimes treated as fixed costs by many European companies, while fixed assets can be more fluid, since not only can they be sold, but also rapidly sold and leased back as required, sometimes depending on what kind of net income figure the troubled company wants to show in its next annual report. Therefore, this chapter starts with a discussion of the divestment of major entities, and ends with a discussion of improvements in normal cash management (via better management of inventories, receivables, payables and so on).

4.4 Five examples of activities spun off in major turnaround situations

It is not certain that a troubled company has anything at all which can rapidly be spun off. The possibility for such a move depends on many factors, including:

- the attractiveness of the product range concerned

- the organization of the company into separate and logical profit centres

- whether separate factories are used by different strategic business units

- whether the accounting system is arranged in such a way that the income, cost and profit structure of the potential spin-off candidate can be rapidly determined without any major 'reworking of the books'

- whether a logical candidate exists as potential purchaser

- whether interest rates are low and the overall business climate is such that it favours expansion plans primarily based on acquisitions. (This was certainly the case at the time of writing, year-end 1998/99.)

Let us illustrate what five well-known and substantial companies have done in the area of *major divestments in turnaround situations:*

a. *Chrysler Corporation* sold off its whole defence division in the first quarter of 1982. This made it possible for Lee Iacocca to proudly claim that Chrysler had 'shown a profit once again'. (Please note the far-from-unusual mixture of operating results with non-operating/non-recurrent items.)

b. In 1998, after decades of unsatisfactory profits, *General Motors* put their whole component manufacturing operation, *Delphi* (with some 200,000 employees), on shares, while initially retaining a majority holding.

c. During the first few years of the 1980s, loss-making *Massey Fergusson* (Canada) cut their worldwide work force from 68,000 to 27,000, while at the same time closing or selling no fewer than 18 factories, including a machinery manufacturing company sold to IBH of West Germany.

d. While turning around the ailing 'Nordstjernan', the flagship of the Swedish Johnson Group, a number of very different companies and/or activity areas were rapidly sold off. This not only generated cash. It also helped provide an undivided management focus on Nordstjernan's future core business, that is, its construction activities. In 1988, one major competitor, ABV, was purchased and merged with *Johnson Construction Company* (JCC) and in 1997 another (SIAB) to form what was to become the largest construction and property group in the Nordic and Baltic Sea area.

e. Earlier in this chapter we mentioned *Beatrice*, a US$9.3 billion food conglomerate which in 1984 paid US$2.7 billion for Esmark Inc, which in turn had not yet fully digested Norton Simon, another conglomerate. The merger made Beatrice about as large as Procter & Gamble. However, as a result of the purchase, Beatrice had also increased its debt from less than $1 billion to over 5 billion dollars, financed at an average interest rate of about 13 per cent. Beatrice's portfolio of companies now included a number of non-food companies such as *Avis Rent-a-Car*, *Wesson Oils* and *Lackawanna Leather Manufacturers*. The 'solution' to the very heavy debt load? A number of companies (which did not fit the Blueprint for the Future Group) were sold off to the tune of US$1,400 million, bringing the debt down to more manageable levels.

While the first four examples (Chrysler Corporation, GM, Massey Ferguson and NCC) were sell-offs of existing operations, long owned by the troubled company, the last case (Beatrice) is quite different. Here, the *selling off of major corporate assets in the acquired company was an integral part of the acquisition plan itself*. The successful spin-off of these companies after the acquisition was even a *prerequisite for the deal*. Otherwise, the purchasing company would have been dragged under by the terrific debt load and by the associated debt servicing burden at a 13 per cent interest level.

The seller and the buyer of non-essential assets or non-core businesses might each have very different motives.

Seen from the seller's viewpoint, in a typical turnaround situation, asset selling is only a means to a noble end, that is, to create enough breathing space for the management to save the company and be able to fully attend to – and reinforce – its future core business.

After major mergers, asset stripping may be a self-inflicted necessity in order to bring down the debt and debt-service to manageable levels. This has been true for many 'leveraged management buyouts' financed by high-yield junk bonds, and usually also fuelled by a big CEO ego. The most spectacular and well-documented case might be the *Rjr Nabisco* case, documented both as a full-feature film and in a well-researched book by Brian Burrough and John Helyar, called *The Barbarians at the Gate: The Fall of Rjr Nabisco*, HarperCollins, 1991.

Undervalued assets might be another key driving force, both for buyers and sellers. In 1999 one of the major forest-owning companies in Scandinavia – Assidomän, 50.2 per cent owned by the Swedish state – was blocked from excessive timber selling (to the tune of SEK 2,500 million), since forests are regarded as a national asset which cannot be played around with for short-term financial purposes.)

Many buyers of substantial assets or whole companies have been encouraged by the need to create enough critical mass in their present or future core business. Thus, the realization of the 'Europe 1992' plan, that is, the creation of the borderless European Common Market, triggered a host of mergers and acquisitions (including some hostile takeovers), both before and after the magical 1992 date.

This early merger fever was by no means limited to companies having their headquarters within the European Common Market. Although Sweden and Finland were initially not part of the European Common Market, many Swedish and Finnish companies eagerly tried to be part of the action. They acquired substantial footholds within the Common Market and thereby grew both in size and importance to the industry. Through foreign acquisitions they increased the likelihood of remaining among just a handful of survivors in each mature industry.

4.5 The 'selling' of Société Générale de Belgique, Belgium's largest industrial holding

Parallel with this EG-driven (nowadays EU-driven) development, the number of cross-border 'raiders' increased. The Italian 'Condottieri', Dr Carlo de Benedetti's 1988 attack on Belgium's 'old lady', (Société

Générale de Belgique (SGB)), represented a major, highly publicized wholesale takeover attempt. Offers in the order of 6,000 to 8,000 Belgian francs were submitted for shares which were quoted at 2,500 francs. Shareholders therefore had the right to expect that – if properly run – the 'old lady' could indeed double or triple her profits.

SGB once controlled one-third of the Belgian economy (plus 70 per cent of the economy of the Belgian Congo!), and used to have a stake in no less than 1,200 companies, spread over 68 countries.

Of course, this highly dispersed arrangement was never rational, and SGB was more or less run as a branch of the Civil Service. During the 1990s, most of these companies were sold off (partly to repay the tremendous debt assumed by the new owners). Most board members and top managers have been replaced, and the ownership further changed.

The attack on Société Générale functioned as a thunderous alarm bell in Belgium, and even throughout Europe. A major, near-mythical holding company, controlling a large part of Belgium's industry and economy, and managed by well-connected (but from a management viewpoint rather unprofessional) public figures, had suddenly been put in play by an 'OPA' (the French abbreviation for a Public Offer), initiated by a non-invited foreigner. Books were written on Carlo di Benedetti's takeover attempt, its causes, intentions and impact (including 'poison pills'), and Suez originally functioning as the 'white knight'.

Even general purpose publications, like the Belgian daily *Le Soir*, suddenly woke up and started providing unprecedented daily reports to the Belgian public. These reports also covered the exodus of SGB board members and line managers as well as the arrival of new, 'hungrier', but also more professional managers with a hard-nosed 'bottom-line' orientation. These individuals were not primarily looking for fancy titles ('Governor' instead of 'Chairman of the Board') or high-level social and commercial connections in Belgium. Rather, they saw the enormous profit improvement potential which could be exploited through the modernization and rationalization of a conglomerate, older than the Belgian state itself. (SGB had actually been headed by a Governor, a title leading to thoughts of cosier colonial days, when Belgium ran the Belgian Congo with the Société Générale as a key instrument. However, in spite of its impressive size, it lacked a normal management team for daily decision-making.)

Although Dr Carlo de Benedetti (simultaneously being the head of Olivetti) did not manage to acquire control of Société Générale de Belgique, he opened the doors to a completely new era, characterized by cross-border, (sometimes even 'unfriendly') takeovers, and a suddenly much increased emphasis on shareholder value and professional management.

Note: In 1998, ten years after the direct attack by Dr Benedetti, 100 per cent of the SGB shares were in the hands of Suez Lyonnaise des Eaux, a French company.

The resulting change in Belgian business and ownership structures has been dramatic. This is partly reflected in the number of Belgian companies no longer listed on the Belgian stock exchange. One of Belgium's two largest banks, *Générale de Banque*, has been bought by Fortis, a Dutch–Belgian services group. The other, *Banque Bruxelles Lambert* (BBL), has been purchased by ING of the Netherlands. The century-old insurance company, *Royale Belge*, has been absorbed by *AXA*, France. (Royale Belge was actually the fourth major Belgian company to disappear recently from the 'BEL-20' index of leading stocks on the Brussels stock exchange). Soon after, France's *Usinor* took a controlling interest in *Cockerill Sambre*, that is, the inheritor of the once formidable Belgian steel industry. The list goes on and on. Others, like *Sabena* the national Belgian airline have for the time being 'linked up' with foreign companies. In Sabena's case, the major new partner is Delta airlines.

The Belgian oil company *Petrofina* – recently proudly introduced on the New York stock exchange as one of only two Belgian companies – was at year-end 1998 expected to be 'the next piece of Belgian family silver to end up on another nation's sideboard'. The quote is from Neil Buckley, *Financial Times'* correspondent in Brussels. He ended one of his articles with a big sigh, saying: 'If only Belgium could seize the opportunity to overhaul its corporate governance system...'

He could equally well have said: If only major Belgian corporations had learned in time to run stringent turnarounds, including massive restructuring when needed, and had known they should move aggressively into leading positions of their own in carefully selected core businesses throughout the new frontier-free European Union, or beyond. Unfortunately, Belgian companies have usually been the prey, not the predator. Too many Belgian companies have been run for the benefit of their directors, passing on little profit to their shareholders, who tended to be either a family or a holding company, not a multitude of demanding shareholders, active on the stock exchange.

Two other European countries with similarly small populations, namely Holland and Sweden, have succeeded better in expanding their own companies over country borders. This might be attributed to true 'stock exchange capitalism', to borrow an expression from Professor Herman Daems, Professor of Strategy and International Management at the Catholic University of Leuven, Belgium.

Viscount Etienne Davignon, a former European Commissioner and one of the few survivors from the SGB debacle, once countered by saying: 'In the frontier-less new Europe, it does not really matter much who owns what.' His opinion was not shared, however, by the workers at the 168 year-old Vilvoorde plant (in Belgium), ruthlessly closed down by *Renault*'s French headquarters at about the same time.

True stock exchange capitalism reached Germany only in 1998–99. Before this time, hostile takeovers were unheard of, boards were seldom bothered by the company's shareholders, and non-performing CEOs were seldom fired. However, in February 1999, BMW's chairman Dr Bernd Pischetsreider, was removed from his position with references to BMW's slow turnaround of Rover. His successor made it quite clear that although Rover would be kept as a separate entity, the turnaround timetable had changed radically.

4.6   Freeing up cash tied up in receivables overdue

Discussing good OCM (operating cash management) is hardly as exciting as the previous discussion about the selling of major entities. A well-run company usually has good OCM, and many readers are no doubt well acquainted with the associated concepts and techniques. However, most turnaround candidates are *not* excellently run companies, and a turnaround manager might find an inordinate amount of

	IF CASH IS MOST IMPORTANT, CONSIDER:	IF PROFIT IS THE KEY CONCERN:
1 Establish if **CASH** or **PROFITS** is the most urgent concern	■ Sale and lease back of buildings and equipment, factoring of receivables, fire sales of product inventory, renegotiating terms with all key stakeholders, rapidly selling off non-strategic assets (perhaps whole SBUs) ■ And do not overlook improvements in *normal cash management*, for example via better collection procedures, stretching vendor credits, better balanced finished stock, lower WIP, and better purchasing policies.	■ Identify 'bleeders', for example unprofitable product lines, markets, customer classes and so on, and eliminate most of them ■ Kill expensive 'pet projects' with little chance of ever succeeding ■ Attack unnecessary parts of the organization, making it smaller and with fewer organizational levels ■ Invest in market development or product and service enhancements where market and customer research indicate substantial opportunities, presently not well exploited.
2 Specify the **AVAILABLE TIME-FRAME** and (if given a choice) the **TARGET TIME-FRAME** for the turnaround: a. to *save* the troubled company b. to *restore it* to acceptable profitability c. to *transform and redirect it* to maximize its chances of achieving long-term success and prosperity	■ IF SAVING the troubled company is the main concern, radical surgery, and a dictatorial management style might be called for ■ RESTORING the company to an acceptable profit level might require downsizing, including the killing of some expensive 'pet projects' ■ To build the 'Future Company' normally requires a redefinition of the company's future 'Business Mission' and (often) selling off what is not part of the company's future core business, while simultaneously investing in strengthening its position in the core business area. Gradually, a 'management team concept' replaces the 'enlightened dictatorship concept'.	
	CUTTING COSTS	INVESTING/EXPANDING
3 Decide if you primarily **CUT** costs, if you primarily **EXPAND** in certain profitability areas, or if you **CUT AND EXPAND SIMULTANEOUSLY**, although in quite different areas	■ Cost-cutting is part of virtually ALL turnarounds ■ Some turnarounds are characterized ONLY by cost-cutting, including the renegotiation of terms with different stakeholders ■ Most turnarounds START with cost-cutting, even to the point of 'shrinking the company'. After this 'retrenchment period', the company is again growing, but in quite different areas.	■ It is wise early on to communicate what shall be the core business of the 'Future Company' ■ Selling of non-core businesses can eliminate loss-making sources and simultaneously generate badly needed resources to create increased strength in the company's future core business ■ Investments and expansion will be based on a FOCUSING STRATEGY, while cost-cutting eliminates many costly PERIPHERAL ACTIVITIES. Normally, cost-cutting *precedes* investments, and it might even be a prerequisite for the latter. Thus, a complete turnaround includes cost-cutting, retrenchment and transformation and freeing up capital and managerial resources for worthier causes.

Figure 4.1   Different emphases: cash vs profit concerns, and 'just saving' the company vs also 'transforming' it

cash tied up in account receivables (A/R), finished stock, work in progress (WIP), or in invoices thoughtlessly paid too early. Therefore, the rest of this chapter is devoted to good OCM, starting with A/R.

A simplistic example might serve to highlight the practical importance of improving the number of A/R days outstanding. Assume that the task is to save a medium-sized company with a turnover of $120 million and with outstanding receivables in the order of $25 million. By *cutting the number of days outstanding to half*, one liberates (that is, frees up) $12.5 million, which can certainly be used for much better purposes.

An excessive number of days outstanding for account receivables (here defined as the value of A/R divided by the average value of net sales per day of the year) tend to reflect not only weak collection procedures, but usually also a number of underlying serious flaws, for example in product quality, logistics, marketing tactics, delivery discipline or invoicing accuracy. Thus, to reduce the number of A/R days outstanding, the turnaround manager might have to face and attack a host of underlying problems.

Many smart customers consciously use such deficiencies in the selling company's setup as an excuse for not paying within the normal number of days. The turnaround manager should also check that the sales department of the troubled company has not allowed its clients extraordinary payment terms in order to clinch badly needed added sales volumes. If it has, the sales organization might in the process have pushed the credit department beyond all reasonable limits, and perhaps also distribution centres, plant managers and so on. This might in turn have aggravated delivery and quality problems and increased already high cost levels, all leading to a further lowering of profit margins.

Therefore, if one intends to bring down accounts receivables from say 80 days to a more reasonable value of 40 days, do not expect that it is just a matter of sending circular letters to all clients concerned!

Turnaround managers usually find that most claims which *exceed 90 days are contested*. Therefore, if these are chosen as a primary point of attack, they threaten to drag the turnaround manager and his already busy executives into both time-consuming and unpleasant discussions. If rapid cash is the main concern, one might be much better off by instead focusing on receivables which are between 40 and 90 days old.

When the oldest outstanding receivables are finally analysed and attacked, the CEO will usually be presented with a complete 'menu' containing all the tricks tried by clients, plus all the mistakes committed by the company itself under severe stress. The situation might be compounded by an earlier reluctance to deal with the situation and/or to correctly evaluate the true value of the oldest receivables (and accept all associated, rather unpleasant write-off requirements).

4.7   Freeing up cash tied up in inventories

4.7.1 Cash tied up in purchased goods or WIP

Cash is usually tied up in stocks in three fashions:

a. purchased raw materials, components and trading products
b. work in progress (WIP)
c. finished goods ready to be shipped.

With the dramatic increase in interest rates around 1980, a lot of attention was suddenly focused on 'capital rationalization', aided by specialized capital rationalization consultants.

Ingoing stock of purchased goods was brought down by the use of just-in-time delivery systems.[2] Cash tied up in WIP (work in progress) was also reduced by kanban systems and other techniques, often originating in Japan.

As late as 1997, Varity-Perkins' diesel engine producing factories in the UK introduced more Japanese rationalization methods, encouraged by a key executive, acquired from Nissan.

Suppliers and clients were called in to examine different sections of the production chain, to provide their opinions and suggestions with regard to ways to achieve a further radical increase in production efficiency and thereby also in production capacity. Detailed information was released to the press with regard to documented or potential productivity gains, for example from more efficient space utilization, shorter transportation stretches between different production stations, a better utilization of existing machine capacity and so on. Their calculation of resulting 'engine production capacity' was quite stunning (and somewhat scary) '500,000 units within five years'. Soon thereafter, Varity-Perkins was acquired by Caterpillar.

High interest rates during the 1980s, combined with the need to free up cash tied down in warehouses, also led to a critical re-evaluation among multinationals of the need to keep local stock in national depots. The goal was to radically bring down stock levels without any lowering of customer service levels. New types of computer-assisted logistic systems were the main tools. SKF, with their 'European Supply and Delivery System', was one of the first in Europe to use regional warehouses serving many national markets. This formula was soon to be successfully copied by the ESAB welding group (as reflected in the ESAB case in Part II).

4.7.2 Cash through improved inventory turns of finished goods

When discussing cash tied up in inventories, one key ratio of great interest is *inventory turns* (that is, the turnover speed of the inventory, expressed as number of times per year), and usually defined as:

$$\frac{\text{Annual Cost of Goods Sold (COGS)}}{\text{Inventory value}^3}$$

Example: Assume that the competition is turning over their inventory 4 times a year while the troubled company only shows 1.5 turns a year. The turnaround manager has then defined not only a *problem* but also an *opportunity* for substantial, quantitative improvement of the troubled company's cash position. The size of this improvement potential can be illustrated by the following calculation:

Assume that your net sales are $100 million, your annual COGS $45 million, capital tied up in inventory $30 million, while your present rate of inventory turns is only 1.5 times per year. Assume that you identify three inventory turns per year to be a realistic target. Although still worse than competition, the change in inventory turnover speed from 1.5 to 3 times would free up $15 million dollars in cash for much more worthy causes.

For the hurried turnaround manager under severe time pressure, sophistication is not his first priority, but reducing the cash tied up in inventory to more reasonable levels.

If he needs to verify if his tentative targets are realistic, this can be done by *benchmarking* against well-run companies in the same or in similar industries. Such reference points ensure that the turnaround expert is not timid, nor indulging in unrealistic 'blue skies planning', but that he tries to achieve realistic targets.

4.7.3 Other positive spin-offs from bringing down inventory levels

Fire sales of obsolete inventory will obviously bring in some cash and bring down the inventory value, thus also freeing up capital in a medium-term perspective. However, getting rid of obsolete or slow-moving stock will also *free valuable storage space, and most likely improve overview and access to the remaining stock.*

A warning: rapid, unconsidered cuts in inventory levels might lead to an undesirable increase in the number of back-orders, which in turn might hurt sales. Such potential negative effects have to be considered and evaluated. In reality, our experience shows that a low, but well-maintained stock can often be associated both with rational logistics and with a good customer service level.

When the worst cash crisis is over, the turnaround manager should also pay attention to how the company ended up with the unacceptably high inventory level. The answer might call for new purchasing policies, but also new logistic principles (just-in-time and so on). Having brought down finished goods levels, methods to bring down *work in progress* (WIP) without hurting either the productivity or the flexibility of the plant should be considered. Certain controls or other procedures might have to be introduced to make sure that the company does not gradually slip back to unacceptable levels of raw materials, purchased components, work in progress or finished goods.

4.8   Stretching vendor credits, whenever possible

One obvious and very important source of cash is the company's suppliers. Stretching the credit time can basically be done in two different ways:

1. *Selectively delaying payment of bills due,* while also taking care not to upset key suppliers who, if offended, might kill the troubled company. (The turnaround of the huge W. T. Grant retailing chain went sour when certain key suppliers simply refused to deliver the goods badly needed for the crucial Christmas period.)

2. Explaining the situation and *negotiating better payment terms and conditions.* This was one of many avenues tried by Lee Iacocca in his elaborate plan to rescue Chrysler Corporation. (Chrysler simply 'postponed' payments to certain suppliers, and/or offered payments in the form of cars instead of cash to others.)

A smaller company, probably with products of more limited general appeal, may not have the same options. If your company's purchase volumes do not match Chrysler's, and if your creative and persuasive skills do not match Iacocca's, item 2 above might be quite a dangerous route, since you are at the same time widely communicating all your problems. This might encourage some banks to call their loans, and some suppliers to deliver only against cash on delivery.

By openly flagging your problems, you might also – like Chrysler Corporation – drop to a 'CCC' credit rating meaning 'that the company's capacity to pay interest and repay principle is predominantly speculative'. This might in reality do you little harm, since hardly anybody is prepared to give a seriously troubled company a loan on acceptable conditions at this point in time. The conclusion is obvious: you have to look for cash primarily from available 'internal' sources, including A/C, A/P, inventory and, of course, potential asset sales, as discussed in several sections of this chapter.

If you are to succeed with an 'open negotiation strategy' you should also be able to demonstrate in a convincing fashion that both suppliers and credit institutions are much better off by supporting your turn-around efforts, than by encouraging bankruptcy. A liquidation balance sheet up your sleeve might be useful, since it can demonstrate in cold figures that *stakeholders are better off if the distressed company is alive rather than dead.* (A 'worst case scenario' used for the calculation of the liquidation value of the company might start out with the following assumptions: Cash + 50% of accounts receivables + 20% of normal inventory value + 50% of PP&E.)

Case Study

WHEN CASH IS MORE IMPORTANT THAN PROFITS

The small company turnaround expert, Renee Fellman, recently illustrated what in this book is called 'When cash is king':

'I start with the cash flow. I set ground rules for what will be paid. Usually, there is not enough money in the troubled company. We will therefore pay absolutely nothing on overdue bills. Essentially, we pay for current products and services with current cash. Then, we cut money-losing projects and decrease costs' (in the remaining core business). 'We negotiate with existent suppliers or find new suppliers who will sell at lower cost.'

'We try to convert the clients into paying by credit card. This almost immediately shortens receivables by 60 days.'

'Only when the cash-flow problem has been fixed can we attack questions like what the company goals are, who is responsible for what, and what the financial and operational targets are.'

Source: Interview with Mrs. Fellman published in *Business Week* on March 2, 1998

4.9 Freeing up cash by renegotiation of loans and repayment schemes

If a rich parent company is prepared to provide the necessary cash, or if the state (or regional authority) is prepared to engage in a bailout, fine. However, this is not a normal situation, particularly not for a small or middle-sized family company.

> Your banker might act as your friend or your foe. However, in a turnaround situation he is likely to act primarily in 'enlightened self-interest'.

> Therefore, one task for a turnaround manager might be to constantly keep the banker 'enlightened' about his own self-interest, and thus make him refrain from calling the loans. (Even long-term loans have an unfortunate tendency to turn into short-term loans when the banker so wants, based on the small print on the rear side of the loan contract!)

Theoretically, a manager might be able to make a bank 'forget' part of a loan, or extend the repayment period, or provide new funds and other measures which might ease the cash squeeze. However, only in exceptional cases should one expect the banker (or other credit institution) to be prepared to go in deeper to cover the bank's already vested interests.

After a successful turnaround, the banker is likely to be exceptionally understanding, friendly and helpful. However, while you are in the densest fog, do not expect too much from him. (Remember that a banker is a person prepared to lend you money when you do not need it, but utterly reluctant to do so when you are in a real squeeze.)

In this chapter, the authors have chosen to abstain from discussing more exotic financing means, including high-yield junk bonds, asset lenders or tiger sharks. We believe a good turnaround manager should be able to succeed without resorting to such extreme and dangerous arrangements which often only tend to deepen the crisis.

> To make a jittery bank manager less jittery, present the broad lines of your turnaround plan to him. Show him, based on objective industry statistics, that your benchmarked targets are indeed realistic. If he still feels tempted to call the loans and force your company into bankruptcy, have your liquidation balance sheet ready, and show him that he has nothing to gain from aggravating the situation further.

4.10 Quantifying the cash needs and the urgency

Before starting to sell off fixed or current assets or undertake other – more or less draconian – efforts to 'liquidify' the balance sheet, the turnaround manager needs a good estimate of how much cash is needed and how urgently.

The 'net quick ratio', that is, the sum of cash on hand, plus accounts receivables divided by current liabilities, might provide a first clue to the urgency of the situation. The time horizon used is of utmost importance. A cash-flow analysis focusing on total incoming and total outgoing cash during the next six months might be quite useless if a detailed short-term analysis of payables due versus receivables expected show that the troubled company cannot meet its payroll requirements on Friday the following week.

A great number of financial ratios are today routinely produced by the accounting department's computers. Such ratios become even more meaningful when related to representative industry-wide statistics, for example from Dun & Bradstreet. In Table 4.1, examples of such ratios can be found. In the table they are grouped into four categories:

■ those describing the company's financial status
■ 'asset utility', that is, those describing how effectively existing assets are being utilized
■ traditional profitability and 'return' measurements
■ employee related data, that is, ratios showing sales, as well as costs and profits per employee.

Table 4.1 contains numerical values for a particular company and for all companies in the same industry.

Table 4.1   Some key ratios used as benchmarks

Ratios	Company data	Industry quartiles		
		Upper	Median	Lower
Financial Status				
Quick ratio (X)	0.4	1.0	0.9	0.5
Current ratio (X)	1.6	1.9	1.4	1.1
Total liability to NW (%)*	232.0	79.3	138.8	301.7
Fixed assets to NW (%)	36.5	35.6	73.0	127.3
Current liability to NW (%)	120.4	63.2	112.4	207.3
Financial charges/sales (%)	2.6	0.6	1.9	3.5
Total indebtedness (%)	56.9	43.9	67.9	89.2

Asset Utility				
Stock turnover (times/year)	4.3	11.5	8.2	5.5
Collection period (days)	29.5	60.2	76.3	128.0
Asset turnover (%)	234.3	216.0	165.8	120.6
Sales to NWC (X)	7.3	8.0	5.2	2.1
Sales to current assets (%)	278.1	251.6	177.4	140.8
Creditors to sales (D)	37.0	34.9	47.0	70.1
Profitability				
Profit margin (%)	0.3	7.6	2.2	0.9
Shareholders return (%)	1.6	36.8	12.9	2.6
Return to assets (%)	0.7	9.3	5.1	1.2
Return on capital (%)	1.4	18.2	10.3	3.4
Return on value added (%)	4.5	7.2	5.1	3.0
Employee (000s)				
Sales/emp. (BFR)	4733	4896	3330	2004
Profit/emp. (BFR)	14	228	102	30
Av. wage/emp. (BFR)	398	613	480	330
Emp. costs/value added (%)	185.0	161.61	110.2	62.2

* NW = Net Worth

Source: Dun & Bradstreet-Euroinform SA.

When industry data are organized as in Table 4.1, they not only provide median values but also quartile values.[4] This makes it easier for the turnaround manager to recognize quickly where his troubled company is situated compared to the competition.

A turnaround manager who moves in on company premises without first undertaking this kind of elementary comparative study of industry statistics is simply unprofessional. Such data help specify the size of the changes necessary first to bring the troubled company to average industry performance, and later to better than average performance, for example as represented by the industry's upper quartile values. (Industry-wide benchmarking is further discussed in Chapter 5.)

The present chapter is not intended to replace a controller's handbook. However, to show the usefulness of certain financial ratios and other performance measurement ratios in a turnaround situation a few definitions and comments are provided below.

As already stated, cash position, cash-flow projections and the company's capability to meet its short-term payment obligations are often the centre of the turnaround managers' interest during the first few months. Therefore, the following ratios reflecting the financial status of the troubled company might be given top priority.

1. The *net quick ratio* (sometimes also called 'the acid test') is simply the net value of current assets after the value of inventory has been deducted, and then divided by current liabilities. (When the resulting value falls below 0.5, this is regarded as a red flag item.)

2. The *current ratio* includes all current assets divided by current liabilities. This value should usually be at least twice as high as the net quick ratio.

3. *Current liabilities* are sometimes also calculated as a percentage of the company's net worth. The resulting value can vary considerably within one and the same industry. This is reflected in Table 4.1, where the median value is 112 per cent, but the upper median only 63 per cent and the lower median over 200 per cent.

A second group of key ratios – also reflected in Table 4.1 – indicates the possibility discussed earlier of actually improving the cash flow by a better use of internal sources of cash. These ratios reflect how efficiently the company is presently using existing assets tied up in inventory, receivables and so on. Such 'asset utilization ratios' include the following three ratios already discussed in greater depth earlier in this chapter:

1. *inventory turns*
2. *collection period* for account receivables (also called 'A/R days outstanding')
3. *accounts payable* in relation to net sales value (or 'A/P days outstanding').

A comparison of the *asset utilization ratios* for the troubled company with benchmarks for 'normal' and 'good' industry performance (represented by the median and upper quartile values) obviously highlights the realistic potential for cash improvements, for instance by:

- *a faster turnover of the inventory of finished goods*, by keeping a lower and/or better balanced inventory

- lowering the *cash tied-up in purchased components* (for example by using more just-in-time delivery) and lowering the amount of work-in-progress (for example by better factory layout and organization, the use of kanban methods and so on)

- a shortening of the average number of *A/R days outstanding*, by better collection methods, faster settling of disputes, possibly also the introduction of a cash discount for faster payments and so on

- a conscious, selective *stretching of the number of days outstanding* for accounts payable, partly based on agreements with certain suppliers.

These possibilities are key instruments to improve the company's cash position, without having to rely on outside financial sources.

The fourth and final group of key ratios (also reflected in Table 4.1) are related to the 'productivity' of the employees, for example sales per employee, or profit generated per employee. If industry-wide comparisons are readily available, and the variation is large, the turnaround manager might choose to analyse in more depth to what extent the observed differences represent very different operating modes within the same industry, for example to what extent the benchmarked companies are engaged in:

a. producing their own components
b. being engaged mainly in assembly, or
c. being mainly in trading of products actually produced elsewhere.

Since the impact of such differences can be very substantial, many turnaround experts prefer not to look so much at *sales* per employee, but at *value added* per employee. Similarly, employee costs measured as a percentage of sales often become less interesting than employee costs in relation to the value added by the company.

Data dealing with the productivity of employees are of substantial interest at a somewhat later stage of the turnaround process, including the identification of obvious spin-off candidates, and/or the calculation of the manpower reduction needed for those parts of the company worth keeping. However, from 'employee productivity data', little information can normally be found of direct value for the immediate improvement of short-term cash-flow.

As soon as the immediate cash crisis is under control, the turn-around manager can start focusing more sharply on *profitability* improvement measures (and measurements), including return on assets. Until such time, 'Cash remains King'. Most of the management actions discussed in this chapter have one common goal: to create the necessary breathing space, allowing the turnaround manager and his team time to undertake other corrective management actions.

4.11 Creditors watching the debt ratio and coverage ratio

The standard industrial statistics reflected in Table 4.1 do contain information about shareholders' return, but do not explicitly calculate any coverage ratio for creditors. However, a banker is supposed to review the coverage ratio, since this reflects the company's capability to cover its debt service.

The coverage ratio is often defined as earnings before interest and taxes divided by interest charges on loans. Another kind of coverage ratio is based on earnings before interest and taxes divided by the sum of interest charges and repayments on the loan itself (that is, partial repayment of the principal).

A creditor is likely to look at the company's *debt ratio*. This is basically a measurement of the exposure of the equity. Again, no fixed rules can be set for a satisfactory debt equity ratio. The more stable the industry and the company and the more regular its cash flow, the higher are the accepted debt levels. However, there are exceptions: for fast moving conglomerate builders, a very high debt ratio and a very low degree of self-financing has normally been fully accepted by the stock-market.

Two Cases

In Europe during the 1980s, Electrolux and Trelleborg were two good examples. At the end of 1987, Trelleborg's shown solidity was down to only 11 per cent while profits per share and dividends per share were at record levels, SEK17 and SEK4, respectively. That high debt level did not worry the stock-market was reflected in the share price, which went from approximately SEK20 in 1983 to

SEK240, that is *12 times higher*, five years later. An obvious consequence of the high debt-to-equity ratio was that Trelleborg's 'own capital' was evaluated at roughly 244 per cent. Such a high evaluation can only be explained by an expectation from the stock-market of a *very high continued capital growth*.

Whatever specific ratio is being used by bankers and other creditors, they all look for the same thing: the troubled company's capability to meet its payment obligations, primarily from the cash generated by its normal operations. They also look at profit and loss statements and the value of collaterals. Deep down, they always want their money back with interest.

Notes

1. Factoring institutions would normally prefer to purchase only selected 'safe' accounts, while the troubled company might continue to be burdened by bad debts and corresponding potential losses. If the factoring institution still buys all receivables they are likely to do this on a 'recourse' basis.
2. In the automotive industry, 'just-in-time' deliveries were regarded as the opposite of over-dimensioned 'just-in-case' stock.
3. The inventory value should preferably be calculated on the average inventory value per quarter, which for the sake of simplicity is often calculated as the arithmetic mean between the value of the inventory at the beginning and at the end of the period. However, in a turnaround situation the manager must also focus on *today's* situation and re-evaluate inventory which is over-valued and still reported, but is in reality 'disappeared' goods. In the turnaround of one warehouse operation, Arpi International consultants found that regional stocks had in reality not been physically checked for the previous three years.
4. The upper quartile represents a company which is positioned so that only 25 per cent of the industry has better values while 75 per cent of the industry has worse values. In a similar fashion the third quartile is being defined as a value for a company which experiences that 75 per cent of companies in the same industry have better values, while only 25 per cent have worse values.

5 The Blueprint for the Future Company, quantitative benchmarks and choice of strategy

5.1 Purpose, contents and structure of this chapter

In a turnaround situation, the last thing the company needs is status quo. Turnaround management is 'change management' under considerable pressure. A new leader is not enough to guarantee intelligent and rapid change. The company needs new goals and strategies, a higher operating pace and a reinforced management team (as shown in the previous chapter). Generally speaking, all employees need a clear picture of a common future worth fighting for, they need to be able to see the way forward, and even to have a new 'marching song'. So how do you translate and communicate the turnaround manager's vision not only to his closest colleagues, as discussed in the previous chapter, but also to the troubled organization as a whole?

This chapter has three main themes:

- It explains the documents most commonly used to *communicate new goals and strategies* throughout the troubled organization, in order to create unity of purpose.

- It describes in great depth *the use of benchmarks* to check that established goals are realistic, that is, achievable, but also shows how to use benchmarks to document the established goals in operational (that is, later verifiable) terms.

- Finally, it discusses strategic choices open to the company. In particular, will the main thrust be to improve the company's internal cost-effectiveness or rather to improve the 'customer perceived value' of its products and services? (Technically speaking, the latter choice is the same as increasing the perceived 'utility' of their products when divided by their price.)

In books on strategy, the choice of strategy is often discussed first, and only later how to document the chosen goals and strategies. However, in a turnaround situation, the order is often reversed. The turnaround manager rapidly has to come up with some kind of Mission Statement. Although it does not contain any numerical goals or timetables, at least it signals that a new time has arrived. The marching orders have changed. The company's future core business and its future Business Mission have at least been proclaimed.

Section 5.3 starts by a discussion of the contents and purpose of a Business Mission Statement as compared to a Blueprint for the Future Company and similar documents often used in a turnaround situation.

After that, the role of comparative benchmarks is highlighted, since these can help to identify underperforming areas of the company, measure the size of corresponding improvement potentials and thereby also strongly influence the corporate strategies chosen and corresponding quantitative goals. Finally (in sections 5.8 and 5.9) the presentation is broadened to cover some of the most pertinent aspects of strategy choice, not least the choice between 'cost leadership' and 'sustained positive differentiation'.

5.2 Meaning and function of the Blueprint for the Future Company

As previously shown, the turnaround manager must often start with austerity measures, including not only hiring freezes, but cutbacks which sometimes amount to considerable downsizing efforts. Although necessary, such activities can easily be misunderstood by employees, as signalling not only the beginning of a retrenchment period, but the beginning of the end for the company.

Therefore, it is important to communicate early on to employees – and other stakeholders – that such austerity measures are necessary to create a *leaner*, *meaner*, more focused, vital, profitable and competitive company. Surgery is necessary initially to save the 'patient', and later to restore the distressed patient to full health.

There are many ways to communicate the fact that the purpose is to save the company, although it must must first undergo substantial changes. Producing and effectively communicating a Blueprint for the Future Company is one way. Such a document demonstrates not only that a future exists, but also what this new future is all about. Knowing the target picture makes it much easier for employees to accept austerity and downsizing measures which might otherwise have been perceived primarily as an expression of slash and burn policies. Even the selling off of whole entities, the closing of product lines or factories, the reduction of manpower, and so on can then be seen in a broader and considerably brighter context.

Communicating the Blueprint for the Future Company normally has strong direct steering effects, since the Blueprint clearly defines:

a. what the company should concern itself with in the future (its Business Mission).

b. which of the existing peripheral activities or projects should be scrapped, downsized, sold off, or at least be given a minimum of management time, financial means and other resources.

From a managerial viewpoint, the function of the Blueprint is:

1. to guide all future investment decisions
2. to prioritize between different ongoing projects
3. to aid the optimal allocation of manpower and other resources
4. to pinpoint areas ready for divestment, closure and so on.

In summary, the Blueprint for the Future Company aids the management team and all employees in the troubled company to focus much more sharply on what is new and what is really important for the survival and prosperity of the company or division.

'A popular child has many names', says a Swedish proverb. In a turnaround situation, key documents providing guidance may be given different names, depending on the preferences of the turnaround manager as well as the company. Our Business Mission, Blueprint for the Future Company, Survival Plan, or our Rescue Scheme can all be heard. Such terms are often loosely defined. This makes a stringent discussion of differences as to their meaning somewhat difficult. The meaning, contents and purpose of the Blueprint has just been explained. In the next section, the Business Mission Statement is discussed and illustrated.

5.3   Blueprint compared to Business Mission, and other terms and concepts

Some turnaround managers, including Per Wejke, prefer to put their main emphasis on a rather brief (10–20 line) *Business Mission Statement*. (A real-life Business Mission Statement used during a turnaround is found a few pages later in this chapter.)

Other managers prefer to talk about the company's new 'marching song', since this term indicates that everybody is from now on moving together at good speed in a clearly indicated direction and with a known goal.

Again, other turnaround experts use even broader concepts which not only cover the goals strived for, but also the means (strategies) to get there. They may refer to such a document as the Rescue Scheme, or the Survival Plan. The latter document can look a bit like the traditional, three-year business plan. However, usually it does not contain all corresponding quantitative details, such as detailed financial data or sales data for each product/market segment.[1]

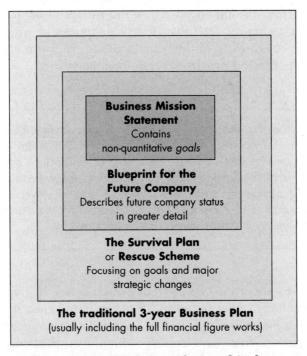

Figure 5.1   Approximate relationship between four terms discussed in this chapter

Figure 5.1 highlights the perceived *relationship* between some of the terms discussed above, primarily with regard to how all-embracing they are.

The briefest operational document is normally a *Business Mission Statement*. This might require only half a page. It is a matter-of-fact statement, pinpointing in unambiguous terms which products and services to provide, in what geographic markets, what key target groups to address and so on. Sometimes, it also specifies the major product lines and the market profile or corporate identity strived for.

Obviously, the Blueprint for the Future Company contains a Business Mission Statement. However, the Blueprint embraces other aspects and is longer. This is logical, since one of its key functions is to convey *motivation and enthusiasm*, not just crisp factual information about the mission ahead. Thus, the Blueprint depicts the future strived for as *highly desirable*. It will doubtless be more satisfying for employees to work in the better-focused, well-run and profitable (although perhaps downsized) future company.

By definition, the *turnaround plan* (or the rescue scheme) contains information on strategies chosen, and also on foreseen major changes in operating modes and structures. Thus, such a plan focuses more on *how* than on *what*. It contains rough calculations of the expected impact of proposed changes on costs, revenues and profits. However, these calculations seldom result in detailed balance sheets and P&L statements for the next 3–5 years, but rather reflect 'the big picture'.

What then about the classic (today often derided) 'business plan'? Such a document may be up to 25 pages long, since it contains all quantitative underpinnings, that is, cost and revenue calculations for the next three to five years, corresponding investments needed, calculation of the capital employed, and the expected return on said capital.

The belief in the usefulness of a formal business plan and corresponding detailed financial projections has diminished considerably during the last ten years. 'Detailed analysis can never replace hands-on action', as one CEO put it.

This is certainly true. However, in a turnaround situation, the bank, the board, the shareholders, or other stakeholders might insist on not simply being served a plausible-sounding Mission Statement or Blueprint for the Future Company and some broad strategy outline, but will require a more detailed document allowing them to analyse the expected impact on the company's P&L statements and balance sheets for the next few years. If so, the turnaround manager will simply have to comply, even if he personally does not find such a detailed document particularly useful when leading the turnaround efforts.

A business plan is often concluded with an *action assignment list*, pinpointing who (or at least which position holder) is responsible for implementing each anticipated change or other important activity, in order to meet specific sub-goals (the latter often called 'critical milestones'). We will discuss such implementation planning in more depth in a later section.

Case Study

ATLAS COPCO TOOLS' BUSINESS MISSION
as defined in their actual turnaround plan,
discussed in Chapter 11

1. Industrial tools

For industrial purposes (in production, maintenance and industrial service activities), the tools division shall market primarily in-house developed and in-house produced air-powered tools under the Atlas Copco brand name.

Further, the division is to market air motors to be used as components, primarily by OEMs. The products are comprised of standard motors, as well as larger series of customer-adapted motors within the power span 0.1 to 10 KW.

2. Industrial systems

To market and deliver fastening equipment and systems, primarily based on Atlas Copco components for electricity or air (as 'drive medium'), intended for large series producers. It shall be possible to adapt our systems for the feeding of fasteners in connection with the assembly process. Systems here means a combination of physical products and services, for example installation, after-sales service and client personnel training.

3. Air line accessories

To provide compressed air users, primarily our existing tool clients, with fittings and components for the distribution and treatment of compressed air all the way from the compressor centre to the place of use.

4. The division's future identity or 'profile', as perceived by customers

For all of the three above mentioned business lines, we are to create and maintain an *Atlas Copco identity* perceived by our clients, and primarily reflected in the following key parameters:

■ high quality products and systems (as to performance data, reliability, and ergonomics)
■ high delivery efficiency
■ superior technical service
■ first-class product information
■ price fully matching the customer benefits provided.

The goal is to be regarded by our own clients as *at least as good as our toughest competitors* in all of our markets classified as 'priority 1 markets'.

Author's note: As can be seen from above, the Business Mission Statement concerns itself with products, key customer classes, markets, services provided, and image in the eyes of key customers versus prices charged.

Whatever turnaround documents are used, and whatever their formal names, two issues remain at the top of the turnaround manager's agenda:

1. *Goals:* '**Where** are we supposed to go from here to achieve what and when?'

   The Business Mission Statement will already cover important goals such as geographic markets, products and product lines, production organization, key target groups, product and service delivery systems, pricing and positioning goals, and so on. Depending upon the turnaround situation and the character of the particular industry, other items might have to be included as well.

2. *Strategy:* '**How** do we get from here to there?'

   The term 'strategy' refers to the broad means and ways through which the agreed goals are supposed to be reached. Strategy documents (whatever their formal name in each turnaround situation) show the planned changes in resources and resource utilization to enable the company to fulfil its 'Business Mission' and to achieve the strived for future status shown in the Blueprint, and to do so within the prescribed time-frame.

It is therefore logical that a substantial part of this chapter will be devoted to *reality checks* of Blueprint contents, particularly as to goals, for example by so-called *benchmarking*.

As will be shown, such benchmarking can either relate:

- to cost levels and *productivity*, or
- to perceived *customer value* (that is, perceived utility of products and services on offer when related to their price).

A separate section will also be devoted to *implementation planning*, briefly touched on above.

5.4 Current status, key trends and benchmarked goals

Before establishing goals, a turnaround manager must first *objectively establish the starting point* for his efforts, that is, *the present status of the distressed company*. This examination includes pinpointing which product lines, markets and so on are loss-making 'bleeders' and why.

To arrive at well-founded conclusions, such a study might sometimes require a revision of the existing accounting system, or at least of the cost allocation principles for common overheads. This is vividly demonstrated by the Atlas Copco Mining and Construction case in Part II.

Second, apart from establishing the true present status, the turnaround manager can benefit substantially from examining *existing trends up to the present*. These might include how slowly or rapidly the company's financial situation has deteriorated and the underlying causes. (For instance, in the ESAB welding case study it is shown that competitors had not understood that the market for manual welding rods continued to decrease by eight to ten per cent per annum, while they continued increasing their production capacity.)

Third, the turnaround manager needs to know what can be regarded as *objectively achievable* by a well-run company operating in the same, or similar, industries.

When establishing or checking quantitative goals for a troubled company, a common procedure is to establish 'the upper quartile' value for all companies in the same or similar industries. (By definition, a company representing an industry's upper quartile is *better* than 75 per cent of its competitors, and *worse* than 25 per cent.) Many numerical examples of 'upper quartiles' were provided in Chapter 4.)

Fourth, the turnaround manager might like to establish some intermediary *critical milestones* reflecting what should be achieved by the troubled company, 6, 12, 18 and 24 months down the line. Such critical milestones – financial or otherwise – must take into account:

- ongoing trends in market demand (for example growth or stagnation, and qualitative changes)
- the company's situation at the very beginning of the turnaround exercise
- the strength of its competition
- the likely mobility or inertia in potential customers' purchasing patterns, including their apparent loyalty to their present suppliers, and typical switch-over costs for them
- the capacity of the troubled company to generate change in the market, specified as to size and speed, while forecasting likely competitive countermoves.

External benchmarks can be most helpful since they show what other companies have been able to achieve. However, any knowledge of this nature must be modified by both a correct evaluation of existing market inertia, that is, the market's resistance to change, and the resistance against rapid change residing *within the troubled company itself.*

Fifth, objective benchmarks can be highly useful if the turnaround manager experiences outside pressure to produce a written, turnaround plan, and to have this document formally *approved* before actually being able to attack all the urgent problems at hand.

If the turnaround manager is a well-established turnaround expert with an impressive track record, he is often given the benefit of the doubt and also a considerable amount of freedom to do immediately what he believes is called for, while regularly informing the board through 'progress reports'. In other cases, the board (or other decision-making entity) might insist on seeing and approving the Blueprint for the Future Company as well as proposed key strategies and – not least – the corresponding investment needs and divestment proposals.

What kind of data then are needed for each of the five items discussed above, and from what sources can they be culled? The turn-around manager has at his disposal many different sources and techniques, outlined in detail in Chapters 7 and 8. Here we will comment only upon the first three of the items listed above:

1. To highlight the *present status* of the troubled company, the turn-around manager will need reliable and up-to-date information as to market position, image and reputation among clients, the strength of competition, existing industrial overcapacity, relative efficiency as compared to competition. He might also like other kinds of cross-sectional analysis, including financial ratios for the troubled company, compared to its key competitors. (The term 'cross-sectional' here simply means that the focus is on *now*, not on *trends* over time.)

2. In contrast, to establish *historic trends* (that is, the second item listed above), time-series analyses (also called 'longitudinal analyses') are necessary to understand how fast the company ended up in its present predicament, and why. Relevant trend analyses will to a large part reflect external conditions such as changes in the demand situation, the market structure and the distribution structure, competition, labour costs in different countries, and/or currency exchange rates. Simultaneously, it is valuable to find out to what extent key competitors have also been hurt by (or perhaps profited from) changes in the competitive and market environment over the last few years. However, disastrous financial results might also reflect the negative profit impact of less successful in-house ambitions. A good example will later be shown in the Atlas Copco Mining case in Part II.

A split on earnings and profits generated by the company's perceived *core business* versus earning and profits (or often losses) from more peripheral activities or new ventures is always of interest in a turnaround situation. This helps decide what is worth saving or even expanding, as well as what to scale back, divest or run in quite another fashion.

3. Also to establish achievable objectives (the third item in the previous five-item list), 'benchmarking against competition' is a key tool. The performance displayed by well-run companies in the same or similar industries helps to specify goals which are not only ambitious but also *realistic*.

5.5   Four more aspects of the Blueprint, needing a reality check

A turnaround manager should certainly not be afraid of 'shooting for the moon, hoping to reach the tree tops'. On the other hand, he must be certain that he can at least reach the tree tops in time, and within existing resource constraints. This is often a survival issue and always a credibility issue. The latter aspect is particularly important if, during the previous two or three years, the troubled company (or division) has repeatedly presented unrealistic goals, plans and budgets which were never met.

A turnaround manager must therefore be able early on to *evaluate critically the realism* of his intended Blueprint for the Future Company, before committing himself and the company to it.

Let us start with two aspects of the Blueprint, concerning internal and external inertia:

1. Does the company already have a *competent management team* in place, able to carry out all anticipated changes? If not, how long will it take to develop the existing team members or get an entirely new team on board? How do management quality concerns influence the time axle for the turnaround plan? (To implement the turnaround plan, the troubled company probably needs more than just the newly arrived turnaround manager. A reasonably complete and professional management team might be a prerequisite to guarantee the quality and the speed of the turnaround.)

2. As shown by several of the six in-depth case studies in Part II, considerable *inertia* might exist, not only within the troubled company, but also in the marketplace served. Even if all desirable management actions are implemented exactly as planned, the market's *response* to these actions may not be as rapid or as strong as expected. (There are many reasons for such 'market inertia'. For instance, it is quite common that existing customers consciously delay their purchasing decisions until they are convinced that the troubled company will indeed survive. For new prospects (presently served by competitors), any contemplated switch to a new supplier in severe distress is not only associated with the same kinds of failure risk, but also with all normal switch-over costs associated with switching to a new supplier. These two factors combined might help explain an unwelcome delay in the expected market impact of the actions undertaken.)

Furthermore, a turnaround manager often finds himself wrestling with two other crucial questions in need of a reality check.

3. Is the sheer volume of proposed actions (many supposed to be taken almost simultaneously) just too great to be handled by the presently available – or easily acquirable – management resources? (Even an outstanding management team has some limitations, as does the rest of the organization, supposed to 'process' all the changes.)

4. Is the projected end-result in itself *realistic*, for example against the background of the actual performance displayed by companies in the same industry?

If in doubt on items 2, 3, or 4, what can a turnaround manager do? Many prefer to discreetly perform a 'sensitivity analysis', that is, a simulation covering a 'best case' scenario and a 'worst case' scenario. (For instance, what happens if actions and associated costs are on schedule, but the expected impact six months late?)

Such sensitivity analyses help pinpoint which actions are absolutely necessary (that is, critical) for the overall success of the turnaround effort, and which actions are in themselves desirable, but not really on the critical path, that is, they do not affect the overall success of the turnaround mission.

When in doubt as to whether contemplated quantitative goals are indeed realistic, *benchmarking against other companies in the same or similar industries* is a tool well worth considering. Later on in this chapter, corresponding techniques and philosophies will be discussed, and representative findings illustrated. *Financial benchmarking* has already been illustrated in Chapter 4, section 4.10. An example of *'value benchmarking* against the y-axis' can be found in the Atlas Copco Tools case study in Part II.

Case

THE TURNAROUND OF BOEING: GETTING THEIR RESCUE PLAN RIGHT – AND IN A HURRY

Boeing only produced $308mn in net profits, that is, less than 1.2 per cent, on their first-half 1998 revenues of $26.3bn. In August the same year, Boeing was split into three units – commercial, defence, and space. New executives were put in charge of each unit. Two of the three were recruited from the outside. A representative of Credit Suisse First Boston Corp. said that Boeing's board was likely to give the chief executive, Philip M. Condit, *only a nine-month period of grace* .

Under enormous pressure, both to deliver airplanes on schedule and to meet the expectations of the board, an *action plan*, or at least a list of priorities was rapidly emerging. The first priority was to remove bottlenecks and get more products out the door in time. The second was to get productivity back to the levels where Boeing was before. The third priority was to redesign the production process to reduce expenditure. To achieve this, the following action list was agreed on:

- massive downsizing of manpower (meaning tens of thousands of jobs)
- modernizing the computer system steering the production process
- reshaping Boeing's relationship with its huge and unwieldy supply chain.

A constantly heard theme throughout the organization was 'pay attention to the bottom line'. Mr Condit's often repeated mantra 'objective data will set us free' simply meant that good decisions require good data, rather than blind adherence to old traditions of outmoded policies. (Main source: *Business Week*)

5.6 Productivity benchmarking and value benchmarking[2]

5.6.1 The relation between productivity and value

Much of the literature on successful, transnational companies creates the impression that low unit costs (mainly achieved through long production runs) are enough to guarantee company survival and prosperity. This is only partly true, as illustrated below.

The truly 'performance-driven company' must simultaneously and continuously excel on *two*, very different, key criteria:

■ high *productivity*, that is, low unit costs, particularly in production and logistics
■ high *customer perceived value* compared to what competition is perceived as offering. (The term 'value' is understood here as utility for the client in relation to the price to be paid by him.)

The concept of the 'truly performance-driven company' is illustrated in Figure 5.2 and its four fields or 'quartiles'.

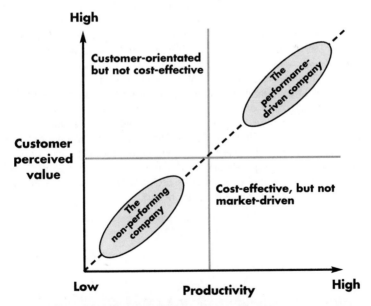

Figure 5.2   The truly performance-driven company
(from *The Performance-driven Eurocompany*, Arpi International SA, 1994 and 1996)

A company which is performing well on the X-axis has, by definition, high productivity. However, although its products are produced at a low unit cost, they are not necessarily highly appreciated in the market place. If so, the company produces low 'customer perceived value'. In other cases, a company's products might be highly appreciated in the market place, but be produced at such a high cost that the products can only be sold at a loss. If so, the company is customer-orientated, but not cost-effective, as indicated by the upper left-hand quadrant of Figure 5.2.

Thus, it is not enough to be *market-driven*, if the company is not *cost-effective*. Nor does internal cost-effectiveness help much if corporate development is not focused on *satisfying market needs* while providing high perceived value to the customer.

Case Study

When the SAAB 9000 car was introduced at the end of the 1980s, it was generally applauded as a highly attractive product. However, the 'industrialization' of the product (that is, streamlining it to better fit a rational production process) was inadequate. The resulting assembly time of over 70 hours per car could, at the beginning of the 1990s, be compared to 50 hours for General Motors and 35 hours for the Japanese. As a result of such a productivity disadvantage, the product could only be sold in reasonable numbers at a loss of about $2,000 per car. This is a good example of an ambitious company having managed to create high customer perceived utility and attractiveness, while simultaneously failing to meet reasonable productivity standards. As a result, SAAB Automobile is today (autumn 1999) 50 per cent owned by General Motors. The introduction of new products, for example the SAAB 9–5, better industrialization and access to cheaper parts via GM's cost-effective purchasing network (and the sharing of components with certain Opel platforms), has improved SAAB's profitability, although the future of SAAB Automobile is still something of a question-mark.

Three pieces of sound advice
(not only for turnaround candidates!)

If you have not already started, first embark on a journey of continuous improvement in cost-effectiveness. Second, be truly customer value-driven, since successful companies evaluate themselves in terms of how their customers see them, and are continually checking, adapting and improving. Third, develop powerful techniques to relate your customers' perceived value structure to your own incremental costs for delivering the products, features and services that your customers desire.

5.6.2 Productivity benchmarking

When multinational companies – distressed or not – decide to 'benchmark', that is, to compare themselves with other performance-driven companies (often called 'best practice' or 'best-in-class' companies), the purpose is usually threefold:

1. to establish the size of the *improvement potential* available
2. to establish *how* the best practice company has achieved its observed 'leading edge'
3. to establish *market-related 'value targets' as well as internal 'productivity targets'* and corresponding improvement programmes.

In Figure 5.3 some aspects of typical productivity improvement programmes are indicated below the X-axis. Either the main emphasis is to improve the quantity and quality of the company's *output*, or to maintain the same output with less *input*, that is, using less resources. As will be shown by several case studies, the latter goal can be achieved by 'flatter' organizations, fewer indirect staff, more automation, simpler procedures, closing of factories, higher loading of remaining factories, and so on. In the ESAB case, no less than 30 factories in different countries were actually closed!

Closely linked to *productivity enhancement programmes* are a number of popular productivity improvement tools, such as *time compression, BPR* (business process re-engineering), and *TQM*.

The detailed case studies presented in Part II are all accompanied by performance diagrams. These illustrate the objectively documented, very substantial productivity improvements actually achieved during the turnaround period in question. Productivity improvements have often been more crucial than growth.

For *value benchmarking* (that is, along the Y-axis) a similarly rich variety of tools has been developed over the past few years.[3] Many are related to what has traditionally been called market research, customer opinion research, competitive studies, brand image comparisons and so on. The competitive radar diagram technique illustrated in Figure 5.6 can pinpoint the relative importance of up to 30 evaluation parameters and simultaneously the company's relative performance on each of these dimensions when compared to competition.

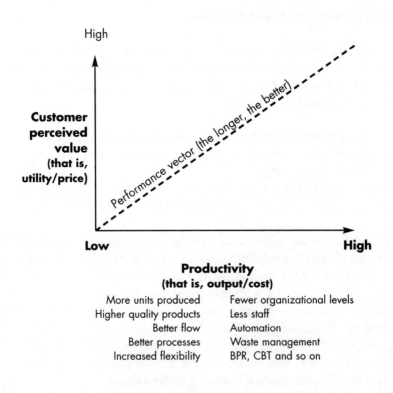

Figure 5.3   The performance-driven company's 'performance vector'
(from *Transnational Benchmarking Practice*, Arpi International SA, Brussels)

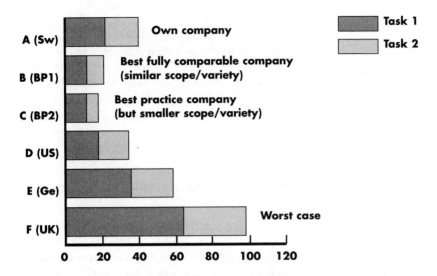

**Figure 5.4   Productivity benchmarks: cost per unit
6 companies in 4 countries**

(from *Transnational Benchmarking Practice*, Arpi International SA, Brussels)

Case Study

PORSCHE BROUGHT BACK FROM BANKRUPTCY: STRATEGY AND SOME PERFORMANCE BENCHMARKS

In 1986, Porsche's sales peaked at over 55,000 cars. In 1992, sales had plunged to only 14,362 cars, a fall of 75 per cent, resulting in losses of US$133 million.

Most experts believed it was now too late to save the company. However, a new CEO, Wendelin Wiedeking, was called in. He had a few cards up his sleeve.

He slashed the workforce by 17 per cent, and quickly hired two Japanese efficiency experts. To get the message across that inventory had to be cut dramatically, he personally chopped off the top half of a row of shelves. (This is an excellent example of what has been called 'gestures with high symbolic value' in this book.)

In 1996, an unusually inexpensive (US$40,000) Porsche 'Boxster Ragtop' was introduced. Earnings doubled to about $55 million on sales of $2 billion, while waiting time for a new Boxster was still about 12 months, one year after launching the model. In September, an all-new Porsche 911 'Carrera' was rolled out. This was seen by many as the culmination of an impressive turnaround. During the fiscal year ending on July 31, 1997, unit sales had increased by 77 per cent to 34,000 cars, more than twice the 1992 figure.

The following performance key ratios highlight 'the mechanics' behind this turn-around. The new 911 was produced in 60 hours, instead of in the 120 hours its predecessor took. Two layers of management were cut out of the organization. The 'time-to-market' was cut from seven to only three years. The number of parts suppliers has been cut from almost 1,000 to only 300, and the number of defective parts was reduced by 90 per cent. Towards the end of 1997, when the turnaround was basically concluded, sales and marketing were expected to be the next objectives for another major overhaul.

Main source: Business Week

5.6.3 Examples of profitability benchmarks for selected industries

Speed is often the key word. Boards, banks, shareholders, and most employees expect and hope that drastic actions will soon be taken to save the company. In such a climate, it is often undesirable to wait for a full-fledged benchmarking study. The turnaround expert might instead choose to rely on what is sometimes called 'fast and dirty' benchmarking. This approach has at least three endearing features:

1. Benchmarks – as well as the turnaround plan based on them – can be presented within a few weeks to bankers, board members, shareholders, employees, media and so on. ('Things are finally happening!')

2. The correspondingly more limited set of data (and the simpler underlying logic) are more quickly grasped by the stakeholders concerned. More full-fledged and usually more complex benchmarking studies do not only require more time. They also tend to be a bit confusing, particularly to outsiders who do not necessarily know the product lines, customer classes and so on, as well as a correct reading of a comprehensive benchmarking study might require. Such studies therefore require more explanations and invite reservations and discussions of underlying assumptions and so on.

3. Necessary actions can be initiated (and the results seen) several weeks earlier. If the troubled company is in a loss-making situation (and/or risks running out of cash), *speed* in implementing corrective actions is much more important than the precision of the underlying data. (Stopping massive losses three weeks earlier does not *sound* very impressive. However, a difference of three

weeks in stopping the bleeding can often save more than the turn-around expert's annual fee!)

Many well-known turnaround experts have chosen to create and maintain their own databases which contain pertinent key ratios for selected industries.

One good example is Professor Ulf af Trolle – to whom this book is dedicated. On a dozen occasions, he saved troubled Scandinavian companies of substantial size. He was simply known throughout Scandinavia as 'the Company Doctor', a title he appreciated.

The existence of such a database makes it possible early on not only to *predict* likely turnaround candidates, but also to *move in* on the company's premises more rapidly to address the situation when the corresponding assignment is received.

A turnaround expert who has not kept a personal database, and who doubts the reliability of available in-house data, might initially have to rely on statistics published by governmental offices, industry associations, or commercially available on-line databases. (These are discussed in considerable depth in Chapter 7.)

Balance sheets for the previous few years of the troubled company and its major competitors are useful. So are industry-specific and company-specific articles written by financial analysts. (Chapter 7 provides many examples.)

In each developed country there is a Central Statistical Office providing benchmarking data for all companies belonging to a particular industry. Such company information is usually sorted with regard to company size, region, or other key variables. Additional computer runs to fit more exactly the turnaround manager's specific needs can often be ordered on a commercial basis and be available only a few days later.

An example of *financial key data* for one particular company, compared to corresponding averages, upper quartiles and so on for the same industry, has already been presented in Chapter 4, section 4.10.

On the next few pages we present industry-wide *profitability* benchmarks for agglomerates of UK companies engaged in 'mature and undifferentiated consumer durable goods', as compared to companies engaged in other kinds of capital goods. This tailor-made material was

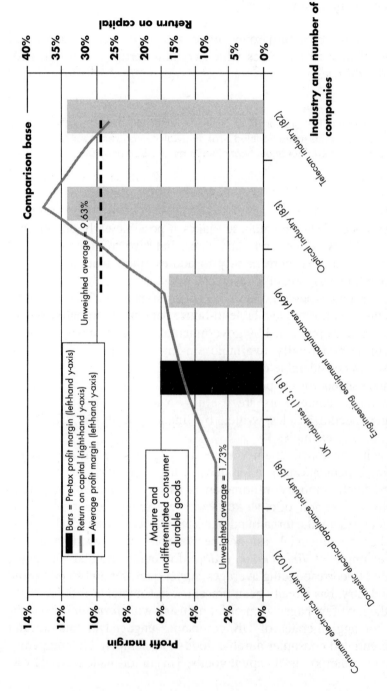

Figure 5.5 Profit margin (%) and return on capital for selected UK industries
(Arpi International SA, Brussels, based on ICC UK raw data)

purchased from a UK data provider, but is based on official UK statistics (see Figure 5.5).

NOTE ON RAW DATA USED FOR FIGURE 5.5

Raw data used in Figure 5.5 for the UK are taken from *UK Industrial Performance Analysis*, published by ICC Business Publications, 1997/98 edition. This publication contains a breakdown of the 13,1811 UK companies which have the highest yearly sales values.

1. The *consumer electronics industry* is a subdivision of the broader sector 'Electronics Industry'. Other industries in the latter sector are: computer equipment distributors, computer equipment manufacturers, computer services, computer software houses, electronic component manufacturers, electronic component distributors, printed circuit manufacturers, scientific and electronic instruments manufacturers and telecommunications industry.

2. The *domestic electrical appliance industry* is a subdivision of the sector 'Electrical Industry'. Other industries in the latter sector are: electrical contractors, electrical Installation equipment manufacturers, electrical wholesalers and lighting equipment industry.

3. *UK Industries Ltd* simply represents a compilation of all the 13,181 companies submitted for analysis.

4. *Engineering equipment manufacturers* is a sector comprising: agricultural equipment industry, defence industry, heating and ventilating equipment, hydraulic and pneumatic equipment and machine tool manufacturers'. (It is close but not completely identical with what is called Verkstsandindustri in Sweden.)

5. *Optical industry* is included in the consumer goods industry, the latter also consists of antiques and fine art, giftware industry, horticulture and garden centres, jewellery trade, photographic industry, record industry, sports equipment industry and toy industry.

6. *Telecommunications industry* is a subdivision of electronics industry, described in item 1, and contains producers of, for example, portable phones and associated strongly differentiated services.

5.6.4 Value benchmarking: two real-life examples

On the next pages is an example of benchmarks arrived at through cross-border industrial market research, in this case undertaken by Arpi International through face-to-face interviews.

Studies of the same type have been undertaken for other multinationals, including the Tarkett-Sommer group (that is, one of the six companies making up the case study section in Part II) and Volvo Penta, in up to six countries each.

One more example of global 'value benchmarking' against competition is provided by the bar chart in the Atlas Copco MCT case study, section 12.2.5. (MCT stands for Mining and Construction Techniques, obviously a highly international and highly competitive field.)

Case Study

THE TARKETT GROUP PINPOINTS ITS COMPETITIVE EDGE USING RADAR DIAGRAMS[4]

The Tarkett-Sommer group is the largest flooring company in Europe and the second largest worldwide.

With its cost-cutting phase completed, group management focused its sights on defining and building a strong competitive advantage, based on internal organisational efficiency coupled with high external market efficiency. Lars Wisén, president of the Tarkett group 1990–98, explains: 'By using our customers' own perceptions and value systems as a benchmark, instead of our own subjective ideas, we have been able to systematically create better customer value'.

Brussels-based consultants, Arpi International, were asked to lend their expertise to this effort. Using a technique developed for market and competition analysis studies for Volvo Penta in six countries, consultants from Arpi International conducted face-to-face management interviews with flooring wholesalers and dealers in three of Tarkett's important markets. These findings were summarized in a series of highly precise 'radar diagrams'.

Radar diagram

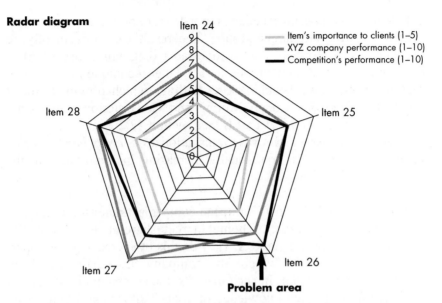

Measuring impact: Radar diagrams helped Tarkett track their competitive performance on no less than 30 competitive evaluation criteria; based on input from Tarkett's wholesale and retail clients in three countries. The information was gathered during face-to-face interviews by Arpi International multilingual consultants. Similar studies have been done for Volvo Penta and other companies.

Figure 5.6   Tarkett-Sommer benchmarking against its competitors through industrial field research

5.7 Cross-border 'value' benchmarking to aid the choice of strategy

In consumer markets particularly, it is often not the *objective* tangible characteristics of the product or service that matter, but the consumer's *subjective* perception of what he gets in relation to what he has to pay. Only the company's present, previous and potential customers can provide such evaluations.

Traditional market research, consumer behaviour research or customer satisfaction studies are increasingly being replaced by *comparative benchmarking studies of perceived customer value*.

Already the term 'benchmarking' indicates that such comparisons must be *objective and quantitative*. Comparisons are made against other organizations, not least against one or more high-performing competitors having an excellent reputation among customers representing the relevant target group.[5] The result can conveniently be presented in the form of competitive radar diagrams (Figure 5.6) or through more traditional bar charts. The latter technique is used when presenting the value benchmarking findings which provided crucial inputs for the Atlas Copco Mining and Construction turnaround, presented in Chapter 12 of Part II (see section 12.2.5).

There are many reasons why transnational or *'cross-border' value benchmarking* is now dramatically increasing in importance in the new frontier-free Europe.

1. To survive and prosper, European companies increasingly have to *compensate the loss* of home market share in earlier heavily protected domestic markets. They do this by increasing their operations in countries where the company has earlier not been strongly represented. In such markets, the company obviously has much more limited knowledge of client attitudes and purchasing motives. Performance-driven Eurocompanies therefore feel that they rapidly need to increase their limited share of non-domestic markets to gain sufficient European-wide critical mass. Their success to a large extent depends on properly understanding markets previously insufficiently known to them, including the understanding of how customers in many different countries (with differing traditions, tastes and preferences) evaluate competing product and service offerings.

2. The typical Eurocompany today faces not only new geographic markets and new target groups, but also new competitors, shorter product life-cycles and more rapidly changing customer preferences. This further increases the need to continuously make sure that the company's products, as well as its customer service and other offerings are fully competitive, *value-wise* as well as *cost-wise*. Knowledge about the company's relative standing versus competition (as reflected in competitive radar diagrams) also provides a good basis for *market-adapted pricing*. (Today, market-adapted pricing means something quite different from yesterday's passive adaptation of prices to competitive products. Thus, value benchmarking provides important inputs to optimal pricing and marketing activities as well as to the company's product development process.)

The previous text[6] is largely applicable to other kinds of cross-border activity, fuelled by the ongoing *globalization* of many industries.

HOW CAN AN INTERNATIONALLY OPERATING COMPANY BENEFIT FROM VALUE BENCHMARKING IN MORE CONCRETE TERMS?

1. It can correctly and in great detail evaluate its own *competitive position* as perceived by selected key target groups in different national markets.

2. Value benchmarking can substantially aid the subsequent improvement process not only by defining the type and size of improvements needed, but also *who to learn from* (that is, 'the value leader'), including the philosophy and techniques used by the best performers on the value dimension.

3. The performance-driven company can use such information to adjust its products, service levels, pricing structures, ways to deal with client complaints and so on, in order to *systematically sharpen its competitive edge* wherever it really counts, that is, for 'critical success factors'.

4. Through more advanced analytical techniques – such as conjoint analysis and other so called multi-variate statistical techniques – an internationally operating company today can even evaluate the likely attractiveness of potential product feature combinations and other *'value packages' not yet seen in the marketplace*. Thus, value benchmarking aids the product positioning of, as yet, non-existent products.

5.8 'Distinctiveness', seen as an alternative to ruthless cost-cutting or lower unit costs through acquisition of more critical mass

Recent literature on globalization and structural changes within the European Union has perhaps tended to exaggerate the crucial importance of economies of scale through more critical mass. An alternative corporate strategy can sometimes be to develop, and maintain, a positive differentiation or other kind of *distinctiveness*, which is perceived as putting the company and its products favourably apart from most of its competitors.

These two strategies (getting unit cost down, as compared to creating more customer perceived value) call for highly different skills and different management emphasis. The former strategy calls for *ruthless and continuous cost cutting*, not least in production and distribution, but often also in administrative overheads, sales and marketing. In contrast, the value enhancement strategy places the key emphasis on *market-driven value creation*, that is, the company's products and services must be perceived as sufficiently different to justify a premium price. (The premium price aspect is here of fundamental importance, since 'positive differentiation' and 'incremental value creation' are normally associated with the adoption of incremental cost.)

However, the *distinctiveness must also be sustainable (and actually sustained) over time*. To achieve this requires *market-driven, continuous product development, firmly backed by value benchmarking*, including customer satisfaction and customer retention studies.

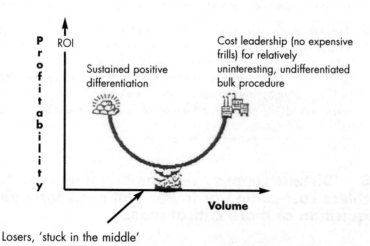

Figure 5.7 **The U-Curve illustrating alternative strategies**
(Arpi International management seminar material)

The moment such a market-driven company gets complacent (that is, 'fat and lazy') and loses touch with its key target groups, the whole distinctiveness strategy on which the company relies tends to fail. The company then becomes just another 'me-too' company (with an unreasonably high cost level), and it is rapidly subjected to the same kind of ruthless price competition as any non-differentiated company. The difference between the cost-cutting and the value creation strategy in a turnaround situation might be illustrated by the following U-Curve (see Figure 5.7), loosely based on the more rigid presentation by Professor Michael Porter.

5.9 More on 'cost leadership' versus 'superior value' companies

The contents of the Blueprint for the Future Company and the corresponding optimal choice of strategy partly depends on industry characteristics, including the industry's competitive realities. It also depends on the troubled company's own size, resources and capability profile, as discussed in the following.

Just as one can make a distinction between *productivity benchmarking* and *value benchmarking*, it might be useful to make a distinction between two broad categories of companies based on what kind of products or services they produce.

1. The first group contains companies producing *mature, relatively undifferentiated* (and often difficult-to-differentiate) *products*, that is, products which tend to be perceived by their customers as broadly interchangeable with those offered by the competition. Such companies tend to choose a strategy which emphasizes critical mass, providing long production runs and cost-effectiveness in all company functions leading to low unit costs.

2. The second group contains companies primarily striving to create higher 'customer perceived value' through more 'distinctiveness'. Such companies do *not* primarily try to achieve a sustainable competitive advantage through superior size and/or ruthless cost-cutting, but rather through 'positive differentiation' closely linked to product characteristics, services provided, and the company's overall marketing approach (including many 'soft variables' such as superb image, strong brand name and so on). In a nutshell, these companies are *value-driven*, rather than cost-driven.

The more a company is able to distinguish itself positively from its competitors, the more it can avoid outright price competition. Unfortunately, in real life, few producers of mature industrial products can create and sustain a substantial competitive advantage in the form of 'customer-perceived added value'.

For producers of mature industrial products, for example Siemens and ABB, high cost-effectiveness – in production, distribution and service – is a must.

Low unit costs for mature, undifferentiated products has traditionally been created primarily by gaining sufficient size (and eliminating part of the competition in the process) by merging with major competitors and absorbing smaller competitors.

Needed: More cross-border European mergers

In 1994, Japan had four producers of heavy locomotives, the US two, and Europe a dozen, many state-subsidized. It is pretty obvious that a restructuring of the 'borderless' European market for locomotives, trains and trams was called for. Today, only a handful of European survivors are left.

The increased critical mass created helps to lower the company's unit costs. However, the increased size can sometimes also improve the 'value side', by improved presence and image in the marketplace. The creation of a large company with a *global reach, impressive combined research and delivery capabilities* and so on, tends to increase its credibility and attractiveness. This is true whether we talk about automobile component manufacturers, pharmaceutical companies, or financial services, where merger-mania is widespread in 1999.

If a performance-driven company succeeds in applying the success formula explained earlier, that is, adhering to the principle 'never to add cost if customer-perceived incremental value does not increase as a result', and 'always cut costs if resulting price decreases are more important to end-users than associated decreases in perceived customer value', it will also enjoy certain beneficial consequences from a strategy choice viewpoint.

■ Old strategies which have become ineffective (at least in selected key target groups) will tend automatically to be abolished or substantially adjusted. (Several of the turnaround cases in the second part of this book represent dramatic changes in strategy, sometimes based on worldwide 'value benchmarking'.)

■ Contemplated unprofitable new activities, including new products and services which are not possible to implement in a 'value-to-cost-efficient' fashion, will tend to be *abandoned at an early stage*, before they have resulted in any expensive misadventures. (Two such typical misadventures are described in the Atlas Copco Mining case in Part II.)

5.10　How to avoid being a 'me-too', 'stuck-in-the-middle' company

European companies likely to get killed well before the year 2000 include companies which are neither big nor efficient enough to have an obvious unit cost advantage (as cost leaders), nor able to create sufficient positive differentiation (distinctiveness) to get a substantial premium price for their products. We refer here to such unlucky companies as 'stuck-in-the-middle' and they are obvious turnaround or up-for-sale candidates.[7]

Whether you prefer to look at the U-curve in Figure 5.7 or at the performance diagram presented in Figure 5.6 is irrelevant. A good manager is likely to arrive at the same conclusion and define the same success formula for his company.

A truly performance-driven company never adds cost to its products if research does not show that the (customer perceived) incremental added value is greater than the additional costs incurred for the value creation. The correlate is equally true: always cut costs when the cost advantage will exceed the perceived decrease in perceived customer value.

In a turnaround situation, one of the first tasks is to evaluate the company's productivity, that is, *cost efficiency*. Thereafter, it is time to evaluate the company's performance along the 'value axis', that is, if the company is value-driven, by excelling for those variables which are important to its clients. (In one of the two Atlas Copco cases later described, the management team was certain that their products were perceived as much too *expensive*. In reality, market research – including benchmarking against competition – proved that buyers worried more about not receiving sufficiently rapid *after-sales service*. They wanted more 'value', not lower prices.)

Case Study

HOW AUTOMOTIVE BUSINESS MISSIONS HAVE CHANGED OVER TIME

During the 1960s (when Bo Arpi was heading the Volvo Group's Central Marketing staff), Professor Howard Perlmutter of the Wharton School of Business and Finance energetically sold the concept of GISCs (Global Industrial Systems Constellations). He did this so successfully that most European car makers thought they had no chance of survival if they did not rapidly produce at least one million cars per annum. This forced many smaller 'speciality producers' like Mercedes, BMW and Volvo (all operating in the so-called 'executive car segment') to ponder their own future.

Surprisingly, it was the European giants (such as Fiat) that started having profitability problems, while the more specialized executive car producers were generally doing fine.

However, towards the end of the 1990s, German car producers such as Daimler, BMW and Volkswagen all 'went shopping' in order to buy foreign car manufacturers and name plates. In this way, they tried to achieve *geographic balance, a complete product spectrum* and *economies of scale*.

On 17 November 1998, the recently merged *Daimler/Chrysler* was quoted on the New York stock exchange, and workers in Auburnhill, Michigan, were served German Apfelstrudel to celebrate the event. Their German colleagues were enjoying 'corn on the cob' (often associated with animal food in Germany), celebrating this highly ambitious cross-border, cross-cultural endeavour. Admittedly, the merged vehicle producing company was only number 3 in the world (after General Motors and Ford) but their stock value was 50 per cent higher than that of General Motors and 25 per cent higher than that of Ford Motor Company.

A few years earlier, *BMW* had purchased (most of) British Leyland, and the right to the Rolls-Royce brand name. As a result, BMW was suddenly also covering most automotive market segments via a more dispersed production and distribution network.

Also the *Volkswagen Group* (under Ferdinand Piëch, whose grandfather was the famous Ferdinand Porsche) took over the full product range – from a new version of the old Beetle to the A8 Audi luxury limousine. They also acquired the right to use the Lamborghini, Bugatti and Bentley brand names.

In contrast, the *Volvo Group* had chosen to stay with a more narrowly defined Business Mission. They tried to remain a 'niche producer' who did not serve all market segments and definitely stayed away from the most price-competitive small-car segment. Although Volvo in 1997 was only number 13 in the world with regard to car sales volume, their profit (after tax) when related to sales was 5.4 per cent. The Volvo Group's combined return on capital during 1992–97 was an impressive 13 per cent. Few competitors could match such figures. In 1997, Volvo actually made almost twice the profits of Volkswagen, although the latter company's turnover was approximately three times that of Volvo. Expresssed in absolute value, Volvo made more profit than either *Renault* or *BMW*, and almost matched the profit shown by the much bigger *Fiat Group*.

Tuve Johannesson, president of Volvo Cars, said 'Thanks to our very different Business Mission concept, we are today less dependent upon the business cycle than most of our full-range competitors. Our annual profitability is actually more dependent upon where we are in our own product renewal cycle and how many attractive models we can build from only two platforms (down from previously three).'

But being small and profitable also makes a company an obvious prey. During 1998, Volkswagen approached Volvo, but was discouraged. As world demand for automotive vehicles weakened further it lowered the value of automotive shares, and also made it cheaper to acquire Volvo. Towards the end of 1998 it was announced that Volvo Cars was going to be acquired by Ford.

Ford's recently retired chairman, Alex Grotman, forecast that only two European automotive producers would survive in the longer-term. Even though the production technology has changed, making it possible now to produce cars in shorter series than before, very important cost advantages are still linked to the producer's size, for instance in purchasing and R&D activities.

The future core business of the Volvo Group will now be heavy vehicles (not least heavy trucks) where Volvo already enjoys a respectable image and world market share, and where they can easily reinforce their position, for example through acquisitions. However, Volvo's recent acquisition of more than 10 per cent of the shares in Scania was not exactly seen as a welcome gesture by the Wallenberg sphere.

5.11 Company size and strategic emphasis

Below are some viewpoints on how company size tends to influence the choice of turnaround strategy. For the sake of simplicity, companies are here classified as small, medium or large.

1. Small companies often find that what is a good strategy choice for a big player in the same industry is seldom the right choice for the small company. A small firm has to evaluate carefully whether it really has both the *creativity* and the *resources* necessary to first create and then sustain distinctiveness, or if it can perhaps acquire sufficient size fast enough (and thereby better cost effectiveness) to match bigger competitors. (Key strategic advice: 'Never attack a bigger and stronger player in his own home market while copying his own strategy! You are bound to lose.')

2. Contrary to what business literature often indicates, the middle-sized company's in-house access to capacity, technology, capital and skills are not necessarily of critical importance for success. A well-run, middle-sized company can surprisingly often gain access to the technology, capital, production capacity and so on which it lacks, through various forms of alliance.

    If capable of creating and maintaining 'distinctiveness', a middle-sized company usually has quite a good chance of survival and prosperity. However, it might first need to maintain and reinforce a strong position in its domestic market (or in selected key market segments) while later expanding organically into the same kind of market segments in other countries.

    Some middle-sized companies have succeeded by narrowly focusing on providing superior service to one or more limited market niches (but in several countries). This seems to be a particularly successful strategy if these niches have been badly served by 'fat and lazy' national giants having their main focus on other market segments.

3. For large companies, it is crucially important to pinpoint exactly where economies of scale are of key importance for growth and profitability. Is it in the creation of a continuous flow of *new products*, as for pharmaceuticals? Is it in *components sourcing*, as for consumer electronics? Is it driven by *superior branding and promotion*, as for packaged foods? Or is it in the number and location of *retail service points*, as for consumer banking?

Obviously, a turnaround manager cannot disregard the relationship between size and valid strategies open to the troubled company.

However, as shown by both the Allgon and ESAB cases, he might sometimes be able to change the rules of the game. In Allgon's case, this resulted in a quadrupling of the company's turnover. In ESAB's case, a highly daring and original strategy moved the company from the verge of bankruptcy to becoming No. 1 in Europe, and No. 2 in the world.

5.12 Implementation planning, including the allocation of responsibilities

Benchmarking to establish cost targets and perceived value targets is fine, but what about the *subsequent implementation?*

To achieve established goals and do so under considerable time pressure, all members of the full orchestra must play the same tune, but on different instruments, to produce the desired result. The allocation of action assignments is therefore an integral part of the turnaround process. The turnaround manager has to ask himself:

'What individual (or future post holder, department and so on) is responsible for which part of the overall turnaround programme to ensure that agreed strategies are followed, goals achieved, critical milestones respected, so that the Blueprint for the Future Company becomes a reality, and not just another dust-collecting document?'

Implementation planning basically consists of the breaking down of the total turnaround programme into discreet, logical action blocks or assignments. Each of these must have a clearly identified beginning and end as well as operationally defined (and therefore easily controllable) goals or sub-goals, called *critical milestones*. Producing a corresponding *action assignment list* is just one way to make sure that each player really understands his part and assumes full responsibility for it.

Obviously, in the final analysis, it is the *turnaround manager himself who must take full responsibility for the implementation of the turnaround plan*. His assignment allocation list initially only exists in his own head. However, as the turnaround proceeds and the management team is reinforced and activated, there is also likely to be a change in the turnaround manager's operating mode, including the degree of delegation used and the assignment lists or other documents used to facilitate increased delegation. (This gradual shift has been highlighted in Figure 3.2.)

Notes

1. To facilitate the discussion in the rest of this chapter, the term normally used is the Blueprint for the Future Company, or just the Blueprint. The reader who so prefers can instead think in terms of an all-embracing statement, covering quantitative goals, strategies, financial calculations, and an implementation plan showing the allocation of responsibilities.

2. The following text (section 5.6) is based on Arpi International's publication *The Performance-Driven Eurocompany*, Brussels 1996.

3. For an excellent discussion of productivity and value benchmarking, its tools, techniques, terminology and practical use for business decisions, the interested reader is referred to Bengt Karlof's book *Benchmarking: A Signpost to Excellence in Quality and Productivity*, John Wiley, paperback version 1994. The following year a 'Workbook' volume was published by the same author and editor.

4. This text is extracted from a 'One Step Up' brochure, and was approved by Lars Wisén of the Tarkett group. The complete text and associated performance graphs can be found on the website www.arpi.com – in English as well as in German.

5. Although not yet called 'Benchmarking', this was standard practice when Dr Arpi was in charge of the Volvo Group's first central marketing research department. This is documented in Bo Arpi, *Planning and Control through Marketing Research*, Hutchinson of London, 1970.

6. From the publication *The Performance-driven Eurocompany*, Arpi International SA, 1994 and 1996.

7. This is a direct quote from a speech given by Dr Arpi at the Sheraton Hotel in Stockholm during the first major Swedish seminar on company strategies, to maximize the benefit derived from 'EEC 1992'. This seminar was held in autumn 1988, attended by 270 top Swedish executives. As shown by later developments, this forecast held up pretty well.

6 Rebuilding the new management team and creating a new team spirit

6.1 Purpose of chapter

If the turnaround is to succeed, and preferably also result in a lasting success, serious attention must be paid to the creation of:

- a new – or at least strongly improved – *management team*
- a new *team spirit* and often also
- an entirely new *corporate culture*.

It is the responsibility of the turnaround manager to make sure that each manager, as well as the full management team, functions well. However, it is not enough that the top management group and its members perform as expected. New values, attitudes, thought patterns and behaviour must also penetrate to lower organizational levels. Together they constitute a new corporate culture, which is not created overnight. An overview of related issues is found in Figure 6.1.

The turnaround manager can speed up this process by communicating clearly with many employees, and perhaps also by announcing a small number of 'symbolic' decisions which are broadly communicated throughout the whole organization, noticed and understood, as a signal that a new era has indeed dawned.

A new top management team – or at least an interim one – can be in place fairly quickly. This chapter deals with issues related to the rebuilding of the team, including some tough issues such as:

- Who is worth keeping and who has to leave
- Why and how to fire executives

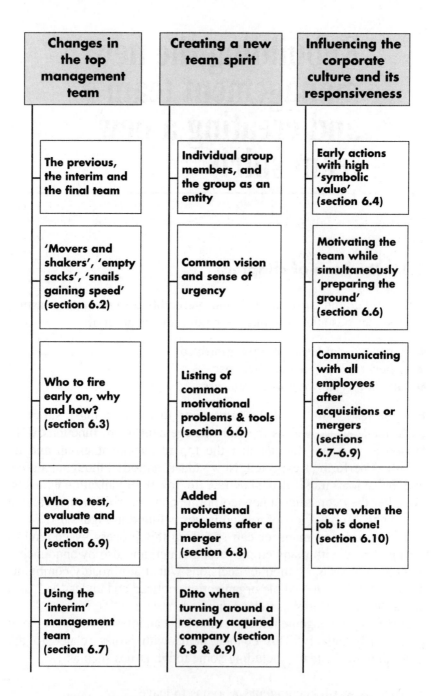

Figure 6.1   Overview of Chapter 6 contents

- Finding key replacements in time
- Making the new team function effectively
- How to build a new team spirit
- Actions of a 'symbolic nature', communicated throughout the organization, to influence corporate values and behaviour.

6.2   'Movers and shakers', 'empty sacks' and 'snails gaining speed'

Through his initial information gathering process (covered in Chapters 5 and 7), and by observing the way managers currently tend to solve their assignments, the turnaround manager can usually quickly conclude which individuals he can definitely build on, and which do not really belong on his management team.

One turnaround manager used to classify the executives found in the troubled company into three groups:

1. *Movers and shakers*. (These are people who really get a kick out of a challenge and start attacking problems whenever asked to do so.)

2. *Empty sacks*. (However much the turnaround manager talks, pulls, kicks, or screams, there is no movement, except of a purely defensive nature.)

3. *Snails gaining speed*. (These are often managers who were either mistreated and/or never given a fair chance under the previous management, but who now have started discreetly blooming, encouraged by finally seeing their initiatives appreciated.)

What percentage then of the old management team normally has to be replaced? The answer primarily depends upon two things:

1. How tough the turnaround situation is. (Is there enough time available to wait for the 'snails gaining speed', or must an experienced management team be put in place quickly in order not to jeopardize the turnaround?)

2. The general quality of managers and other key position holders already available in the organization and their willingness and capacity for change.

The authors have been involved in turnarounds where all members of the top management team have had to be relieved of their duties right away. We have also been engaged in turnarounds where most of the previous management team could be kept. However, in such cases, the management team usually had to be subjected to heavy doses of group work, including strategic planning sessions, sometimes even computer-assisted simulations showing the likely impact of contemplated strategic moves on both external markets an on internal cost structures. (Several examples of such 'activity-based costing' simulations in turnaround situations are found in Chapter 8.)

6.3 Who to fire early on, why and how

When a new, fully empowered turnaround manager arrives on company premises, employees *expect* – many even *hope* – that drastic things will finally happen. If little seems to happen, they tend to get disappointed.

Some types of firings or demotions should preferably be done rather rapidly. Individuals who should be fired on the spot and under substantial limelight and fanfare are:

■ Individuals found to have *committed fraud*. (Kickbacks from non-optimal vendors, or using company resources for private purposes and so on)

■ One or two key executives who carry the *'historic' responsibility* for bringing the company into this mess. (One, the previous CEO, has usually already been forced to leave the company before the turnaround manager arrives. If he is still around – even in a new role – be prepared for big trouble and split loyalties!)

■ *Obstructionists*, that is, managers who systematically try to undermine your authority, question your actions in public, create enemy camps, delay the implementation of decisions taken, and so on.

Turnaround management is no boy scout picnic. Often, it is more like warfare, perhaps on ten different fronts simultaneously. Under these circumstances, the turnaround manager (and the company itself) cannot afford to have cheats or counter-productive forces around.

In such cases, do *not* wait for the replacement to arrive. It might even be an advantage to live without one or two key managers for a while and study the quality and potential of their subordinates. Perhaps they are ready to take on larger missions?

Another managerial category contains those who do not try, as well as those who hesitantly but dutifully try but are so far from a satisfactory performance that one cannot afford to wait for them. Most of these managers should be replaced or at least removed from their present positions. They might have been grandchildren of the company's founding father, good golfers, excellent story tellers or charmers in general. Others might have survived simply by managing to avoid anybody's critical attention for many years.

For this category of well-meaning non-performers, there is hardly any point in creating striking examples. Smoother methods can be used.

The first measure is simply to tell the individual in question that *his performance has been found wanting and encourage him to find employment with another company*. 'Discreet reversed executive search' and the use of 'outplacement services' should be considered. Within the context of a multinational company, one might also be able to find a less demanding position with another organizational entity for honest, but under-performing managers.

Although the turnaround manager might have to operate like a 'dictator', he still has to observe all the *laws, rules, regulations and traditions in the countries concerned*. Otherwise, the company might get *sued, get bad publicity, or have to deal with a striking work force* – and this on top of all the other pressing company problems. (US managers, temporarily operating in a continental European environment – and used to more liberal US 'hire and fire' policies' – have belatedly learned this lesson the hard way. Authoritarian Finnish executives assigned the task of running recently purchased Swedish subsidiaries have in several cases run into serious trouble. So have Swedish managers, who seriously underestimated the power of the German *Mitbestimmung* rules, which are rather different from their toothless Swedish counterparts, called 'MBL'.)

Fortunately, boards, employees, and union leaders are normally not stupid. Properly informed and consulted, they can often show a considerable understanding for the removal of non-performing executives, particularly if more capable talents are waiting around the corner.

In stark contrast, European unions have tended to get very active (and sometimes very difficult to deal with) if and when *a massive downsizing of the overall payroll is suggested*, say a cutback by 15–30 per cent. Both the scope and purpose is then quite different. Massive downsizing is proposed to bring down costs. In contrast, when firing non-performing executives, the key purpose is *not* to save money, but to get a better and faster responding management team, capable of taking the company into much greener pastures – and making it stay there.

REWARD FRIENDS, REPLACE UNHELPFUL PRIMA DONNAS

In 'close to sudden death' cases, by definition associated with severe cash problems, the turnaround manager might have been forced to stand 'hat in hand' for months, often having to accept rather bad treatment from suppliers, key clients, credit providers, and so on. However, at the end of a successful turnaround period, his day has come. It might now be time to identify who were the company's friends, and who made the turnaround process exceptionally difficult.

Having organized and improved the debt structure, it might be worthwhile to re-evaluate the company's main bank connection in the light of what you have recently learned. You might also like to have a second look at your list of preferred suppliers. Perhaps it is now time to reward those who stood by when times were bad. After all, they took a substantial risk to help save your company.

6.4 Early actions with high 'symbolic value'

A number of other actions should be taken early on, partly out of necessity, partly to send important signals throughout the organization, but also to show what the turnaround manager really stands for.[1]

Among necessary early actions in a turnaround situation, the following are common:

- general *hiring freezes*

- delays, reductions or the complete *abolition of many investment plans*

- *centralizing control*, including the approval by the turnaround manager himself of all cheques and purchase orders – at least for the first four weeks. (It is surprising how much one can learn just from this simple administrative procedure!)

- *MBWA* (management by walking around), asking pertinent questions all the time – even seemingly simple and uninformed ones – while always insisting on quick answers (and certainly not expecting a thick report or a defensive memo some two weeks later).

Actions which are not always necessary, but have a substantial symbolic value might include the following:

- Selling off spectacular company cars (and company planes, if any), which were extensively used by the previous CEO, both for business and pleasure.

- Closing the executive dining room, forcing top executives to mingle with lower level managers. (The turnaround manager might himself choose to rotate between different in-house eating facilities, where he will also get an excellent idea about the existing mentality and opinions broadly held.)

- Insisting that top management starts seeing real customers and real end-users instead of hiding on the executive floor, removed from everyday reality.

- Insisting that executives get personally acquainted with the company's products and those of the competition. (Thus avoiding the common marketing myopia syndrome caused by being too well insulated.)

- Talking to people at least three levels down in the organizational pyramid, while disregarding the formal organization chart and normal reporting patterns.

GETTING AT&T'S TOP MANAGERS TO START MOVING: 'JUST GO DO SOMETHING !' (AND ENJOY THE STOCK OPTION)

Towards the end of 1996, John R. Walter was appointed chief operating officer of AT&T. Coming from another company and even another industry, he was impressed by the degree of *inertia, arrogance, bureaucracy* and *politics* which characterized AT&T. Obviously, the corporate culture had to change. ('Change managers' were in short supply.)

'Ninety-five per cent of the people who come into this office want *me* to make the decision,' said Walter. 'I ask them, what do they think we should do, and then I tell them to do it. My God, just go do *something.*' (Source: *Business Week*)

Another way to encourage delegation, individual thinking and a broader identification with the bottom line was to increase the number of employees who would enjoy stock options. Earlier, stock options had been reserved for the top two layers of management, while Walter sought shareholder approval to add two more organizational layers, that is, approximately 9,000 managers.

- Being in the office at 7 a.m. Start the first, one-on-one meeting at 7.15. (Or why not start with a 'power breakfast'?) Larger meetings with the full management team can start as early as 8 a.m. sharp. The participants might certainly grumble, but the message will no doubt be understood.

- Forbidding all first-class travel, if not justified by special professional reasons, and/or agreed in advance.

- Cancelling the next (even if already planned) extravagant and expensive sales conference. If needed, plan it on a shoestring budget, with more emphasis on good content and effective style than on luxurious surroundings. (Some managers call these 'flash meetings'.)

6.5 Building the new management team: what is meant by 'new'?

Whether most of the former executives are replaced or are still around, the use of the term 'the *new* management team' can still be justified, since old attitudes and habits of its members have to change both radically and fast. Such a change typically includes the following aspects:

■ a dramatic increase in the *interest and respect for facts*, to the detriment of long-established myths, unfounded rumours and defensive story telling

■ the constant search for new and fresh ways of doing things *cheaper, better, faster*

■ much more effective *cross-functional* and *cross-border cooperation*

■ simpler, but more effective *communication patterns* (usually reflected in fewer, shorter memos, and more reliance on face-to-face communication)

■ longer working hours and *more effective meeting patterns*

■ *systematic organization building* (flatter, simpler, clearer, more goal-orientated)

■ *strong identification* with the Blueprint for the Future Company, and with the ongoing efforts to realize the grand vision it represents.

Early on, the new – or at least rejuvenated – management team will find all its members fully engaged in a busy period, characterized by:

■ a *critical analysis* of the old ways, while simultaneously defining new and better ways to do things

■ the gathering and analysis of *pertinent and objective information* on which subsequent decisions can reliably be made

■ *redefining the company's Business Mission* and creating the Blueprint for the Future Company, as was discussed in great detail in Chapter 5

■ *decision-making* (strategic and tactical, as well as more mundane)

■ *implementation of the actions* reflected in miscellaneous strategic documents, while scrupulously respecting associated time and cost frames

- *implementation of other desirable changes* which might represent quite a radical break with long established company traditions.

After an intensive and highly successful turnaround of a forklift truck manufacturer, an exercise which lasted almost two years, Dr Arpi was told by an enthusiastic 62-year old executive: 'When you started working with us, I thought "this guy brings chaos on us". In retrospect, these two years have constituted one hell of a business school. Just a pity I was only allowed to graduate close to my retirement date.'

A strong management team is not only important when it comes to saving the troubled company under its new CEO. To our mind, it is the responsibility of any turnaround manager to see to it that the company is not only temporarily saved, but gradually develops a strong, independent, *top management team that can run the company – and run it well – after the turnaround manager himself has left the company* for other assignments. There is at least a 50 per cent chance that his successor will be found within the management team he leaves in place when the turnaround has been successfully concluded. (The purpose of any therapy is not to make the patient permanently dependent on the constant availability of a particular doctor, but to make the patient healthy and independent.)

Case

At Digital Equipment, an internally recruited, new CEO found it difficult to introduce badly needed changes.

Between 1992 and 1996, Digital fired 36 of its 40 top executives. Among the four survivors was Robert Palmer, who succeeded Ken Olsen, the man who had built Digital. Olsen had by then acquired cult status. *Fortune* magazine called him 'America's most successful entrepreneur'.

However, such long and repeated success is often dangerous. Management principles, once proven successful, tend to be adhered to long after they have become obsolete. The CEO tends to be surrounded by yes-men. He tends to think he knows all the answers, and can do nothing wrong. (This was equally true for Roger Smith of General Motors, and for P. G. Gyllenhammer, the chairman of Volvo for two decades.)

When Ken Olsen finally transferred his powers in order to help introduce the long overdue, radical and rapid changes, it was to a DEC insider, who was also his loyal friend. Unfortunately, the new man, Robert Palmer, indoctrinated during the Ken Olsen era, tended to apply identical values, priorities, procedures and management practices. He was obviously not the right 'change manager'.

In such a situation, an externally recruited CEO is usually a better answer.

'OUTSIDER' CEOs – THEIR INITIAL CREDIBILITY PROBLEM, AND HOW TO SOLVE IT

John R. Walter had been running the Chicago-based printer company R. R. Donnelley & Sons Co. before being head-hunted as president and chief operating officer of AT&T. Not knowing the industry, he contacted other 'outsider' CEOs. These included Eastman Kodak's George M. C. Fisher, Sears' Arthur C. Martinez, IBM's Gerstner and Stephen M. Wolf of US Air. Their advice: 'Initially, you are a foreigner. Therefore, watch your back. People are going to tell you to your face that they want to be part of your team. Do not believe that.' One middle manager at AT&T expressed it differently: 'John Walter has not yet *earned the right* to criticize us'.

However, when Walter without any pre-warning walked into a room where 100 sales managers met, and started to discuss the issues facing the company in 'a town meeting format', he was greeted with a standing ovation. (Compare what has earlier been said in this book about a turn-around manager using 'hangar meetings' and so on to quickly arrange face-to-face meetings with large numbers of employees – not only top managers – and engage in two-way communication, rather than lecturing the audience).

6.6   Motivating the new management team

Obviously, the rejuvenated management team is a key instrument for creating increased momentum and a sense of new direction throughout the organization. Although the full team is needed for this purpose, in the final analysis, the turnaround manager cannot delegate his personal responsibility for:

■ 'Driving' and psychologically motivating the top management team

- Constantly increasing the team's effectiveness and action-orientation
- Sending strong steering signals throughout the rest of the organization.

Expressed differently, the top management team is both a *target* and an *instrument* for his efforts. Only in this way can the turnaround manager achieve maximum impact throughout the troubled organization.

How can this be achieved in real-life? A few helpful clues are listed below:

a. *Motivation and a feeling of common purpose*: turnaround situations generate a variety of positive and negative forces. Some forces tend to scare and demotivate. Others can be *important motivators*. ('Finally I got a chance to prove my mettle!') The turnaround manager can help the process by removing unjustified fears and simultaneously providing *a feeling of common direction and opportunity*.

b. *Change is a necessity, not an option*: employees must be informed and influenced until they fully understand and accept that change is not only *imposed* upon the company by a newly arrived manager, but that *change is absolutely necessary*, and that it can provide employees with a highly rewarding personal experience.

c. *The personal angle*: a turnaround manager must understand that most employees tend to wonder *what is in it for me?* ('Will it lead to a new career path, interesting new job contents, a better working environment, stimulating challenges, or primarily to more work of the same type as before, plus the risk of losing my previous stature or – perhaps even my employment – with this company?')

d. *The importance of the first impressions and first decisions*: the first impressions of the newly arrived manager and his first actions will cast a long shadow. Therefore, be sure that you *move ahead* in a fast, even-handed and correct fashion. Do not delay making some high-profile, tangible decisions early on. These will signal to the organization that you are not only 'a mover and a shaker' in general, but that you also appreciate what needs to be done.

e. *Maximum speed helps to identify and retain managerial talent*: the higher the *speed* and the *quality* of the changes made, the easier it usually is to retain the most valuable employees and to attract first-class players from the outside. On the other hand, hesitant foot-draggers ('deadwood') are normally scared by decisive actions, since these imply that they will also have to move faster. Thus, *high speed* can be a helpful tool, also from a human resource management viewpoint.

f. *Making sure that people really understand what is required of them and why*: they must be provided not only with a general sense of urgency, but also with a sense of a common direction reflected in clear-cut goals and individual tasks, well worth fighting for. Demand much, but at the same time see to it that *you provide both strong leadership and a strong sense of common corporate direction!* (Although many might accept an 'enlightened dictatorship' for the time being, in the long run, the turnaround manager must *train others to think and act* pretty much on their own, although within the agreed strategic framework.)

g. *Improving group dynamics in the rejuvenated management team*: the turnaround manager is well advised to spend considerable time on improving the inner workings of the new management team. (The same might be true also of other groups, including some cross-functional and/or cross-border project groups.) The following pointers might be helpful:

- The turnaround manager must not only be capable of assessing the *company*'s strength and weaknesses, problems and opportunities, but also the strengths and weaknesses of the *management group*, and how its members interact.

- He must help build trust, mutual support and respect for all the team members. Thus, the turnaround manager must be particularly careful how he criticizes individual behaviour as well as intellectual reasoning power.

- Individuals must be helped to communicate better, particularly over functional borders or country borders, and to work better together for maximum combined impact (externally and internally).

- He will have to repeatedly, almost constantly, clarify objectives and priorities. This helps to make them remembered, and fully 'operational' when translated into day-to-day actions.

■ He might even consider using more formal educational tools, preferably in-house seminars closely linked to company specific cases. In these endeavours, he might choose to be assisted by an experienced, well-briefed outside consultant. (Chapter 8 of this book provides many examples of how the latter can contribute.)

In some parts of the world, including the US and Scandinavia, it has been common for a turnaround manager to short-cut the usual slow information process by personally and directly addressing all employees, or at least several hundred employees at a time, together often representing several layers of the formal hierarchy.

As already mentioned, Jan Carlzon's turnaround of Scandinavian Airlines Systems (SAS) included regular 'hangar meetings' with up to 600 individuals at a time. In this way, he could make sure that everybody had received the very same message, fast and without any 'message distorting communication filters' so often found in large organizations.

It takes a strong and rather likable personality with good communication skills to fully exploit the latter approach. Still, most employees appreciate the fact that the turnaround manager is not hiding somewhere on a remote executive floor, but has chosen to address them personally. He does not even have to be a smooth-talking charmer. If he is just an honest person conveying an impression of professionalism, valid turnaround experience and substantial integrity and human understanding, a mass meeting approach must be considered a valid tool. In this way, company news can be released rapidly, and unfounded rumours and worries responded to.

Such a speech can also be a first, important step to influence the corporate mentality, enhance the spirit of employees and encourage them to actively contribute, while conveying to them a clear-cut vision of the future and the means of getting there, in terms understood by everybody.

6.7 Evaluating the interim management team

The turnaround manager – even if working 16 hours a day – cannot possibly himself carry out every analysis, do all the planning and implement all the necessary actions. This is neither possible nor desirable. Ideally, he should have a *management team* at his disposal from day one. This team should ideally be motivated by a strong will to attack and correct the present deplorable situation, and possess the corresponding professional capability.

Unfortunately, on arrival, the turnaround manager is *not* likely to find such a well-functioning, highly motivated and professional management team in place. (If so, the company would hardly be in a turnaround situation!)

At least in a medium-term perspective, it is the turnaround manager's responsibility to create a fully satisfactory top management group. Until this has been achieved, he might simply decide to use the top executives presently available. Of course, he will put most of his trust in those who seem capable and willing, and who display a good dose of common sense.

Members of the existing management team must be tested and critically evaluated before their final fate is announced. For lack of a better term, while its members are still being tried and tested, this group might be thought of as 'the interim management group'. It is seldom completely identical to the old management team, nor to the final team.

The turnaround manager has rich opportunities to evaluate the growth potential of each manager and to decide who to keep, who is capable of soon assuming a larger spectrum of responsibilities, who should be trained for future roles, and who is found so wanting that he must be replaced. The management team will be so engaged in problem analyses, data gathering, interpretation of findings, suggestions as to long-term strategies and short-term corrective measures, that there will be no lack of input to the evaluation process.

Even when the turnaround manager already knows the answers, it is a good idea to discuss both strategic issues and action programmes with the full interim management team. Not only does this make it easier to evaluate members and group dynamics, but executives participating in such discussions can identify more easily with the necessary actions, spread the message throughout the organization and defend the necessary actions with vigour.

> It is the responsibility of the turnaround manager to evaluate the members of the top management team, personally fire incompetent managers, negotiate and close employment deals with newcomers, and to see to it that the interim management works smoothly and effectively.

6.8   Motivational problems after a merger, perhaps over country borders and involving several cultures

To build and motivate *one* management team is certainly demanding enough. So what about the situation after a merger or an acquisition affecting two management teams, representing two different corporate cultures, and perhaps also representing two or more countries? How does one integrate team members from different corporate and national cultures and make them work effectively together towards a common goal?

Below is some pertinent advice, primarily based on three sources:

1. Price Pritchet's book, *After the Merger: Managing the Shockwaves*, Dow Jones-Irwin, 1985.

2. Recommendations by Business International, reflected in their client report '*Making acquisitions work*'.

3. The two authors' combined experience from several cross-border, post-merger turnarounds. This includes assignments after the merger of Asea with Brown Boveri into ABB, generally regarded as one of the more successful cross-border mergers.

Six pieces of post-merger advice

1.   Always explain *why the merger took place, why now*, and what *common benefits* can be expected from it.

2.   Provide the new (that is, the combined) company with a clear-cut *new identity* as early as possible – based on the perceived future common strength, rather than based on 'rear-mirror' nostalgia.

3. Clarify if the purchased company (or the smaller of the two merged companies) is supposed to *keep its own operating mode*, or if it will rapidly be integrated with the larger company. Stating that 'nothing will really change' is seldom believable and normally not true. If the expected integration is to be limited to only certain areas (product-wise, country-wise, function-wise and so on), explain this.

4. If the intention is to change to a *new common company name*, do this early, even if this will create considerable initial confusion among both employees and clients. The change to a new corporate identity might call for outside expertise and substantial external (as well as internal) costs. When the hotel chain 'Western International' changed its name to the briefer, but close-sounding 'Westin', the associated corporate re-identification measures were estimated to cost no less than $70 million. When one of the two companies affected by a merger finds itself in deep financial distress, such re-identification costs might be quite a heavy extra burden, well worth careful consideration before going ahead with the name change.

5. Recognize the enormous thirst for *reliable information*, primarily experienced *within the purchased company*. Even if no firm, financial plan yet exists, keep communicating. (Guesses by employees are usually much worse than any later known reality!)

6. Do not keep quiet until all the details of your Blueprint for the Future Company have been sorted out. You just make people nervous. You lose momentum. At least one of the two organizations to be merged is likely to be almost paralysed until their employees know what is in store for them.

Jockeying for positions, infighting, power struggles, and guessing games will take too much time and energy away from the business. In the meantime, markets are likely to be badly served by worried and demotivated employees. Since speculations and internal battles divert attention from much more constructive pursuits, this situation should not be allowed to go unattended for long.

Of course, your basic strategy must be sound, and your pre-acquisition analysis reasonably accurate. Thereafter, the advice is obvious: move quickly and decisively!

DEUTSCHE BANK ANNOUNCES RAPID INTEGRATION AFTER HAVING ACQUIRED BANKERS TRUST

In May 1997, Rolf-Ernst Breuer became CEO of Deutsche Bank. His predecessor, Hilmar Kopper, spent huge sums on pushing the bank into investment banking. Breuer's initial mission was to start making money, partly by using years of experience gained in the bank's investment and trading departments.

In November 1998, it was suddenly announced that Deutsche Bank was to acquire Bankers Trust (USA) for DM17 billion. Provided US and European union regulators approved, as well as the shareholders, the merger of the two organizations would create the *world's largest bank*. This time, a much swifter and more determined integration effort was foreseen than the rather leisurely pace shown when Deutsche Bank had acquired Morgan Grenfell. Four ambitions were communicated at the very outset:

a. The buyer decided to announce the 'cruel' decisions early on.

b. These included cutting 5,500 jobs, presumably corresponding to a saving of US$1 billion by year 2001.

c. Deutsche Bank announced they would ask existing and new shareholders to come up with DM4 billion, that is, approximately 40 per cent of the takeover cost.

d. To make sure that the best revenue-generating managers did not defect to rival institutions, Deutsche Bank earmarked DM400 million as 'golden handcuffs' incentive payments.

Several examples of problems associated with mergers and particularly with *cross-border mergers*, have been discussed in previous chapters (for example the three cases in Chapter 1, section 1.3; and the Spanish, two French and one Swedish/French case, all discussed in Chapter 2, section 2.6). Other company-specific examples can be found in the many case studies scattered throughout the book, including the four in this chapter dealing with Digital Equipment (DEC), AT&T, Deutsche Bank/Bankers Trust and Asea Brown Boveri (ABB).

6.9 Advice to a turnaround manager running a recently acquired company

Assume that you have been appointed turnaround manager for a recently acquired company. What – apart from what has already been said – do you then have to take into consideration? The following items might be worth considering:

a. *Pass on information to the acquired company concerning the parent company*: its history, corporate philosophy, value systems, strengths and weaknesses. Try to help the acquired entity orientate itself toward a new identity and a new future – a future which might be at least as rewarding as the old one. (However, you are not there to brainwash people on behalf of the parent company, so do not overdo it!)

b. Clarify the practical consequences of likely *new reporting relationships*. Acquired companies constantly complain about ill-defined power structures, confusing lines of authority and tangled relationships. In Europe, particularly since 1990, cross-border deals are increasingly common. Only 30 per cent live up to pre-merger expectations. This underlines even more sharply *the need to consider language problems, cultural differences, discrepant management practices* and *different modes of communication*.

A few examples of contrasting management practices

Formal versus informal decision-making, respecting the hierarchies versus 'tearing down the pyramids and flattening organizations', secrecy versus open information, 'big sticks and big carrots' versus more subtle steering principles.

It is obvious that a successful turnaround manager in a post-merger situation must understand (and respect) the two company cultures and, preferably, speak the relevant local languages. (Ideally, he should be able to behave like a chameleon, cleverly adapting to the particular environment in which he happens to be operating at each point in time!)

c. Even if the turnaround manager is formally responsible only for the well-being of the *acquired* company, he must in reality be prepared to work also within a much broader corporate structure, with new – and partly unsettled – reporting relationships. In one recent case, the acquired company was:

■ reporting to a Swedish executive vice president along the 'product line dimension',

but also to

■ a French 'country manager', and
■ to a Swiss PRC ('parent company responsible').

Such a '3-dimensional management perspective' was common within ITT during Harold Geneen's heyday. Further, different parts of the same legal entity often reported directly ('on a solid line basis') to quite different Group Managers, located at ITT World HQ in New York, or at a regional HQ, for example ITT Europe in Brussels.

ITT: Splitting the local legal entity

From a reporting viewpoint, SEL in Stuttgart was split into half a dozen profit centres, including those for public switching, private business communications, military equipment, consumer brown goods, and consumer white goods. The legal SEL entity was quite another matter. A turnaround manager must be able to operate effectively also in such a complex environment, which might be quite different from anything he has previously experienced.

---

d. While busily building his new management team, defining the new Business Mission, and identifying the Blueprint for the Future Company, the turnaround manager must be realistic enough to recognize that in a post-merger situation *many parties are likely to be scheming behind his back.*

The owner limiting the degrees of freedom

Perhaps many at headquarters want the production of the troubled company moved somewhere else. If so, both the local factory and the local R&D department might soon be closed. A Blueprint which does not acknowledge such realities might be rather useless. Its formal approval becomes a necessity.

CROSS-BORDER CULTURAL SHOCK: THE CREATION OF ABB

On Monday 10 August 1987, the merger between Asea (of Sweden) and Brown Boveri (of Switzerland) was announced. Both companies were over 100 years old, highly respected and even regarded as national treasures. Each had a strong corporate culture.

Cultural clashes could be expected for many reasons: the two companies had long been in competition, they had different home countries with different value systems, and they were run according to very different management principles.

One of the authors (Dr Arpi) worked with some post-merger problems, including certain products (for example surge arresters), being produced both in Sweden and in Switzerland. The perceived characteristics of the two companies at the time of the merger are reflected in the following informal notes from this assignment.

'Compared to Asea, Brown Boveri is more centralized. Asea has for quite a few years worked with far-reaching decentralization and with smaller business units, responsible for their own P&L statements. While business unit managers within Asea know their cost and revenue structure by heart, their counterparts within Brown Boveri put their trust in group management, the wisdom of the central financial department, and the perceived overall excellence of the company. As to R&D, the engineers at the Ludvika plant in Sweden usually stop their development efforts if further efforts would make the product too expensive for the market place. "Incremental costs then exceed the customer perceived incremental value." Such a reasoning is rather foreign within Brown Boveri. There, product development has often been allowed to continue until many products (including many types of surge arresters) are so expensive that they have difficulty meeting world market prices. Sometimes they can therefore only be profitably sold in very small and highly specialized niches. (Example: protection of installations in case of a nuclear attack.) Asea seems to be fairly good at developing new products at acceptable speed, and also getting them to the market in time. In contrast, Brown Boveri are responsible for several impressive, quite ground-breaking innovations, but they often failed to commercialize them successfully in time. (Examples briefly mentioned seem to cover a broad range, from catalytic converters to liquid crystal screens.)'

While checking the order processing system for surge arresters, it was observed that several weeks could pass before an order received from a client was even *formally confirmed* by Brown Boveri. The marketing director concerned expressed his regret, but explained that each and every customer order had to go to the central financial department for '*risk evaluation*'. Few had considered what impact this delay had on the company's perceived responsiveness to client needs.

After some discussion it was agreed that *all* orders in the more stable currencies and for low-risk clients and markets (plus all other orders which did not exceed a certain threshold value) could be confirmed on the spot by the marketing director himself. Thus, only more problematic cases had to be referred to the central 'risk evaluation' unit.

The overall impression at the time of the merger was that Asea was more marketing-orientated and certainly more profit-orientated, while Brown Boveri was more research-orientated, and with an organization that was heavily centralized. As a result, many of Brown Boveri's middle managers had a somewhat limited insight into the revenues, costs and profitability associated with their own area of responsibility. The 'bottom-line orientation' was not as obvious as within Asea, which was run by Percy Barnevik, who had a controller's solid background.

Against this background, it came as no surprise that 'cultural shock' set in within the Brown Boveri organization. The merger was often perceived there as a 'takeover by the aggressive Swedes'. *To facilitate the merging of the two organizations into a cohesive whole, ABB early on established their corporate headquarters in Switzerland.* (There is a striking similarity with the Tarkett case in Part II. Having acquired the equally large Pegulan organization, Tarkett moved its headquarters to Germany.)

It is of great importance for the interim team to get rapidly from the strategy formulation phase to the actual plan implementation phase. Without waiting for approval of the complete Blueprint for the Future Company, they must attack numerous practical problems and deficiencies in different areas. Some of these have little direct bearing on the Blueprint for the Future Company, but must still be effectively addressed.

In summary, in a post-merger, cross-border turnaround, all the normal turnaround pressures are increased. The future place of the troubled company in the overall corporate structure has not always been decided. Even the acquired company's birthright might be in doubt. Under these conditions, the task of building, motivating and retaining an effectively operating management team takes on important new dimensions.

6.10 Enjoy the turnaround, but leave when the job is concluded!

A turnaround manager can afford to be satisfied with a job well done, but he should not become complacent, nor hang on longer than necessary. The typical length of different kinds of turnaround has already been discussed in Chapter 3, section 3.14.

How long a particular turnaround manager should stay on board also partly depends on the arrangements made at the beginning, as shown by the following three real-life examples:

1. In the first case, the turnaround manager was a young and 'hungry' man operating within the context of a major multinational organization. He was given the turnaround assignment to prove his mettle and growth potential. It was also clearly indicated from the very beginning that if successful, he would rapidly become CEO of a considerably larger group of companies.

2. In the second case, the turnaround manager was an experienced manager around the age of 60. He was given this assignment as a way of concluding his career in a challenging fashion. It was understood that he would stay onboard until the age of 65. Afterwards, he retired to Australia, with the company's blessing, but retained some board functions in the UK. (His appreciation of London's theatre life was a strong contributing factor.)

3. In the third case, the turnaround manager was an external consultant ('manager for hire') contracted for the explicit purpose of carrying out a particular turnaround operation. It was agreed that he would stay in this role for at least nine months, maybe longer if the situation so demanded. Consultants from Arpi International have often worked in this fashion in different company, country and language areas.

Most of the turnarounds carried out by Per Wejke and reported in Part II have taken between two and four years. This was true for the Atlas Copco Tool case and for the Atlas Copco MCT case. However, the Allgon case, which included quite spectacular growth ambitions, fell into the six–eight year bracket. The latter time-frame also applies to the ESAB and Tarkett cases, characterized by equally spectacular growth and internationalization ambitions, leading to a dominating market position, each company becoming No. 2 worldwide.

The young, hungry executive mentioned above was rewarded with another, much bigger assignment immediately after completion of the first turnaround, which took two-and-a-half years. The older executive in the second example discussed above was allowed to stay on board for a few more years than were strictly needed for the turnaround assignment as such.

If an 'outside' senior consultant is used (as in the third case), he should certainly not be allowed to hang on at all costs, particularly if the troubled company no longer needs his presence on a full-time basis. Perhaps he might be invited to stay on the board of the saved company for one or two years. From this new platform, he can actually ensure that what he set in motion is also correctly concluded.

Initially, such a board arrangement might be combined with one or two consulting days a week, to help the new CEO to get rapidly into the overall picture. However, such extended consulting assistance must never be forced upon the new CEO by the board, and it should be terminated whenever the new CEO feels that he knows the company sufficiently well. (Obviously, if the new CEO mishandles the remaining implementation stages of an agreed upon turnaround plan, he might simply have to accept whatever assistance the board decides to provide!)

A turnaround expert should normally leave when his assignment is over and the company is in decent shape and in good managerial hands. The original assignment is then finished.

If the turnaround manager (as in the Allgon case) stays on for more than two to four years, it is often because he has in reality assumed a new responsibility, for example to generate *spectacular international growth and shareholder value* on a longer-term basis. (In the Allgon case, the company became the winner of the Stockholm Stock Exchange Award, because of the company's quite spectacular performance.)

Note

1. Some of the examples provided in this chapter have already been briefly mentioned in the overview chapter, that is, in Chapter 3.

7 Where to get plan input data

7.1 Purpose and contents of this chapter

Two related questions are dealt with in this chapter:

1. Where does the turnaround manager find the necessary information, that is, *what kind of sources* are normally open to him when designing his Blueprint?

2. How does he go about *using these sources* – from company employees and outside experts to on-line databases and CD-ROMs?

The present chapter is not meant to replace standard text books on market and competitive research, controllers' manuals, or books on group dynamics or interviewing techniques. The focus in this chapter is rather on what is different, or particularly *pertinent*, when gathering information in a turnaround situation.

The contents and usefulness of a Business Mission Statement and a Blueprint for the Future Company were discussed in Chapter 5. There, the use of quantitative benchmarks to establish turnaround-related goals (as to costs, productivity and customer perceived value) were also discussed.

This chapter begins with a brief recap of the previous benchmarking discussion, followed by an overview of topics covered in the present chapter.

Benchmarks provide valuable information as to what is achievable in real life by a well-run company in the same or similar industries.

Expressed differently, benchmarking is *done to ensure that turn-around goals are neither too modest nor overly optimistic*. Although the Blueprint itself may not explicitly recapitulate all such benchmarks, they are nevertheless crucial for goal validation purposes.

However, externally derived benchmarks cannot be turned 'automatically', that is, heedlessly into company-specific goals for the troubled company. They may first have to be modified with regard to the following company-specific factors:

- The *quality* of the reinforced management team, including its capacity to analyse and understand problems correctly, as well as to *implement* vigorously any necessary changes.

- The *corporate culture*, that is, the traditions and value systems of the troubled company, and how rapidly these can be changed, if and when needed.

- *Cash flow problems* (or lack of venture capital) delaying otherwise highly desirable actions, which would put too much strain on limited financial resources.

- The external *credibility* of the company (including the turnaround manager and his management team) among creditors, suppliers, clients and so on. (Low credibility substantially restricts the degree of managerial freedom and often excludes certain types of solution.)

- The troubled company's *ownership structure*, including the possible existence of a rich, sympathetic and patient parent company.

- In which *country* (or countries) the turnaround takes place. (Laws, traditions, preferences, expectations and, in a unionized company, the attitudes and behaviour that can be expected from the unions.)

- The strengths and weaknesses of existing *intra-company systems*, procedures and controls and the extent to which these are adhered to.

Thus, while benchmarks, by definition, are primarily based on comparisons with other companies, the Blueprint or rescue plan must also take into consideration a large number of specific *in-house factors* of the nature illustrated above.

The rest of this chapter deals with other sources and techniques for information gathering, than those linked to formal benchmarking.

Table 7.1   Information sources discussed in Chapter 7

In-house sources		External sources
Document-orientated	People-orientated	All types
Accounting data and financial reports	One-on-one interviews	Tailor-made, company-specific market and competitive research (incl. benchmarking against competition)
	Group discussions	
	The individual assignment	
Business plans and other strategy documents	The group assignment	Existing published industry studies of an *ad hoc* nature
Following a typical order from receiving it, until shipped and paid for	Interviewing employees having recently left the company	Interviewing industry experts
		Free Internet information, for example via websites
		'Pay-as-you-go' professional databases
		CD-ROM based information
		Business TV channels, linked up to both printed media and websites (for example Time Warner – CNN)
		Emerging new sources, encouraged by new technologies and rapidly falling prices

7.2   The most obvious in-house sources

The most obvious in-house sources include:

■ standard accounting data and *financial reports*

■ access to the *controller's department* for further-going explanations and analyses

■ a (perhaps already outdated) *business plan* or similar strategic document showing what the troubled company's previous management team tried to do, and why

■ additional information gathered through *MBWA* (management by walking around) on company premises, while observing and talking to people

■ more organized *meetings*, either in the form of one-on-one discussions or in the form of group discussions. (The latter term may cover meetings with the top management team, with existing project teams or new project teams, and *ad hoc* meetings for a particular purpose.)

The use of internal *accounting reports* is discussed in the next section. The systematic use of *employees* as key information sources is considered in Section 7.3, which ends with a discussion of MBWA. External sources are covered in section 7.4.

7.2.1 Internal accounting data

Customary accounting data, reports and key ratios, usually supplemented by more occasional in-house reports or statistics, can normally highlight the operating mode as well as the efficiency of different company functions. Above all, from them, the turnaround manager can rapidly identify 'bleeders', that is, unprofitable products, markets, divisions and so on.

Example of pertinent key ratios

The 'hit rate' achieved among quotations made, loading figures for different machine groups, the time spent within the R&D department on different types of development projects, the average number of days outstanding for receivables, preferably broken down on different product lines, markets and/or customer groups.

A more complete discussion of financial data used in connection with a typical turnaround is found in Larry Goddard, *Corporate Intensive Care*, York Publishing, 1993.

'CREATIVE ACCOUNTING' AT GROWTH-ORIENTATED VIACOM, THE ENTERTAINMENT COLOSSUS

Under the 74-year old chairman and CEO, Sumner M. Redstone, Viacom Inc. grew from 7,000 employees in early 1994 to 83,000 in summer 1997. By then, Redstone controlled 67 per cent of Viacom's voting stock and he still ran the company like an unfocused mom-and-pop operation. Even his credo sounded like a platitude: 'Growing Viacom to its maximum potential is the goal.'

Viacom's growth has mainly been through acquisitions. These include the debt-financed acquisition of Paramount. In March 1997, Redstone vowed to get Viacom's long-term debt of $10.2 billion down to 'between dollars 6 billion and 8 billion by 1999'. Since Redstone did not want to sell any major assets (except a few radio stations), this supposedly meant a slower growth for MTV Networks, Simon & Schuster, and Blockbuster. Perhaps one would also experience more examples of creative accounting. 'Viacom has been there before', as *Business Week* put it.

In 1994, Viacom acquired Blockbuster. It immediately wrote off US$318 million, corresponding to two-thirds of Blockbuster's tape inventory.

When Blockbuster later started selling from the radically written down inventory, sales margins for the next four quarters shown were in excess of 40 per cent. Such superior financial results were badly needed in 1995, since Viacom would have been required to pay up to $680 million to shareholders, if the company's stock had failed to achieve certain price targets. When the last of these crucial price-target hurdles had been successfully cleared (during the third quarter of 1995), the artificially inflated Blockbuster margins just vaporized. (For the next four quarters, Blockbuster margins fell by 14 percentage points back toward their historic average. However, financial analysts now tended to interpret this 'margin squeeze' as proof that Blockbuster was in deep trouble. Blockbuster's previous owner, Mr Huizenga said 'Blockbuster is in reality doing fine. It is just hurt by earlier accounting tricks. Blockbuster has been made the culprit, when it should not be. In my opinion there was more (merger-related) creative accounting than Wall Street knew.'

On March 3 1997, *Business Week* stated: 'Thanks to the Blockbuster accounting and the lacklustre performance posted by many of the (Viacom) units in 1996, the 1997 comparisons are bound to look terrific. The stage is then set for Redstone to collect popular acclaim for piloting Viacom to a stellar 1997!' (In reality, Viacom's stock lost half its value between 1993 and the summer of 1997 – when the Viacom stock was trading close to book value. As a comparison, Disney then traded at over three times their book value.)

Moral

A turnaround manager should accept nothing at face value. Rather, he should expect that accounting data might be *artfully manipulated* (or even 'cooked'), to cover the true size of actual losses, particularly in certain pet project areas.

On closer scrutiny, he might also find that *financial reserves* (shown in the books) are much *too small* in relation to the actual size of underlying problems and exposures. This might for instance be true in areas such as claims, unsettled law suits, stocks not properly evaluated, product quality problems which will later lead to high guaranty costs and so on.

By just 'snooping around', he might find other 'skeletons in the cupboard' that nobody has dared to mention before. (It might be a key client on the verge of leaving, or a competing product introduced at half the price of the company's own pet product.)

Even keeping such reservations in mind, internal accounting data is still one of the most logical starting points for any turnaround exercise.

7.2.2 The controller: a reliable source, or part of the problem?

In several turnaround cases in which the authors have been involved, it was necessary to fire the controller. Typical reasons are reflected in the following cases:

1. In the first case, the controller turned out to be a drug addict who skillfully managed to let the company finance her purchases by rather artful manipulation of accounting figures. These facts were only revealed when the turnaround manager *forced her to take a holiday* for the first time in five years. (She had previously refused to take a holiday because she was scared of what might happen if somebody else was in charge of the accounts while she was away.)

2. In a second turnaround case, there were wide discrepancies between the reported 'preliminary' monthly results and the 'final' monthly results reported only ten days later. *The variances seemed inexplicable.* On closer scrutiny, it turned out that the controller was a former school teacher who had decided that business life was probably more fascinating than teaching. After three weeks of reschooling (paid for by state funds) and substantial and very

creative rewriting of his CV, he managed to land a position as controller of a medium-sized company belonging to a well-known multinational group. Although he did nothing dishonest to line his own pockets, his spurious accounting led to erroneous management conclusions and severely flawed managerial decisions. After this was discovered, the multinational group to which the troubled company belonged had to reopen their accounting books and revise their consolidated results downwards, a somewhat embarrassing situation for all concerned.

A note in passing: Six months later, the same individual contacted Dr Arpi. The 'controller' had now completed an equally brief marketing course, and wondered if Dr Arpi could perhaps help him find a job as a marketing manager 'which seems to be much more interesting than being a controller'.

3. In a third case, the controller was a young, bright, good-looking, and extremely self-confident female who reported to a recently arrived, sales-orientated general manager who was rather gullible. She started her career by declaring that the multinational group's well-established accounting system was unsuitable for the purpose at hand. She was going to introduce a 'better and much more flexible' accounting system, chosen by herself. In the meantime, the CEO was told not to worry. *'Provided sales increase by 50 per cent, costs are likely to fall accordingly.'* (Needless to say, this was a highly personal and utterly false interpretation of Professor Bruce Henderson's so-called 'experience curve'. For mature, undifferentiated products – say a beer can without a label and no beer in it – the experience curve indicates that costs might fall by 25–30 per cent, if the accumulated production volume, that is, the experience, *doubles*, but certainly not when it only increases by 50 per cent.)

When the truth about 'the new accounting system' was revealed, this forklift truck producing company found itself not only without a reliable accounting system but, even worse, without reliable accounting data. The management team *thought they had made a huge profit* during the previous year. In reality they had been *running up substantial losses* while 'buying market share', partly based on the erroneous interpretation of existing strategic literature mentioned above. In the country in question, the *whole industry*, trying to copy the 'aggressive new pricing strategy', was losing money!

Moral

In a turnaround situation, *never accept accounting data at face value.* You must know both *what* lies behind the figures and *who* stands behind them.

So what do you do about an incompetent controller? If you are an expert on financial matters yourself, you might decide to fire him rapidly. Otherwise, think twice. A critical turnaround situation does not necessarily get less critical by thoughtlessly calling in external auditors.

> The last things you need at such a critical stage are widespread rumours that the 'books are cooked' and that the situation in reality is much worse than earlier reported. Remember, you are there to *save the company*, not to kill it off!

7.2.3 The business plan and other strategic documents

On arrival, the turnaround manager is likely to find a number of budget documents, business plans, strategy documents and so on. Perhaps nobody – with the possible exception of the departed CEO – actually believed in their contents. More likely than not, the business plan contained both *exaggerated sales figures* and *underestimated cost levels*, and the author probably knew it.

When business plan goals have not been reached, it is usually because of one (or both) of the following two factors:

1. The goals were *never realistic*
2. The corresponding action plan was either non-existent or *never stringently implemented*.

Some turnaround managers find it useful to establish the reasons for the troubled company's present situation. 'Benchmarking' against competition helps to determine if the ambitious goals were *ever* realistic. If yes, what about the actions taken to reach them? Expressed differently: was there a strategic *planning deficiency*, or *an implementation deficiency*, or possibly both? The following two questions are usually worth considering:

1. Were the actions *never listed*, or at least never listed in such a way that one could later easily determine if they had been implemented as expected?
2. Were the actions *never professionally executed* within given time and cost frames, and to what extent did each action achieve its intended purpose?

An '*ex post facto* audit' might answer both questions. Some turnaround managers feel they do not have the time to engage in such fault finding exercises. Instead, they tend to regard old business plans as dust collectors, which obviously only had one use – to buy a bit of extra time for the outgoing CEO.

From previous business plans, the turnaround manager might find an indication of what went wrong, including symptoms of underlying managerial weaknesses. However, when it comes to deciding what now urgently needs to be done from the strategic viewpoint, the old business plan (or similar document) is usually worthless. After all, had the plan been good and professionally executed, the troubled company most likely would not have found itself in the present mess.

In summary, reading an old business plan or other strategic document found in the archives might be useful if it provides the turnaround manager with information on the following aspects of the troubled company:

■ Did the old management team know how to plan and calculate professionally and realistically, or had they become experts at 'selling hope, disguised in figures'?

■ Was the previous management team primarily weak in planning or weak in execution, or possibly both?

■ Did most of the errors in planning originate in 'erroneous assumptions about the outside world', or rather in an over-estimation of the speed, professionalism and impact of their own management actions?

■   Which external plan assumptions were seriously unrealistic? (For example the general market development, inflation rates, currency exchange rates, competitive moves, or the likely market response to their own marketing actions?)

■   What might the old strategic documents tell about the 'value system' within the company at large, and particularly within its previous top management team? (Creative or old-fashioned? Market- or production-orientated? Down-to-earth or blue skies planners?)

7.2.4   Acting as cross-functional trail-blazer and detective

MBWA can take many forms, as will be discussed in section 7.3.6 and in the Tarkett case study. In the present section, only one particular type is illustrated, namely walking, talking, and carefully listening, but all the time systematically following a 'horizontal trail' (that is, applying a cross-functional approach).

By stubbornly *following a selected process or procedure* from beginning to end, and constantly asking *pertinent questions of* the individuals met, the turnaround manager can often rapidly learn a surprising amount. As an example, he might decide to start from a trade receivables review, and then follow the complete process – and all associated activities and paperwork – from the time of a sale or an order placed until the final invoice has been paid by the client.

Even following just *one concrete case or transaction* might sometimes be quite revealing: was the invoice sent on time? Was it complete? Was the shipment of goods complete as to quantity or quality? Did our performance provide the customer with an excuse not to pay, or to pay late? Were reminder notices sent on time? With what kind of results? What is our policy for future sales to the same client when his receivables due are not paid? Are future shipments blocked manually or by the computer? Who, if anybody, has corresponding override rights? Are

stringent reports issued concerning receivables overdue? How are top management and the marketing director normally notified? What kind of actions do they
usually take on this basis – if any at all? Why not in this particular case? Is there
an improvement or a deterioration as to receivables overdue? Why? What can be
expected in the future if no change takes place?

Questions asked during MBWA must be *highly specific*. 'Is this
price really in line with our existing price lists and the approved
discount conditions for this customer at the purchased quantity? Are
the *payment terms* offered here really in line with established
company policy? Do you think that our company's *policy* with regard
to payment terms and discounts is sound?'

The process of following one cross-functional trail seemingly has
many similarities with a classical management audit, but it does not
have the same broad scope or key purpose. During a turnaround
manager's MBWA, the emphasis is on *rapid learning* rather than on
strict *control*.

7.3 Employees as key sources

7.3.1 One-on-one interviews

Discussions with employees a few levels down provide an excellent
way to get to know the general atmosphere in the company. One-on-
one interviews with each key executive are also an excellent way to
get to know their ways of reasoning, and the scope and limitations of
their managerial perspective. Individuals who are primarily defensive
and 'rear-mirror orientated' are less useful to the turnaround manager
than those who have some bright ideas for the company's future, how
its operating mode can and ought to be improved, and so on.

ONE EXAMPLE OF A REVEALING ONE-ON-ONE INTERVIEW (verbatim)

New CEO: So we seem to agree that the present productivity in the assembly section is far from acceptable and that we need to increase productivity by at least 30 per cent.

Production manager: Could not agree more.

New CEO: So what do you suggest should be done about it?

Production manager: We are going to fight and succeed.

New CEO: That is certainly the right spirit. Perhaps you could point out one specific area where actions could be taken right away to improve productivity. Where would you like to start?

Production manager: We are going to persevere.

New CEO: Yes, indeed, but *how* do you suggest we go about this productivity problem in more concrete terms?

Production manager: (now obviously frustrated) Do you not believe in me?

(This manager had no idea about where to *start* the necessary improvements. Nor was he 'managing' his present area of responsibility in any meaningful sense. As a result, he was later subjected to 'reversed executive search'. Here the term is used almost as a synonym to 'outplacement' but with one noticeable difference: the company did not have to tell the executive first. Instead, he was very happy about a job offer discreetly provided by an external head-hunter. This saved his face and provided an interesting new career with another company.)

A SECOND EXAMPLE OF A REAL-LIFE ONE-ON-ONE INTERVIEW (WITH A HAPPY END)

Bo Arpi: (to the R&D director in the troubled company) The sales and marketing people tell me they have a problem. Their standard sales contract says that each delivery of this type includes a service manual and a spare parts list. However, many clients have told me they have not received a spare parts list even 24 months after they took delivery of the product. Would you like to comment?

R&D Director: The clients are right, although the problems are limited to only some of our products.

B.A.: How come?

R&D Director: Our spare parts lists are very complex since they must cover all possible variants of that particular model.

B.A.: It must certainly be a complex task if it takes you two years to produce such a list. Tell me how thick is the spare parts list for an average model, and what does it cost to edit and print it?

R&D Director: It is not just a simple list, but quite a thick binder. Last time I checked, it cost us approximately US$110,000 for each model.

B.A.: Does this not strike you as unusually expensive?

R&D Director: No, I have carefully checked prices with three different suppliers, and the price we pay seems to be quite normal for a printing and editing job of this size.

B.A.: If you divide the $110,000 by the number of units you have typically sold by each model during the last two years, what figure do you arrive at?

R&D Director: (after spending a minute on his pocket calculator) Over $5,000 per unit sold. (*Note:* A 'unit' is here a forklift truck.)

B.A.: Does this not strike you as unreasonably expensive?

R&D Director: When you put it in relation to our product cost, I have to agree.

B.A.:	If you have only built 22 units of *each model* during the last two years, you can hardly have sold all that many units of each *variant* either?
R&D Director:	No, most existing variants have *not been sold at all* during the last 24 months. However, we still have to document them in our spare parts list, in case a client buys one. This is what makes the spare parts list production such a complex and expensive thing.
B.A.:	Who then decides on which variants should be offered in each national market place?
R&D Director:	My function (the R&D function) only specifies all variants which it is *technically possible to build* with available components, while fully respecting safety and mean time-between-failure requirements. Then I assume it is up to the marketing department to decide which and how many variants they want to offer in each national market.
B.A.:	Is your impression that most of the variants which your department specifies as *technically possible to build* are later also offered to the marketplace as *commercially available*? Do you mean that no 'commercial filters' are introduced by the marketing department to limit the number of commercially available variants?
R&D Director:	To the best of my knowledge there are at present no such filters. The marketing people tell me they need to maintain maximum flexibility to be able to meet all potential customer requirements.
B.A.:	Please do me a favour. Tell me by this afternoon how many units are produced on average each year for every *model*, and also how many *variants* are potentially available.
R&D Director:	(later the same day) For a typical model, we build between 4 and 30 units per year. As to *variants*, there are – at least theoretically – 2,400,000 variants, most of which are of course *never* built.

Comments

A simple question about a seemingly isolated problem here led to the *unearthing of a much larger problem*. (Starting out asking about the delay in spare parts catalogue deliveries finally led to a discussion of the number of existing variants on offer, with repercussions far outside the spare parts catalogue area.)

The line manager involved had seemingly followed sound procedures – for example he had checked catalogue printing prices against three suppliers. However, *he never spontaneously started to think cross-functionally*. Dividing the spare parts catalogue costs by the number of products actually sold of each model simply fell 'outside of his area of responsibility', since he was not responsible for sales. This is a typical example of a good functional manager who had not yet learned to operate within a 'cross-functional mind set'.

The previous CEO was described as a 'very nice guy'. Unfortunately, he was also characterized as a 'conflict-avoider at any price'. As a result, he had preferred to talk to only one functional head at a time. This had hardly encouraged *cross-functional thinking and cooperation* over departmental borderlines.

7.3.2 Group discussions

Discussions with groups of executives provide the turnaround manager with the opportunity to evaluate *group dynamics*. He can note the degree to which a common consensus exists for specific issues, which individuals tend to talk more than others, who tends to just agree most of the time (not providing much personal input), who is showing off to satisfy his or her big ego, who strives to arrive at a compromise by acting as a 'spokesman for all', or who likes to report clearly deviating opinions, and so on.

Obviously, a turnaround manager will consciously try to *influence* existing group dynamics, including opinions and behavioural patterns. There are many subtle tools available for this purpose. He might provide factual feedback, comment upon suggestions made, encourage those who have good ideas, but are too shy to speak up without direct encouragement, and so on.

Example

In connection with two successful turnarounds, Dr Arpi was asked to run group dynamic sessions with the complete management group for two days a month during a nine-month period. The results achieved manifested themselves in many ways. A much clearer common understanding of the company's problems became quite obvious. Finger pointing at other company functions and departments stopped. The appreciation of other company functions increased, so did coopera- tion over functional borders. In a slow-reacting company perhaps bound by many traditions, such sessions can help create a 'sense of urgency', including an under- standing of the importance of rapid (but still fact-based) decision-making and subsequent rapid implementation of 'corrective management actions'. A real-life example of such a group discussion can be found in the case study below.

To change group dynamics usually takes considerable time. This process can seldom be telescoped into a limited time span. Locking up the whole management team for two days in a country inn or at a coastal hotel might be a good way to solve one or two clearly delin- eated problems. However, to fundamentally change existing manage- rial attitudes and behavioural patterns takes time and systematic effort. Ideally, it should go hand-in-hand with a change in daily working patterns and cooperation modes.

CASE: GROUP DISCUSSION TECHNIQUES IN A TURNAROUND SITUATION

The general setting for the group discussion reproduced below is a meeting with all functional heads and all regional managers in a major distribution organization for construction material. Bo Arpi (B.A.) has been called in as a 'strategic planning consultant' by the recently appointed managing director, expected to lead a major turnaround effort in an imperturbable family-owned company that lost $19 million the previous year.

B.A.:   I have called this meeting to discuss what can be done to improve the profitability of this company.

Let us for the time being just leave all manpower considerations aside and instead focus on what aspects of this company's operations can be *changed* or *done differently*. Give me one example of what might be changed.

The Group: (Complete and massive silence, but no unfriendly attitudes.)

B.A.: Let us start by focusing on your present product range. What might be done there?

Regional manager: Nothing.

B.A.: Why do you think so?

Regional Manager: Mr S., the founder of this company, always emphasized that we must remain 'a full-service company'. Thus, we must be able to offer every article that competition is able to offer. No product range cut-backs are therefore possible.

B.A.: Interesting. Thank you very much. Then what about *price changes*? Could you for instance sell more if you lowered your prices, or, alternatively, increase profits by raising prices?

Executive vice president, 60 years old: Competition does not allow us to increase prices above the existing market level. If we were to lower them, we would invite murderous price competition. To stop price wars, we have our industry association which meets once a month and discusses the market outlook and related matters. (Big smile.) I happen to be the chairman of this industry association.

B.A.: If I understood you correctly, you cannot increase prices, nor lower prices.'

Executive vice president: That is correct.

B.A.: So what do you suggest we do? Shall we just retain the same products, prices and cost structures as those of last year, register another substantial loss, gradually destroy the share capital of this company and perhaps be forced to liquidate it?'

All: (Deep silence. Most participants uncomfortably looking down, adjusting their ties, obviously unhappy, but without any clue as to what actions might be considered.)

Comments

This was a proud old family company with a very strong company culture. It had been run in an authoritarian way. Few had ever questioned the wisdom of the founding father, or the judgement of his son. The culture and the value system were certainly not adapted to the rapidly changing market and competitive conditions of today.

To make this group of 'maintenance managers' (instead of 'change managers') embrace a modern top management viewpoint, B.A. ran regular strategic planning meetings with the full group, during a nine-month period. Simultaneously, Arpi International conducted detailed profitability studies for over 100 specific product/market segments, assisted by a computer simulation model, providing overview and transparency, not earlier available. Each product/market segment contained ten different 'profit contribution levels'. (This technique is fully explained in Chapter 8, where some numerical findings from this particular turnaround case are also shown.) As a result, the participants could now, for the first time, clearly see and fully understand how the original gross margin associated with a given segment was step-by-step eroded by different kinds of costs and what, if anything, remained.

Apart from showing the present cost and revenue structure, the same computer-assisted model was later used to simulate the likely profit impact of contemplated changes as to pricing, product mix, customer target mix, order structure and so on.

7.3.3 The individual assignment

Allocating individual assignments is often an excellent way to gather facts, opinions and ideas, and to activate key players. It is also an excellent way to evaluate the capacity of each individual. (Is he/she a 'mover and a shaker'? Does he/she run fast with the ball, or is he/she full of inertia? Is he/she only really creative when it comes to finding excuses for not delivering what was expected on time?)

If two individuals are given the same assignments, each should normally be informed about this 'parallel' arrangement and the reason why it has been chosen. Each individual should be asked *not* to cooperate with the other person on this particular assignment, since possible variations in the answers received are of interest to the CEO, who can himself easily consolidate the answers later on. Expressed differently, the turnaround manager does not want to be presented with watered-down compromises at an early stage.

7.3.4 The group assignment

Group assignments are important since they tend to encourage cross-functional cooperation and cross-functional thinking. However, they are also an excellent way to create consensus as to the true nature of a major problem and its best solution as well as to elucidate certain opportunities which should not be missed. A cross-functional group might be asked to start working immediately for at least two hours the day it was set up. This arrangement has certain advantages. For instance, the turnaround manager can rapidly make sure the assignment is correctly understood and that work on finding a solution has started without unnecessary delay.

If the group does *not* start working right away, a functional manager might easily slip back into his own department and perhaps even start 'digging defensive trenches' together with his staff. Therefore, you might call a 2½-hour meeting. Later, you only use half an hour yourself to introduce the task and then leave the group to use the subsequent two hours to attack the task.

By allocating a rather short time period for the completion of a group assignment, the individuals concerned are forced to cooperate and also to concentrate on what is really essential. A classical SWOT[1] analysis might be initiated this way (even though experience shows that some formal 'editing' of the group's findings by an outside expert is usually needed before the findings are sufficiently specific and operational, that is, action-orientated).

Another useful trick is to run a SWOT analysis during an evening session and to *provide structured feedback* the following morning, and then ask the group to list what *concrete action* they feel should be considered for each listed Strength, Weakness, Opportunity, and Threat. For each SWOT item that was listed the previous evening, the group can be asked to produce two concrete actions worth considering. In this hands-on fashion, 'paralysis through analysis' can be avoided and action-orientation regained. (Many participants have usually participated in SWOT analyses before, but most have never been asked *what to do* about the listed items.)

7.3.5 Individuals not working for the troubled company

To check how the company is perceived by the market and by other interested parties (including stakeholders), and in what respect the company must improve in order to survive and flourish, the turnaround manager might choose to *interview outside sources* (major suppliers, key distributors, key clients, former employees, and so on).

In the Tarkett case, detailed in Part II, the turnaround manager spontaneously emphasized the importance of such sources. It is a powerful way to catch early on critical 'warning signals' not yet picked up by 'intra-company sensors'. Such signals from the outside world might be particularly important to a proud old (and perhaps also old-fashioned) company where many employees have preferred 'to remember old victories' rather than observe ongoing competitive moves and rapid changes in the marketplace.

The turnaround manager might choose to carry out some of the external interviews personally while asking an industrial market research company (or a senior management consultant) to carry out the remaining interviews in order to arrive at a more well-rounded and more representative picture.

7.3.6 Learning from 'management by walking around'

Instead of waiting for (and then being forced to rely on) cleverly 'filtered' in-house reports, a turnaround manager should make it a habit early on to walk around, ask questions, and insist on quick answers. (Long memos arriving later have an unfortunate tendency to ingeniously cover up many unpleasant realities, rather than putting an urgently needed spotlight on them.)

One particular type of MBWA has already been illustrated in section 7.2.4, namely 'the pursuit of one cross-functional trail'. More MBWA examples will be provided in the Tarkett case study (section 14.10).

Just walking around, meeting employees, asking relevant questions, and standing firm will provide the turnaround manager with an excellent 'feel' for the company, its value system, the loyalty and professional quality of its co-workers and perhaps also highlight certain weaknesses with regard to existing products, tools, administrative procedures and policies. (In an international turnaround situation language capabilities are an obvious prerequisite.)

7.4 External information sources: an introduction

The use of in-house sources has already been illustrated with reference to accounting reports, business plans, one-on-one interviews, group discussions, MBWA, including the pursuit of a specific 'horizontal trail' (for example tracking the processing of an order up to and including the time when the payment has been received).

The prudent turnaround manager is well-advised to remain sceptical of most in-house sources, particularly uncorroborated pieces of information and accompanying subjective explanations and impressions. He must make sure that the information provided is reasonably *correct*, and does not only reflect wishful thinking. He therefore needs to *cross-check* information.

Verification against other in-house sources is sometimes possible, for example by using:

- other in-house reports
- individual conversations during MBWA
- individual assignments given to 'young and hungry lions'
- parallel assignments given to several individuals
- in-depth studies of a particular issue on company premises
- group discussions (preferably with several groups, seeing a given problem from different angles).

Doubtful in-house statements can often be checked against *external data sources*. The validating source may be:

- an external industry expert
- a published industry report

- a tailor-made *ad hoc* study, commissioned by the turnaround manager
- findings from on-line database search (later described).

'External' individuals even closer to the company – like stake-holders – might also be worth consulting, including:

- key suppliers
- major distributors and/or
- key clients and selected salesmen
- perhaps even bad-debt cases, but also
- executives who left the troubled company at their own initiative during the previous two years.

It is far from unusual to find a troubled company having both a weak internal reporting system and also basing most of its endeavours on quite flimsy external data as to markets, competition and technological developments.

In such cases, the turnaround manager must add pertinent and reliable external information from whatever sources are available to him. The rest of this chapter delineates different kinds of *external information sources*.

As has been shown in Figure 7.1, these sources include:

- market research and competitive studies, tailor-made for the distressed company's needs
- published industry-wide studies
- computer-assisted database search, and information available on CD-ROM, and nowadays even
- 'hybrid media'.

For instance, the same conglomerate (say Time-Warner) might publish one or more periodicals, own several TV stations, and be up on the World Wide Web with its own sites. These might include not only stored TV clips of previously distributed programming contents, but also on-line, real-life TV programmes sent via 'streaming techniques'. All this can be supplemented by offering a manager verbatim printouts of the text used in previous business-related TV programmes, for example an interview with a key competitor or client. In 1999, the quite rapid merger of TV sets, computers, CD-players and so on hastens this development, to the point that whatever is written here is likely to be outdated in a few years.

7.4.1 Tailor-made market research and competitive studies

Market research and *competitive studies* are today regarded as standard managerial tools. In a turnaround situation they can prove to be particularly useful. They help pinpoint both problems and opportunities and assist the necessary reorientation. They address fundamental questions, such as the following:

What are the *size and growth rates* of our different product/markets segments? What is our company's *share* in each segment? What are the corresponding shares for our key competitors? *Why* have some of them been more successful than we have? Is it because of *superior products, pricing, service, distribution* or something else? Which promising product lines, markets and market segments should we stay in and which ones should we preferably *leave*? What is the best strategy for our chosen future core business? What is the best 'exit strategy' from product/market segments we should get out of?

7.4.2 Purchase of existing market research studies

Before ordering any expensive tailor-made *new* study, the turnaround manager should obviously consider the possibility of buying an *already existing* research report. The acquisition of such a report might save both time and money. It is a way of rapidly acquiring valuable information, and without having to pay the total cost for the study. (Corresponding costs are shared with many other organizations).

Several professional organizations regularly undertake industry-wide studies and then make them available on a commercial basis. A turnaround manager new to the industry, might have some difficulty finding them. However, surprisingly many market research directories (even 'directories on directories') do exist. These constitute a logical starting point when trying to track down published research reports. In the process one often also stumbles upon pertinent branch organizations (for example in foreign countries), previously neglected publications, and even the names of relevant industry experts.

A few examples of pertinent English language directories (gleaned from Bo Arpi's bookshelves) are listed below:

1. Lorna M. Daniells: *Business Information Sources*, University of California Press, 1993.

   Lorna M. Daniells is a former reference librarian at the Baker Library of Harvard Business School. This is the third edition of her classical reference work. She covers not only books and directories but also sources available on-line or on CD-ROM. One of the strong points of *Business Information Sources* is that it compares a particular source to related books. It also contains lists of trade journals and statistical sources for *specific industries*.

2. Hiram C. Barksdale and Jac. L. Goldstucker: *'Marketing Information', A Professional Reference Guide*, Georgia State University, 1993.

   Barksdale and Goldstucker are marketing professors of Georgia State University. Their standard work was originally published in 1982, and they are assisted by a panel of marketing experts from 21 corporations and universities. The first part of the book is a guide to associations and organizations. The second part contains a bibliography of more than 4,000 books, periodicals, software and audiovisual materials organized into 27 subject areas, including 'Health Care Marketing', 'Nonprofit Marketing', and 'Services Marketing'.

3. Arlington Management Publications: *Marketsearch* (previously called *International Directory of Published Market Research*), paperback version June 1986.

Several directories on marketing information sources only focus on a particular geographic area such as Europe or Latin America. Among such titles can be mentioned the following:

1. Gale Research: *European Directory of Marketing Information Sources*, 1991.
2. *European Compendium of Marketing Information*, paperback version July 1992.
3. Christine Shaw: *A–Z of UK Marketing Information Sources*, paperback version November 1984.
4. Schaffer: *Business Information Sources of Latin America and the Caribbean*, 1982.

The examples given above represent only the tip of the iceberg. The fact that some of the reference books are several years old does not usually prevent them from listing still valid publishers, addresses, names of annual publications, highlighting a particular industry and so on.

The general availability of modems and Internet 'service providers', plus the corresponding search tools (like Netscape or Internet Explorer) make it possible for a turnaround manager (or one of his assistants) to initiate a *database search for supplementary information*. Each such search effort might include the simultaneous scanning of a large number of websites and/or commercial 'pay-as-you-go' databases.

If this scanning covers commercially available ('professional') databases, as discussed in Chapter 7, section 7.4.3, he will normally be able to identify rapidly not only pertinent *information* as such (for example on markets, competitors and technologies), but also relevant *sources* (publications and individuals) which regularly cover a particular industry of interest to him.

Professional information providers often put parts of their research findings on the Internet free of charge in order to inform the user of the existence of their full report, its contents and price. Normally, the full report can be ordered on-line, which once again saves valuable time.

For an industry with great economic importance and with a broad common appeal, like the automotive industry, an impressive number of sources is always available. For the automotive industry, just a few are mentioned below:

1. The *Financial Times* regularly covers the automotive industry in great depth. Corresponding information is made available on-line, for example via the *Financial Times'* own 'FT Profile' service, but it can also be reached via other information service providers, who differ depending on country.

2. Another source regularly and deeply involved in international automotive studies is the *Economist Intelligence Unit* (EIU), also located in the UK.

3. Certain universities, not the least in the US and in Europe, are deeply and continuously devoted to the automotive industry, and can as a result provide pertinent automotive information. (This is for instance true for the *University of Michigan*.)

Specialist publications – many also available on-line – exist even for the automotive components' industry, which has rapidly become global. *Automotive Components Analyst* is a newsletter and management report published monthly by the *Financial Times*. *World Automotive Components* is an annual report published by The Economist Intelligence Unit (EIU).

For industries of more restricted interest, the existence of ready-made research reports is less likely. Contacting, for example, Frost & Sullivan in London might be useful. This organization publishes a large number of market research studies (although not necessarily carried out by their own organization). In an annual directory, Frost & Sullivan list all the studies made available by themselves.

There are even 'Directories on Directories', for example *World Data Base of Business Information Sources*, covering 35,000 organisations, publications, and databases as well as thousands of pertinent websites. This title is described later in this chapter. Today, such information is increasingly provided either on CD-ROM, or found via on-line database search. Therefore, the number of *printed reference directories* is tending to decrease rapidly. They are too cumbersome to search through compared to a CD, and their contents too outdated compared to on-line information.

The impressive amount of data which can be generated through 'clear text search' of up to 3,000 databases at a time may be rather intimidating. Previously, when computer scanning was more expensive, the analyst operated with much more exactly targeted 'search profiles'. These included specific product classification codes, geographic area, type of 'happening' (for example investments in new factories), and were for cost reasons limited to only a few information sources.

Today, it is still advisable for a turnaround manager (or his assistant, outside consultant and so on) to identify early on the relevant standard industry classification code (SIC code) for the particular industry and product range in question. This code might help save time and money by limiting the search to what is of most direct interest in a given turnaround situation. (The turnaround manager certainly has more important and urgent tasks than sifting through large amounts of largely irrelevant information produced as a result of a too broadly or vaguely defined search profile.)

Periodicals	Periodicity	Issues per year
Automotive Components Analyst – newsletter	monthly	12
FT Automotive Quarterly Review	quarterly	4
World Automotive Manufacturing	monthly	12
Automotive Emerging Markets	monthly	12
Motorsport Business	monthly	12
World Commercial Vehicle	monthly	12
Automotive Environment Analyst	monthly	12

Publications

Transplants and Beyond: The internationalisation of the world's automotive manufacturers

EMU and the Automotive Components Industry: Strategic opportunities and threats in new Europe

The World's Car Manufacturers: A financial and operating review (2nd edn)

Supplier Partnering: Making partnerships work

Intelligent Transport Systems: A review of technologies, markets and prospects

The Car Aftermarket in Europe (2nd edn)

Safe at Any Speed?: The growth prospects for safety-related automotive technology

Automotive Materials: The challenges of globalisation and technological change

The Japanese Automotive Industry in Europe

Automotive Logistics: Optimising supply chain efficiently

Korea's Automotive Future

The Global Truck Industry: Markets, players and future prospects

The Unique Vehicle Market of India

The Automotive Sector of the Middle East: A market for the new millennium

Mercoaur's Automotive Industry

The Chinese Automotive Industry: Pitfalls and opportunities to 2010

The Mexican Automotive Industry: Prospects and opportunities for the future

The Polish Automotive Industry

The Directory of Polish Automotive Component Manufacturers

The Czech and Slovak Automotive Industries

The Hungarian Automotive Industry

The Global Emissions Report: Commercial opportunities from emissions regulations

Electric Vehicles: Prospects for battery, fuel cell and hybrid powered vehicles

World Class Vehicle Environment Performance: Strategies for success

The Global Automotive Components Annual Report 1999 Edition: *A strategic review of markets, players and product*
Who Owns Who in Global Automotive Components 1999: *The world's 100 top players and subsidiaries analysed*

Figure 7.1   Examples of automotive reports and monthly newsletters published by just one source, *Financial Times*

A turnaround manager seldom has the time or the inclination to undertake the database search himself. He should still make sure that this important tool is not forgotten, but effectively used. (Whether he uses external search experts or a fully qualified employee found on the company's premises is irrelevant here.)

Several books exist on how to use on-line resources for business purposes. One respected book is *On-line Resources for Business: Getting the Information your Business Needs to Stay Competitive*, by Alfred Glossbrenner and John Rosenberg (John Wiley & Sons, paperback version September 1995). Part III of this book contains pertinent advice on how *to hire and use a third party to perform custom-designed marketing research* and other business research. A book with a similar theme published around the same time is *Directory of Directories on the Internet: A Guide to Information Sources*, by Gregory B. Newby, paperback, January 1994, Information Today Inc.

Today, directories tend to be more specific, and available on several media, or on a combination of media. (For instance, the buyer of a CD-ROM gets 12 months' free updates via the Internet). A few examples of more recent directories are:

1. *Directory of Financial Sites on the Internet*, Release 1, with CD-ROM, paperback, Pitman Publishing, 1997.

2. *The Worldwide Directory of Market Research Reports, Studies and Surveys 1998*, paperback, Cambridge Scientific Abstracts, 1998.

3. *World Database of Business Information Sources* (published by Euromonitor plc, London, and Euromonitor International, Chicago, on an annual basis) lists no less than 35,000 different information sources on a CD-ROM. However, this database is also available 'live' on the Internet. It covers other databases and publications (from annual reports and market reports to trade associations, statistical publications and syndicated surveys). Related titles are:

    ■ *World Directory of Business Information Websites*
    ■ *World Directory of Non-Official Statistical Sources*
    ■ *World Directory of Marketing Information Sources*
    ■ *World Directory of Business Information Libraries.*

The organization behind these reports, that is, Euromonitor, is certainly not alone when it comes to similar endeavours. However, it

Report titles that match your query: (2 matches)

Date	Report Title
6/98	THE WORLD MARKET FOR **BEER**
4/96	**BEER**

Euromonitor Report: S2BR
THE WORLD MARKET FOR BEER
Date: Jun-98

Purchase Marked Chapters

CHAPTER TITLES (Click on a chapter title to view a detailed list of records.)

☐ INTRODUCTION $ 20.00

☐ EXECUTIVE SUMMARY $ 420.00

☐ WORLD MARKET OVERVIEW $ 760.00

☐ OPERATING FACTORS $ 320.00

☐ LAGER $ 580.00

☐ ALES AND STOUT $ 360.00

☐ MARKETING STRATEGIES $ 580.00

☐ CORPORATE STRATEGIES $ 520.00

☐ DISTRIBUTION STRATEGIES $ 380.00

☐ MAJOR COMPANY PROFILES $ 2220.00

☐ MINOR COMPANY PROFILES $ 1740.00

☐ FUTURE OUTLOOK $ 500.00

Purchase Marked Chapters

Next Chapter   TOC Chapters   All Details

Figure 7.2   On-line search to identify valid research reports, and buy them on-line (chapter by chapter)

It is also possible to download the findings. (This example starts from a turnaround manager introducing the keyword 'Beer'. As a result, two research reports were found. The contents of the most recent one and the price per chapter is displayed on the computer screen. Database used: Euromonitor.)

is a highly respected source with a clearly international scope and good intuitive 'search engines'. The authors have therefore chosen to show in section 7.4.4 what is currently available from this particular information provider, although on different media.

Should a turnaround expert need a crude set of *world market forecasts*, or numerical estimates of the market shares enjoyed by different companies or brands, he can find such information commercially available today on CD-ROM disks, for example from Euromonitor. Such sources, and how to use them effectively, are discussed later in this chapter.

It is sometimes difficult to choose between buying a book, a CD-ROM, or 'download' information from a website. CD-ROM is quicker to search than the other two media, and the CD-ROM is always available. The Web is updated more often, but might take much longer to search, and not least, to print the relevant findings.

If the turnaround manager (or one of his assistants) would also like to look for *professional books*, 'www.amazon.com' will usually provide all the desired information, even for books out of print. The corresponding computerised search process is broadly described below.

LOOKING FOR A PROFESSIONAL BOOK ON A GIVEN SUBJECT?

On the World Wide Web, one finds www.amazon.com. This organization keeps track of close to five million titles, including most professional books, often even those out of print. A search for books on our subject, 'turnaround management', might follow the steps indicated below.

1. On your computer, go to http:\\www.amazon.com. Specify that you are interested in books, rather than in VHS cassettes or in music on CD.

2. You will find a listing of over 30 subjects, from 'Arts & Music' to 'Young Adult'. Choose 'Business'. The computer will confirm that you are interested in 'Business & Investing'.

3. If you specify (through 'key words') that you are interested in 'turnarounds', the computer might (1999) provide you with nine suggested titles (including how to turnaround a baseball league or a small church). If instead you introduce 'Corporate Restructuring', the computer will provide you with 23 titles.

---

4. If you click on one of the books which seems to be particularly pertinent to what you are looking for, you may enjoy three added benefits. First, you might be able to get an idea about each book's
contents, either through a review displayed on-line or by access to
the book's list of contents. Second, the system might tell you what
other books were usually purchased at the same time by those who
purchased the book you are presently contemplating. Third, the
system might tell you under what specific classification heading these
books can normally be found on the Amazon system, for example
under 'Corporate Restructuring'.

5. In a similar fashion, the analyst might, in less than 15 minutes, identify perhaps 20 potentially relevant books, find out when and by
whom they were published, what the price is and so on.

6. Finally, Amazon provides the opportunity to order directly on-line.
The user can at the same time specify whether the book should be
sent individually as fast as possible, or be sent in one package,
together with other ordered books, somewhat later. After having
provided one of your company's credit card numbers and its expira-
tion date, your order will be confirmed, the estimated shipping time
indicated, as well as the total cost, including transportation charges.

7. The 18 different search categories made available to somebody
interested in business and investing are shown below:

General	Harvard Business School Press
Accounting	Industries & Professions
Audiobooks	International
Biographies & Primers	Investing
Book Bargains	Management & Leadership
Business Life	Marketing & Sales
Careers	Personal Finance
Economics	Reference
Finance	Small Business & Entrepreneurship

7.4.3 Using charge-free Internet information versus more professional databases

An impressive amount of unbiased information about industry trends, major competitors, and the marketplace today resides in external databases. These can be approached on-line from a PC equipped with a modem.

When Dr Arpi started his Brussels-based consulting company more than 20 years ago in 'pre-PC days', his first 'assistant' was not a person, but a portable Texas Instrument 'Silent 700' computer, with an acoustic modem and bubble memory. The very first top management assignment (for the Valmet Group of Finland) was clinched in a hotel room in Stockholm. Eight metres of paper filled with pertinent industry data was silently but impressively produced by the portable computer terminal in front of a rather surprised business area manager, who had never seen anything like it before.

Strangely enough, turnaround managers *still tend to under-utilize external on-line databases*. Why, is somewhat difficult to understand. After all, highly knowledgeable individuals have taken the trouble to write relevant articles, reports, and sometimes even books, about the troubled company's competitors and the industry. Later, library experts have painstakingly read this material, classified it, and put it on a mainframe computer for easy access. Is it then too much to ask that turnaround managers (their assistants, or somebody else within the troubled company) actually *look* for this information and *select and digest* what is relevant, for example from a marketing and competitive viewpoint, or for product evaluation purposes?

As previously mentioned, many executives do not even know the SIC (standard industry classification) code for their own key products. Perhaps they believe that such a 'strange' identification number is only meant for the customs department, while bearing little relevance to their own decision-making problems and information needs?

Such a laid-back attitude by a CEO might be excused if the company he runs already has a superb market research department. Unfortunately, experience shows *that few companies in distress can brag about their outstanding market research departments*.

A search of international databases usually provides four different kinds of information:

1. *Numerical data* about sales, markets, production, investments, and so on, perhaps even accompanied by 3–5 year forecasts, or at least indications of growth trends.

2. Pertinent references to specific *books, articles, research reports* and so on which cover the areas of direct interest, plus a brief description ('abstract') of their main contents. (If such article abstracts are not available, a researcher can – as an alternative search strategy – limit his search to articles where the chosen key word(s) can be found either in the article title or in the first paragraph of each article, thus saving search time and money.)

3. Information about which *trade publications regularly monitor the troubled company's industry* and might therefore be worth subscribing to and/or contacting.

4. The *names of authors* who time and time again seem to *cover a particular industry*, and who are therefore obviously very well-informed. (Example: for the *Financial Times*, the earthmoving equipment industry and corresponding global markets are usually covered by just one or two experts. For executives operating in the said industry, it might be highly worthwhile knowing their names.)

Specialized journalists are often pleased to hear from their readers (particularly if the journalists have reason to believe that you might also be an interesting future source for information gathering or verification). Half a day's discussion with a specialized journalist who has a long, deep and completely unbiased involvement with your particular industry, might be *much more useful than just spending another day on the troubled company's premises, listening to guesstimates, revitalized myths and defensive theories*. Outside sources can reveal dangerous misconceptions and antiquated frames of reference which are ready for the scrap heap.

Information freely available on the Internet is primarily provided by the source itself. The source therefore 'controls' what is said about itself. Obviously, it is rather unlikely that a company will publish information which is negative with regard to the company, its behaviour, products, prices, and so on.

When mentioning on-line databases, many tend to think only about information that is freely available on the Internet, since this has been discussed by the general media to saturation point during the 1990s. Unfortunately, many managers seem to have forgotten that other more well-balanced (that is, more neutral, varied and 'professional') databases exist that offer substantial advantages. This calls for an explanation.

An alternative to charge-free information available on the Internet is *professional, commercial databases*. Their contents are usually fed, classified and controlled by a professional organization. (It might be a university library, a branch organization, a specialized magazine like *Business Week*, or a daily business paper, like the *Financial Times*). Such information is not preselected to benefit a particular company.

However, since the source can seldom make this information available free of charge (like a website owner does), the information user usually has to pay for getting access to information contained in professional databases. However, fees are negligible in relation to the corresponding importance of the success of the turnaround assignment. To scan professional databases via a PC does not take long, and it does not cost much. In a turnaround situation such database search can provide invaluable information. Turnaround managers should regard professional databases as one of several important sources during the execution of their turnaround assignments.

Professional databases have at least two obvious advantages:

1. They have much *richer* and more *varied* contents than websites. They often also carry a 'historic backlog', which might go back five to eight years (in contrast to charge-free Internet information, which normally only covers the last 12 months).

2. Information contained in professional databases also includes material *unreservedly critical* of a particular company, its products, strategies, pricing, market behaviour and so on. Also, such articles often contain *comparisons with competing companies* in the same industry and industry trends.

To recap: professional databases provide the following five types of information:

1. Identification of pertinent sources, including books, articles, research reports and so on, which cover the troubled company's own industry (or its client industries), including the relevant product range, distribution network, market structure and so on. Such information is normally of substantial interest to a newly arrived turn-around manager, particularly if he comes from another industry.

2. Quantitative data illuminating the size of sales, markets, production volumes, and investments, often broken down into geographic areas, main product classes and so on, and often accompanied by industry forecasts.

3. Information about individual companies, their problems and successes, their relative strength (for example as reflected in market share), and (often critical) viewpoints on their choice of global strategy, and on recent changes in their strategies. Such articles might even have been broadened to cover the dynamics of a whole industry, including its key players.

4. The names of authors who regularly cover certain industries and product ranges and who therefore are of interest as potential information sources, quite apart from what they have published.

5. Computer links to products (reports and so on) which can be purchased from the same source or affiliated sources.

Data freely available on the Internet are certainly still of some interest. Such information primarily shows how a particular company (for example a competitor) likes to 'position' itself. This includes what kind of features, capabilities, and strategic moves they like to emphasize. A successful company might also choose to present their latest financial data free of charge on the Internet, culled from their official financial report, albeit normally accompanied by some 'explanations' and 'interpretations' originating in their PR department.

When in doubt, financial information freely available on the Internet should *be supplemented by the full financial reports* (for example from Dun & Bradstreet, a company also available on an on-line basis). The use of professional databases will always 'add more meat', and sometimes also correct the rather skewed perspective arrived at by studying only Internet sites or official company reports.

7.4.4 Market and competitive information available on CD-ROM

A relatively new medium for carrying information about industries, markets and products is *the CD-ROM disk*. Technically, a CD-ROM can be regarded as falling somewhere between external reports and database search. The storage capacity of a CD-ROM far exceeds any normal research report. Convenient search tools stored on the CD itself make it possible to select rapidly only the relevant parts of all information available.

CD-ROM diskettes represent a rapidly expanding media type, and it is difficult to give an overview of this highly dynamic field. A few examples are given below.

If a turnaround expert needs a first set of world market forecasts, has a computer with a CD-ROM drive, and is prepared to part with approximately 2,000 dollars, the following CD-ROM might be of interest: Gale Research, *World Marketing Forecasts 1997*. (Windows version, published in October 1997, and most likely annually thereafter.)

A second example from another respected source is *World Consumer Markets 1997/98* from Euromonitor plc, 60–61 Britton Street, London EC1M 5NA, UK. The same company provides many other CD-ROM-based business products, including:

■ *The World Database of Business Information Sources* on CD-ROM 1999
■ *The World Database of Consumer Brands and Their Owners* on CD-ROM 1999
■ *World Marketing Data and Statistics 1999* on CD-ROM
■ *World Marketing Forecasts 1997* on CD-ROM.

The *World Consumer Markets* CD^2 contains information on approximately 20 different consumer industries or 'product classes', and perhaps 330 individual consumer products. Back data for 1992–97 are presented for 49 countries. The user is provided with the option to present the material he has selected in graphic form through facilities provided on the CD-ROM itself.[3]

A few more CD-ROMs, used for somewhat different purposes, might be worth mentioning:

- CDs listing all companies in a particular country, sorted by industry classification codes, regions and so on. This provides an easy *overview of competitors* and/or *key clients*. Today, most national telephone companies sell such disks or provide them free of charge.

The national German phone company calls its product *Gelbe Seiten für Deutschland*, and markets it through Deutsche Telecom Medien GmbH, abbreviated 'DeTeMedien'. Their Belgian counterpart, BELGACOM, distributes their Belgian Guide on CD-ROM originally under the name 'Business CD, release 1.0', 1998. Similar arrangements can today be found in most European markets, and with quite good 'search engines' provided on the CD-disk itself. The CD can therefore be used in many different ways, for example to count the number and geographic distribution of companies in a particular industry or trade, and without ever having to leave the desk.

- *Financial information* for all share-based companies above a certain size, usually accompanied by financial comparisons with the previous few years. For all German *Aktiengesellschaft* such a CD product can be purchased from CD-ROM Verlag & Vertrieb, Frankfurt.

- *World Marketing Data and Statistics 1999* covers macroeconomic trends in 209 countries, spanning a 20-year time period. (Example of data provided: annual tourism expenditure in Portugal, number of passenger cars in use in South Korea, or housing conditions in Japan.)

- *World Marketing Forecasts 1998* contains macroeconomic forecasts related to demographics, country economies, consumer expenditure on a dozen product categories, the use of credit cards, advertising expenditure, food consumption, and so on. However, retail distribution patterns are also well covered.

The two last mentioned reports are from the previously mentioned Euromonitor company. They also produce a CD-ROM containing a 'World Data Base of Consumer Brands and Their Owners'. For example, if you are involved in the turnaround of a company producing premium beer and you are interested in all premium beer brands sold in the US, this CD-ROM would rapidly provide the turn-

STRUCTURE OF INFORMATION SEARCH ON EUROMONITOR'S CD-ROM *WORLD CONSUMER MARKETS*

1. Choose among 15–20 *product classes*. (Those for 1997 are listed below.)

2. Choose a *product* within a given product class, as exemplified for the product class 'cosmetics and toiletries' below. (In total there are 330 individual consumer products.)

3. Choose among 5 *world regions* or choose the world as a whole.

4. Select one country (or several *countries*) within the region (49 countries are covered).

5. Decide if you are primarily interested in monetary *values*, in *volumes*, or in both.

6. Ask the system to produce a *spreadsheet* displaying the requested data.

7. Use the *graphic* facilities (available on the CD-ROM) to produce, for example, bar charts, highlighting what interests you, *and/or* 'cut and paste' them into other Windows-based applications.

8. Recent 'data modelling features' now make it possible to turn all values into dollars, to express them as value per capita, to calculate the average annual growth rates, and so on.

Listing of 15 broad product classes:

Automotives, clothing & footwear, consumer electronics, cosmetics & toiletries, disposable paper products, domestic electrical appliances, drinks, food, home furnishings, household cleaning products, housewares, leisure goods, OTC health care, personal goods, tobacco.

Listing of 13 'products' within the product class 'consumer & toiletries':

Baby care products, bath & shower, colour cosmetics, deodorants, hair care, men's shaving products, oral hygiene, perfumes & fragrances, shaving products, skin care, skin care products, sun care, sun care products.

around manager with a list of all the brands owned by companies based in the US, with detailed profiles of these companies.

The speed of CD-ROM readers is today (1999) over 30 times faster than they were when introduced. Prices both for the CD drives and for the duplication of CD disks are rapidly falling, which will boost their practical use. Simultaneously, the storage capacity increases while the search engines are becoming much more sophisticated.

All these factors combined encourage the further growth of CDs as carriers of market and competitive information. In connection with a turnaround, the acquisition of just a few carefully selected CDs might rapidly and substantially assist in getting quite a good picture of an industry or trade and corresponding trends.

7.5   Other data-gathering sources and techniques

During a turnaround of a petrochemical industry (and most other processing industries) 'manpower headcount' is seldom a major concern. In an insurance company (and many other service-orientated industries) it is.

When turning around a 'people-intensive' company, the turnaround manager has to ask himself: 'How much of our total workforce – and of their totally available working time – is absorbed by:

■ different product lines?
■ different customer classes or market segments?
■ different key tasks?'

If he sees an office with, for example, 120 individuals diligently working away, the three questions listed above might assume substantial importance. In such a situation, a *suitable form of time studies* might come in handy, since the results can highlight the time demands (and thus the costs) generated by different customer classes, product or service categories and even by different kinds of task.

To establish the actual use of available time in an office environment, it is often not even necessary to use 'continuous' time studies, or even to use an external observer. (The latter might not only disturb the working pattern he is supposed to study, but also might be resented as a 'spy'.)

In a turnaround situation, where people are motivated to find obvious weaknesses and implement badly needed changes, a *self-administered frequency study* might be enough. Such a study can be arranged along the lines described below.

Each participating individual is equipped with a *reporting form*, preferably small enough to be kept in a shirt pocket. A small apparatus (with a timer and a gong) is introduced in the office. At randomized points in time, 16–20 times a day, it generates a non-aggressive sound, like a small gong or a modern doorbell. When the sound of the gong is heard, each participant quickly makes three pencil marks, all in the same column of his form, and then reverts to the previous activity.

One mark indicates the *type of activity* he is engaged in. A second mark shows the type of physical *product or service* that his work is related to. A third and final mark indicates the *customer class* served, if any in particular. An example of the front of a self-administered study form (once successfully used by Arpi International among sales people and office workers in an insurance company) is shown in Figure 7.3, to illustrate the basic principle.

Correctly planned, introduced and monitored, this kind of time study can rapidly provide a surprising amount of valid information. A numerical example might illustrate this: assume that 120 individuals on average make 18 markings per day throughout a five-day working week. In only one week this generates a unique database comprised of more than 10,000 observations. Further, each such observation provides information not only about the task performed, but about customer class served and product class affected.

Provided that (a) the working week chosen for the study is *representative* of a longer time period, and (b) that the observation moments have been *randomly* chosen (in the statistical sense, and aided by the apparatus earlier described), these 10,000 observations taken together will (only ten days after the study commenced) provide the turnaround manager with a correct and representative picture of how much of the available working time is consumed by:

■ different tasks
■ different customer classes
■ different types of products and/or services.

> Thereafter, the *time demands* originating from different customer classes, product classes and tasks can be expressed in *monetary units,* since the cost of each personnel category is known within the company.
>
> These costs can then be compared to the *revenues generated* by the same customer categories and product/service categories.

In a turnaround situation this kind of information usually provides a *strong impetus for change.* The participants in the study spontaneously tend to get interested in the result of the study. Particularly if rapid and continuous feedback of findings (for example each morning) is given, it prepares the ground for a broad discussion of:

■ tasks which should be *eliminated* or performed in a cheaper fashion
■ products or services which are *not correctly priced*
■ whether to *drop or serve differently* those customer classes that at present require an inordinate amount of time, without generating corresponding revenue and a positive profit contribution
■ sales bonus programmes which do not correctly reflect the size of underlying sales efforts
■ products or services which should be *cost reduced* or dropped altogether, since the revenue generated does not match corresponding costs.

Assume that one week's self-administered frequency studies have produced over 10,000 recorded observations, and that all of these are stored on a computer. A more penetrating computer-based analysis, described below, can now rapidly be made and presented for a discussion of suitable measures. Such a supplementary analysis – which more closely links tasks with products and customer classes – should highlight:

■ what kind of *time-consuming tasks* are associated with the handling of a particular, unprofitable customer class
■ how the time required to generate $1,000 in sales is *very different from one kind of product/service to another*
■ how the 'task profile'(that is, working pattern) differs between different customer classes and product categories

■ differences in working patterns between different personnel categories.

Admittedly, like all techniques, self-administered frequency studies are associated with potential pitfalls.[4] This is particularly true:

■ if the reporting forms used are *too complex* or otherwise not suitable for what should be observed and reported by the employee

■ if the overall *purpose of the study* is misunderstood or psychologically not accepted

■ if the *personal integrity* of each individual is not protected, for example if he believes that his individual form is going to be critically scrutinized by his boss (rather than be pooled together with forms from at least four other individuals before any results are presented to his superior).

The next chapter contains a description of even more advanced data gathering and computer simulation techniques, making it possible to pinpoint the exact 'capacity demands' made on the troubled company, not only in the area of office workers, but throughout all company functions and how they relate to each and every product/market segment served.

Such advanced techniques are *not* part of the average turnaround manager's toolbox. However, when correctly used, they have proved to be *extremely powerful tools* both from *an analytical and an educational viewpoint*. Thus, they provide an excellent factual basis for tough decisions.

Front side of 2-sided checking form (approximate time of observation, more exactly indicated by the gong)

Presently ongoing task or occupation

	7.15	7.45	8.15	8.45	9.15	9.45	10.15	10.45	11.15	11.45	12.15	12.45	13.15
Selling													
Follow-up of client contacts													
Claims handling													
Damage limitation													
Planning and organizing													
Other office work													
Travel time													
Waiting time & interruptions													
Meal breaks													
Remaining working time													

Ongoing work can broadly be assigned to these insurance types

	7.15	7.45	8.15	8.45	9.15	9.45	10.15	10.45	11.15	11.45	12.15	12.45	13.15
Motor vehicles													
Private persons													
Major producers													
Small producing companies													
Other companies													
Home insurance													
Freight insurance													
Not possible to assign to product categories													

	13.45	14.15	14.45	15.15	15.45	16.15	16.45	17.15	17.45	18.15	18.45	19.15	19.45	20.15	20.45	21.15	21.45	22.15	22.45	23.15	23.45
Selling																					
Follow-up of client contacts																					
Claims handling																					
Damage limitation																					
Planning and organizing																					
Other office work																					
Travel time																					
Waiting time & interruptions																					
Meal breaks																					
Remaining working time																					

	13.45	14.15	14.45	15.15	15.45	16.15	16.45	17.15	17.45	18.15	18.45	19.15	19.45	20.15	20.45	21.15	21.45	22.15	22.45	23.15	23.45
Motor vehicles																					
Private persons																					
Major producers																					
Small producing companies																					
Other companies																					
Home insurance																					
Freight insurance																					
Not possible to assign to product categories																					

Name . . . . Date . . . .

Figure 7.3   Form for self-administered frequency study in an insurance company

Notes

1. SWOT = Strong points, Weak points, Opportunities and Threats.
2. In 1998 this CD received first prize in the competition arranged by DPA (Directory Publishers Association)
3. A listing of Euromonitor's CD titles and their contents can be found on their website: www.euromonitor.com
4. The self-administered frequency study technique, its strengths and weaknesses, pitfalls and so on was originally described in great detail in a book called *Planning and Control through Marketing Research*, by Bo Arpi, published by Hutchinson, London 1970.

8 'Penetrating the fog': activity-based costing (ABC) in three turnaround situations

8.1 'Capacity demands' put on the company

In many turnaround situations, it is obvious from the outset which products, customer classes, and so on are unprofitable. In other situations (say a warehouse operation handling thousands of different articles), sharper analytical tools might be needed to pinpoint the true profitability situation, for example for each product/market segment.

This chapter demonstrates a technique – *activity-based costing*, (ABC) – which might help turnaround managers in complex, fragmented or blurred situations. First, the ABC concept is defined. Then, the knowledge gained and the impact on subsequent turnaround decisions are illustrated by three real-life cases, representing very different industries. These cases cover a major metal wholesale operator, a globally operating marine satellite communication provider, and a car manufacturer supplying the aftersales market for parts and accessories. One of the two authors, Dr Arpi, was heavily involved in all of these cases.

The conceptual starting point for the ABC analyses is simply that a company exists to serve certain client needs, which place a burden on the company in the form of 'capacity demands'. To be of value to its shareholders, the company must also serve these client needs so cost-effectively that it produces an acceptable profit. *Which* needs to serve are normally specified in the company's Business Mission Statement.

In a turnaround situation, it is *particularly important to understand how and to what extent different kinds of company resources (manpower, space, capital and so on) are being consumed by the different product/market segments served.*

In this chapter we will therefore focus on the 'capacity demands' put on the company by:

- different product/market segments served
- different customer classes (including customers of different size)
- different geographical markets served.

Technically, capacity demand considerations can be broken down into three groups:

1. What is the capacity demand when the company is being run on a 'business as usual' basis, that is, with the present loading levels, organization, methods, techniques, customer service levels and so on?

2. What reduction in capacity demand would there be if certain product/market segments were abolished, served less intensively, or were handed over to others, for example cooperating but quite independent distributors?

3. How fast and to what extent will a reduction in capacity demand result in a decrease in corresponding costs, and to what extent will a reduction in demand primarily result in (more) underutilized manpower and facilities?

8.2 A definition of activity-based costing

Below is a definition of activity-based costing which covers *both* the frame of reference developed by Professor Ulf af Trolle as early as around 1955 (and very successfully used throughout Scandinavia) *and* the much more recent ABC 'consulting fad' of the 1990s.

ACTIVITY-BASED COSTING (ABC)

Instead of allocating chunks of common costs to different cost carriers via simplistic allocation keys, activity-based costing starts with the company's *available resources* and shows how these are actually being 'consumed' by different kinds of *activity* and the 'capacity demands' these activities put on the organization. Such capacity demands might originally be

---

expressed as time demands, space demands, or demand for capital. Later, all these kinds of demand are expressed in *monetary units*.

To clearly show causes and effects, *cost formulas* can be created which contain the most important 'cost drivers'. The formulas show the relative weight attached to each pertinent cost driver, and the way these influence the capacity demands put, for example, on a department or function.

If the size of the cost drivers is known for each product/market segment, then so are the costs to serve a particular segment. Thus, the *net profit* generated by each segment is also known. Several intermediary 'profit contribution levels' might also be defined. For instance, 'profit contribution level 1' might show what remains of the gross profit generated by the segment in question after all the segment-related marketing and sales costs have been deducted.

8.3 A more complex analytical model accommodating many product/market segments and multiple profit contribution levels

Figure 8.1 represents a first attempt to highlight the *capacity demand concept*, as developed and used in this chapter. In Figure 8.2, this model is further developed. The comments below relate to both models. Later, their practical use and usefulness in turnaround situations will be discussed.

In the middle of Figure 8.1 is a 'black box' representing the troubled company and all its resources. To the left have been indicated different customer classes, national markets and product/market segments currently served by the company. The arrows to the left of the 'black box' represent the capacity demands placed on the company, its resources and functions. Such capacity demands can be of many different kinds (for example demands on time, space, equipment and capital) and manifest themselves in many different company functions (from sales and order processing to shipping and invoicing, and, later on, guarantee matters).

'Black box'

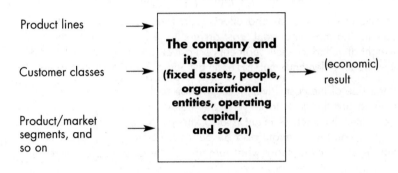

Product lines

Customer classes

Product/market
segments, and
so on

The company and
its resources
(fixed assets, people,
organizational
entities, operating
capital,
and so on)

(economic)
result

Note: This simplistic model will be further developed later in this chapter.

**Figure 8.1   Capacity demands made on the
troubled company: the basic concept**

To the right of the rectangle in Figure 8.1 is an outbound arrow. This represents the combined economic result of serving all the existing product/market segments and so on, through the present organizational structure, with currently available equipment, methods and so on.

In a turnaround situation the combined economic result derived from all product/market segments served will normally be *negative*. This means that the cost for the resources utilized to serve the present product/market segments *exceeds* the revenues generated by the same activities. The capacity demands are simply too great (or the revenue generated too small) to produce an acceptable profit.

By definition, the conceptual model in Figure 8.1 is an oversimplification of a much more complex reality.

To arrive at a more useful tool in a turnaround situation, the previous model must obviously be refined, particularly in the following aspects:

■ The 'black box' in Figure 8.1 must be further developed so that it explicitly deals with each important company function. Only in this way can the 'capacity demands' placed on each of these functions be correctly analysed.

■ The optimal way to identify product/market segments must be determined so that subsequent profitability findings can facilitate the drawing of correct conclusions and thus speed up subsequent corrective management actions.

■ One needs to identify the major 'cost drivers' and, through cost equations, show how these influence the capacity demands put on the company. This means that one must observe and approximately measure to what extent different types of internal company resources are being occupied or 'absorbed' when the company is serving (perhaps up to 100) different product/market segments.

■ As a result, quantitative formulas can be developed which show the approximate relationship between different product/market segments on the one hand and resulting 'segment-specific' costs, revenues and profit contributions on the other. (These calculations usually call for a computer-assisted approach.)

■ Finally, capacity demand formulas have to be turned into monetary values (instead of just reflecting time, space and capital demands and so on).

Figure 8.2 represents a development of the previous conceptual model. At the bottom of the figure is an illustration of how costs (of different origins and sizes) are generated in each company function (F1 ... F10) by two different cost carriers here representing two different product/market segments. Real-life examples of numerical cost formulas used in a turnaround case are found in Figure 8.3.

The cost formulas found in Figure 8.3 (although we have not shown the correct values here) were used during the turnaround of a major metal wholesale and warehouse operation, discussed later.

The cost formulas provided in Figure 8.3 relate only to:

■ the sales function
■ the delivery trucks, including their drivers
■ the material handling equipment used in the stocking area.

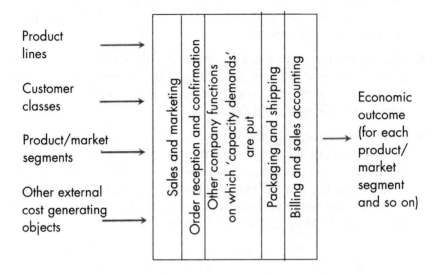

Q1: what costs are generated in each function when a particular product/market segment is *served* by the company?

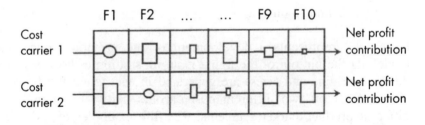

Q2: how much of the original gross margin in a given product/market segment remains when all the costs for the 'capacity demands' generated have been deducted?

Figure 8.2   The troubled company (its different functions and the costs generated within each function)

Costs in the sales function

The number of order sheets × DM31.37 + the number of 'order lines'*) × DM12.61 + the number of small clients × DM109 + the number of medium-sized clients × DM218 + number of major clients × DM436.

(a) *Costs for trucks with drivers when operating within the company's own terminal:*

Number of delivery routes × 15.45 minutes × DM1.69/minute + number of visits to different 'loading stations' × DM8.1 to DM16.1 (depending on which of five loading stations is used) + the number of loaded order lines × DM2.6 to DM7.5 (with the lowest value representing smaller stainless steel articles and the higher value representing heavy steel products such as cold-rolled steel rods).

(b) *Costs for delivery trucks with drivers when working in the field:*

Number of routes × DM21.3 + number of delivery locations × DM52.4.

(c) *Costs for utilized fixed handling equipment (cranes, and so on):*

Number of order lines × DM9.1 to DM18.2 (the exact figure depending on what type of product was loaded, with the highest value typical for construction material).

Note: These formulas were constructed in such a way that they could be used to highlight not only the capacity demands in the present, highly troublesome situation, but also the likely impact of changes in sales volumes, product mix sold, customer classes served, and so on.

An example of a resulting cost and 'profit contribution' table, measured at ten different 'contribution levels', is shown in Table 8.1.

* *Terminological note:* The term 'order line' here means one item (that is, one 'line') on an order sheet.

Figure 8.3   Example of cost formulas used during an actual turnaround of a metal wholesale operation to establish net profits (or net losses) for each product/market segment served

Similar cost formulas (reflecting demands on time, space and capital) were constructed for other company functions, such as personnel permanently engaged in the stocking area, interest on tied-up capital (differentiated for different kinds of product), costs for the physical premises occupied, for centralized data processing and common administrative overheads.

When the gross margin generated by each product/market segment is 'bombarded' step-by-step by one type of cost at a time, it is quite easy for a manager to see how and through what kinds of cost the original gross margin in each market segment is eroded. An example is given in Table 8.1.

The remainder of this chapter is not primarily devoted to how one can define such cost formulas or how to calculate the profitability outcome. Rather, the main emphasis is on the *practical use* of such techniques in three different turnaround cases, not discussed elsewhere in this book.

Table 8.1 shows the findings for one particular product/market segment. First, the gross margin generated by this particular segment is shown, then what remains of the gross margin after deducting all the marketing and selling costs related to this particular segment. The remaining amount is called 'profit contribution level 1' or 'CL_1'. (Within the troubled wholesale operation, the term 'marketing contribution' was preferred to CL_1.)

As other kinds of cost are gradually introduced, other kinds of contribution level (called CL_2 to CL_{10}) can be calculated. As a result, it is now possible for the turnaround manager to see clearly how the original gross margin for a particular product/market segment has been eroded – or 'absorbed' – step-by-step by different kinds of cost until a net loss is actually reported at 'contribution level 10'.

Since computers were used for this study, the same profitability findings could be presented:

■ not only in absolute monetary amounts for each segment, but also

■ as the net profit (or net loss) per 'order line' shipped to each segment, or

■ as the net profit (or net loss) generated per kilo of product shipped to the same segment.

Table 8.1 Example of computer output showing how the original gross profit in a particular product/market is 'wiped out' step-by-step by different kinds of cost

Note: Behind each cost item below there is a cost formula in operation similar to the ones displayed in Figure 8.3

	Activity-based costs of specified types	Remaining part of the original gross profit	Corresponding values if the costs for under-utilized capacity are also taken into account
Gross profit		GP = 75097	75097
Sales force cost	10840	$CL_1 = 64257$	59797
Stocking area empl. costs	13893	$CL_2 = 50364$	41797
Truck + driver (when in-house)	2582	$CL_3 = 47782$	38350
Truck + driver in the field	1434	$CL_4 = 46348$	30950
Interest on stock	19008	$CL_5 = 27340$	9855
Interest on receivables	5000	$CL_6 = 22340$	4855
Data processing costs	12600	$CL_7 = 9740$	−7745
Fixed handling equipment	3000	$CL_8 = 6740$	−12245
Physical premises	34800	$CL_9 = -28060$	−61945
Administration overheads	15000	$CL_{10} = -43060*$	−76945

* The last line shows the difference between revenues and costs (for different kinds of 'capacity demand').

For logistic deliberations, weight was obviously a key concern. For administrative issues, the number of order lines was of greater interest.

Finally, the top management team had the option to either disregard the costs for underutilized capacity, or (let the computer) 'force them out' according to one of three available allocation keys. (For some company functions and analytical purposes, the *number of order lines* seemed to be a better allocation key than *weight* or *value*. However, thanks to the extensive use of the 'cost driver' and 'activity-based costing' concepts, most costs had already been correctly allocated, exclusively based on the real capacity demands generated by different cost carriers, such as different product groups or customer classes.

8.4 Advantages of 'bottom up' costing instead of 'top down' costing

What has been illustrated differs radically from the often used, rather crude 'cost allocation' schemes. It might therefore be worth repeating the key characteristics of the techniques used:

1. The ABC costing technique just discussed can be said to represent 'synthetic costing' or 'bottom up costing', rather than 'top down' (that is, classical allocation) costing. In the former case, *activities* are seen as generating *capacity demands* which are later all expressed in monetary terms. In the latter case, chunks of money are allocated to different cost carriers based on simplistic 'allocation keys' having little to do with the actual activities in different company functions.

2. If the primary cost drivers and their relative weight and impact are correctly identified (usually through field studies) for each important company function, a set of *mathematical formulas* can be constructed. These reflect how different activity types and activity levels generate quantifiable 'capacity demands' which can all be translated into costs. (For a more complete description of common ABC terminology, the reader is referred to section 8.2. Examples of real-life cost formulas have been shown in Figure 8.3.)

3. Cost formulas might be used not only to calculate the present profit contribution (or losses) associated with each product/market segment, but also (within certain limits) to describe the likely

consequences of contemplated changes (for example in activity levels, product mix, customer mix, service levels and so on). This is *extremely important in a turnaround situation.*

Expressed differently, ABC techniques can be used for descriptive as well as predictive purposes. In a turnaround situation, the former aspect is closely related to the question '*Where and why are we losing money?*' The predictive aspect is more closely related to the question '*What shall we do, and with what kind of expected impact, for example on profits?*'

In a turnaround situation, the computer-assisted costing technique discussed here can be used not only:

■ to identify *product/market segments* which are 'bleeders'

■ to identify what *activities* have primarily contributed to create the net loss in a given product/market segment

■ To determine how much *prices* would have to be increased in order to cover all costs in one or more particular product/market segments

but also:

■ to highlight the likely cost and revenue impact of a contemplated new *customer structure*

■ to show the cost impact of an improved *order structure*

■ to identify the decrease in capacity demands in case certain products, customer classes or national markets were *abolished* (or served in a less intensive fashion)

■ to determine what the resulting impact would be on net profits if prices for a given product line were *increased,* for example by 20 per cent, while this move was predicted to generate a drop in corresponding sales, for example by 15 per cent. (Thus, the computer-aided model can, within reason, be used for certain types of 'price sensitivity simulations'.)

As shown by the above examples, the numerical model (primarily expressed through a set of cost equations) can be used in three significant fashions:

- to *describe* today's situation
- to *forecast* the impact of changes in the company's environment
- to *simulate* the likely impact of contemplated management actions.

Although ABC techniques generate detailed and specific cost and profitability data highly useful in most turnaround situations, they can seldom meet the criteria for truly scientific studies. However, in a turnaround situation 'the proof of the pudding is in the eating'.

Expressed differently: if the techniques used lead to *clarity, overview, correct decisions*, and tend to speed up the actions taken and encourage managers to think harder and more clearly, then they have been good enough for their intended purpose.

The following examples from a major metal warehouse operator, a global marine communication company and an automotive producer will demonstrate the practical usefulness better than any general description.

8.5 ABC techniques applied to a national warehouse operator for metal products

'Synthetic costing', as previously described, was extensively used by Arpi International even before the arrival of the PC, and long before activity-based costing became something of a consulting fad at the beginning of the 1990s. (Before the PC, an 'unintelligent' computer terminal was simply linked up to a suitable mainframe computer.) The cost formulas provided in Figure 8.3 (although not showing the exact values) were used during a turnaround exercise of *a major steel and metal wholesale group operating with five substantial regional warehouses.*

Illustration of the 'cost driver logic' used: it is not unusual for a company's own truck fleet and drivers to spend up to 30 per cent of their time in the company's own terminals, waiting for paperwork to come through, goods to be loaded and so on. Obviously, this time has little to do with the distance to different clients to be served or their size. Expressed differently, it is not a *distance-dependent* or *customer-dependent* activity, but to a great extent a *product-dependent* activity. For instance, the loading of cold-rolled steel bars might require both loading assistance and special loading equipment, like overhead cranes. If these overhead cranes are a scarce resource, several trucks might have to wait in an in-house truck queue before they can load the cold-rolled steel. All these factors combined might mean that the loading of one 'order line' of cold-rolled steel will take *ten times as much* in-house terminal time as loading one order line for a simpler to handle product type. Such real-life facts are seldom reflected in the 'cost allocation keys' decided on by a central financial department. Activity-based costing (ABC) is much more likely to take such realities into account, since it is based on observation and *measurements* of underlying activities.

In the particular turnaround situation at hand, corresponding cost formulas were never intended to meet high scientific standards. However, they did their intended job by:

■ helping to highlight which product/market segments still produced a net profit contribution and which were loss makers. ('*Where* do we bleed?')
■ clearly illustrating how the original gross margin generated by each product/market segment was eroded step-by-step by different kinds of costs. ('*Why* do we bleed?').

In this particular turnaround case, the activity-based costing exercise obviously filled a descriptive purpose, and provided a decision base. However, it also fulfilled an important *educational* purpose. As described more fully in Chapter 6, the latter aspect might be almost as important as the former one. In the particular turnaround case here referred to, the troubled company had largely been run by *unimaginative 'maintenance managers' who felt that nothing should, nor indeed could, be changed*. Thus, inertia was the rule, not the exception.

So, how did their mindset change? Presented with ABC-based highly detailed cost and profitability figures (reflecting 10 contribution levels in more than 100 product/market segments), these managers gradually started discussing:

- badly needed *price increases*
- customer classes which were obviously given *too much service*
- the introduction of a *fixed service fee* for small orders below a certain amount
- the possibility of carrying out many activities in quite a different and much cheaper fashion.

Step by step, these discussions (encouraged by the new CEO and his external senior consultant) helped to turn the *warehouse-bound 'mainte-nance managers'* into *enthusiastic 'change managers'*. And in a turn-around situation, change managers are indeed the kind most needed, while status quo defending managers are considerable obstacles.

The first major price increases (around 30 per cent) were *not* intro-duced for the company's steel products (regarded as quite central to the company's core business). Instead, more peripheral products were chosen. When few negative client reactions were observed to these price increases, and competition also started increasing their prices (considerably more than raw material prices might have justified), substantial price increases were also gradually introduced *for main-stream products.*

While the industry association was particularly proud of 'having avoided ruthless price competition' for cold-rolled steel among its members, *the ABC analyses undertaken showed that the whole industry was probably losing about $15 'per order line', each time a cold-rolled product was shipped.* Obviously, the industry association was not inclined to believe this. The senior consultant finally received permission from his client to show the client's actual cost study figures to the industry association. After having considered their own in-house use of overhead cranes for cold-rolled steel, corresponding truck queues, the need for loading assistance for the drivers and so on, the association members finally – although reluctant and somewhat embarrassed – accepted the ABC findings as characteristic of the whole industry.

Price fixing throughout the industry was obviously illegal. However, simply providing the members with an accurate fact base as to true costs was enough to make all major suppliers gradually increase their prices for cold-rolled steel products until they also completely covered all related handling and distribution costs.

Table 8.2   ABC computer output for two different product/market segments in the same industry

	Activity-based cost of indicated types		Remaining part of the original gross profit	
Note: Behind each cost item below there operates a cost formula similar to the ones shown in Figure 8.3				
	(Segment 1)	**(Segment 2)**	**(Segment 1)**	**(Segment 2)**
Gross profit	–	–	634	359
Sales force cost	138	45	496	314
Stocking area employee costs	65	34	431	280
Truck + driver (when in-house)	29	13	402	267
Truck + driver in the field	50	18	352	249
Interest on stock	168	41	184	208
Interest on receivables	18	12	166	196
Data processing costs	105	34	61	162
Fixed handling equipment	27	17	34	145
Physical premises	149	84	–115	61
Administration overhead	89	32	–204	+29

Conclusion: Although Segment 1 starts with a gross profit almost twice that for Segment 2, the latter at least covers its ABC-based costs. In contrast, Segment 1 produces 'capacity demands' larger than its gross profit. Thus, it is a 'bleeder'.

In Table 8.2 there is a comparison between the cost and profit contribution structure for two product/market segments. One represents cold-rolled steel.

8.6   Using ABC analysis to evaluate managerial performance in a turnaround

After having pinpointed the profitability of different product/market segments (and thereby automatically also the profitability of whole product lines and whole customer classes), one question remained:

how can a turnaround manager use such ABC-derived data to also *evaluate the performance of managers carrying a P&L responsibility?* Staying with the metal wholesale turnaround case, this question is addressed below.

Many different 'contribution levels' had been calculated and presented for each product/market segment. Which of these contribution levels was then best suited for evaluating present managerial performance and establishing new managerial objectives?

After considerable discussions in the management team, one basic principal was agreed on: a manager shall only be made *responsible for the costs* (and resulting profit contribution levels) over which he *has almost full control*. In this particular turnaround case, it was therefore decided that all managers with P&L responsibility should primarily be evaluated at 'contribution level No. 8'. In practical terms, this meant that they were made responsible for all kinds of cost, with the exception of:

1. costs for the (much too big and expensive) central computing department and
2. costs for the (much too big and expensive) warehouse buildings, which they were forced to use by a board decision.

If a manager is not allowed to decide to move away from a luxurious, centrally located, but too expensive building, or if the manager is not allowed to 'escape' the costs generated by a central EDP department (partly over-dimensioned for pure PR purposes), then his performance is more correctly measured before such costs, that is, at an earlier profit contribution level, for example CL_8.

What happened to the central EDP department and to the equally impressive, but too expensive, warehouse buildings which were not the responsibility of either product line managers or regional managers?

1. The EDP department (containing 54 individuals) was rapidly sold off ('outsourced') to a computer services company providing services to many clients. The troubled company then purchased only the necessary services from the same outfit for approximately 50 per cent of their earlier costs. (The speed of the services provided actually improved.)

2. After the conclusion of a very successful turnaround which took less than two years, the whole metal wholesale operation was sold off to its major supplier of metal product who wanted to 'integrate forward'. However, the warehouse buildings remained in the hands of the old owner. He rightfully regarded the buildings as a highly interesting investment in a longer-term perspective. However, the rent paid to him by the new warehouse operator was adjusted downward to a more competitive level.

In parallel with the turnaround activities already described above, the troubled wholesale operation was subjected to substantial downsizing efforts. However, rather than 'cutting 15 per cent over the board', it was now possible to:

- *selectively cut in certain areas*, while
- *expanding in other, more profitable areas*, and
- simply increasing prices in others.

In connection with the downsizing, the computer-assisted ABC simulations were very useful in pinpointing both where and how deep to cut. The existence of an objective and substantial fact-base also helped convince the employees of the absolute necessity of the downsizing measures taken.

8.7 Application of ABC-based simulation techniques to the automotive aftermarket

The ABC techniques previously described can successfully be applied to a wide range of different industries. They can even be applied to several layers of the vertical distribution chain within the same industry, as shown below with a case from the automotive aftermarket.

The selling of vehicle spare parts and accessories to the aftersales market is usually a highly profitable business. Even so, certain product/market segments might be 'bleeders', or at least produce an unsatisfactory net profit contribution.

Senior consultants from Arpi International were once asked by a vehicle manufacturer to investigate their cost structures and the resulting profitability situation for a large number of vehicle product/aftersales market segments. A distinction was first made between slow moving parts, fast moving parts and TBA-articles, that is, tyres, batteries and accessories. Simultaneously, no less than eleven different distribution channels were identified and analysed. These included mail order and selling over-the-counter to end-users as well as active selling by the car dealer's representative when he systematically visited independent garages and service stations.

Through techniques similar to those used in the metal wholesale case discussed earlier in this chapter, the gross margin as well as the profit contribution at different contribution levels were highlighted for a large number of vehicle product/aftersales market segments.

In this particular case, the cost investigations (and subsequent computer simulations) were extended until they covered no fewer than three different layers of the vertical distribution chain, namely:

1. the vehicle producer's 'industrial system level'
2. the vehicle producer's 'wholesale level'
3. the 'dealership level'.

The resulting multi-layer ABC study provided several important advantages not previously discussed:

1. What might be described as 'finally being able to piece together a puzzle whose many elements were previously dispersed throughout the organization'.

2. Allowing 'the objective measurement of the existing organizational tension between different layers of the same distribution chain'.

The first aspect is discussed in section 8.7.1. below, the second in section 8.7.2.

8.7.1 Piecing together an excessively fragmented cost/revenue puzzle

In a huge multinational operation, with many highly specialized departments, and with profit responsibilities held by many different individuals, it is often extremely difficult for any executive to have a complete and, at the same time, reasonably detailed picture of what is really going on. (In an automotive aftermarket operation, one manager might only be responsible for car radio sales. Another manager might be responsible for several product lines, including car radios, but only for those sales which go via mail order.)

If computer-assisted ABC studies are used, they encourage the *combination of information from many sources*, where each source is only representative of one particular piece of the total puzzle. In the automotive aftermarket case, such pieces of information were combined in one all-embracing model. This created an overview which earlier had not existed anywhere within the multinational organization. The model also encouraged and facilitated consistency cross-checks, not earlier possible.

As a result of this approach, each individual information provider could soon after be given an objective feedback which went far beyond his normal, limited area of responsibility and extended his professional horizon. The complete findings (presented in the form of spreadsheets) represented a clear-cut framework for decision-making, not only as to commercial transactions and prices, but also as to organizational structures.

8.7.2 Pinpointing and measuring 'organizational tension' within a distribution chain

The automotive aftermarket study discussed here contained no fewer than *three* different levels of the *same vertical distribution system*. It therefore became possible to identify the *origins of existing organizational tensions* and even to measure their size. These tensions turned out to be rooted in economic, that is, quite rational, but previously badly understood reasons, since nobody within this three-layer structure had earlier been in possession of detailed profitability data for more than one distribution level at a time. The practical consequences are discussed below.

Can a car manufacturer increase his sales of spare parts to the existing fleet of his own brand of vehicles? He obviously cannot increase the number of accidents in order to increase the corresponding sale of spare parts. Also, he can only to a very limited extent influence how far the vehicles will be driven each year, and thereby the number of spare parts sold due to normal wear and tear.

Against this background, the vehicle manufacturer discussed in this case had chosen to put considerable pressure on his network of authorized dealers to sell factory guaranteed original spare parts aggressively to *independent* garages operating in the same geographic region who repaired his brand of vehicles. However, such pressures by the vehicle manufacturer had repeatedly been met with considerable resistance by the car dealers. The activity-based aftersales studies referred to here finally highlighted the reasons why, and in quite clear-cut numerical terms. The bar graph in Figure 8.4 helps to explain the situation.

A car dealer incurs incremental costs in selling spare parts to independent garages located in his own geographic area. First, he must invest in a truck, second in a travelling salesperson, and third often in mobile stock to be kept in the truck. Thus, the dealer is *forced to carry extra costs* of a type and size that he is not otherwise used to when selling spare parts used for a vehicle being repaired in his own garage.

These ABC studies showed that the active selling of spare parts to independent garages (by visiting them) was the *least profitable activity* in which a car dealer could engage. However, seen from the car manufacturer's viewpoint, the same kind of sales activity produced not only an additional sales volume, but also a highly attractive net profit at the manufacturer's level (see the third bar group in Figure 8.4).

The ABC findings clearly demonstrated that an impressive part of the gross margin was rapidly absorbed by the added costs for such 'active field selling' to independent garages. And that was not the end. On top of this, the independent garage would insist on – and actually receive – a substantial *discount* (from the list price) before buying any parts at all. This discounting, plus the incremental selling costs earlier mentioned, *more than wiped out the profit margin* for the 'authorized car dealer', as shown by Figure 8.4.

The tension between the vehicle manufacturer on the one hand and his dealer network on the other could now be highlighted in *objective, quantitative terms* (as reflected in the third pair of vertical bars). By showing the conflicting economic realities experienced by the two

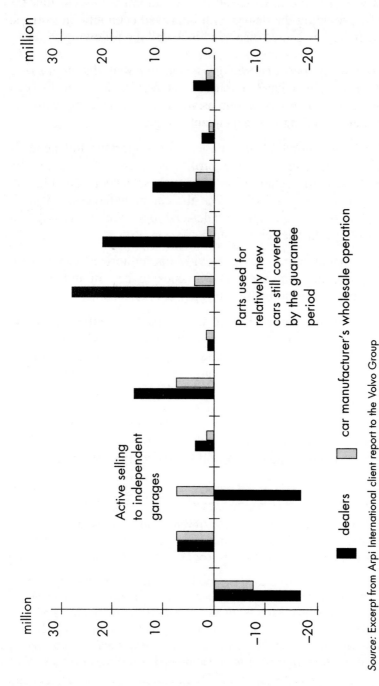

Figure 8.4 Car parts – comparison of resulting net profits for the car manufacturer and for his authorized dealers, when activity-based costs have been allocated to 11 different distribution channels

Source: Excerpt from Arpi International client report to the Volvo Group

parties, it was possible to focus on how to diminish this tension, for example by providing the dealer with improved economic incentives. Tension-reducing measures discussed included the following:

- *Differentiating between the gross margin* that the authorized dealer received for parts purchased for repairs done on his own premises, and the gross margin associated with the more cumbersome 'active' selling to independent garages.

- Establishing common sales targets for important independent dealers, then pooling all the profits generated throughout the vertical distribution chain from sales to these accounts, and finally *splitting resulting profits* between the car manufacturer's wholesale operation and his appointed dealership network according to a pre-agreed profit-sharing formula.

- The car manufacturer could provide his authorized dealer with extra economic compensation for sales to certain independent garages pre-agreed to be high-priority client accounts.

- The car manufacturer himself would pay the expected 'trade discount' directly to the 'high-priority retail clients', say, once a month. This would make the sales activity more profitable for the car dealer, and reassure the manufacturer that he was not paying extra incentives for parts actually used by the dealer.

The final solution is not revealed here. However, the ABC-based profit information for both layers of the distribution chain created an objective and sound foundation for all subsequent negotiations.

The multi-layer, computer-assisted cost/revenue model allowed a simulation of the likely profit impact (for different layers of the vertical distribution chain) of any contemplated new cooperation programme.

Discussing a quantitative, common fact-base tends to change the relationship between the different parties in a given distribution chain. Instead of trying to make money at each other's expense, a 'cooperative partnership' might be established which serves *both* parties well. (Some strategists would say that the participants then move from a 'zero sum' game to a 'win-win' game.) In some turnaround situations, new types of cooperation over existing organizational borders can be quite crucial to the success of the turnaround efforts. Thus, ABC studies might add a new angle to the 'stakeholder' discussions in earlier chapters.

8.8   Complete computer simulation of a troubled company, all its distribution channels and product lines

As shown in Chapter 7, time utilization studies of certain company functions can provide a broad range of information immediately relevant and useful for many important turnaround decisions. However, ABC-based computer simulations might cover *all* company functions and activity areas. Thus, they are usually even more useful.

In a typical turnaround situation, activity-based costing does not focus so much on the production function, which is already quite well researched, but on what really occupies the company's sales force – its order reception departments, stocking and shipping departments, the spare parts department, the invoicing department, and so on.

When the *time, space* and *capital* spent on different products, markets, and customer classes have been analysed and translated into costs, a realistic picture of the real profitability of different product/market segments has also been created. Myths and unrealistic hopes for the future can therefore be abandoned and the perspectives broadened. This is a valuable contribution to any turnaround process. While almost unheard of only ten years ago, ABC-based computer simulation techniques are today increasingly used by some turnaround experts for two key reasons:

1.   Computer simulation of the troubled company, its distribution channels, product lines and key customer classes provides an excellent and coherent overview of all aspects of the troubled company's entire business, including all product/market segments and their real profitability. ('Bleeders' or 'feeders'?) Subsequent strategic and tactical decisions are easier to make. Decisions taken will also be more easily understood by the individuals affected. ABC analyses have prepared the ground.

2. Clever computer simulation of a troubled company is also one of the *most powerful educational tools for in-house use*. The reason is obvious. Such education does not start with high-flown theories, but with down-to-earth facts about the troubled company itself. The participants can rapidly learn by analysing the company's present situation, and can apply different 'magnification levels' for different analytical purposes. Carried to its logical conclusion, such computer-assisted training can include *simulation of the likely consequences of contemplated management actions* (commonly known as 'what if' simulations). As shown, such tools have repeatedly and successfully been used to help overcome 'departmental myopia' and to force near-sighted managers to apply a broader cross-functional perspective for the good of the company as a whole.

Employees in many troubled companies tend to cling to long-held attitudes, traditions and behavioural patterns, even when these are sub-optimal, unprofitable and/or unnecessary. In such 'sleep-walking' cases, hard-nosed, factual computer simulations of revenues and different types of costs in each product/market segment might serve as eye-openers. Managers are automatically encouraged to review and evaluate critically and constructively their present operating mode, including procedures, values, behaviour, and so on.

The latter is of great importance, since people in troubled companies often tend to become transaction-orientated rather than management-orientated. Myopia has replaced overview. Working *hard* has become more important than working with the *important issues*, that is, investing time and money primarily in the most important and most profitable product/market segments.

The structure of the simulation model itself guides the actual fact-gathering phase and the later structuring and combination of the information into a coherent whole. The techniques used to *gather* information needed for such simulations are by no means ground-breaking. However, the way in which corresponding information – usually from many different sources – is *combined*, is rather special, and will often provide a new perspective on the company and its activities.

8.9   A marine satellite communication case

Once, four senior consultants from Arpi International were called in to have 'a last look' at a seemingly doomed marine division. The board had already taken the tentative decision to close down the division which produced and marketed systems for marine satellite communication as well as high-frequency (HF) radios for ships. However, a four-week moratorium had been granted to allow confirmation of the wisdom of this decision.

Last-minute activity-based costing studies – along the lines earlier discussed – showed that 80 per cent of all 'capacity demands' placed on the Marine Division were *not* associated with the new satellite communication systems at all, but with many generations of tailor-made HF systems on ships located all over the world. An excerpt from the consultant's presentation to the board is found below.

CONCLUSIONS PRESENTED TO THE BOARD OF A MARINE SATELLITE COMMUNICATIONS DIVISION (BASED ON ACTIVITY-BASED COSTING AND COMPUTER SIMULATION)

'The board of the marine division has recently suggested the closing of its satellite communication activities. One of the reasons given was that a typical satellite communication order contains no fewer than 130 order lines. Therefore, SATCOM orders supposedly generate a diversified and very substantial activity level, assumed to have contributed to the recent severe losses within the marine division.

These assumptions are contradicted by the following facts. The SATCOM activities represent only 16 per cent of all tenders and 11 per cent of all orders received, if spare parts orders are excluded. The latter figure falls to an almost negligible 3.5 per cent of all orders handled when spare parts orders are also included.

Compared to these activity level figures, it is interesting to observe that the SATCOM activities generate no less than 30 per cent of the division's total turnover and 28.5 per cent of its net profits.

Although each SATCOM tender and order contains many "order lines", these are to a large extent *identical* from one tender or order to the next.

Expressed differently, the SATCOM business is largely *standardized*, while the HF-radio business is extremely varied, fragmented and handling-intensive (for example 85 per cent of all activities in the warehouse stocking area are HF-related). Expressed differently, HF radio places exorbitant "capacity demands" on the organization, while the more recently introduced SATCOM business is much more standardized, smoother, and puts fewer demands on the organization.

In the tables in front of you, the gross profit for SATCOM as well as for HF radio are indicated. So are ten different kinds of cost (each representing different kinds of capacity demand). The resulting profit contribution, measured at no less than ten different profit contribution levels is also shown. Our findings imply that the tentative decision to close down the SATCOM operation must be re-evaluated. Instead, the extremely high cost levels for HF radio activities must be studied, and actions taken to reduce them by approximately 30 per cent.'

As a result of the new studies, four key decisions were taken:

1. The jungle of internally developed HF radio systems was replaced by a *smaller number of externally developed HF systems*, purchased at 70 per cent of internal costs for comparable systems.

2. *Spare parts prices for old systems were dramatically increased* to include the very time-consuming system-identification and fault-finding work done by highly knowledgeable experts within the spare parts department. (This department was often contacted 'on-line' by a ship situated on the other side of the globe).

3. *Shipping and billing methods were tightened.* Shipping three different parts ('just in case') and then waiting an average of 152 days before two of the three parts had been returned (when the third could finally be invoiced), was no longer acceptable commercial behaviour.

4. *The satellite communication product line was resurrected.* Helped by the Falklands War (when Her Majesty's ships rapidly needed modern satellite communication equipment, and price was not even *discussed*) the marine division became highly profitable. The following year it proudly received the Scandinavian Airlines Systems' much coveted 'Annual Export Award'.

8.10 Summary of the practical usefulness of ABC-related techniques

In the Chapter 7, the use of a particular kind of time-study technique was illustrated. It could be used to highlight how the total available time of a sales force is in real life allocated with regard to:

■ different tasks
■ different product lines
■ different customer classes.

In this chapter, this kind of analysis has been substantially extended. The ABC analyses shown here cover:

■ many types of 'capacity demand' (other than time demands)

■ many different company functions (other than the sales function, illustrated in Chapter 7)

■ many kinds of 'cost driver' (representing the basic underlying factors which primarily decide the size of the capacity demands generated)

■ and (as in the car aftersales case) several layers of a vertical distribution system.

  The use of such sophisticated (and also more complex) 'cost and profit' simulation techniques requires a process-orientation, reliable measurement techniques and canny computer utilization. The sheer size of the calculation tasks involved can be illustrated by the following example:

■ a product/market matrix often containing *100* different segments
■ *ten* 'cost and profit' contribution levels for each such segment
■ the costing formula (behind each cost contribution level) typically containing *three to five* different cost drivers
■ up to *three* different distribution levels covered by the same simulation exercise.

The above description implies that over 10,000 values will be calculated. This explains why a computer is needed.

8.11 Are ABC analyses worthwhile in a typical turnaround situation?

Although useful, these techniques can hardly be regarded as standard tools in a turnaround situation. However, if and when correctly used, they have proven to be:

■ effective tools to replace existing *myths* by *facts* (since 'cause and effect' relationships are focused via cost drivers and cost formulas)

■ excellent tools to *resolve conflicts* (between different organizational entities and their key representatives)

■ powerful *educational instruments* to increase the knowledge level in the management group, and elsewhere

■ a robust *eye-opener* which reduces confusion, stagnation and inertia and hastens long-overdue *management action*.

Like any other tool, ABC-based 'cost and profit' simulation techniques can be misused. These techniques can never produce better results than the quality of underlying studies and measurements, including the correct identification of the most pertinent cost drivers, and how they affect the capacity demands put on different functions, departments, distribution layers and so on, as previously illustrated.

Given sufficient time (and with all the knowledge provided by hindsight), any university professor can no doubt find weaknesses in the techniques discussed here, including cost formula design and underlying measurement techniques.

However, in real life – and particularly in a pivotal turnaround situation – the quest is not for exactness, but for information which:

■ is at least *better* than earlier available information

■ provides a *sufficiently good basis* for significant decisions which must be taken (usually on an urgent basis).

The best test of ABC-based tools and techniques used in connection with a turnaround is therefore:

■ whether they provide a *basis for sound decision-making* (that is, leading to decisions which one does not have to later regret)

■ whether they tend also to *generate cooperation, interest, understanding and action-orientation*, not only on the part of the top management team, but throughout large sections of the troubled organization.

In a chapter of this nature, it is tempting to start discussing a number of technical concepts, for example fixed costs versus variable costs; separable costs traceable to only one cost carrier versus 'common costs' for several cost carriers; costs which rapidly disappear if an activity is dropped versus costs which tend to remain, even after the revenue creating activity has been abandoned. However, this is *not* a controllers' handbook. Instead, we have assumed here that these distinctions are well known to, and respected by, the turnaround manager, or – if not – that he brings in the necessary expertise.

Assuming that over half of the analysed product/market segments show losses rather than positive net-profit contributions, what kind of management actions are normally considered? In this chapter, we have touched on some of them. They include:

■ stopping activities in certain product/market segments

■ dropping certain product lines or models

■ dropping unprofitable customer classes

■ serving certain customer classes in a less expensive fashion

■ increasing prices for certain unprofitable products and services

■ operating in a simpler and less expensive fashion, while simultaneously reducing associated paperwork

■ changing the facilities, tools and methods currently used, for example in the area of logistics

- starting information, communication and educational programmes throughout the company in order to give employees a clearer picture of the situation in different product/market segments, of the (relatively few) activities from which the company makes a profit, and the (many) current loss-making activities and so on

- making real-life field tests in one or two product/market segments to find out more about the market's response to different kinds of management actions before introducing them on a larger scale.

8.12 Do the time pressures allow ABC studies?

One pertinent question remains unanswered. *Is there really time for sophisticated, computer-aided simulations* (as described in this chapter) *in a grave turnaround situation?* The answer depends on the turnaround situation itself, the turnaround manager's preferences, and the expertise available to him.

The planning, implementation and analysis of a more limited self-administered *time study* (at randomized points in time as described in Chapter 7), does not have to take more than three to four weeks. This time-frame is completely compatible with the time-frame available for most turnaround exercises.

What then about the much more ambitious and complex ABC-based computer simulation techniques described in this chapter, where many information sources, cost carriers, cost types, distribution layers and so on are involved? Two to three months is the minimum time typically needed to gather, process and present the information in a suitable format. However, in an industry with heavy seasonal variations, such a study might have to be repeated a few months later in order to ensure that the findings are indeed 'representative' over time.

In this case, the earlier indicated time-frame of two to three months might have to be extended to perhaps six months before a valid and truly representative fact base exists. On top of this, another three months might pass before all resulting 'educational activities' have been concluded and the results seen, for example in an increased awareness of the troubled company's key problems and an increase in its managers' willingness and readiness to attack these problems in a systematic and effective fashion.

The turnaround manager must himself decide if he needs this kind of sophisticated information base, and if he has sufficient time to wait for its realization. In other words, it is up to him to decide whether he should primarily 'shoot from the hip' (without any previous sophisticated data gathering) or if he can afford to proceed a bit slower, with the obvious advantage of later being able to confront the organization with a comprehensive and objective fact base calling for immediate corrective management action.

> In real life, most turnaround managers will settle for a compromise. Thus, they are likely to attack the most obvious and substantial problems without delay, and simultaneously initiate studies which will only be truly useful later on.

One recently arrived CEO in a troubled company expressed it as follows: 'The big, low-hanging apples I will attack immediately, without any sophisticated tools. To find the smaller fruits, perhaps hidden higher up, I might need a ladder or other suitable tools. That is where I believe a good consultant and his more sophisticated toolbox has a role to play.'

8.13 Living happily without consultants and advanced analytical techniques?

Successful turnaround managers typically have big egos. This is often reflected in their speeches and their book titles. Example: *Mean Business – How I Save Bad Companies and Make Good Companies Great* (Albert J. Dunlap, 1997, published by Simon & Schuster's Fireside Books. Dunlap is also known as 'Chainsaw Al', or 'Rambo in Pinstripes'.) One more example might be justified. The second turnaround of Chrysler Corporation was followed by a book called *The Seven Laws of Business that made Chrysler the World's Hottest Car Company,* by its former CEO Robert A. Lutz (John Wiley & Sons, 1998.)

Such turnaround artists seldom acknowledge that they use both senior consultants and some pretty advanced analytical tools. In reality they use both, but often downplay their own reliance on external market research and external management consultants. Instead, prominent space is usually allocated to their own MBWA.

'Chainsaw Al' in fact devotes a whole chapter to what he calls 'Fire all the consultants'. In it, he first demeans consultants and their use, then discusses his own substantial respect for and close cooperation with C. Don Burnett (a partner of Coopers & Lybrand), characterized by the author as 'one of the few outsiders who can influence my thoughts and decisions'. Dunlap's advice to other turnaround managers is clear-cut: 'Develop a long-term relationship with one multi-faceted consultant, but no more'.

Then follows a lyrical description of the many important functions played by such a hand-picked senior consultant: (He) 'gets me up and running, identifies opportunities, feeds me invaluable information, and then formulates a plan that has been shaped and influenced by me'.... (Such a consultant) 'helps me organize a plan of action, providing an opportunity to jump-start the company'.

Equally important, Dunlap specifies that he does not rely on the senior consultant 'to make my decisions or give me a scapegoat for the corporation's past misdeeds'. He continues by saying that in a turnaround situation the senior consultant 'must work for and report directly to the chairman of the board and/or to the CEO, not a division head'. If something is really going to change, the consultant's recommendations will 'need the driving force of the person at the very top of the organization chart'.

In this book, we have used less provocative chapter titles than 'Chainsaw Al'. However, our opinion about the best use of management consultants in a turnaround situation is pretty similar. One of the two authors, Per Wejke, has repeatedly – and highly successfully – been in the turnaround manager's 'hot seat'. He has then used consultants if and as needed. (Some of the findings from such cooperation with outside experts will be presented in connection with the six case studies in Part II.) In contrast, Bo Arpi has typically been the senior consultant called in to help a recently arrived CEO, expected to turn around a troubled company rapidly. Their combined experience means that the turnaround process and its toolbox have been highlighted from two different and highly relevant vantage points.

Capable senior consultants have a rich and varied toolbox. Only weak consultants try to sell the turnaround manager 'a ready-made cure in search of a disease'. Experienced turnaround consultants should be able to select both relevant and powerful tools which will 'do the job', nothing more nor less.

A turnaround situation is not the ideal time to send in a busload of young MBAs, however bright. In this book, many examples have illustrated when, where and how a senior consultant can be used, what analytical tools he might apply, and the benefits often derived from such a cooperation.

This book is not meant to provide an overview of all these tools. However, in conclusion we recap some earlier-mentioned tools which are closely related to improving:

■ either the troubled company's *perceived customer value*
■ or the troubled company's *cost-effectiveness.*

The truly performance-driven company is one which *excels on both axes*, as shown in Figure 8.5 (see also Figure 8.6). All six in-depth case studies which follow recount how the troubled company's *cost-effectiveness and productivity have been improved.* (The results are shown in thought-provoking 'performance graphs'.)

Most of the cases also illustrate how the *perceived customer value* has been improved. (The Atlas Copco Mining case and the Tarkett case are two good examples. In both cases, cross-border industrial market research and 'value benchmarking' were used.)

A good turnaround manager is capable of not only cutting costs, but also improving perceived customer value. The former activity is of primary importance early on, just to save the company. An improvement in perceived customer value is normally a prerequisite for the company's longer-term health, that is, to make the company grow and thrive, while providing increased shareholder value. (The turnaround of Allgon under Per Wejke is an excellent example of how to radically increase shareholder value to such levels that Allgon was declared 'winner' on the Stockholm Stock Exchange.)

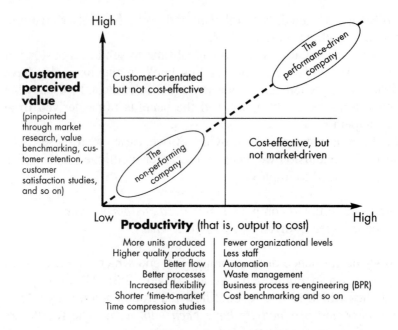

Figure 8.5   The performance-driven company
(Arpi International SA, 1996, *The Performance-driven Eurocompany*)

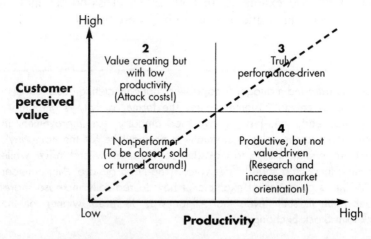

Note: Companies in the first quadrant are typical turnaround candidates (or possibly even closure or divestment candidates). Many companies in the second and third quadrants are also manifest turnaround candidates. Basically, what the turnaround manager tries to do is to change and 'reposition' the troubled company so that it can occupy a proud place in the 'truly performance-driven' quartile.

**Figure 8.6   The performance-driven company
seen from a turnaround perspective**

Part II

'Taking it to the Course': Six Complete Turnaround Cases

Chapter

9	The Allgon Case Study	246
10	The ESAB group restructuring the European welding industry	265
11	Atlas Copco Tools	295
12	Atlas Copco Mining and Construction	313
13	Almex	327
14	The Tarkett Case	335

Chapter 9
The Allgon Case Study
List of Contents

Introduction		**247**
9.1	**The company's development up to 1990**	**248**
9.2	**The troublesome situation in 1991**	**249**
	9.2.1 The Orbitel debacle	249
	9.2.2 The US subsidiary debacle	250
	9.2.3 Friction with the part-owners of a jointly owned German sales company	250
	9.2.4 The 1991 situation: a summary	251
9.3	**Functional analysis of Allgon's problems**	**252**
	9.3.1 An old company faced with a young company's problems	252
	9.3.2 Management and organization	252
	9.3.3 Foreign sales and production companies	253
	9.3.4 Market contacts and market know-how	253
	9.3.5 Product programme evaluation	254
	9.3.6 Administrative procedures and information flow	255
9.4	**Problem awareness within the organization itself**	**255**
	9.4.1 The old president's viewpoint	255
	9.4.2 Attitudes among headquarters' staff	256
	9.4.3 The board's view	256
9.5	**Management change and the first strategic moves**	**257**
	9.5.1 Profile of the new president	257
	9.5.2 Priority 1: cleaning up after the Orbitel disaster	257
	9.5.3 Appointing a new head of the systems division	257
	9.5.4 The new group management team	258
9.6	**Changes in the organizational structure**	**258**
	9.6.1 Clarification of responsibilities and performance evaluation criteria	258
	9.6.2 New reporting relationships for the foreign sales companies	259
	9.6.3 Analysis and paralysis versus decisive actions	259
9.7	**Marketing and customer contacts**	**260**
9.8	**Improving the product programmes of the two divisions**	**261**
9.9	**More rapid decision-making**	**261**
9.10	**Performance diagrams showing this turnaround's impact on sales, profits, and so on**	**262**
Notes		**263**

The Allgon Case Study[1]

Introduction

The Allgon company has been probably the most talked about newcomer on the Stockholm Stock Exchange since the late 1980s. Its spectacular growth and increase in shareholder value justify its place as a case study in this book. From a turnaround management viewpoint, it is particularly interesting to note how the company has constantly redefined its Business Mission in the light of changing markets and technologies. By cleverly anticipating and using such changes to their own advantage, Allgon serves as an example for many other companies in industries characterized by rapid growth and rapid technological change.

Allgon is also an example of the transition from a relatively small company run by an entrepreneur to becoming number two in the world, managed by a professional team focusing on a fast-growing niche. From a position as an almost unknown company, Allgon is today well known and respected. During a five-year period, the market capitalization value of the company grew almost one hundred times and the share price increased by more than thirty times.

In 1980, the family that owned Allgon decided to focus the available resources on products for mobile phone systems, that is, particularly on antennas (mounted on portable phones or on vehicles carrying such phones, or antennas used in connection with stationary 'base stations'), as well as on certain components contained in the base station. Since the antennas can both receive and send signals, corresponding equipment is often known as 'wave propagation' products. This concentration was a risky undertaking since, at that time, it was far from clear that mobile telephone systems would grow at such an incredible rate.

The owner put the company on the right course, while displaying a rather unusual mix of vision and willingness to take calculated risks. Ten years later, when the company was facing certain difficulties, he recruited a successor with substantial experience from international business operations. The cooperation between the two individuals was smooth and productive and contributed to the impressive later achievements.

Allgon's manpower grew from 140 to 700 in five years. High performing executives and technicians were added to the company. The very strong growth of the market in mobile telephone systems no doubt helped Allgon, but the company also knew how to benefit from this industry trend. Sales grew sevenfold in five years and profits rose accordingly, as shown by the performance diagrams included in this case study.

9.1   The company's development up to 1990

Allgon was founded in 1946. It started as a manufacturer of relatively simple *car aerials*, but later went through a number of important changes as to product range and market scope. This can be illustrated by a few examples.

When the market for household TV reception aerials grew, this sparked quite a change in Allgon's market focus. During the 1960s, the company took another important step forward by establishing itself as a supplier of antennas for professional needs, primarily for military applications, but also for civil use. These changes in market and application focus were accompanied by a considerable increase in the company's technical competence.

From approximately 1975 to 1985, Allgon focused on land mobile radio (LMR) and related technologies. When this particular market segment showed signs of being saturated, Allgon investigated other market opportunities. It found one in a market quite different from their earlier application areas, in the market for cellular telephony.

Allgon's Swedish location was a strategic advantage, since the world's first commercial cellular telephony system was NMT, developed by the Nordic countries.

Allgon grew rapidly during the latter part of the 1980s. As shown by the performance graph (Figure 9.1) the company reached a sales level exceeding SEK200 million in 1990. Earnings developed well during 1988 and 1989, and in 1990, they corresponded to about 8 per cent of invoiced value. Then a number of unfavourable events occurred which called for turnaround activities.

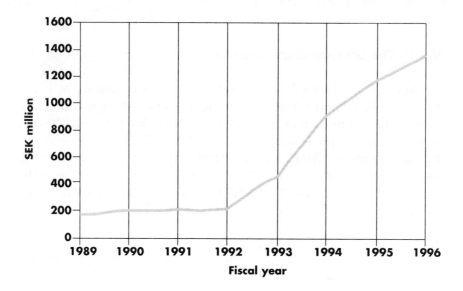

Figure 9.1   Allgon: invoiced sales 1989–96

9.2   The troublesome situation in 1991

9.2.1 The Orbitel debacle

One of Allgon's two divisions, the systems division, had directed most of its development efforts to serve the needs of Orbitel, a British telecommunications company. Many observers believed Orbitel would soon become the leading supplier of base stations for GSM, a well-known pan-European cellular system for portable telephony. As a result, Allgon received orders from Orbitel for base-station components amounting to more than SEK100 million.

However, for a number of reasons, Orbitel's GSM project failed. Ericsson's development of GSM base stations turned out to be ahead of Orbitel's. In 1991, Ericsson bought Orbitel and immediately discontinued the Orbitel base station project.

Allgon's situation now became very serious. The company had already purchased and received inventories corresponding to about SEK35 million, to be able to service the Orbitel contract. (Writing off these inventories would have wiped out approximately half of Allgon's shareholder's equity!).

9.2.2 The US subsidiary debacle

On top of Orbitel's predicament, it became obvious that in the latter half of 1991, Allgon's American subsidiary was also rapidly deteriorating. This company had been acquired only a few years earlier, and it was focused on *land mobile radio systems*. The US company was regarded as an excellent base for a strong activity in vehicle-mounted antennas used for cellular telephony. A prerequisite for this new activity was the systematic transfer of technology from Allgon in Sweden to the US subsidiary. However, due to:

- inadequate US management
- poor cooperation between the American subsidiary and its Swedish parent
- a serious lack of understanding within the US entity that a transfer from land mobile radio to cellular technology was a must

the P&L of the American company deteriorated rapidly. The company showed a considerable loss in 1991.

9.2.3 Friction with the part-owners of a jointly owned German sales company

In Germany, a sales company had been started with a local German partner on a 50/50 ownership basis. This sales company was highly profitable, since the German market (before the arrival of GSM systems) was a technically isolated market with limited competition, allowing for high prices. As a result, the German market actually accounted for almost the entire profit of Allgon.

However, the relations with the German partner were strained. In Allgon's opinion, the German partner seemed to manoeuver in order to assume 100 per cent control over the German sales company.

9.2.4 The 1991 situation: a summary

On the bright side, Allgon had focused on very promising and fast growing markets and developed considerable technological expertise in corresponding areas. However, the company was also faced with a number of extremely serious problems which could endanger the company's whole existence.

The 1991 situation can be summarized as follows:

1. A very real risk existed of losing half the Allgon equity, since already purchased components for the Orbitel project had no real market value.

2. The systems division had no order stock because of the cancelled order and an otherwise very limited customer base. (The systems division had neglected to develop customers other than Orbitel for a long time.) As a result, the marketing competence within the division had deteriorated and clearly become inadequate.

3. Growing losses in the American subsidiary caused by an erroneous product and market focus.

4. Substantial friction existed between the two 50/50 owners of the very important German sales company, which was Allgon's major profit producer.

After more than 15 years as head of Allgon, its managing director – who was also by far the dominant shareholder of the company – decided to retire. The board welcomed this management change since necessary measures could now more easily be implemented by a new managing director (less bound by company tradition or personal commitments). The key mission for the new CEO was to *urgently safeguard the future of Allgon*. This mission is here regarded and described as a 'turnaround case'.

9.3   Functional analysis of Allgon's problems

9.3.1   An old company faced with a young company's problems

Allgon was not a particularly young company in 1991 since it was founded back in 1946. However, Allgon's problems in 1990 and 1991 were typical of a young company displaying rapid growth. With all important strategic decisions taken in the early 1980s, the company had radically switched focus and was faced with the very challenging cellular technology. Thus, for all practical purposes, the problems met were similar to those faced by a much younger company still in its 'rapid growth' phase.

9.3.2   Management and organization

In 1990, about 150 people were employed in the company. Half of them were white-collar employees, half blue-collar workers. Seen from the outside, the company seemed to be quite well organized, with two clearly defined divisions (each being a separate legal entity), and a small head office function.

However, in reality the company did not function according to this organization chart. Delegation 'downwards' did not function. Most issues instead tended to float upwards, to the president's desk. The group president therefore got involved in most matters, big and small. This resulted in an extremely high workload, but also in a very slow decision-making process.

The lack of delegation had two roots. The president was 'helpful and service-orientated'. However, he also had great difficulty telling his key managers that they should make their own decisions within their area of responsibility. His steering principles reflected the fact that Allgon, only a few years earlier, had been quite a small company. This allowed him to personally get involved in all kinds of decision.

The second reason was the fact that the two division managers reporting to the president simply lacked managerial competence. (They had no formal training and limited practical experience as managers. They also lacked many of the personality traits required to lead other people.)

The Allgon organization had simply become too dependent on its president, even for minor issues. The organization was not staffed or run in a fashion that allowed for the handling of a critical situation, characterized by fast technological change, and many serious problems occurring simultaneously.

9.3.3 Foreign sales and production companies

In 1990, Allgon had (fully or partly owned) sales companies in Germany, Great Britain, France, Italy and the US. Production took place in Sweden, the US, and to some extent also in Germany.

There was a lot of friction between the Swedish organization and the two companies in the US and Germany.

From a *sales and marketing* point of view, little or no control was exercised from the Swedish HQ. *Administrative* and *financial* controls were also very weak. So was the technical cooperation. The sales companies were originally only created to sell the products of the Allgon antenna division, for example vehicle-mounted products, a typical and *rather standardized* consumer product. However, the foreign sales companies manipulated and manoeuvred in order to sell the complex products of Allgon's systems division as well. These included components to base stations for mobile telephony which required *much more technical competence* than existed in the foreign sales companies.

While the French company was profitable, and the German company was *very* profitable, the US company reported heavy losses, and the English and Italian companies moderate losses. The lack of good financial control systems for the foreign entities certainly did not help.

9.3.4 Market contacts and market know-how

The success of the *antenna (or mobile communications) division* was not primarily based on in-depth market knowledge, but originally on a very competitive product programme. In light of the fast growing antenna market, there had been an obvious shortage of products, and Allgon was better placed than most competitors to supply the required volumes.

254 of 400 INTERNATIONAL TURNAROUND MANAGEMENT

However, the managers of this division, which also handled vehicle-mounted antennas for mobile communications, *had very few end-user contacts*. This resulted in a severely limited knowledge of real-market needs. When the market finally matured, the marketing and sales competence within Allgon was clearly inadequate. This first became apparent in the US and the UK.

For Allgon's systems division, the situation was even worse. This division had few contacts with its potential customer base, since it had been entirely focused on the Orbitel order. When this customer vanished, it became obvious that the systems division had few customers and few contacts with potential customers. The only remaining volume customer was a US agent, selling Allgon's components for stationary 'base stations' for cellular communication networks. However, the relationship with this customer was also problematic and characterized by distrust. (It did not help that the whole sales staff of Allgon's systems division lacked the competence, as well as the skills and personality necessary to be successful sales people. In fact, all of them were replaced within the first 12 months of this turn-around exercise.)

9.3.5 Product programme evaluation

The antenna division's products

The product programme of the antenna division, also handling all *vehicle-mounted antennas* (used for hand-held GSM phones and other mobile communications units), was perfectly in line with actual market needs. From a group-wide profit viewpoint, it was also this product programme that ensured Allgon's survival. It largely compensated for the division's many shortcomings in marketing skills as well as in the effective control of their rather free-wheeling foreign-sales companies.

The systems division's products

In Allgon's systems division, the situation was quite different. As already stated, Orbitel's failure made not only their product stock obsolete, but also a substantial part of all ongoing R&D efforts, since Orbitel's competitors had all chosen very different technical solutions.

The only systems division product which sold in large quantities was a range of *base station antennas*, which was well received in the US. However, these sales were handled by the US agent, who posed many problems for Allgon.

In summary, Allgon's systems division had a weak product range focused on European needs, and an extremely weak marketing and sales team.

9.3.6 Administrative procedures and information flow

Allgon's administrative function was more like a *registering* function than one which really provided information for the effective *steering and control* of the different units of the Allgon group.

Administrative routines were cumbersome and slow. Monthly and quarterly reports took much too long. This in turn caused corresponding decision-making (and 'corrective management action') to become unacceptably slow. Another consequence was that information available at any point in time was often too outdated or otherwise inadequate. These deficiencies contributed to the difficulties in trying to guide, monitor and control Allgon's foreign sales companies.

9.4 Problem awareness within the organization itself

9.4.1 The old president's viewpoint

Allgon's president and main owner was quite aware of the serious situation. However, he could not personally see any viable way forward. He was of the opinion that it was almost impossible to attract really competent people to Allgon, since the company was small and little known. Furthermore, he assumed that the Swedish-based Ericsson group, which needed many engineers with the same competence, was regarded as a much more attractive company to work for.

Although this opinion was partly correct, the president overlooked the fact that many individuals actually prefer to work in a smaller organization, providing more room for individuality, personal initiatives and independence from excessive bureaucracy. Although the president recognized the *need* for more delegation (and making Allgon function more as laid down in its organization chart), he did not personally know how to bring this change about. He therefore actively welcomed a successor.

9.4.2 Attitudes among headquarters' staff

Generally speaking, there was a very limited understanding among the HQ staff as to the seriousness of the overall situation. Their formal educational level was low. (While Allgon's key field of activity was indeed 'high-tech' in 1991, there *was only a handful of university engineers* working for Allgon at that time.)

On the *commercial side*, the available knowledge and experience was both limited and inadequate. Only a few of the salespersons had a university education, in spite of the fact that many customer contacts required very good technical and commercial skills. Headquarters' staff could not generally grasp the size of the problems facing the company or the underlying reasons, or they preferred to think that these problems were just a result of 'temporary unfortunate circumstances' about which they could do very little.

9.4.3 The board's view

In 1991, the board consisted of two external board members and three internal directors, including the president. All five individuals were substantial shareholders in the company, but also highly entrepreneurial personalities. They tended to have a professional focus on the company and its problems. Their unanimous decision was to recruit a new president from the outside.

9.5 Management change and the first strategic moves

9.5.1 Profile of the new president

Since no suitable candidate could be found within the company, the board took the decision to recruit a new managing director 'from the outside world'. The new managing director was in his mid-fifties, and had thorough experience from several export-orientated multinationals. A senior person with this particular background was supposed to add to the company's credibility, both internally and externally. His previous experience of turnarounds and associated restructuring was also a strongly contributing factor.

9.5.2 Priority 1: cleaning up after the Orbitel disaster

The first task was to deal with the cancelled order from Orbitel. A team from Allgon's systems division repeatedly visited Orbitel to try to make them accept delivery of what they had indeed once ordered. However, it was obvious that Orbitel would have no use for the products ordered and were not inclined to take delivery.

The remaining possibility was to *negotiate reasonable conditions* for the cancellation of the order. This was handled by the new president together with two sales managers who had no earlier involvement in the situation. An important negotiating strategy to arrive at a rapid settlement was to use the considerable embarrassment felt by Orbitel because of the discontinued project. Early on, *Orbitel therefore agreed to pay the full cost price* for all the components that Allgon had bought for the execution of the Orbitel order. As a result, Allgon's own equity was not hurt, and no equipment write-offs had to be made.

9.5.3 Appointing a new head of the systems division

As earlier explained, the systems division completely lacked orders. Furthermore, it had almost no customer (or potential customer) contacts. This represented an extremely serious situation for Allgon.

It was obvious that the person in charge of the systems division lacked the management skills and business know-how to address the situation. Therefore, the new company president decided to replace the old divisional manager by a person who:

1. had thorough knowledge of the cellular telephone industry
2. was very customer-orientated
3. was extremely entrepreneurial.

This person was rapidly identified and employed first as sales manager of the systems division. Later he was given total responsibility for the systems division. Under his management, the division rapidly grew and prospered, helped by a much improved and broadened product range and an extended customer base.

9.5.4 The new group management team

Although functioning fairly well in a short-term perspective, it was apparent that several members of the group management team would have to be replaced later on. Actually, within two years *all* members of the old management team were replaced.

Today, Allgon is a medium-sized company with 750 people and sales in excess of SEK1,500 million. Managerial requirements and skills are both different and more pronounced than when Allgon was just a small, SEK200 million company. The replacement of most members of the old group management team was a prerequisite. (So was a change in existing delegation principles, as described in the next section.)

9.6 Changes in the organizational structure

9.6.1 Clarification of responsibilities and performance evaluation criteria

In order to substantially improve organizational efficiency and shorten the response times, the work in the management group was restructured. It was made clear to the divisional managers that they were to carry full responsibility for the financial results of their own divisions, and also for the capital tied up in them. The roles of the financial manager and the technical director were simultaneously better defined than had previously been the case.

9.6.2 New reporting relationships for the foreign sales companies

The foreign sales companies had – in a somewhat vaguely defined fashion – reported to the *president* of Allgon.

When it had been clarified that all foreign sales companies (with the sole exception of the American subsidiary) should only deal in *vehicle-mounted products*, they could rapidly and logically be instructed to report directly to the divisional manager in charge of the said products.

This measure simplified reporting considerably and cut down communication times. It also off-loaded group management, which could now devote its time to other, more urgent issues. (As expected, many of these changes were met with considerable resistance from some of the heads of the foreign sales companies. Those who worried more about their personal reporting status than about the proper functioning of the organization were replaced.)

The American subsidiary constituted a special problem. It had primarily been acquired in order to provide a manufacturing base in the US. However, its product programme was not competitive, and its P&L showed a substantial loss. Since chances of rapidly improving the situation were non-existent, it was decided to close down the production, sell off the premises, but keep a small sales team to serve the US market.

9.6.3 Analysis and paralysis versus decisive actions

In retrospect, the reader might conclude that the actions described here did not require a lot of sophisticated analysis, but primarily *decisive management action*.

A company has often found itself in a crisis situation just because of a repeated lack of managerial action, and not as a lack of analysis *per se*. Some individuals within such a company are usually aware of what should be done, but no action is ever taken. The growing crisis might scare top management to such an extent that no crucial decisions are taken at all. The top management team is simply 'paralysed'.

One contributing factor to such inertia is the close personal ties which block the top man from implementing desirable changes, since the changes are negative for his old friends or colleagues. The turnaround expert, in this case a new company president, is there to act, that is to manage the company. While the old president might have been a cautious 'caretaker', the new person must be his opposite, that is a 'change agent', making long overdue changes happen, and happen rapidly.

Fast decision-making and rapid (sometimes even ruthless) *implementation* are often the keys to success in a turnaround situation. This was certainly true for the Allgon case, described here.

9.7 Marketing and customer contacts

The amount of time spent with customers was very low in the (vehicle) antenna division, and almost non-existent in the systems division. This lack of an extensive customer interface is common to many crisis companies, and one important reason why they experience problems.

In the systems division, a new sales manager who was extremely customer-orientated and entrepreneurial was brought on board. Over the next 12 months, he replaced his entire sales staff in order to get a team that was willing 'to listen to signals from the marketplace'. As a result of the increase in customer orientation, divisional sales *grew more than tenfold* in a five-year period.

Throughout Allgon as a whole, and not least by the management group, very substantial emphasis was put on nurturing customer contacts to make the company more effective in responding to changing market needs.

As a result of the spectacular company growth rate (which started in late 1992), many young individuals could now be employed. As a result, the average age of the individuals working in Allgon dropped to 29 years! It was important that these young and well-educated people were encouraged to learn and to understand the driving forces of Allgon's business, forces which were only partially of a technical nature, but also market-driven.

9.8 Improving the product programmes of the two divisions

For reasons explained earlier, the product programme of the systems division was very weak. The product programme of the antenna division had also begun to lag behind competition, particularly when the earlier heavy and fixed-mounted car telephones began to be replaced by smaller, hand-held portable phones.

The problems in the systems division were gradually solved by a determined effort to increase the headcount and simultaneously improve manpower quality. This (in combination with the arrival of a strongly customer-orientated division manager) led to a radically improved systems division product programme in a remarkably short time.

In the antenna division, *the switch to hand-held portable phones meant that the antennas were now no longer separate, but built into the telephones themselves.* This created an OEM business which was quite new to Allgon. In a short time, the market for antennas in hand-held phones actually became considerably larger than the market for vehicle-mounted antennas. The new OEM focus required a new antenna division manager, applying a truly market-orientated approach, and such a man was therefore employed.

Together with changes earlier discussed for the systems division, all this meant that Allgon had changed not only its product ranges, but also its attitudes in favour of a market-orientated view, including a great awareness of – and responsiveness to – the customers' needs.

9.9 More rapid decision-making

When major changes in a company have to be made, speed in the decision-making process is often crucial. It saves costs, and substantial revenue advantages can quickly materialize. There is no doubt that a medium-sized company which, like Allgon, has most of the major share holders on its board, enjoys a big advantage as compared to companies where the board members are anonymous representatives of all shareholders.

A turnaround of a major division of a big company is often very different from the Allgon turnaround discussed here.[1] Rapid decision-making there is the exception rather than the rule in big corporations. Many layers of headquarters' management might be involved.

Approvals by the board might be delayed, and so on. Political manoeuvring among top managers might not only delay, but sometimes even completely block, sound decision-making.

In the case of Allgon, the situation was much more favourable. All board members were big Allgon shareholders. Since the new CEO had also been given the opportunity to purchase a substantial amount of Allgon shares on favourable conditions, the company's best interests coincided with 'shareholder value' concerns in a way that is far from common in many other turnaround situations.

In this case, important decisions could rapidly be made and implemented, including the change of strategic focus, the appointment of new key managers, the reshaping of the organization, the development of the two product ranges, the closure of the US plant, and so on.

9.10 Performance diagrams showing this turnaround's impact on sales, profits, and so on

In five years, Allgon's *sales* increased sevenfold, from SEK200 million to SEK1400 million. From a loss in 1991, *net income* increased to SEK75 million in 1994. *Operating income* was close to SEK90 million the same year. (Figures 9.1 and 9.3 reflect this.) In a nutshell, Allgon became the star of the Swedish stock market.

From the many earlier mentioned contributing factors to this success story, it might perhaps be worth repeating the following:

1. The rapid *elimination of unprofitable elements* (that is 'bleeders'), while at the same time *aggressively developing the viable and profitable elements*. Thus, a good turnaround manager should be able to 'use the brake and the accelerator simultaneously' (although for different aspects of the business).

2. The rapid *competence improvement* among managers and other key staff, with regard to knowledge, skills and attitudes.

3. The development and communication of a *new Business Mission* (and Blueprint for the Future), which was later adhered to at all times.

4. The obvious advantage derived from a highly competent, responsive board, most of its members being important shareholders.

This allowed for the aggressive pursuit of a cure for the company, while simultaneously providing excellent shareholder value. (Between 1992 and 1996, the dividend increased from less than 20 öre to close to 1 crown, that is a five-fold growth in only four years, see Figure 9.2).

Charts showing the dividend development and other performance aspects follow.

Notes

1. The key source for this turnaround case study is Per Wejke, not only co-author of this book, but as CEO, also responsible for the Allgon turnaround, hailed by the Scandinavian business press as an outstanding achievement. *Finanstidningen*, 31 December 1993: 'Best of all the shares quoted on the Stockholm stock exchange this year was Allgon, a company previously close to bankruptcy. An investment of SEK6200 towards the end of last year is today, only one year later, worth SEK50,460.' Or, as *Veckans affärer* put it: 'Incredible Allgon!'

   Analyses of annual reports and the production of corresponding performance diagrams ('score cards') has been carried out by Mr Marcus Fogel from Arpi International's Brussels office.

2. Compare the ESAB case, where the success was to a large extent dependent upon the inertia among major competitors!

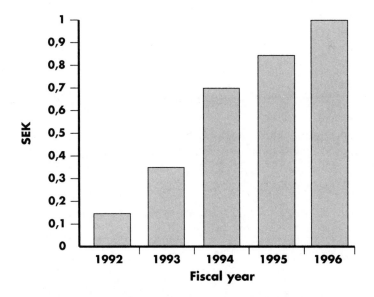

Figure 9.2   Allgon: dividend per share 1992–96

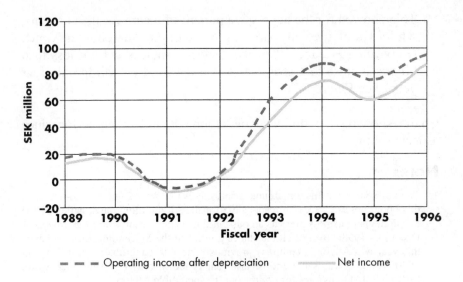

**Figure 9.3   Allgon: operating income
and net income 1989–96**

Chapter 10
The ESAB Group restructuring the European welding industry

List of Contents

Background		**267**
10.1	**Industry-wide overcapacity in a not particularly price-sensitive market**	**268**
10.2	**The four phases of the turnaround, using Igor Ansoff's growth matrix**	**269**
10.3	**Overview of the 12-step strategy used**	**271**
	10.3.1 Step 1: 'Kill all lingering hopes'	271
	10.3.2 Step 2: 'Cleaning up ESAB's own act': radical changes in ESAB's production structure	272
	10.3.3 Step 3: 'The industrial clean-up statement'	273
	10.3.4 Step 4: ESAB's systematic elimination of industrial overcapacity	274
	10.3.5 Step 5: Rationalization of product ranges without disturbing markets	275
	10.3.6 Step 6: Establishing a short-term brand strategy	276
	10.3.7 Step 7: Establishing a medium- and long-term brand portfolio strategy	277
	10.3.8 Step 8: Revising the pricing strategy	279
	10.3.9 Step 9: Introducing a 'parallel' sales force strategy	280
	10.3.10 Step 10: Matching the countries, brands, product portfolios and strategies	281
	10.3.11 Step 11: Organizing for change	282
	10.3.12 Step 12: Heavier customer orientation and a new distribution structure	284
10.4	**Looking closer at two of the cells in Igor Ansoff's 'growth matrix'**	**285**
	10.4.1 Introducing old products in new markets (1986–88)	286
	10.4.2 Expansion mainly based on new products sold in new markets, or new market segments (1986–90)	287
10.5	**On management style and the importance of the ESAB board**	**288**
Score Cards: **Performance charts for this turnaround**		**290**
Notes		**293**

10 The ESAB Group restructuring the European welding industry*

Background

During the late 1970s, the Gothenburg-based ESAB welding company became so unprofitable that it was threatened by split-up or bank- ruptcy. Underlying driving forces included:

1. *the disappearance of the demand for manual welding products from European shipyards and a subsequent decline in oil rig production*
2. *a gradual switch from manual welding techniques to more advanced (semi-automatic, fully automatic, and robotic) techniques[1]*
3. *in the area of solid wire, ESAB met new competitors, namely the steel works 'integrating forward'*
4. *the abolition of a 'stocking subsidy' paid by the Swedish state to counteract business cycles.*

The demand for manual welding consumables steadily diminished by 8–10 per cent per year. As volume dropped, and producers' fixed costs remained unchanged, the whole industry came under severe price pressure, leading to losses. The fact that the market segments for solid wire and flux core wire simultaneously grew could not offset ESAB's losses.

---

* This case study is based on one half-day interview in Gothenburg on 19 October 1998 by Dr Arpi with Mr Bengt Eskilson, former president and CEO of ESAB, and two further 3-hour interviews in Brussels with Mr Bo Sandqvist, executive vice president of ESAB at the time of the turnaround, plus Dr Arpi's own notes and reports from the time of the turnaround. Valuable assistance as to financial performance data for the turnaround period were provided by Mr John Forsell, still with the ESAB Group. The authors take this opportunity to thank all three for their valuable input.

For 5 years, Arpi International assisted the ESAB Group in imple-menting the following strategy. It resulted in the company becoming the leading European player (30 per cent market share) with the most modern production facilities for welding consumables, the lowest production costs, and the highest price level. Through acquisitions in the US and elsewhere, they also became number two worldwide.

10.1 Industry-wide overcapacity in a not particularly price-sensitive market

Around the mid-1970s the whole welding industry seemed to live under the assumption that there was soon going to be a major *increase* in steel consumption in Europe. In the light of this, major investments were made, or at least planned, in new steel producing facilities (for example the huge 'Steelworks 1980' project in Northern Sweden). Investments were made to increase the capacity to produce both more welding consumables and more welding equipment.

A hand-held welding stick represents a very small part of the overall cost of the end-product being welded. Industrial market research repeatedly showed that buyers of welding consumables were in reality not very price sensitive. In spite of this, many producers of welding consumables acted as if the welding market was soon going to grow very substantially, if only consumables prices came down. Instead of increasing sales, this only led to a further increase in the already substantial stock of welding consumables. This in turn encouraged many competitors to drive their prices even further down. Simultaneously, the steel industry integrated forward, and as a result increased their production of certain welding consumables, not the least solid welding wire for semi-automatic welding. In this way, the steel producers tried to make better use of the existing capacity in their rolling mills. When the resulting production increase met a demand weakening by 8–10 per cent per annum, consumables prices were driven further down.

To the ESAB Group, it became increasingly obvious that many competing producers of welding consumables were not able to clearly distinguish between the net impact of the following factors:

1. the changing *size of the market demand for welding products*
2. the changing *composition* of the demand as a result of *changing welding processes*

3. the impact of temporary business fluctuations as compared to long-term trends
4. the *falling prices* for welding consumables, not least for handheld welding rods.

To survive and prosper, ESAB needed to get their own product costs *down*, and the industry-wide price level for consumables *up*. This case shows how both these goals were achieved.

10.2 The four phases of the turnaround, using Igor Ansoff's growth matrix

Although the work by the Harvard professor Michael Porter was well-known to ESAB's management team, a slightly older frame of reference was often used to discuss relevant strategic choices and 'alternative growth vectors'.

Professor Igor Ansoff, one of the very first 'strategy gurus' introduced the concept of a 'growth vector matrix' containing 4 cells:

1. expansion by using old products in old markets
2. expansion by using existing products in new markets
3. the introduction of new products in old markets
4. the introduction of new products in new markets.

		PRODUCTS	
		Present products	**New products**
MISSION	**Present markets served**	Market penetration	Product development
	New markets served	Market development	Diversification

Figure 10.1   Growth vector components
(Ansoff, *Corporate Strategy*, 1968)

ESAB's development can reasonably well be described using this frame of reference. However, in ESAB's case, top management decided to start out one step ahead of the 'market penetration' phase. Thus, they first undertook what they called an internal 'critical evaluation and cleaning-up phase'.

The resulting frame of reference and associated time-frame specific for the ESAB case are reflected in the following table.

1. Critical self-evaluation and 'cleaning up the mess' in existing markets. (The selling of non-core businesses and low-yielding assets improved cash-flow and slimmed the balance sheet.)	*Squeezing the balance sheet* Time period: 1979–1983
2. Acquisitions in European markets where ESAB was already represented, acquiring major competitors, operating with product types already well-known to the ESAB Group.	*Market penetration* Time period: 1983–1987
3. Introducing established welding products in new markets (like Asia and the US, primarily by acquisitions of a well-established company in each such market).	*Market development* Time period: 1985–1989
4. The introduction of new products (to both old and relatively new markets).	*Product development* Time period: 1986–1990

The exact measures taken and the overall strategy used are depicted in great detail in sections 10.3.1 to 10.3.12 of this case study. After that, in section 10.4, we will look closer at two particular cells in Igor Ansoff's growth matrix, while describing ESAB's strategy in even greater detail.

10.3 Overview of the 12-step strategy used

10.3.1 Step 1: 'Kill all lingering hopes'

As long as even one or two companies in a shrinking industry believe that the shrinking demand is just a 'temporary set-back', the industry is not likely to ever succeed with the necessary restructuring and resulting reduction of overcapacity. 'Killing all lingering hopes' then becomes a cornerstone for the more enlightened players.

Correspondingly actions taken by ESAB included prominent publication in their annual report of the continuously shrinking industry demand, followed by equally disappointing forecasts showing a further steady shrinking of the expected demand for manual welding products. Reasons quoted were the diminishing demand from ship-yards and from the off-shore industry, and an ongoing switch from manual welding processes to semi-automatic welding and a mechanization (or automation) of many welding processes. ESAB's own pessimistic forecasts were accompanied by expert statements, also from customer industries, that there would never be a return to what was earlier regarded as 'normal' welding market conditions.

To make sure that the message had been received, understood and believed, all key European competitors were invited by ESAB to Sweden, ostensibly to celebrate the company's 80th birthday. The guests were again confronted with utterly gloomy forecasts, this time presented by a well-known international industry expert. One guest commented: 'I thought this was a birthday party, not a funeral.'

THE ESAB CASE

Major problems	Key actions taken
■ Overly optimistic forecasts throughout the industry	■ 'Kill all lingering hopes strategy' (section 10.3.1)
■ Getting rid of industry-wide overcapacity	■ 'Industrial clean-up' statement (section 10.3.3), followed by systematic elimination of competitor's overcapacity (section 10.3.4)

■ Too many consumable brands, product lines, and products	■ Product range rationalization (section 10.3.5) and new brand strategies (sections 10.3.6 and 10.3.7)
■ Depressed price levels	■ New pricing strategy, based on new cost and market share realities (section 10.3.8)
■ Latent post-acquisition confusion (for example as to what brand to use where, and what products at what price, and so on)	■ Systematic matching of brands, countries etc., using a 'product portfolio versus market share matrix' (section 10.3.10)
■ Too many small customers too intensely served, and the big ones not always given the right kind of attention	■ New distribution structure, heavier (big) customer orientation, more added value in services provided (section 10.3.12)
■ Central and Eastern Europe threaten to become low-cost production base for competing consumables exported to Western Europe	■ Aggressive acquisition activity by the ESAB Group to control the situation (section 10.4.1)

10.3.2 Step 2: 'Cleaning up ESAB's own act': radical changes in ESAB's production structure

In 1980, the ESAB Group had too many factories, many with very low capacity utilization. Therefore, during 1981–83, a number of ESAB factories producing welding consumables (for example in Holland, France, Norway and Denmark) were closed.

Factories for alloyed electrodes were specialized to a much higher degree. (This followed a pattern recently used by, for example, SKF and Electrolux throughout Europe. This was not a coincidence, since the CEO of SKF was a member of the ESAB board.)

The now improved loading of ESAB's factories, combined with a specialization of their factories, led to much lower unit costs in production:

1. Already the longer production runs, the higher loading per factory, and retaining the most modern factories in the industry, provided a 10 per cent cost advantage.

2. Another 10 per cent was gained through lower purchasing price, as a result of the larger volumes purchased (and partly because of the larger lots purchased each time).

In comparison, the competition were stuck with diminishing volumes and increasing production costs, and were forced to increase their prices, if they were to stay in business with a profit.

The price increases needed were in the order of inflation +4% per annum.

ESAB's cost advantage more than offset the increase in transportation costs, which resulted from each factory now having to serve a larger geographic area. The earlier concept of 'keeping a national factory primarily for our domestic needs' had become completely obsolete. Elimination of all fixed costs for the closed factories (SEK 10–15 million per factory), and a radically reduced products range produced in each factory, led not only to lower unit costs, but also to improved product quality.

Another logical consequence of the fact that each remaining factory was serving many markets was that the factory managers now had to report to ESAB group management, *not* to the country manager in the country where that particular factory was geographically located. Resulting changes in reporting patterns and power structures were not appreciated in all quarters. Still, economic calculations could clearly justify the changes introduced.

10.3.3 Step 3: 'The industrial clean-up statement'

The ESAB Group issued a policy statement that ESAB was prepared to 'actively contribute to a restructuring of the whole industry', and to help loss-making competitors out of the business at a lower cost to them than if they had chosen to restructure or close on their own.

This 'industrial clean-up' statement (published in ESAB's annual report, but also mentioned to business journalists) was enough to encourage several competitors to make discreet individual contacts with ESAB's president. Competitors had by now finally found out that they could probably live quite happily without their previous engagement in unprofitable welding products.

For major European competitors, such as BOC, Philips and GKN, the welding operation represented less than 10 per cent of their turnover, and was therefore of highly marginal interest as compared to their core businesses. Without any outside prodding by ESAB, they might simply have kept absorbing losses in this rather peripheral business area.

10.3.4 Step 4: ESAB's systematic elimination of industrial overcapacity

There were two main reasons why ESAB wanted actively to be engaged in the reduction of industrial excess capacity:

1. To *remove existing overcapacity* to stop existing producers from continuing to produce large volumes at incremental costs.

2. To *stop new players from entering the market*, based on production capacity purchased at rock bottom prices. Their low fixed costs would no doubt have encouraged cut-throat pricing.

For many European competitors, their welding operations represented a very small part of their total turnover. In some cases, it was only 1–3 per cent, that is of completely marginal interest as compared to the owner's core business. As already mentioned, an unfortunate result of this situation was that many a mother company felt able to 'afford' to continue carrying annual welding consumable losses in the order of SEK30–50 million (US$5–8 million), without seriously hurting the overall economic viability of the mother company.

In this situation, the CEO of ESAB, Bengt Eskilsson, chose to approach the board of such companies with the following question. *'What would you say if I invited you to a welding consumables project with a payback period of only two years?'*

As expected, most board members said they would respond very favourably to such a proposal, and accept it without much discussion. Mr Eskilsson could then continue his presentation, by saying to the company's owner:

> You are presently losing SEK30 million a year on your welding consumables operation. ESAB is prepared to acquire your welding business at a fair equity value minus our own costs for the restructuring of the business in order to arrive at a profit level of 15 per cent return on the capital employed. (In your particular case, the equity is SEK60 million, and the restructuring costs also 60 million. We are therefore prepared to take over your welding operation as well as corresponding costs. Since you are presently losing SEK30 million a year, this arrangement corresponds to a two-year payback, when seen from your own viewpoint!

This kind of reasoning, although certainly somewhat unusual, was rather convincing. Many competitors therefore decided to accept the offer provided according to the 'ESAB formula'. ESAB's 'purchase' of many of its competitors could also be executed without any negative impact on ESAB's P&L statement. Any difference between equity value and price was introduced into ESAB's balance sheet as 'negative goodwill'. The restructuring costs were later charged against this 'negative goodwill', without any negative influence on ESAB's P&L statement. (Sometimes, when the 'negative goodwill' was bigger than the total restructuring cost, the impact could actually be positive.)

The impact on the industrial overcapacity is reflected in the fact that ESAB closed no fewer than approximately 30 production units for consumables during the 1980s, while concentrating their production to the remaining, most modern and cost-effective entities.

10.3.5 Step 5: Rationalization of product ranges without disturbing markets

Production methods found in the different acquired companies were technically compared. Similar methods for low volume products were combined into one, thus reducing the number of methods of production by the ESAB group. Production of such low-volume products was concentrated in one factory.

However, from a marketing and branding viewpoint, the same welding stick was often packaged in several different boxes and sold under different brands (for example one blue box with the brand name 'Arcos', and a yellow box branded 'ESAB' accompanied by its previous number, well-known to the welder. Since the welder was sometimes likely to notice a slight product difference, the product was sold as 'recently upgraded'.

Market research undertaken by Arpi International showed that while buyers tended to be fairly flexible in their purchasing behaviour, *welders were extremely conservative and change-resistant craftsmen*. The latter often refused to work with 'new' products, recommended by their foremen or by the purchasing department. Intentional 'mishaps' could easily occur in their work as a consequence of product changes imposed on them against their will. For that reason, the composition, branding, marketing, and so on of high-volume electrodes was handled with utmost care in order not to irritate clients or affect sales.

10.3.6 Step 6: Establishing a short-term brand strategy

Considerable rationalization benefits could rapidly be enjoyed in areas such as production, product range harmonization and logistics. However, it was decided not to try to rapidly move clients (or welders) from one brand name to another, even if both brands belonged to the ESAB Group.

If a product, previously used by a customer, disappears from the market, the customer (knowing that he is forced to change products anyway) is likely to also look at competing products, including those not produced by the ESAB Group. It is then difficult to maintain the market share of the acquired company. For example, if a company has a 20 per cent market share and acquires another company with a 15 per cent market share, it would not end up with 35 per cent, but perhaps only with 25 per cent. If the company that acquired a second company is not capable of later maintaining the combined total sales volume represented by all earlier existing and recently acquired brand names, the term 'buying market share' is simply a misnomer.

10.3.7 Step 7: Establishing a medium- and long-term brand portfolio strategy

Through their extensive acquisition activities, the ESAB group had acquired eight different brands. Many of these were only used nationally or in a few European countries. To attack the brand portfolio problem, all brands were sorted initially into the following categories:

1. *major brands* to be kept in a longer-term perspective

2. *transfer brands* to be gradually and carefully phased out through a systematic effort, but at a pace that ensures that the 'purchased customer base' remained intact

3. *phase-out brands:* these were usually minor brands which could be phased out more rapidly to save costs, without any major negative impact on ESAB's overall sales volumes and profits. In this case, retained products were usually assigned to a high-volume brand.

> Generally speaking it took on average about *three years* to systematically 'transfer a customer base' from one brand to another. This required not only sound strategic thinking, but subsequent systematic action in a number of areas such as sales, branding, packaging, logistics, sales force steering, and so on. (We have oversimplified the process here, which in reality distinguished, for example, between *brands* and *product names*, and which brand could be used by what sales organization.)

The removal of the factories from the control of any particular country manager has already been mentioned. A similar organizational arrangement now had to be introduced, with regard to the management of all the brands of the ESAB group. At its peak, the ESAB group had no fewer than nine different brands for welding consumables. In 1990, these nine brands had been brought down to only four in Europe, namely:

1. ESAB
2. Filarc (formerly Philips)

3. Murex, mainly in UK
4. Arcos, and
5. Alloy Rods, a brand name mainly used in North America.

For welding machines, the brand reduction went even further – only the ESAB and Murex brand names were used in Europe.

Also, for consumables, the ESAB and Murex brands were earmarked early on as the only two long-term brands to be retained. Other brands were treated as intermediary, to be systematically phased out.

Apart from phasing out whole *brands*, the ESAB group was also phasing out many *products*. An interesting way to phase out products was to price them out of the market. When doing this, ESAB group management was often surprised to find how price-insensitive the welding consumables market actually was. In spite of systematic and regular price increases by the ESAB group, many a brand earmarked to be phased out was often still being purchased by many clients, and therefore generating an increasing margin. However, around 1993, only two international brand names remained, that is, ESAB and Filarc. (For flux cord wire, the Filarc name is still used. The brand Alloy Rods is also still used, but only in the US.)

The earlier very strong link existing between a brand, the producing factory's location, and the corresponding logical 'home market' for the product had by now been abolished in favour of international brands and specialized factories, each serving many markets. To ensure correct strategy implementation, each sales company was given a PCR (parent company responsible), that is a specially earmarked executive who was a member of the group management. Such an individual (in close cooperation with the business area managers for consumables and welding equipment) had to balance a particular market's interest versus corporate-wide goals and strategies as to, for example, optimal brand utilization in an international context.

The function of the PCR, as well as deciding the optimal, 'product portfolio' for different markets and marketing purposes, is further discussed in sections 10.3.10 and 10.3.11. There the reader will also find the 'product portfolio/market share' matrix used by the ESAB group for strategic purposes.

10.3.8 Step 8: Revising the pricing strategy

The turnaround strategy and associated growth strategy provided ESAB with many production cost benefits.

Whenever the ESAB Group doubled its production of a particular product, overall product costs (here including sales and administration costs) tended to decrease by at least 10 per cent. To this ('experience curve effect') could be added the benefits derived from reduced fixed costs as a result of fewer factories, higher factory loading figures, and the use of only the most modern and efficient factories among all those acquired. Finally, raw material purchasing prices fell by another 10 per cent, as a result of the larger volumes purchased.

In the retained factories, ESAB invested substantial amounts to increase productivity and quality. Further important savings followed from the concentration of product management and R&D to ESAB headquarters in Gothenburg.

After the lowest production costs in the industry and a substantial strategic market share in each major market (usually 20 per cent or more in the country in question) were reached, a two-pronged pricing strategy could then be introduced:

1. It was clearly communicated to competition that ESAB by now had the *lowest product costs in the industry*, and that ESAB could therefore, if necessary, 'afford' to engage in a price war with disastrous effects on the profitability of its competitors. If a competitor's volume fell even further as a result, he would be faced with more unabsorbed fixed costs, calling for price increases, not decreases.

2. ESAB could *increase its prices to a sound level*, a move that was usually quickly copied by its remaining competitors. (Thus, ESAB often became the 'price umbrella' for competitors, although the latter could never touch ESAB's own profitability level.)

In order to avoid unnecessary price competition, but still benefit from substantial sales volumes, ESAB also made an agreement with a major Finnish steel producer (today called Fundia, but previously called Dalsbruk). The agreement meant that Dalsbruk produced solid welding wire for both companies, while refraining from marketing the product themselves. ESAB instead became the marketeer for both. In this way, product costs could be kept low, while direct price competition could be more limited.

Early on, ESAB widely communicated that they had the lowest product costs in the industry. This was initially a bluff, but developments gradually made the statement reflect the reality.

As already pointed out, the reasons for this cost advantage were:

- ESAB's most modern factories in the industry
- higher factory loading (after closing a substantial number of factories)
- longer product runs for many standard consumables
- lower purchasing prices because of ESAB's substantial and growing size.

For low-priority 'transfer products', further aggressive price increases could be used to speed up the process of transferring clients to other, somewhat less expensive, but still ESAB-owned products and/or brands.

Increasingly, the pricing policy applied was seen in relation to both the *strategic position* of a brand in a given geographic market, and also the *strategic market penetration goals* established for the same. Here the 'product portfolio/market share matrix', discussed in section 10.3.10, had an important role to play. So did the PCR.

10.3.9 Step 9: Introducing a 'parallel' sales force strategy

Initially, it was decided to keep *several sales forces operating in parallel* under different brand names.

Even if most end-users suspected at the back of their minds that the ownership of their normal welding products supplier had changed, end-users were much comforted by the fact that they continued to both meet the *same sales person* and also buy the *same brand* and the *same product numbers* as earlier. (No obvious reason therefore existed for a buyer to change his earlier established purchasing behaviour.)

Germany became the only exception to the 'parallel sales force rule'. There, an over-ambitious general manager – for cost-cutting reasons – insisted on combining the three earlier existing sales forces. As a result, three different brand names and three logos were put on some sales people's business card. The result was a substantial confusion in the German marketplace and a rapid reduction of the Group's combined German market share. (As already pointed out, one can only truly 'buy market share' if later one is also fully capable of actively *managing the acquired market shares*. This calls for good brand and product line management, but also a strategic management of existing sales forces.)

10.3.10 Step 10: Matching the countries, brands, product portfolios and strategies

Initially as a descriptive tool (and later used as a strategic goal-setting tool), each country was placed in one of the nine 'cells' in a 'product portfolio versus market share' matrix. This matrix had no doubt borrowed certain traits from Boston Consulting Group's (BSG's) portfolio thinking.[2]

		Width of product portfolio		
		Full	**Limited**	**Severely limited**
Market share	**High**	Cash cow ('milk and enjoy')		
	Medium		'Cash and invest'	
	Low			'Get out' or 'try new formulae'

Figure 10.2   Product portfolio versus market share matrix

Countries displaying a full brand portfolio and enjoying a high market share are obviously associated with the cell in the upper left-hand corner of the matrix. (Such a placing corresponds to a typical 'cash cow' situation.)

The square in the lower right-hand corner represents countries where ESAB had both a severely limited portfolio and a low market share. Here, the recommend strategic choice was to leave the market-place, or to try again in a new way.

In the centre of the matrix lies a cell, called 'Cash and invest'. This cell represents countries with a positive cash-flow, but also with a need for more investments.

In a 'dynamic perspective', that is seen over time, most ESAB countries tended to move along a diagonal 'growth vector', starting in the lower right-hand corner and finishing in the upper left-hand corner. However, whenever the direction was reversed, this was a clear sign that 'corrective management actions' were called for.

The use of an analytical framework of this nature facilitated the discussion of the need for brand names and product lines – and their best use – in relation to each sales company's particular market position, and its future market share goals.

10.3.11 Step 11: Organizing for change

If brand names acquired through company acquisitions are too rapidly and thoughtlessly 'folded' into the acquiring organization, experience shows that up to *80% of the acquired market share can be lost within 12 months*. If so, a company with a 15% market share, who has just acquired a company representing another 10% market share will certainly not enjoy a 25% combined market share one year later. The ESAB experience states that the likely combined market share would only be (15% + 20% × 10% =)17 per cent, since intelligent brand management was lacking.

Members of ESAB's executive committee therefore decided early on to rapidly stop national managers from following their natural urge to 'continue killing their recently acquired old competitor' (by ruthlessly and thoughtlessly cannibalizing the latter's customer base), and thereby also killing the valuable brand loyalty just purchased. From 1982, each national market had its own PCR person. This person very often had to assume the role of both educator and referee.

As might be expected, the rapid accumulation and implementation of new concepts (group factories, group brands, growth matrixes, and so on) and new steering and reporting principles were too much for some country managers. This was also reflected in the number of countries where the national top management team had to be replaced. (Within the ESAB group, this was for example the case in Germany, Italy, Norway, France, the UK, Switzerland, Austria and Singapore.)

The removal of the specialized factories (serving many markets) from the control of any particular country manager has already been discussed. The old cord was cut. Instead, the total product management, R&D functions and factories were now put directly under ESAB's group management.

Of key importance for success was to make sure that group-wide concepts and strategies were correctly handled, for example with regard to:

■ group-wide strategies
■ group-wide brands
■ group-wide factories
■ group-wide financial plans.

To help sort out the strategic position of the ESAB group and its brands in each national market, and to determine in which growth direction to move, the earlier discussed 'product portfolio/market share' matrix was used – and that in three different ways: as a descriptive, educational and strategic tool. Such decisions were primarily taken by group management, but with heavy inputs from the business area manager concerned. The PCR (for each sales organization) then closely monitored the subsequent implementation.

A long-needed reinforcement of the group's central marketing organization started in 1983. This rapidly resulted in much better and more well-founded marketing plans, and also in more sophisticated communication strategies, identification schemes, and so on.

To avoid any confusion between ESAB as a brand and ESAB as a group, it was decided to change both the logo and its colour for the ESAB group, while retaining the well-known yellow logo for ESAB as a brand. Such brand and corporate identity strategies could only be developed centrally, and the adherence to them was the responsibility of the PCRs.

10.3.12 Step 12: Heavier customer orientation and a new distribution structure

A conscious effort was made to gradually supplement the earlier, somewhat single-minded focus on products and production, which is often encountered in a predominantly engineering-orientated environment. A more market-orientated perspective was called for. Seminars for ESAB managers were run all over Europe to discuss *outside-in* instead of *inside-out* management thinking.

Parallel to this enhanced market focus, ESAB also strived to become much more *customer-orientated*. *'Who is our customer?'* and *'How to serve our customer'* became the central themes:

a. As a tangible result, *new products* started being developed in very close cooperation with certain demanding and knowledgeable end-users.

b. ESAB also started studying *their own clients' logistic needs*, including the material flows in their clients' production processes, and corresponding client stocking requirements, the client's (real or imagined) need for just-in-time shipments, and how cost levels could rapidly be brought down (for both parties) by an increased degree of cooperation and logistic optimization over company borders.

In line with the said change, traditional sales people were turned into 'key account managers', now fully equipped to analyse their customers' needs and replenishment plans in substantial depth. Each key account manager was now able to make a complete profitability calculation, encompassing not only the ESAB Group, but all steps up to and including the end-user. The slogan 'ESAB – your partner in welding' was now introduced to further underline the *cooperation aspect of the new client relationship*.

Obviously, ESAB could not handle the medium-sized and small clients in the same individual and highly intensive fashion as described above.

Germany might serve as a good example. Arpi International, the Brussels-based consulting company, undertook extensive studies of the German welding customer structure and also carried out on-site interviews with German welders, with their foremen and with the purchasing individual who formally placed orders for welding consumables and equipment. They arrived at two key conclusions:

1. An impressive number of small German clients was directly served by salesmen from ESAB (or by ESAB recently acquired) sales forces. However, corresponding profit margins were not enough to cover the selling costs.

2. Most of the salesmen who had for years dealt with small and inconsequential clients were usually quite incapable of successfully approaching major German clients.

This problem was solved in two ways. *First*, small German clients were referred to independent wholesalers, who were promised that this time around the new ESAB wholesaling strategy was not just a temporary 'fad', but a serious long-term ESAB policy worth investing in. *Second*, a large part of the existing ESAB sales force was replaced by more experienced sales individuals, capable of opening doors to major German companies at the right organizational level.

Europe-wide, no fewer than 23,000 medium-sized and small ESAB clients were diverted to 1,500 ESAB distributors. From a geographic viewpoint, these were already closer to the smaller ESAB clients and could better serve their actual needs.

10.4 Looking closer at two of the cells in Igor Ansoff's 'growth matrix'

Most of the acquisition activities discussed in section 10.3.4 can be characterized as increased European 'market penetration', that is growth based on products and markets already well-known to ESAB. However, referring to Igor Ansoff's 'growth vector matrix', the ESAB group also grew in two other ways, namely by:

■ introducing old products in new markets
■ introducing new products in new markets.

These expansion strategies are discussed in the following sections.

10.4.1 Introducing old products in new markets (1986–88)

One 'growth vector', according to Igor Ansoff's corporate growth model (reproduced in section 10.2), is for a company to grow in *new* markets, primarily based on already well-known products and technologies. Ansoff prefers to call this strategy 'market development'.

From 1986 to 1990, such a growth strategy was actually used by ESAB, primarily in the following market areas:

1. Acquisitions in *Asia* (not least in India), to which some of the West European ship building activities, as well as many of the off-shore rig building activities had been moved.

2. The *US*, where major growth could be expected (at least as soon as the second international oil crisis had been successfully terminated). The 1989 acquisition of L-Tec (Linde Technology) and Alloy Rods represented the realization of this North American strategy. Through this bold move, the ESAB group became No. 2 in the US, and could 'balance' the largest player, including limiting his desire for dumping products cheaply in the European market.

3. Acquisitions in *Eastern Europe* (Hungary, Czechoslovakia and Poland), markets which were then seriously under-developed, and where a rapid growth in welding products could soon be expected.

When the wall between East and West Germany disappeared, ESAB was afraid that the low production costs in Central and Eastern Europe were going to be used for export to Western Europe, and that a competitor in the welding business might realize this possibility. ESAB group management therefore decided without delay and 'as a noble act of self-defence' to *acquire control of the leading manufacturers in Hungary, Czechoslovakia, Poland, and former East Germany*. The former ESAB-owned pre-WWII factory in East Germany would never be able to produce electrodes at competitive cost levels, when labour costs in East Germany were raised to the same levels as in West Germany. Therefore, the leading companies in Hungary and Czechoslovakia were acquired 100 per cent, and with quite favourable conditions for personnel reduction. The Czech factory already had quite new production facilities for solid wire, but needed investment in an electrode factory. By also acquiring a minority share of a Polish factory, ESAB in reality *acquired good control of welding consumables exports to Western Europe.*

The chosen ESAB strategy for Central and Eastern Europe was later found to have been an excellent move. Today, these factories produce to the same quality standards as other ESAB factories, and they can therefore also export to Western Europe.

10.4.2 Expansion mainly based on new products sold in new markets, or new market segments (1986–90)

Parallel to the 'old products in new markets' growth pattern just described, ESAB also followed another growth strategy, based on *new products in new markets* (or at least in new market segments). As described below, this diversification strategy was sometimes triggered by an acquisition having had a more traditional main thrust, although producing highly interesting side effects.

When ESAB bought the Philips welding consumables operation, ESAB acquired both new technological knowhow, and a better access to certain highly specialized market segments. Philips was the company that originally specified the technical requirements for offshore welding. These later became law. Thus, through the Philips acquisition, the ESAB group could suddenly meet all existing offshore welding requirements. From ESAB's own viewpoint, this can be described as 'growth via new products' in previously badly penetrated market segments.

ESAB's own R&D efforts also provided vehicles for growth. Some of these efforts were focused on welding wires used in connection with semi-automatic and fully automatic welding – so called flux cord wire and solid wire. (Such wires do not need special protective coatings, since they are protected from oxidation during the welding process by a shielding gas. Welding sticks used during manual welding are different: they carry their own special protective coating.)

Since an industry-wide switch was underway, from manual to automatic welding, ESAB's R&D efforts with flux cord wire and solid wire also contributed to ESAB's continued growth.

Asea had long been major ESAB shareholders. At the beginning of the 1990s, when ABB was founded, Asea's ESAB shares were moved to Incentive, an important holding company in the Wallenberg sphere. As a result, ESAB was never a part of the important merger between Asea and the Swiss company Brown Boveri, which created ABB, that is Asea Brown Boveri.

On 22 August 1994, the now healthy and much enlarged ESAB group was sold to the international investment company, the Charter group, for SEK3,400 million. This price tag should be compared to the situation around 1980, that is at the beginning of this turnaround case, when the ESAB Group was on the verge of bankruptcy.

10.5 On management style and the importance of the ESAB board [3]

Bengt Eskilsson's management team consisted mainly of 'hands-on' managers, that is doers. Paperwork was kept to a minimum. Calculations were often crude, but rapidly made, and decisions followed almost immediately.

Things were then set in motion. We moved so fast that competition often did not understand what we were doing, and they often had no alternative but to accept our proposals.

To be able to act so rapidly, and even take substantial risks, the full permanent support of the board was a prerequisite for success.

ESAB's board was indeed highly qualified. It included Curt Nicolin, Gösta Bystedt and Kjell Högfeldt. Of particular interest was Gösta Bystedt of Electrolux, since he could provide extremely valuable experience of how Electrolux operated (in the area of white goods), when it came to their handling of multiple brand names obtained in connection with their many foreign acquisitions.

For the rest, the ESAB Board consciously allowed Bengt Eskilsson to operate extremely fast, and even take substantial risks, as long as the agreed high-level strategy was followed.

The fact that most of the members of ESAB's turnaround management team were *doers*, is reflected by the fact that most of them reappeared later on as managing directors of other substantial companies operating in highly dynamic industries. (Torsten Körsell went to Allgon (a communications company), Lars Brodd went to Stiga (sporting goods), and Anders Träff to Nordico (earlier known as KF Industries). Of ESAB's line managers during the turnaround period, only one is still with ESAB.

The fast-moving line managers, often out on the road, were backed up by two excellent staff executives. These are still with the ESAB group.

How did ESAB – once a company tottering on the verge of bankruptcy – secure an inflow of young talent? During the beginning of the 1980s, ESAB had *systematically picked all the best students from the Chalmers Technical University and employed them as 'trainees'*. When the 'turnaround team' disappeared later on, many of these youngsters were able to take over.

One more person of great importance to the success of the ESAB turnaround ought to be mentioned. A young outgoing executive, primarily with an international marketing background, Bo Sandqvist, was recruited from the Mölnlycke Group, well known for their successful international marketing. Sandqvist brought a lot of badly needed 'modern marketing thinking' into ESAB's predominantly engineering-orientated environment.

On his arrival, only three MBAs could be found at ESAB headquarters, and these were primarily to be found in the accounting department. Sandqvist was an excellent, multilingual conceptualizer, who could present and explain ESAB strategies, product portfolio models, market segmentation ideas, and so on, both within the ESAB group and to important external target groups, including financial analysts, if and when needed.

Thus, while Eskilsson restructured the European welding industry, Sandqvist provided the conceptual framework which was a prerequisite if the organization was to fully understand and follow. He also helped to introduce modern marketing thinking in an originally somewhat hostile engineering-dominated environment, which had previously tended to regard modern marketing and its terminology as both strange and of limited practical usefulness.

In 1990, Bengt Eskilsson terminated his position as CEO of ESAB, but remained as chairman of the board.

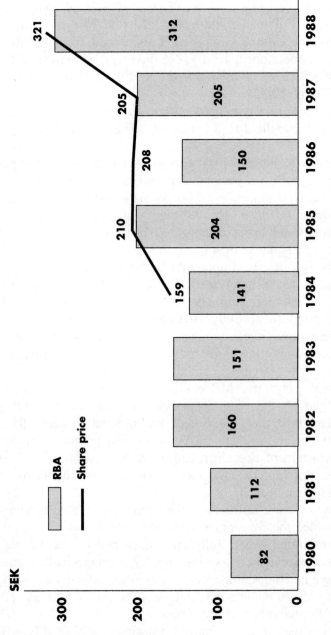

RBA = ESAB accounting term, primarily reflecting return *after* financial items, but *before* certain 'allocations' and taxes. The allocations reflected deviations versus plan in reserves, inventories, and so on.

Figure 10.3   The ESAB case: RBA and share price developments

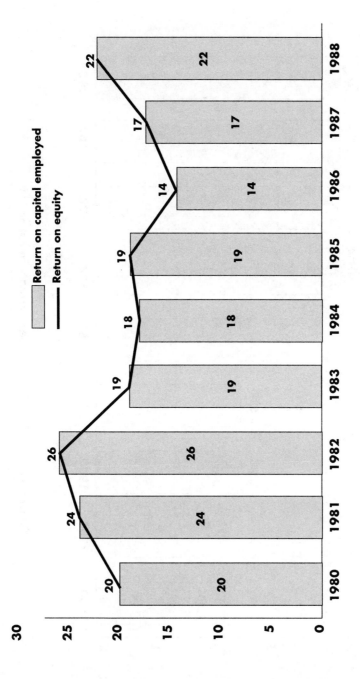

Figure 10.4   The ESAB case: return on capital employed and on equity

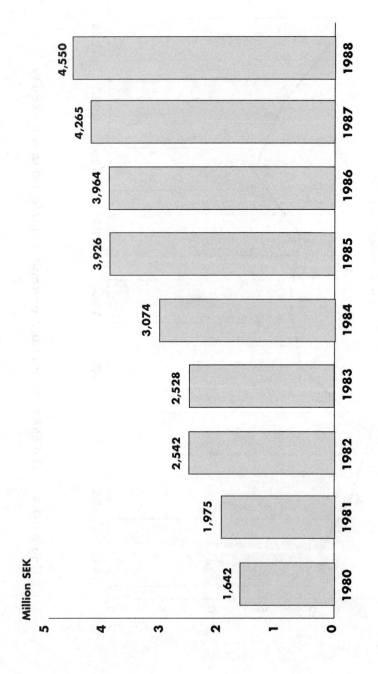

Million SEK

1980	1,642	
1981	1,975	
1982	2,542	
1983	2,528	
1984	3,074	
1985	3,926	
1986	3,964	
1987	4,265	
1988	4,550	

Figure 10.5   The ESAB case: growth in turnover

Notes

1. Some technical obstacles blocked the complete replacement of manual welding by automatic welding. 'Welding rods' for manual welding are often used outdoors, for example on construction sites during road and bridge building activities, and in naval docks, where tankers or oil rigs are under construction. For such applications, welding robots can seldom be used. Sophisticated welding robots are more commonly found along the production line in a car factory.

2. However, seen from the viewpoint of BSG's original four-cell diagram, ESAB was highly unorthodox. Instead of getting out of a typical (that is shrinking and unprofitable) 'dog market', ESAB actively invested in the dog market!

3. This section is based on two tape recorded 3-hour interviews with Bo Sandqvist (then executive vice president) and a subsequent 3-hour discussion with Bengt Eskilson (then president of ESAB). Both have seen and approved the material in this section on 'Management Style'. The same subject is also covered in the Tarkett case, where a full-page illustration of 'The key traits of "The Scandinavian Management Style"' can be found.

Chapter 11
Atlas Copco Tools

List of Contents

Introduction to the Atlas Copco Tools case		**296**
11.1	**The Atlas Copco group and its tools division**	**297**
11.2	**The situation before the turnaround interventions**	**297**
	11.2.1 The board's perception of the tools division's general viability	297
	11.2.2 The very costly international sales organization	298
	11.2.3 Divisional morale and motivation	298
	11.2.4 A blurred divisional business concept	299
	11.2.5 Excessive cost levels	299
	11.2.6 Summary as to the root causes	300
11.3	**Actions taken to address the situation**	**301**
	11.3.1 Appointment of a new president	301
	11.3.2 Evaluating the competence of the divisional management team	302
	11.3.3 Clarification of the future business concept	302
	11.3.4 Improving the cost efficiency of the sales organization	305
	11.3.5 Production structure and production overcapacity	306
	11.3.6 Production planning and factory layouts	307
	11.3.7 Product development finally guided by profitability criteria	307
	11.3.8 Summary with performance graphs	308
***Score cards:* Performance charts for this turnaround**		**309**

Atlas Copco Tools

Introduction to the Atlas Copco Tools case

Atlas Copco Tools was the smallest of the three main divisions of the Atlas Copco group. Growth had been slow and profitability low. The product lines of the two largest divisions, components and rock-drilling equipment, had developed into advanced systems or engineered products. As a result, the whole Atlas Copco group (not the least the group's foreign sales companies) had adapted its operations and cost levels to the requirements of these two largest divisions.

In contrast, Atlas Copco Tools had a product line mainly consisting of relatively inexpensive standard products with squeezed margins which could only support a truly lean organization. The tools division no longer sat comfortably within the Atlas Copco group. Serious doubts existed as to the possibility of achieving growth and sound profitability. There had even been discussions on the possibility of the group divesting itself of the whole tools business.

With a new turnaround manager on board, major weaknesses were rapidly identified and suitable actions taken. The Business Mission was reviewed and reformulated in an operational fashion. Target key cost levels were established, and cost saving programmes implemented.

A network of specialized tools sales companies was created in the most important industrial markets. This had a dramatic effect on tools' sales, efficiency, and profitability. Excess production capacity was eliminated. Product development was focused on certain products with a good profit potential instead of supporting the expensive philosophy of providing 'a complete product range'. From having represented only one-tenth of Atlas Copco's turnover, the tools division (today called the industrial division) grew to one-third of the group's total turnover. The industrial division is today the world market leader in its chosen core business.

This case also illustrates that often different businesses cannot be handled by simply applying a 'group-wide formula', but certain ones might require their own arrangements.

11.1 The Atlas Copco group and its tools division

Atlas Copco is a well-known multinational group, with headquarters in Sweden. The group is famous for compressed air and hydraulic equipment used in industry, mines and heavy construction work. Major product lines are compressors, rock-drilling equipment and industrial power tools. The Atlas Copco group is established all over the world. It is one of two world leaders in their chosen core business areas.

In 1980, the tools division – covered by this case – was still the smallest of the group's three divisions, and only accounted for ten per cent of overall sales. Through this turnaround and subsequent actions described in this case, this division grew to represent one-third of Atlas Copco's turnover.

11.2 The situation before the turnaround interventions

11.2.1 The board's perception of the tools division's general viability

The division's profitability had been unsatisfactory for quite some time, and it had even shown losses. As a result, the board of the Atlas Copco group had repeatedly questioned the general viability of the tools division. There was also a widespread feeling that perhaps the tools division did not 'fit very well' into the Atlas Copco group. Some individuals even contemplated selling off the tools division.

As already stated in the introduction to this case, the tools division had been adversely affected by the general developments in the two bigger divisions – those for rock-drilling and compressors. There, the development had moved away from standard products towards specially customer-adapted products or 'engineered' products. These products needed more software development and other kinds of technical support. This influenced the organizational development of the whole Atlas Copco group – including its sales organization – in a fashion not adapted to the needs of the tools division. However, this gradually increasing discrepancy was not generally observed and acknowledged by top management.

11.2.2 The very costly international sales organization

For a long time, the Atlas Copco group had well-established sales companies all over the world. These sales companies were responsible for the combined sales of products from all the three major divisions (that is rock-drilling, compressors and tools). From a cost allocation viewpoint, products from the three divisions were carrying common sales and administrative costs in pretty much the same way. For the tools division's relatively inexpensive products, this led to a situation where the division and its products had to carry far too high a share of marketing, sales and administrative costs.

One more factor worked to the disadvantage of the tools division; managers in the foreign sales subsidiaries personally benefited from an incentive system. A major component of this incentive system was based on invoiced sales value. This in turn encouraged a somewhat narrow focus on the more expensive products, represented by the compressor and rock-drilling divisions. It was generally regarded as both more profitable and more prestigious to work with the more expensive products emanating from these two divisions, than to work with the products coming from the struggling tools division.

11.2.3 Divisional morale and motivation

The morale within the tools division was low since the viability of the whole division was constantly being questioned. The tools division had no fewer than four different presidents during the previous nine years. Partly as a result of this, the 'strategic focus' of the tools division had constantly been changing. Desperation had been replaced by confusion and a feeling of mental fatigue.

The last divisional head before the turnaround exercise felt that he did not enjoy full support from headquarters. It was also very difficult for him to attract and recruit good people to tools from the other divisions. In contrast, the best people in the tools division were often actively looking for a 'promotion' to one of the other two (much bigger) divisions. These divisions seemed to offer a career-hungry individual much better opportunities.

11.2.4 A blurred divisional business concept

Particularly in a crisis situation, it is imperative to select and concentrate activities according to a well-defined *business concept* or *Business Mission*, as discussed and illustrated in Chapter 5. However, before the turnaround described here, the business concept of the tools division was not clearly defined, particularly not from a practical, 'operational' viewpoint. (The word 'operational' here means that it provides concrete guidance for everyday decisions and activities.)

Instead, a broad range of very different (and sometimes outlandish) 'business opportunities' tended to be discussed endlessly within the tools division. The time spent on such peripheral issues distracted attention from important key tasks, including that of rapidly improving divisional profitability.

11.2.5 Excessive cost levels

Since price levels were largely decided by world market prices, the unsatisfactory profitability of the division must primarily have been due to excessive cost levels.

Just three examples:

1. The division had *too many production units*. As a result, most of them were *underutilized*.
2. In relation to the volumes sold, *overhead costs* in production, administration and sales were far *too high*.
3. Logistics and material management also left a lot to be desired, resulting in *high inventory levels* and *high obsolescence costs*.

This unfortunate situation had to be addressed at a time when the closing of a factory met with exceptional resistance in Sweden, where Atlas Copco had their headquarters. The then recently introduced legislation, prescribing active employee participation in decision-making ('MBL'), was skillfully used by the unions. They often managed to slow down or even stop major changes, including any badly needed major restructuring. The basic question of whether such actions were urgently needed to save the company and safeguard its commercial viability, was often ignored.

11.2.6 Summary as to the root causes

Many factors had contributed to the development of the division's highly problematic situation. These factors included:

- weak leadership
- excess capacity
- too high marketing and administrative costs
- excessive production overheads
- an expensive international sales organization, which had not been created to meet the particular needs of the tools division.

Lack of clear-cut support from most of Atlas Copco's top management might be added to this list, as well as a rather widespread doubt about the division's long-term viability, contributing to a sense of uncertainty throughout the tools division.

As for most other cases, a list of key problems and corresponding key actions has been compiled for increased overview. The corresponding list is to be found below.

ATLAS COPCO TOOLS CASE

Major problems	Key actions taken
1. No clear-cut operational focus and no definition of what the tools division 'was really all about'.	1. Formulate, write down and communicate the division's future Business Mission.
2. Weak leadership, frequent previous changes of CEO.	2. Appointment of a new CEO (also being the turnaround manager) who stayed on board for several years.

ATLAS COPCO TOOLS CASE (cont'd)

Major problems	Key actions taken
3. Low divisional morale and motivation. Strange working patterns in the management team.	3. Conscious efforts to increase operating focus, improve cooperation and enhance team spirit and motivation.
4. Excessive production capacity in all five factories.	4. Close four out of five factories.
5. Too high overhead costs (particularly in administration, production and sales).	5. Establish clear-cut cost targets and close follow-up of their gradual achievement.
6. Expensive but not very cost-effective international sales organization.	6. Create a new foreign sales organization, fully dedicated only to the tools products.
7. Product development projects too often leading to unprofitable products.	7. Tougher policy: abolish or send back for redesign if cost and profitability targets not met.

11.3 Actions taken to address the situation

11.3.1 Appointment of a new president

Atlas Copco's group management decided to give the tools division a 'last chance'.

A new president was recruited from outside the group who had had a previous assignment within Atlas Copco ten years earlier. As a result, the new executive was fairly well acquainted with the group. However, he was *not* part of the tools division, nor linked to previous management mistakes.

Comment: This is a typical case where an *external turnaround manager should be recruited.* A man raised within the troubled division for a long time normally becomes too much 'part of the system'. A new man can see things with fresh eyes and also be given the benefit of the doubt.

11.3.2 Evaluating the competence of the divisional management team

When the business situation in an organizational entity has deteriorated to a point where a radical turnaround programme must be implemented and a new president brought in, the lack of confidence in the organization's future usually penetrates both the board and the division's own top management team. Sometimes, the latter simply has to be replaced in its entirety.

In the tools' case, the competence of the members of the management group was quite acceptable, in some instances even good. However, there was a great need to change the overall mentality and the working mode of the management group. As earlier discussed (in Chapter 3), this is often the case when a full-fledged turnaround situation has been allowed to gradually develop over a number of years.

11.3.3 Clarification of the future business concept

There existed no clearly defined divisional business concept which the full management group could agree on. There was a certain general consensus about what the division 'was all about'. However, the 'business concept' or 'business idea' was so vaguely formulated and so non-operational, that it gave very little concrete help when it came to 'focusing' and 'prioritizing'. As a result, time and time again, valuable managerial capacity was wasted on investigating various highly peripheral projects 'which *perhaps* could save the division'.

During a two-day meeting with the whole management group, and assisted by an external consultant, the future Business Mission of the tools division was agreed on. It was clearly delineated to avoid any highly subjective interpretations later, and immediately put in writing.

The clarification of the division's Business Mission meant that all managers within the division finally knew exactly:

1. which *customer needs* to satisfy

2. what the corresponding *product programme* should be, and

3. which *customer groups* were to be served.

Thus, all executives knew not only what to work with, but – equally important – what *not* to work with, since it was not part of the division's Business Mission or the division's core business. (As to terminology, the reader is referred to Chapter 5.)

It was now possible for the management group to become *goal-orientated*. The team could now – at last – fully concentrate on what the division was actually supposed to concern itself with. This clear-cut, new focus quickly led to a radical improvement in managerial efficiency and productivity. Again, we can see this process as a confirmation of the planning procedures described in Chapter 5.

In a subsequent step, the responsibilities and corresponding authority of each member of the division's management group were clearly defined. Action plans were agreed upon and closely monitored to ensure that they were implemented in time, within agreed cost frames, and with expected results. (ITT – once the fifth largest company in the world – pioneered the concept of highly detailed computer-stored 'action assignment lists' and accompanying strict follow-up procedures to ensure plan adherence, goal achievement and continued pressure on managers to really 'manage'.)

ATLAS COPCO TOOLS' 'BUSINESS MISSION': AS DEFINED IN THE STRATEGIC PLAN FOR 1982

1. Industrial tools

For industrial purposes (in production, maintenance and industrial service activities), the tools division shall market primarily in-house developed and in-house produced air-powered tools under the Atlas Copco brand name.

Further, the division is to market air motors to be used as built-in components, primarily by OEMs. The products are comprised of standard motors, as well as larger series of customer-adapted motors within the power span 0.1 to 10 KW.

2. Industrial systems

To market and deliver systems, primarily based on Atlas Copco components for electricity or air (as 'drive medium'), intended for large series producers. It will be possible to adapt our systems for feeding fasteners in connection with the assembly process. By systems, we mean here a combination of physical products and services, for example installation, after-sales service, as well as training the clients' own personnel.

3. Air line accessories

To provide compressed air users, primarily our own existing tool clients, with fittings and components for the distribution and treatment of compressed air all the way from the compressor centre to the place of use.

4. The division's customer perceived profile

For all of the three above mentioned business lines, we are to create and maintain an *Atlas Copco identity* perceived by our clients in the following key parameters:

- high quality (as to performance data, reliability, and ergonomics)
- delivery efficiency
- superior technical service
- first-class product information
- price fully matching the customer benefits provided.

The goal is to be regarded by our own clients as *at least as good as our toughest competitors* in all of our markets classified as 'priority 1 markets'.

Authors' note: As can be seen from the above, the Business Mission Statement concerns itself with products, key customer classes, markets, services provided, and image in the eyes of key customers versus prices charged.

Weekly management group meetings were introduced in the tools division. Key decisions, often long overdue, could now rapidly be taken, after allowing sufficient time for adequate analysis. The management team of the tools division finally started to function as a professional management team.

11.3.4 Improving the cost efficiency of the sales organization

One of the key reasons for the unsatisfactory profitability of the tools division was the high costs charged to their product lines by Atlas Copco's foreign sales companies, who were primarily equipped and staffed to service the needs of much more complicated Atlas Copco products, such as compressors and rock-drilling equipment.

The new president of the tools division could only see one, rather radical, way to solve this dilemma. He decided to create separate foreign sales companies solely for the tools products, that is companies completely dedicated to and organized around the needs of the tools division's own products. Early on, he realized that this would probably meet with heavy resistance from many Atlas Copco executives. He therefore made it a firm condition for accepting the new position that he was allowed to start a fully dedicated tools sales company in Germany, the most important European market for industrial power tools.

The board's early approval of this prerequisite later turned out to be quite crucial. When the fully dedicated tools sales company was to be started in Germany, several headquarter executives actively tried to kill the idea. However, the president of the tools division pushed through the decision, fortunately being able to refer to the pre-agreed conditions on which he had accepted this difficult turnaround assignment. (His previous knowledge of the Atlas Copco corporate culture was no doubt also helpful; he had been able to anticipate correctly the substantial resistance emanating from corporate sources outside the division itself.)

The new German sales company, exclusively established for the products of the tools division, performed quite well. As a result, during the next few years, similar fully dedicated tools sales companies were established in all important industrialized countries. This increased the marketing muscle behind the products from the tools division and boosted their sales, while simultaneously making it possible to keep the cost levels in line with what was needed for (and possible to carry by) tools products. As earlier stated, these did not require the same degree of sophistication, nor the same high cost levels as the more complex and demanding product lines from the other two Atlas Copco divisions.

11.3.5 Production structure and production overcapacity

In spite of constant rationalization drives elsewhere, the overall production structure for tools had not changed for many years. All their five production units were still seriously oversized. Available surplus production capacity had simply been 'spread out' according to some kind of 'fairness-to-all' principle. This led not only to guaranteed underutilized capacity in all production units, but also to very high unit product costs, including high costs for production administration, which obviously had become increasingly complex and politicized.

One solution was *to rapidly close at least two of the five factories.* This was initially regarded as something that could simply not be done, since 'Atlas Copco's corporate culture' (at that time) did not allow the closing of factories. Furthermore, it was very difficult to implement a far-reaching factory closing decision, because of the then recently introduced Swedish legislation regarding employee participation in the managerial decision-making process and its interpretation by the unions. This might call for an explanation.

Among unions, there was a widespread belief that they had 'the right' to approve or disapprove the closure of a factory, a division or a company. In reality this was not the case. Instead, a rather complicated information process had to be adhered to. The misunderstandings emanated from the fact that this information process had been called a negotiating process, which was a misnomer.

Even so, the information process was both new and complex. The situation was further aggravated by the fact that the Swedish economy was simultaneously rapidly deteriorating, creating a loss of jobs and employment, which made the unions even less inclined to accept 'downsizing' for whatever reason. However, although the 'negotiations' were tough and often unpleasant, the final decision-making rested with the company's top management.

Under the new president, the first factory was rather rapidly closed and the buildings sold. Shortly afterwards, another factory was closed down. The resulting concentration to *only three production sites* (instead of five) substantially helped to improve the tools division's financial situation.

A few years later, two more of the remaining three factories were closed. After this, all tool production took place in one factory located in Scandinavia, plus one assembly unit in Holland. The latter unit was justified because of its much closer location to the important markets in Western and Central Europe.

11.3.6 Production planning and factory layouts

At the start of this case, the factories of Atlas Copco Tools had a highly traditional production planning system. Thus, 'rolling' sales forecasts were issued on a quarterly basis. These were then transformed into production programmes, purchasing plans, and so on. However, because of the highly fluctuating demand situation in the tools market, forecasts were highly unreliable, resulting in almost permanent problems reflected in low-delivery efficiency combined with too high stocking levels.

As part of a new production rationalization programme, tool's production planning process was thoroughly reviewed. This resulted in a complete change of production philosophy. Instead of letting the production programmes be entirely based on sales *forecasts*, the production levels were instead to be based on sales *actually achieved*, with priority given to those products which were most badly needed.

Simultaneously, the physical layout of the most important tools plant was changed from groups of similar machines (for example a milling machine group and a drilling machine group), into a *flow-orientated layout*, optimized for the most important key components.

Taken together, these changes resulted in a *tripling of the inventory turnover*, while simultaneously achieving a much improved delivery efficiency and an improved customer service level.

11.3.7 Product development finally guided by profitability criteria

Formal profitability calculations had long been submitted for all new product development projects within the tools division. However, the most common reason for approving a new tools project had not been its expected high profitability, but rather that the new product was regarded as (somehow) 'essential' in the product line, although in a rather vague and undefined sense. As a result, many R&D projects had been started and pursued within the tools division, although the majority of these projects resulted in unprofitable new products.

This operating mode (and associated mentality) was immediately abolished by the new president. If a product development project did *not* show an acceptable profit potential under realistic assumptions, the project was either outright *discontinued* or returned for *redesign*. Over time, this change in R&D policy contributed quite substantially to the general profit improvement within the tools division.

11.3.8 Summary with performance graphs

The symptoms observed and the corrective management actions taken in this case are typical of many turnaround cases. One of its most important aspects is to 'revive' and 'restart' a demotivated, distracted, sometimes even paralysed, management team, and also to make sure that this team devotes its time to the right issues, while abolishing peripheral issues of little relevance to the success of the company or division in question. Specifying the Business Mission helps greatly. The rapid implementation of necessary actions is the logical consequence.

What had haunted the tools division was an unwillingness to pinpoint 'root causes', and take the necessary decisions, particularly when these included some uncomfortable elements, including making people redundant or diminishing the stature of some old friends. While a Business Mission Statement had guided the most urgent corrective management actions, a Blueprint for the Future Company helped to guide the *subsequent highly profitable growth in selected core areas.*

Through a subsequent aggressive acquisition strategy, this Blueprint could be realized. As a result, the tools division grew and developed into what is today known as *Atlas Copco's industrial division.* This at present accounts for approximately one-third of Atlas Copco group-wide sales, while still showing a very healthy profitability.

The following graphs (Figures 11.1, 11.2 and 11.3), show the constant growth in sales and profitability, also the abnormally low-capacity utilization in 1981, the year when this turnaround case started.

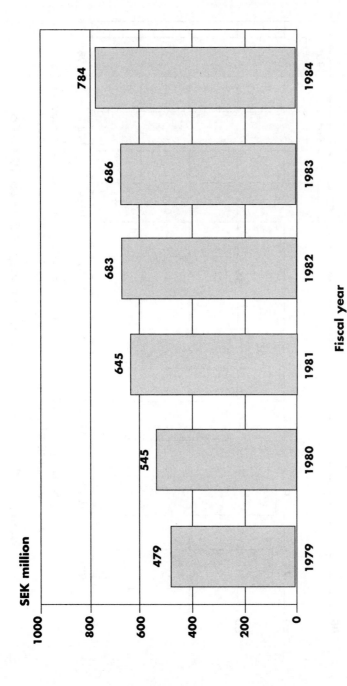

Figure 11.1   Atlas Copco Tools: sales development 1979–84
(Company Reports)

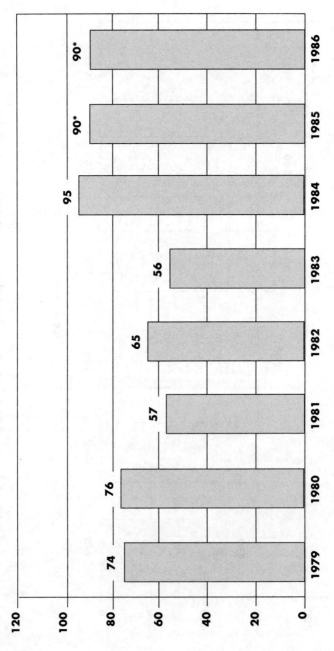

* Capacity utilization for 1985 and 1986 has been estimated to at least 90 per cent, although formal measurements stopped in 1984. Figures from previous years are based on published data.

Figure 11.2   Atlas Copco Tools: capacity utilization 1979–86

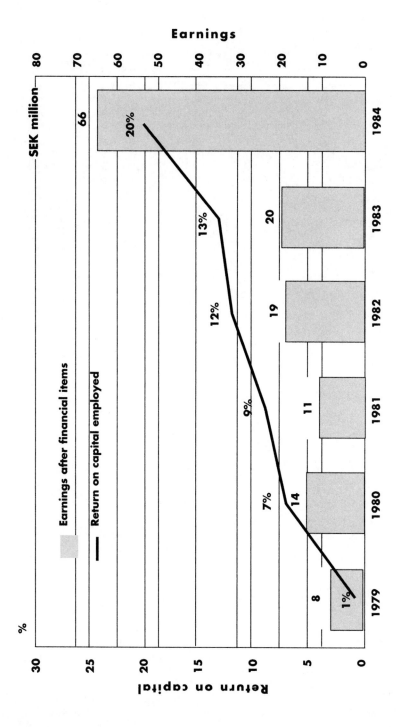

Figure 11.3 Atlas Copco Tools: development of earnings and return on capital employed
(Company Reports)

Chapter 12
Atlas Copco Mining and Construction

List of Contents

Introduction		**314**
12.1	**Situation before the turnaround intervention**	**315**
	12.1.1 The company, the MCT division and its products	315
	12.1.2 The managerial situation in 1984	315
	12.1.3 Studies to pinpoint the root causes	316
	12.1.4 Two specific projects, two major problems	316
12.2	**Actions taken**	**317**
	12.2.1 Creating a new management team and a new team spirit	317
	12.2.2 Profitability measurements and allocation principles for common costs	317
	12.2.3 Speeding up and cost reducing the robot rig project	319
	12.2.4 Closing down the Cleveland (tunnel boring) unit	320
	12.2.5 Strategic customer satisfaction research kills misconceptions	321
	12.2.6 Summary: key actions and key results	323
Note		**323**
Score cards: **Performance charts for this turnaround**		**324**

12 Atlas Copco Mining and Construction

Introduction

When the turnaround started, Atlas Copco's Mining and Construction division was the undisputed world leader for many types of rock-drilling equipment used in mines and construction work. The division employed 2,500 individuals and had factories in several parts of the world. Still, the MCT division showed an unacceptably low prof-itability. Sales grew slowly. So did the overall market.

The case illustrates how a turnaround manager, by focusing on only a handful of actions, can radically improve company performance and profits. The main reason for the unsatisfactory profitability was too high in-house costs, not least for R&D. Already the closing of one manufacturing unit, while giving a new focus to a very expensive development project, had led to dramatically reduced cost levels.

In order better to understand the customers' opinions and their decision-making criteria, a worldwide customer survey was under-taken. The results showed that MCT's customers did not experience product characteristics, or price, as a major problem, but slow and inefficient after-sales services was. The implementation of a completely new programme to address these deficiencies further improved the company's reputation, market position and profits.

Apart from excerpts from the worldwide market research findings, the normal performance diagrams for the full turnaround period have been included.

12.1 Situation before the turnaround intervention

12.1.1 The company, the MCT division and its products

This case describes the turnaround of the mining and construction division of the Atlas Copco group (abbreviated to MCT, while today it is instead called CMT for Construction and Mining Techniques). This division was previously regarded as the 'heart' of the Atlas Copco group.

In the 1950s, through the so-called Swedish drilling method, Atlas Copco became a world leader in rock-drilling. Later, it became a world-wide leader in *mechanized rock-drilling* with an impressive range of drill rigs for different purposes. (Normally, multiple drills are operated in parallel. Later, dynamite is used to clear large volumes of ore.)

In the 1970s and early 1980s, the world market for MCT's products had stopped growing. As a result, MCT's profitability suffered. The compressor division now took over as the most profitable and fastest growing part of the Atlas Copco group. MCT had become a problematic, loss-making division with a doubtful future.

12.1.2 The managerial situation in 1984

The MCT division had been headed by no fewer than five presidents in a little more than ten years. This contributed to:

■ a lack of strategic focus
■ a lack of sustained efforts over time, and
■ weak motivation throughout the MCT division.

In April 1984, the president of the MCT division decided to leave his position. A contributing reason was that he felt a lack of support from group management. He therefore also left the Atlas Copco group.

The limited support was easy to understand. MCT's profitability had seriously declined. In fact, the once glamorous division now was a loss-maker. The cooperation within the division's own management group was also characterized by substantial and continuing friction.

12.1.3 Studies to pinpoint the root causes

What were then the root causes? Were product prices too low, product costs too high, or both?

To pinpoint the underlying problems in an objective fashion, *benchmarking studies* were initiated by the newly appointed CEO. These studies highlighted:

a. how the division was scoring on 'customer perceived variables', such as quality, service, and price, and
b. in-house cost levels.

The huge *PIMS database* was used to provide further analytical reference points, and as a starting point for a critical review of the strategies used.

The main reason for the unacceptably low profitability was found to *be too high cost levels* in several functional areas.

The problem was made worse by the fact that no member of MCT's divisional management assumed his full responsibility for certain significant cost items. The strong-headed managers of MCT's three subdivisions simply *did not accept the cost allocations* decided by the central finance function, although the subdivisions certainly needed and even welcomed the activities which generated the costs in question.

The previous head of MCT had simply not been strong enough to enforce a correct and complete cost allocation system and get full acceptance for its results. *The surrealistic consequence was that the three subdivisions continued to report excellent profitability, in spite of the fact that the whole MCT division* (that is the three subdivisions) *showed losses.*

12.1.4 Two specific projects, two major problems

The Cleveland tunnel boring project

The MCT division had acquired a Cleveland-based manufacturer of tunnel boring machines.[1] This acquisition turned out to be an economic disaster since the US product was technically unreliable. As a result, every customer delivery resulted in a loss. Substantial costs were incurred both on modifications on customer sites, and later on guarantee work.

The internally developed robot rig

The most important internal MCT development project – at least with regard to costs – was the development of a robot rig with an integrated, built-in computer (for steering purposes). The project's management group had chosen to develop their own computer hardware in-house, instead of using standard hardware readily available on the market. The explanation given for this was that the environmental requirements for a rock-drilling rig were so demanding and unique that a dedicated computer had to be designed.

Likewise a unique programming language had been designed to cope with the special requirements. The total world market for this type of drill rig was not more than 10 to 20 units a year. It is therefore easy to see the problems associated with providing efficient support for such a unique product sold in small quantities, spread over all five continents.

12.2 Actions taken

12.2.1 Creating a new management team and a new team spirit

The replacement for the departing president was recruited within the Atlas Copco group. The choice fell on the president of another Atlas Copco division, Per Wejke.

The new president quickly found that cooperation within the MCT management group had severely deteriorated. Therefore, his first important task was to *re-establish mutual trust, as well as efficient cooperation* within the management group.

Reintroducing sound economic thinking was reasonably easy. It could rapidly be achieved. However, reintroducing a new (and more normal) cooperative atmosphere in the management group took much longer. Stubborn personalities first had to be convinced. When too stubborn, they simply had to be replaced by better 'team players'.

12.2.2 Profitability measurements and allocation principles for common costs

The managers of the three subdivisions were able to establish their own accounting practices. These did not include the concept of carrying each subdivision's part of the common costs of the full MCT division. (For instance, the heads of the subdivisions did not acknowledge their responsibility for covering any costs for data processing, common information systems, or finance.) Consequently, each subdivision proudly reported satisfactory, but *highly misleading profitability figures*.

By decentralizing most of the common functions sub-divisional managers could finally be made fully accountable for all costs incurred by their operations. This in turn led to a renewed focus on costs and a very considerable reduction of remaining central overheads. (The latter were now scrutinized and evaluated in a much more active and critical fashion.)

Agreement was reached on correct allocation keys for any remaining common overheads *and common accounting principles* were established for all subdivisions. As a result, a correct, complete and fully accepted view of the profitability of each subdivision finally existed. This in turn made it much easier to rapidly implement all the

---

ATLAS COPCO MINING AND CONSTRUCTION

Key problems	Key actions taken
1. *Management problems* a. Instability	1. *Management improvements* a. New CEO, staying on board during full turnaround period
b. Lack of focus and motivation	b. Clear statement of the division's future Business Mission
c. Too little understanding of end-user attitudes and concerns	c. Worldwide customer satisfaction study, correcting earlier held false impressions
2. *Too high costs* a. Incomplete cost allocation and no assumption of full cost responsibility by subdivisions	2. *Cost reductions measures* a. Reduce and decentralize 'common' resources, insist on new cost allocations, and on new accounting and performance measurement principles

ATLAS COPCO MINING AND CONSTRUCTION (cont'd)

Key problems	Key actions
b. Expensive in-house robot rig project	b. Switch to standard computer hardware and software. Reduce project team
c. Loss-making Cleveland tunnel boring subsidiary	c. Reduce time-to-market. Close foreign subsidiary. Move technological knowledge. Centralize marketing efforts much more closely

necessary rationalization activities. Through these, costs were finally brought down to quite acceptable levels, compatible with cost levels in other similar (and 'benchmarked') companies.

12.2.3 Speeding up and cost reducing the robot rig project

The robot rig project engaged a project group consisting of no fewer than 40 individuals. Most of these actually had very little experience with the rock-drilling products already available from competitors. They also knew very little about the world market for rock-drilling products.

The first decision was to stop the in-house development of computer hardware and of corresponding, specially designed, programming language.

Instead, the project group was ordered to select the most suitable hardware and programming language, already available on the market. In this fashion, the resources needed for the robot rig project could be brought down to *less than half*. The project's completion time was also reduced from 'somewhere in the future' to about one year, a dramatic cut in the 'time-to-market'.

The next step was to combine the special development group for the robot rig with the already existing development group for more conventional drilling rigs. This organizational *integration increased efficiency, while radically reducing costs.*

Taken together, these robot rig measures saved MCT SEK20–30 million annually.

12.2.4 Closing down the Cleveland (tunnel boring) unit

The tunnel boring machine, produced by the recently acquired company in Cleveland, caused losses amounting to SEK60–80 million annually. The causes were multiple. First, the Cleveland product was simply of a highly questionable quality. Second, their factory was heavily underutilized. Third, marketing efforts (and associated extra-ordinary technical costs) were too widely scattered geographically. There seemed to be no way to make this operation profitable reasonably fast, or even at all.

There were also some 'political' concerns. This acquisition had been made with the personal involvement of several members of the board of the Atlas Copco group, as well as by members of the board of Atlas Copco, North America. The delicate task of the turnaround manager was to convince these two boards to accept the necessary decision, that is *to simply close the Cleveland unit.* The convincing of all top managers concerned took a couple of months. Not only discussions, but also new analyses were now called for. (As a result, when the decision was finally taken, the tunnel boring machine project had probably been better analysed than most other Atlas Copco projects!) *Facts could finally prevail over gut feelings and unfounded technological enthusiasm.* Six months after the closure decision, cost levels had fallen to a level corresponding to an annual saving of SEK50 million.

The closing of the Cleveland unit did not mean that any important knowledge was irretrievably lost. The technical knowhow associated with the Cleveland tunnel boring machines, was systematically transferred to Sweden. There, the product was fundamentally redesigned. When reintroduced in the marketplace it was done so in a much more controlled fashion.

12.2.5 Strategic customer satisfaction research kills misconceptions

When a sales manager cannot produce the volumes or margins expected by him, he is often inclined to state that 'we need less expensive products with much better performance to increase our profit margins and market share'.

When MCT's insufficient profitability and slow sales growth were discussed, similar in-house 'explanations' were often heard. (The products were 'too expensive and their performance not sufficiently superior to that of competition'.) *In reality, Atlas Copco MCT was already world market leader* (or not worse than number two) *for many of its product lines*, including the very important hydraulic rock drills.

To stop misconceptions and unjustified internal criticism of MCT products and product performance (rather than high internal costs), the top management team decided to let an independent consulting firm undertake an objective worldwide study of the customers' rating of MCT products and services compared with that of leading competitors. Corresponding findings showed in no uncertain terms that MCT customers were satisfied or even very satisfied, with the MCT products' performance and even with their price levels. (One graph from these studies, Figure 12.1, accompanies this case description.)

Instead, rather unexpectedly, widespread dissatisfaction was reported with MCT's spare-parts service, and the time it took to get technical support. It turned out that a rapid and high standard of after-sales service was much more important than product price. MCT's customers had to calculate their own total production cost over a long time period, and the length and frequency of the end-user's 'down-time' was therefore an item which had not been officially observed within MCT.

This belated understanding led to a number of MCT programmes and activities to ensure that MCT customers would in future receive much improved after-sales service. It is difficult to calculate exactly how much this service enhancement contributed to MCT's substantially increased profitability (see Figure 12.2) over the next few years, but it was no doubt a strongly contributing factor.

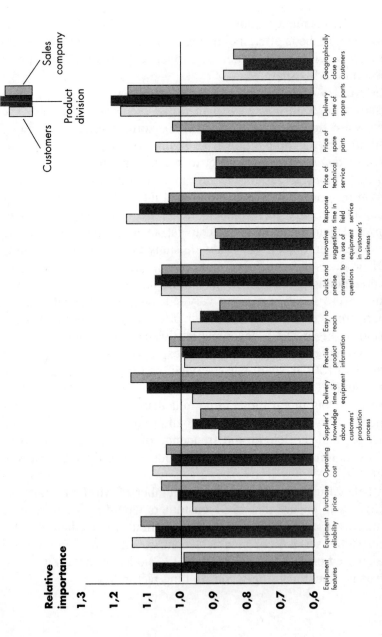

The three sources:

Sales company

Product division

Customers

Relative importance

Figure 12.1   Perceived relative importance of different MTC features within MCT HQ, within foreign sales companies and among end-users

12.2.6 Summary: key actions and key results

The seven most pertinent aspects of this turnaround case were probably the following:

1. clarifying the Business Mission to provide sharper focus
2. changing the spirit, and reorganizing the work pattern of the management group
3. changing the accounting and cost-allocation system, while making sub-divisional managers assume their full cost responsibility
4. using standard hardware and software for the internally developed robot rig
5. closing the Cleveland tunnel-boring operation, while still benefiting from corresponding knowhow
6. providing much stronger focus on after-sales service and highly reliable products than on a further increase in the technological development pace (since MCT was already the world leader)
7. a substantial strengthening of the extremely important international sales organization.

Taken together, these seven activities radically brought down the highly-inflated cost levels and turned a previously loss-making division into one with quite acceptable profitability and satisfied customers. Invoiced sales grew and market shares increased (as shown by Figure 12.3).

Note

1. The term 'tunnel boring' is here primarily used to denote so called 'full-face boring' where the diameter of the drilling equipment coincides with the diameter of the tunnel itself. (This is different from drilling with multiple drills operated in parallel, as described earlier.)

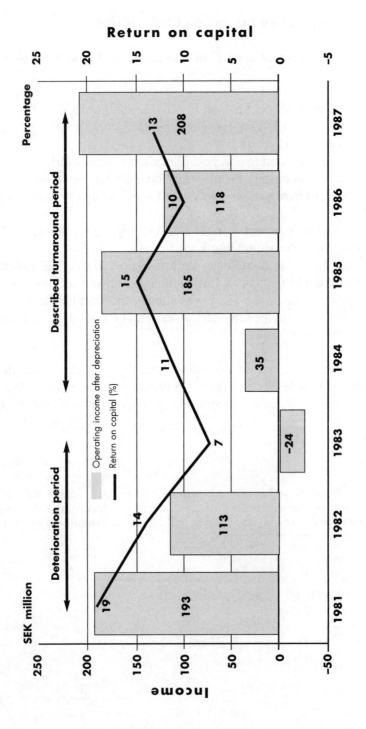

Return on capital

Percentage

25 — 20 — 15 — 10 — 5 — 0 — -5

1987   1986   1985   1984   1983   1982   1981

Described turnaround period

Deterioration period

Operating income after depreciation

Return on capital (%)

13   10   15   11   7   14   19

208   118   185   35   -24   113   193

SEK million

250 — 200 — 150 — 100 — 50 — 0 — -50

Income

Figure 12.2   Atlas Copco MCT: operating income and return on capital 1981–87

(Analyses based on seven annual reports)

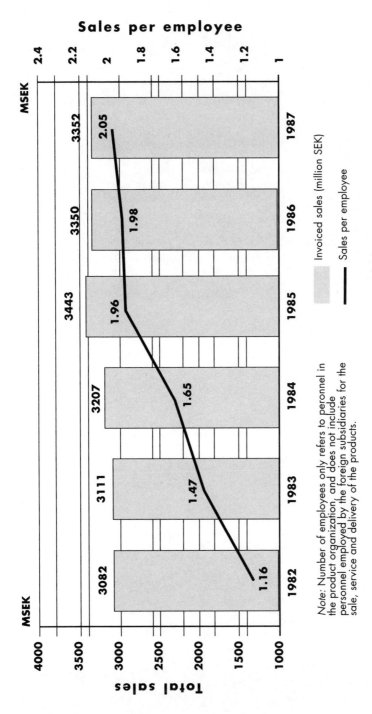

Figure 12.3   The Atlas Copco MCT case: sales value and sales per employee
(Company Reports)

Chapter 13
Almex

List of Contents

Introduction   **328**
    The company, its key products and target groups   328

13.1 Excellent products, but unsatisfactory profits   **328**
    13.1.1   An under-dimensioned central sales organization   329
    13.1.2   More on Almex cost levels, prices and profitability   329

13.2 Key elements of the new action plan   **330**
    13.2.1   Reinforcing the sales organization   330
    13.2.2   The new pricing policy   331

13.3 Results achieved during this turnaround   **332**

Score cards: **Performance charts for this turnaround**   **332**

13 Almex

Introduction

The company, its key products and target groups

Almex is a producer of ticket-issuing machines for public transportation. Such machines can be manual, semi-mechanized, or fully mechanized. The key market consists of organizations engaged in bus operations, that is city traffic and/or long distance traffic. In 1975, Almex was the world market leader for manual ticket-issuing machines. These are primarily used for long-distance bus lines where the fare structure is often so complex that manual assistance is asked for.

However, Almex also marketed semi-mechanized and fully mechanized fare-collection machines, normally used in city traffic or for other short-haul transportation. In this area, Almex met considerably tougher competition, but still enjoyed a decent market share.

13.1 Excellent products, but unsatisfactory profits

In the marketplace, Almex had a very good reputation for technological excellence. A big effort had gone into product development. Almex products were well designed, modern, and were known to perform well.

In spite of this, Almex showed *slow sales growth and unsatisfactory profitability*. (For sales and profitability graphs, see Figures 13.1 and 13.2.)

Around 1975, Almex was acquired by Incentive, an important Swedish holding company, belonging to the Wallenberg group. In light of the unsatisfactory profitability, the new owners decided to reinforce the Almex management team with a new executive, initially to work as a 'second-in-command', but also to substantially increase Almex's capacity for investigations and facilitate an objective but critical review of the validity of existing company strategies. A year later, this person (Per Wejke) took over as president of the company.

13.1.1 An under-dimensioned central sales organization

The manpower at company headquarters for sales and marketing tasks was obviously insufficient. One person handled all sales directly to Swedish clients. A second person handled the agents in all the other Nordic countries. In addition, he also dealt with the German agent. A third person was responsible for all other agents in a large number of different countries. However good the products, this three-person arrangement could hardly be expected to generate a very active sales effort or rapid sales growth.

Outside Sweden, the company's home base, Almex had only one end-user sales organization of its own. This was in Great Britain, a very important Almex market. In all other countries, a wide spectrum of different kinds of agent was used from highly specialized organizations, in for example Germany and Switzerland, to more broadly operating trading houses. The latter obviously had very little chance of understanding the Almex products in any depth, and could therefore not do an effective marketing and sales job. Headquarters personnel made very few field visits to non-Scandinavian markets and the follow-up of foreign marketing and sales activities was rudimentary.

13.1.2 More on Almex cost levels, prices and profitability

Benchmarking against Almex's competitors showed that the company's unsatisfactory profitability was much more closely related to a *pricing* problem than to a *cost* problem.

Almex had traditionally been run in a very cost-conscious fashion, where 'unnecessary' costs were avoided by all means, particularly in the marketing and sales area. A similarly cautious attitude had unfortunately also characterized the company's price increase policy. If any price increases had been made at all during the previous few years, these had been small, and Almex customers and distributors had become used to this pattern.

The conclusion was pretty self-evident: Almex's price levels could be substantially increased, provided that:

a. a reinforcement of the sales force was made
b. Almex's position with key customers was systematically strengthened.

13.2 Key elements of the new action plan

Since Almex had a strong position in the world market, it was logical for it to have good profitability. However, to achieve this, both Almex's sales organization and its pricing policy had to be improved.

13.2.1 Reinforcing the sales organization

The central sales organization, located in Sweden, was increased from three to five individuals. The newcomers were highly qualified, with excellent language capabilities. One was fluent in Spanish, English and German and assumed responsibility for Spain and South America. The other person was fluent in English, French, Italian and Arabic and became responsible for France, Italy, North Africa and several other non-Scandinavian countries.

In Germany, Almex's second most important market, an agreement was reached to acquire the previous sales agency, since its owner was ageing and not very dynamic. In France, an entirely new sales company was started in cooperation with the previous agent, but now with Almex as the majority shareholder. In Italy, a new agent was appointed to replace the previous agent, who had not been sufficiently active.

ALMEX (TICKET ISSUING MACHINES)

Key problems	Key actions
1. *Unsatisfactory profits (although Almex was a world leader)*	1. *Increased volumes, market share, gross margin and net profits*
a. Under-dimensioned central marketing and sales staff	a. Reinforced HQ staff as to quantity, quality and language skills
b. Weak international field sales organization	b. Starting up of own sales companies in Germany and France, replacing the Italian agent, and so on.
c. Weak central sales monitoring systems	c. Performance monitoring against targets, budgets and commonly established plans
d. Too little cooperation between HQ and foreign country organizations	d. Common activity plans and visits to key clients
e. Weak pricing policy and too low price levels (in general)	e. Benchmarking against competition, followed by substantial price increases

The increased manpower within the central sales department now made it possible to monitor progress much more closely and – whenever called for – intervene in major markets. Broader activity plans were developed centrally. From this starting point, national distributors were requested to submit their own marketing plans and sales budgets to Almex's headquarters. The same procedure applied to Almex's own sales companies. Not only were distributors and sales companies now closely monitored, they were also subjected to regular field visits in order to review their installations, performance, action plans and budgets on site, and also to visit key customers together.

13.2.2 The new pricing policy

As a first step, the general price development in each Almex market was studied. So were actual changes in exchange rates and prices of competing products. This analysis was then supplemented by internal production cost analysis, as well as benchmarking against competition. The conclusion reached was that Almex's prices could (in most markets) be substantially increased.

The reinforced marketing team now had both the *facts* and the necessary depth of *expertise and experience* to put a new, and this time a much more aggressive, pricing policy quickly in place. The reinforced marketing and sales management team was also fully capable of rapidly and professionally dealing with the negative reactions which emerged in a few markets.

13.3 Results achieved during this turnaround

From an almost static annual sales volume experienced over several years, Almex's sales *increased by about 40 per cent* during the first year after the changes were introduced. During a five-year period, sales almost *tripled*.

Profits doubled during the first year after these changes were introduced. During this same five-year period profits actually increased by 400 per cent. (See Figures 13.1 and 13.2)

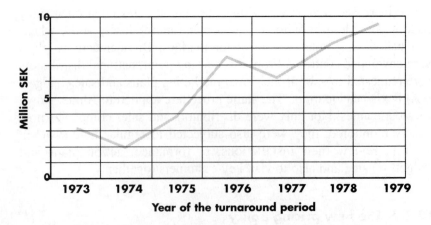

Figure 13.1   Almex – annual results before extraordinary items 1973–79
(Company Reports)

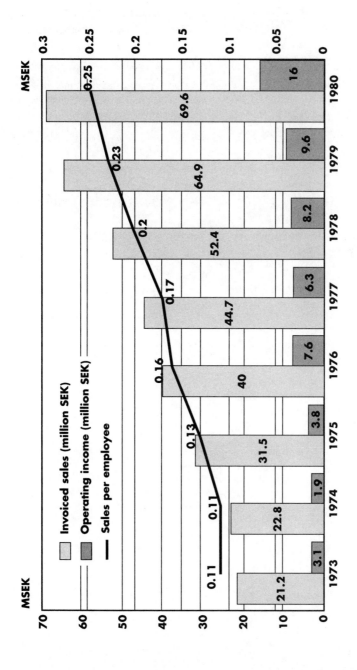

Figure 13.2   The Almex case: sales and income
(Company Reports)

Chapter 14
The Tarkett Case

List of Contents

Introduction		**336**
14.1	**Key stepping stones in Tarkett's development from 1900 to 1987**	**337**
14.2	**Main reasons for the substantial Pegulan acquisition in 1987**	**340**
14.3	**The introduction of badly adapted organizational and strategic concepts**	**340**
14.4	**The turbulent 1987 to 1989 years, including ownership change**	**343**
14.5	**1990: The urgent need to once again find a new owner while restructuring**	**344**
14.6	**1991 to 1993: An even sharper strategic focus and further divestments radically improve profits**	**345**
14.7	**1994: The first of two more ownership changes**	**347**
14.8	**1997: The merger with Sommer introduces a French owner**	**347**
14.9	**Strategic keys to success: core business concentration, internationalization, and two-way cross-border learning**	**351**
14.10	**Simple top management principles might be the most useful ones**	**352**
14.11	**Cross-border cultural shock sets in and the CEO leaves**	**354**
Notes		**359**
Score cards: **Performance charts for this turnaround**		**360**

14

The Tarkett Case*

Introduction

The Tarkett case justifies its place in the present collection for several reasons.

■ *While most of the other five cases have dealt with industrial goods having commercial clients as their end-users, Tarkett's flooring products to a large extent have households as end-users. Thus, this case relates to consumer capital goods (sometimes instead called durable consumer goods).*

■ *The Tarkett case is not only about how to save a deeply troubled company. It also demonstrates how a Scandinavian-based company managed to systematically break out of its Scandinavian home base, and become truly international. This was to a large extent achieved through two very substantial and rather courageous foreign acquisitions, resulting in the location of group headquarters to the European continent, with the Tarkett shares quoted on the Frankfurt Stock Exchange.*

---

* This case study is partly based on six substantial management reports relating to strategy, marketing and pricing issues (including three reports containing findings from 'face-to-face' industrial field market research among flooring wholesalers and retailers in the UK, Germany and France), issued during the course of this turnaround by Arpi International S.A.,Brussels. Of even greater value were three half-day interviews with Lars Wisén, then president of Tarkett-Sommer, Europe's largest flooring company. He was most helpful in *highlighting the management philosophy* of a successful Swedish turnaround manager, running a major group with its headquarters in Germany, but with French owners. The last of these three meetings took place in Frankenthal on 6 October 1998, only a few days before Wisén decided to leave the company, after a clash with the owners, widely interpreted in the press as a result of 'incompatible management cultures'. Financial data (mainly of a public nature) have been put at our disposal by Tarkett-Sommer's chief controller at the time.

336

- *Thus, in the last ten years, this company has not relied primarily on 'organic growth' by a gradual increase in its 'export activities' from its original domestic base, but on bold strategic leaps. These leaps have been associated with radical, multiple changes in strategic concepts, sometimes successful, sometimes less so.*

- *Step-by-step, this case demonstrates the switch from one vision and corresponding strategic concept to quite a different vision and strategy. This change was accompanied by new steering principles and a new management style, initially rather foreign to the German business environment. During the time period covered by this case, the Tarkett group's ownership structure changed not once, but twice. These changes contributed to a high degree of turbulence.*

- *Part of Tarkett-Sommer's success has been linked to finding good answers to the following questions: what to acquire, where, and when? What to divest to save time and money, and to avoid dilution of scarce top managerial resources?*

This case is based on the 'inside story', warts and all. The case description contains a large number of direct quotes. These reflect in substantial detail the management philosophy of Lars Wisén, the group's CEO from 1990 to Autumn 1998, and largely responsible for this success story.

14.1 Key stepping stones in Tarkett's development from 1900 to 1987

Tarkett's sales growth from 1900 to 1965 was negligible, as shown by the curve in Figure 14.1. In 1965, a decision was therefore taken to grow more rapidly through *internationalization*, and primarily through the establishment of foreign sales companies.

Lars Wisén (LW):[1] Tarkett started its internationalization by establishing sales organizations in Scandinavia, Austria, Germany, Holland, and other countries. This is a parallel development to many other Swedish companies at that point in time such as NIFE (batteries), SAB (brakes), and DINOL (anti-corrosion products). Even the Volvo group, (founded in 1927), still had no less than 65 per cent of their cars sold within Scandinavia as late as in 1964. Five years later, 65 per cent of a much larger Volvo car volume went to countries outside Scandinavia. Thus, Tarkett's internationalization drive must be seen as part of a broader pattern common to much of Swedish industry.

However, it gradually became obvious that the Tarkett group could not achieve more substantial international growth through production only in Sweden and it recently established sales companies abroad. Acquisitions were also required, both to broaden the product spectrum and to get access to established brand names and sales channels. The most important of these are mentioned below.

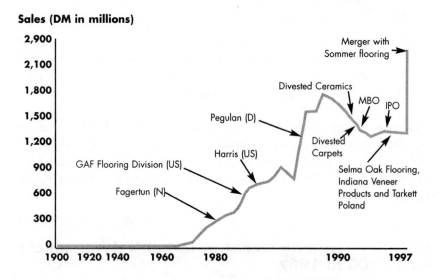

Figure 14.1   The Tarkett history
(Tarkett)

1979–89:   Tarkett purchased Fagertun, a Norwegian company. The well-known *brand name* was kept, and most of its existing customer base, but the majority of the plant was closed.

1982:   Tarkett purchased GAF's unprofitable flooring business, including a US flooring division and a factory in Ireland. (The last two letters in the GAF company name indicate the company's origin as an Aniline Factory. GAF also produced many other chemical products, including asphalt and roof coatings, of little interest to Tarkett.)

1983: Tarkett acquired Harris of Tennessee, US, a company producing and marketing wooden floors. Originally, Tarkett's Swedish headquarters tended to regard Harris primarily as a major sales outlet for Swedish-produced wood products. This was a major mistake. (The Swedes in reality learned a lot from Harris, for example how to maintain low overhead costs and how to develop better skills in sales and marketing.) Together with GAF's US flooring division, the Harris purchase added much to the Tarkett group's *North American presence*.

1985: A new CEO (not yet LW) arrived to head the Tarkett group, from his previous position with Gränges Metallverken. During the next few years, Tarkett rapidly acquired several flooring-related companies, including the very substantial German Pegulan company. (The Pegulan group represented a mixture of flooring activities in many countries. For instance, they produced PVC flooring products in Germany, ceramics in Italy, textile carpets in Austria and in Germany, and folio products in France. Pegulan also sold certain automotive products, including felt products for noise abatement purposes, presumably an interesting growth market.)

Through the purchase of Pegulan, the size of the Tarkett group suddenly almost doubled, from a turnover of DM800 million to over DM1,500 million. However, the latter figure included many non-core products and many loss-making organizational entities. Only through their divestment could the Tarkett Group much later (1996) return to profitability, but now with a somewhat smaller turnover, approximately DM1,300 million.

This case story describes corresponding turnaround measures, including some less than brilliant moves, and then the 'next big leap forward' – the merger with Sommer-Allibert's flooring division reporting a turnover of no less than FF4,100 million in 1996. It ends with a discussion of the 'management philosophy' of LW and the cross-cultural shock finally experienced in 1998 within a group run by a Swede, with headquarters in Germany, but with French owners.

14.2 Main reasons for the substantial Pegulan acquisition in 1987

There were several reasons for this acquisition which suddenly doubled Tarkett's size.

1. Through this acquisition, Tarkett could rapidly acquire a strong market position in the huge *German flooring market*.

2. Pegulan was much stronger in consumer marketing, while Tarkett was very strong in contract marketing (for example where the products were not used by households, but by construction companies and/or in public environments).

3. Pegulan also had products without any direct counterparts from Tarkett, located in Ronneby, Sweden. Some of these products were of little interest. Others had quite a strategic importance.

4. Pegulan had *important client contacts* within the German automotive industry, which was of great potential interest to the Tarkett group, since each vehicle contains both flooring and noise abatement products, for example in the roof and under the hood.

14.3 The introduction of badly adapted organizational and strategic concepts

Among decisions taken immediately after the acquisition of Pegulan in 1985 was the introduction of a (then highly fashionable) *matrix organization*. The new matrix included one product dimension and simultaneously one market dimension. However, this multi-dimensional concept (embracing divisions, business areas, business units, and so on) was quite foreign to most German managers. 'Who is really my boss? I certainly cannot have *two* bosses.' Others worried about exorbitant costs for this kind of 'double management' and 'overlapping reporting systems'. (Some managers even talked about 'multiple accounting systems', previously primarily known by Italian managers and then for purely fiscal reasons.)

Apart from philosophical arguments, it was soon found in real life that the new matrix organization was too cumbersome, too costly and rather difficult to manage.

LW: The matrix tended to create 'too many chiefs and too few Indians', that is too many office-bound managers and too few individuals out on the road, actually selling and carefully observing the needs and reactions in the real marketplace.

Strategically, the Tarkett group had simultaneously decided to implement a new total flooring concept. Corresponding strategy required the Tarkett group 'to be dominant, or at least to be a very substantial player for all types of flooring materials'. From this overriding strategic ambition followed a perceived need to create 'a complete assortment of products for all customer classes'.[2]

Not only was this full-service concept very costly. Many of the required new products were simply 'dreamt up' centrally. Without any previous dependable market tests they hit the final marketplace with mixed results. Many continental wholesalers and retailers were not yet ready to accept the radically new concept of 'purchasing all my flooring products from only one source'. For instance, German flooring distributors were used to buying their wood products from three or four suppliers. For PVC products the purchasing pattern was similar, although the suppliers might be different from those supplying the wood products.

LW: Although households might have been our end-users, the immediate market for the Tarkett group consisted of wholesalers and retailers, and they did not react positively to the total flooring concept. We were probably 20 years ahead of the market with our 'purchase all your products from only one source' concept. The market was simply not yet ready for this, but preferred buying separate products from several producers.

Having recently acquired Pegulan, the president of Tarkett was suddenly responsible for approximately 7,000 employees and a turnover of DM1,500 million. Many of the employees and much of the sales were outside Scandinavia. Good organization and delegation were called for. However, the CEO found it difficult to change his well-established, 'hands-on' way of managing, which was better suited to a smaller organization. Systematic delegation was not sufficiently used. As a result, too many small issues ended up on the CEO's own desk.

> LW: With hindsight, one might say that some Tarkett executives displayed more action-orientation than subtleness or deep analytical proficiency. They were in a hurry and fully dedicated to 'go-go super growth'. As a result, the handling of the 'purchased' German managers was also far from subtle. Only a week after the acquisition, 60 German key executives were invited to a meeting in Sweden to be 'provided with information about the future', including their own. At the meeting, the Germans found that most items had already been decided without any input from their side and with little concern for German traditions and mentality. (Grown men were seen crying with lukewarm champagne in plastic cups. Of the 60 executives and managers working for Pegulan at the time of the takeover, only two remain today. This reflects a combination of two facts: a certain weakness in the managerial quality of the German managers, but also the Swedish buyer's rather clumsy handling of certain highly sensitive personnel issues.)

In summary: the recently much-expanded Tarkett group had:

- too many loss-making sources
- a brand-new strategy not appreciated by the marketplace
- a matrix organization that did not work
- a CEO who found it difficult to adapt his management style to the new realities of a much larger and more international company.

Organization charts and steering principles were not adapted to the new situation. German executives left in droves. Effective cost controls were not in place. 'In many ways', said Wisén, '1987–89 were lost years, although much was learned from all the mistakes committed then'.

14.4 The turbulent 1987 to 1989 years, including ownership change

Pegulan was simply the backbone of the German flooring industry. Seen in a longer-term perspective, Tarkett's purchase of Pegulan was therefore probably *a correct strategic move*. However, in a medium-term perspective, say 1985–89, this acquisition led to both turbulence and a severe strain on the Tarkett organization. The subsequent change in the Tarkett group's own ownership structure added to this turbulence. This is described more in detail below.

The Tarkett group belonged to Swedish Match. In 1988, Swedish Match was in turn acquired by Stora (also known as Stora Kopparberg), probably Europe's oldest share-based company. Stora did not have a reputation for providing a 'swinging environment' for fast-moving, market-orientated managers!

After the previous exodus of German managers, it hardly came as a surprise that several Swedish Tarkett key executives also left as a result of the new ownership. They did not want to be integrated with what they perceived as a 'stuffy, bureaucratic, slow-moving environment, which certainly does not understand consumer marketing, so important for the future of the Tarkett Group'.

At year-end 1989–90, Lars Wisén took over as CEO of the Tarkett group. One month later, he had developed his turnaround plan. On 10 March 1990, the full Tarkett board was presented with this plan, that is, a Blueprint for the Future of the Tarkett group, and the road to get there. A key element of this plan was to move Tarkett's headquarters rapidly from Sweden to Germany.

(LW): We needed to get out of our rather limited Swedish home base. We needed to fully understand that the town of Ronneby in Sweden was not the centre of the world, not even necessarily the logical centre for the Tarkett group, particularly if the group wanted to survive as one of the four to five global players that I envisaged in my scenario.'

Tarkett's board originally opposed the proposed move of headquarters, since they expected quite a violent opposition by the unions, and many other negative consequences. Reluctantly, the board finally agreed that Tarkett headquarters could temporarily (that is for only two years) be located in Frankenthal, south of Frankfurt. This 'temporary' arrangement turned out to work so well that it remained in place eight years later.

14.5 1990: The urgent need to once again find a new owner while restructuring

In May 1990, Stora purchased the huge German Feldmühle company. In connection with this purchase, Stora needed cash. Lars Wisén was informed about Stora's need to sell the Tarkett group, even though the agreed Tarkett turnaround plan had not yet been implemented.

In this situation, Lars Wisén contacted several key competitors (including Sommer, Forbo, Armstrong, and DLW) to find out if one of them was interested in purchasing the whole Tarkett group. These contacts actually resulted in one serious offer in the area of SEK2.6 billion. However, the potential buyer indicated that he was not interested in also taking over the Tarkett group's loss-making textile carpet operation, at that time valued at approximately SEK300 million.

Partly for this reason the acquisition offer was never accepted by Stora. Instead, a well-known financial institution (CSFB) offered their divestment services to Stora's top management, and a new prospectus was under preparation.

However, in the meantime, Wisén found a buyer (an Austrian holding company) prepared to pay good money for Pegulan's loss-making textile carpet operation. As a result, Wisén declared that he did not think the services of CSFB necessary, since the rest of the Tarkett group could either easily find a buyer, or be 'turned around' (by LW) before being sold off.

The constant rumours about the Tarkett group (or miscellaneous parts of it) being sold to one company or another, created a 'mental exhaustion' within the Tarkett organization. This kind of uncertainty had to be dispelled, one way or another. Finally, at the shareholders' meeting in May 1991, the board declared that the Tarkett group was no longer up for sale. A turnaround of the group was now the top priority.

Obviously, *the Tarkett group had to sell off certain unprofitable parts, as well as all parts (profitable or not) which could not be considered part of the Tarkett group's future core business, as reflected in its Business Mission Statement.* (In line with this policy, the ceramic operations were rapidly sold off to Finnish interests, and a second textile carpet factory was sold for DM70 million.)[3]

Thus, after a period of rapid expansion, resulting in a decreasing prof-itability, came a period of *retrenchment*, including selective divestments and a shrinking of the Tarkett group around its redefined core business, now basically defined only as wooden floors and resilient flooring prod-ucts. (The earlier concept of 'a complete product range provided from just one source' was simultaneously scrapped as being both too expen-sive and too little appreciated in the marketplace.)

During this cost cutting and restructuring process, it became increas-ingly evident that certain Tarkett managers were not good 'change managers', but that they functioned well only in a stable environment, when presented with relatively few problems, few radical changes and few demands for hard-nosed implementation of fundamental changes. Parallel to a critical review of available management talent, the number of executive positions was substantially reduced.

14.6 1991 to 1993: An even sharper strategic focus and further divestments radically improve profits

The divestment of Tarkett's non-core businesses and certain loss-making entities *created cash.*

During a period of just two years, 1991 and 1992, no fewer than ten factories were sold. These divestments generated an income in the order of SEK2,500 million.

Both the reduction in overall cost levels, and *the increased produc-tivity* now characterizing Tarkett's resilient (that is primarily PVC) flooring products also contributed to *increased profits* and cash-flows. Indeed, resilient flooring products could now for the very first time be regarded as true 'cash cows', financing other Tarkett activities. Part of this cash was used to strengthen the group's wood flooring operations, particularly via investments in more modern production facilities.

From 1990 to 1993, the Tarkett group delivered a cash-flow to its owner (still Stora), in the order of SEK1,300 million. In 1990, when Wisén had arrived as the new president, the Tarkett group had only made an operating result in the area of DM10 million. At the end of 1992, operating results had quadrupled, and income from sold non-core entities contributed further. (In 1996, the Tarkett group showed an EBIT [earnings before interest and tax] of DM136.3 million on invoiced sales of 1,340 million. Thus, *profits* were up while *turnover* was actually lower than immediately after the Pegulan acquisition. This is typical for any 'retrenchment phase', while aggressive, uncon-trolled growth is often detrimental to good profitability.)

At the end of 1992, *an important two-year restructuring phase had been concluded.* Its key results can be expressed as follows:

- A new medium-term corporate strategy had been defined and, to a large extent, also implemented.

- A well-adapted organizational structure was now in place, with Tarkett headquarters remaining in Germany.

- The future Tarkett management team was to a large extent in place.

- Externally, the Tarkett group had now gained substantial credibility. The group's radically improved track record had impressed not only the marketplace, but also competitors and the financial community.

14.7 1994: The first of two more ownership changes

Stora's top management team had repeatedly been approached by CSFB (that is Credit Suisse – First Boston) concerning a possible sale of the Tarkett group – either as an integrated whole, or in parts. Instead, a 'leveraged management buyout' (an MBO) took place. On 4 March 1994, Stora sold the Tarkett group and in fact received 200 million *more* in purchase price than their own previous estimate of the group's value.

A new top organization, *Tarkett GmbH*, was created. This company was primarily owned by Goldman Sachs Capital Partners and Doughty Hanson. However, members of Tarkett's own top management team were also shareholders in the new venture, and with highly interesting stock options. The change might therefore be characterized as a leveraged management buyout with the full blessing of the former owners. After being able to show even further profit improvements, the Tarkett shares were finally floated on the Frankfurt stock exchange, with GS Capital Partners and Doughty Hanson retaining 65 per cent. The majority owners could put pressure on the new management team. The latter was also motivated by considerable professional pride and interesting stock options.

14.8 1997: The merger with Sommer introduces a French owner

In November 1996, Lars Wisén sent his board a policy letter. In it, he expressed his views about the future of the flooring business, stating that 'only four to five major players will survive, one of them being Tarkett'. Further, he outlined the objectives of a potential acquisition and/or merger activity, listed corresponding acquisition candidates and alternative financial constructions. (Initially, Tarkett's owners seem to have put this policy document rather passively aside with few comments and even fewer commitments.) Tarkett had by now become so profitable and so respected in the marketplace, that it was a highly interesting merger partner. It was unlikely to stand alone for long.

LW: Several potential acquisition objects/merger partners were analysed, including Gerfloor, Forbo, Armstrong, Sommer and DLW.

However, in September 1996, Sommer entered the picture in a more serious fashion. On 5 November, the same year, Lars Wisén had dinner with the president of Sommer-Allibert. Lars Wisén's suggestion was simple: 'If you sell me your flooring division, I will arrange for the Sommer-Allibert group subsequently to get at least a 50 per cent holding in the new Tarkett-Sommer flooring group'.

Provided with a 50 per cent ownership stake in Tarkett, the president of Sommer-Allibert would be able to consolidate Tarkett's figures with Sommer-Allibert's own. Thus, he would become the nominal head of a much bigger company. Heads of French companies of substantial size are often invited to join the French president on his foreign trips. Other benefits tend to follow.

The deal was closed on 3 December 1997. Goldman Sachs and Doughty Hanson were satisfied. They had sold part of their shares in Tarkett at a favourable price, and had made a substantial profit in the process. The president of Sommer-Allibert found himself to be the president of a much larger group, but initially without having to worry too much about how to actually *run* the merged flooring division. This should remain Wisén's responsibility and headache. Wisén would run the new Tarkett-Sommer flooring group out of Frankenthal. He remained there until autumn 1998, when he left his position for reasons later described.

The new Tarkett-Sommer group represented a major global flooring player, with sharply increased (combined) market shares, not only in France, but in many other major markets as well.

Well in advance of the deal, Tarkett had a negotiated credit line of DM1,200 million. Only DM705 million in cash was used for the deal itself (plus the assuming of DM250 million in debt). Although the increased debt-load weakened the group's credit rating, this was not supposed to influence Tarkett-Sommer's future credit costs. Sufficient buffers had already been created for their expected needs in the foreseeable future, and Tarkett-Sommer expected to continue to generate a positive cash-flow.

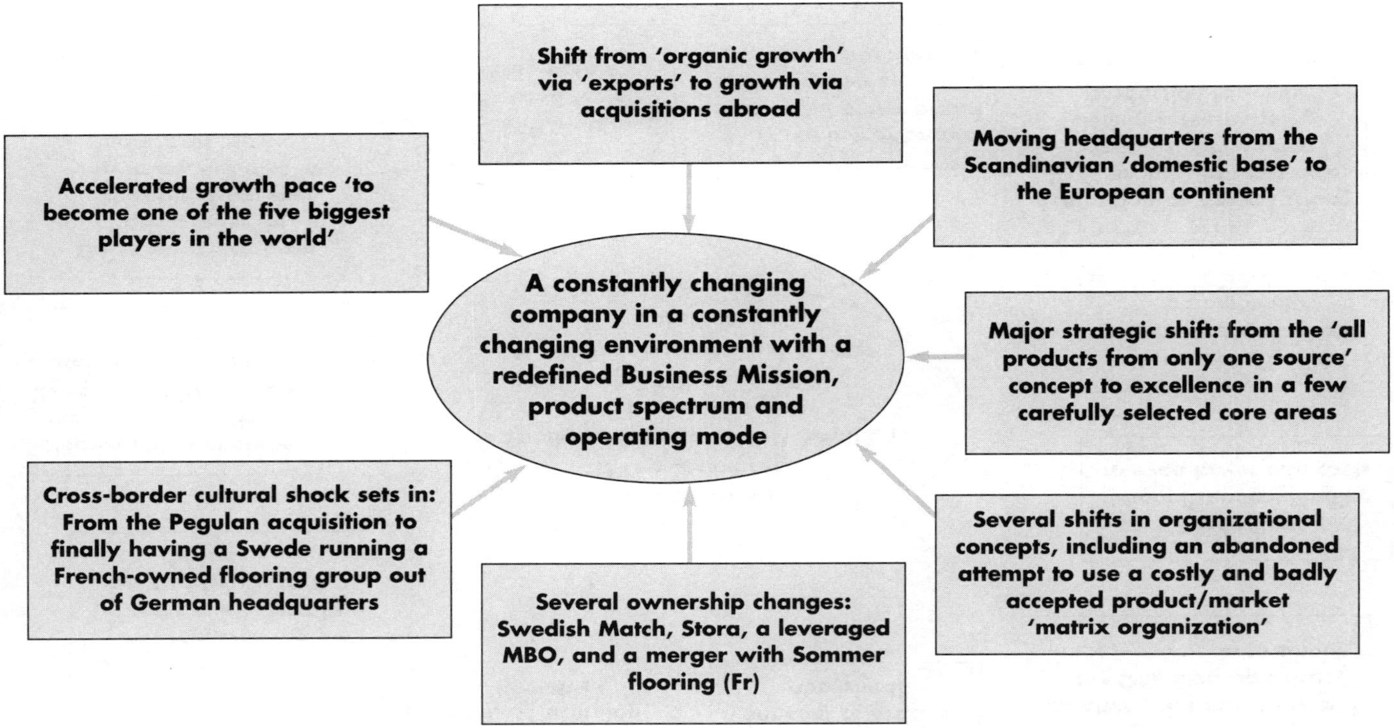

Figure 14.2 Major forces at work in the Tarkett case

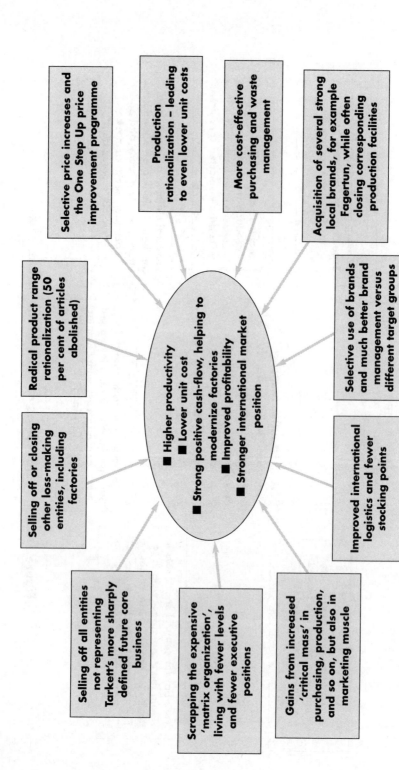

Figure 14.3 Some of the profit improving actions taken

Selective price increases and the One Step Up price improvement programme

Production rationalization – leading to even lower unit costs

More cost-effective purchasing and waste management

Acquisition of several strong local brands, for example Fagertun, while often closing corresponding production facilities

Radical product range rationalization (50 per cent of articles abolished)

- Higher productivity
- Lower unit cost
- Strong positive cash-flow, helping to modernize factories
- Improved profitability
- Stronger international market position

Selling off or closing other loss-making entities, including factories

Selective use of brands and much better brand management versus different target groups

Selling off all entities not representing Tarkett's more sharply defined future core business

Improved international logistics and fewer stocking points

Scrapping the expensive 'matrix organization', living with fewer levels and fewer executive positions

Gains from increased 'critical mass' in purchasing, production, and so on, but also in marketing muscle

14.9 Strategic keys to success: core business concentration, internationalization, and two-way cross-border learning

Previous sections have dealt primarily with the growth, internationalization and turnaround of the Tarkett group (now the Tarkett-Sommer group). What lessons can be learned from the Tarkett's turbulent but successful years 1990–98?

a. A company should stick to what it is *really good at*. In Tarkett's case, this is wooden and resilient flooring products, while avoiding product-range extensions into new, peripheral (and usually loss-making) areas.

b. *Internationalization*, together with increased size is a *key to the future* for most mature industries with rather undifferentiated products. (Tarkett-Sommer's expansion was by no means limited to Western and Central Europe. Eastern Europe as well as Asia were also important expansion areas.)

c. Moving headquarters out of Sweden was a difficult, but strategically correct move. Seen from a group-wide perspective, Sweden today only has a few Tarkett factories, some international logistic functions, and a sales force downsized to meet the needs of the Swedish marketplace itself. As to group-wide R&D, some development work is still going on in Ronneby, but it is limited to certain wooden flooring products.

d. The transition from being a predominantly Swedish organization to being a truly international organization, was only made possible by the physical move to Germany. It also improved the group's image as an international player. It demonstrated to the marketplace, as well as to Tarkett executives of foreign origin, that the Tarkett group places great emphasis on internationalization. Increasingly but belatedly, it also demonstrated its appreciation of capable executives of non-Scandinavian origin. (But the road has been long, and many serious 'corporate culture' errors were committed along the way.)

e. Having acquired Harris, many Swedish executives thought their task was to 'teach' their US counterparts how to operate. Today, the Swedish managers clearly recognize that they have instead learned a great deal from their US operations, not only with regard to cost-effective wood production, but also with regard to marketing and sales, and associated skills and techniques.

f.   As to the US, the Tarkett group might initially have been too polite and hesitant when it came to cancelling contracts with low-performing US distributors. However, today US 'carrot and stick' principles are more generally applied. Thus, good performers are rewarded, lousy performers replaced. The systematic review of 'so-so' distributors has also facilitated the early recognition of improvement possibilities among average performers.

14.10 Simple top management principles might be the most useful ones

LW: I place great emphasis on having happy, interested employees, positive about getting up and going to work in the morning and who are not afraid to speak their mind, or to enthusiastically try new things, and to learn from their mistakes. Employees should not be defensive, nor afraid of making a mistake, as long as it is done in good faith and the mistake is not repeated.

LW: I also believe in an organization in constant change. By frequently changing the formal organizational structure, we have created many openings for ambitious people who otherwise just felt stuck in the same old rut – and, as a result, were rather unmotivated.

In order to allow people to grow, and to turn local managers into truly international executives, Tarkett put international 'job rotation' into system. (Managers tended to accept gladly such challenges provided they felt they would be taken care of, if and when they wanted to return to their home country.)

Bo Arpi asked Lars Wisén if any particular 'management theories or principles' had been especially useful to him. Verbatim excerpts from LW's tape-recorded response follow:

LW: I certainly follow the academic literature and acquaint myself with new, promising frames of reference. I have used such inputs primarily in two ways:

1. More often than not, they 'scientifically confirm' what I have already found out myself in a practical way through my many years in real business life, including my own involvement in several turn-around situations.
2. Admittedly, sometimes the professional literature also gives me impulses to try new approaches.

In the final analysis, I fully recognize that *people make up the company. Front-line people*, including salesmen, are probably more important for our overall success than a handful of individuals at the very top of the company.

I try to encourage an open attitude in several ways. My door is constantly open. *Anybody can pop in and say hello.* As said before, I allow anybody to make a mistake once, as long as they *learn from it*, that is move on without repeating the same mistake. (Reason: complete 'mistake avoiders' also tend to be 'action avoiders', making the company grow stale.)

As to *work morale*, I have for long periods been the first to arrive in the morning and the last to leave in the evening. This sets an example, and therefore I do not have to talk so much about what I expect. People understand.

For the rest, *I believe in MBWA*, that is management by walking around, and talking to people who happen to come my way. ('Have you sold much today? What do you think about our new XYZ?', and so on.) Such MBWA should not always be done in a formal business suit either. Switching to a pullover is one of my ways to *level with the workforce*. Formal meetings with agendas and pin-striped suits might be necessary once in a while. However, such meetings usually do not teach me much about my organization, or about the attitudes of the average employee.

How do I measure *performance*, apart from financial data? It is easy. Once a month or so, I meet with one of our larger clients and I simply ask him what we at Tarkett do well and what we do not do so well. He will usually tell me quite honestly about any slack observed in our performance.

In a turnaround situation, the top guy might have to gradually change. Initially, one might have to be a somewhat dictatorial, but undisputed leader. Later, the saved company might benefit more from me being a 'team coach', who makes others act promptly, correctly and with confidence. This is a very difficult change process for most turnaround managers. Many simply manage to avoid this change process by moving on to another distressed company, needing temporary – but hopefully also enlightened – dictatorship.

Right now, after so much change, this company needs a somewhat calmer period. Let us call it a *consolidation period*. After all, we have sold 30 per cent of the company that existed back in 1987. Simultaneously, we have increased our profits ten-fold. We have new owners several times over. We have moved our headquarters out of Sweden and are today registered on the Frankfurt Stock Exchange. Through the recent (1997) Tarkett-Sommer merger, the size of our flooring operations has doubled. The majority of all these changes have taken place during the last five years. A somewhat more stable (but certainly not complacent) period might now be welcomed by many within the group.

Looking back, the key was really quite simple; just to *make it as easy as possible for our own clients and our clients' clients*. We first had to make our clients aware of what actually generated their profits. However, we also had to be quite aware of what is really attractive to their clients, that is to our end-users. Your own market research studies were most helpful.

In summary, I believe *one should not make things more complicated than they really are*. Yes, it might look quite complex and complicated at times. But in reality, one should try to *simplify*, go for the important things, and so make it easy for oneself. This also applies to the Tarkett turnaround case.

The *symptom* is often found in the marketplace, but the *problem* is usually found within our own organization. Fortunately, the *solution* can also often be found within our company, or at least in *the all-important interface between ourselves and the marketplace*.'

14.11 Cross-border cultural shock sets in and the CEO leaves

Through repeated interviews with Lars Wisén (CEO of the Tarkett group 1990 to autumn 1998), his 'Scandinavian' management philosophy and management style has been well illustrated (as above and Figure 14.4).

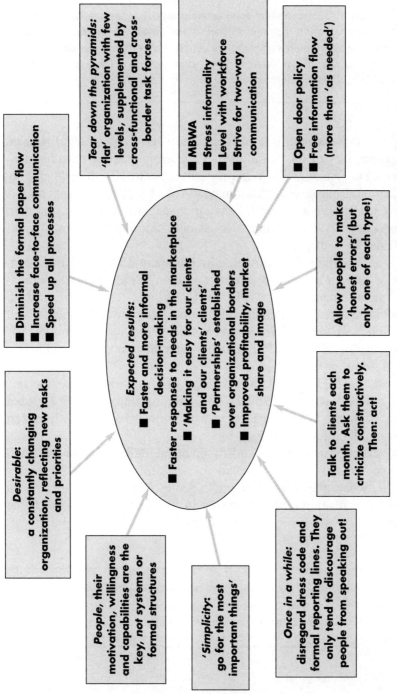

Figure 14.4 Key traits of 'The Scandinavian Management Style'
(Interview with Lars Wisén)

Diminish the formal paper flow
- Increase face-to-face communication
- Speed up all processes

Tear down the pyramids: 'flat' organization with few levels, supplemented by cross-functional and cross-border task forces

- MBWA
- Stress informality
- Level with workforce
- Strive for two-way communication

- Open door policy
- Free information flow (more than 'as needed')

Desirable: a constantly changing organization, reflecting new tasks and priorities

Expected results:
- Faster and more informal decision-making
- Faster responses to needs in the marketplace
- 'Making it easy for our clients and our clients' clients'
- 'Partnerships' established over organizational borders
- Improved profitability, market share and image

Allow people to make 'honest errors' (but only one of each type!)

Talk to clients each month. Ask them to criticize constructively. Then: act!

People, their motivation, willingness and capabilities are the key, *not* systems or formal structures

'Simplicity: go for the most important things'

Once in a while: disregard dress code and formal reporting lines. They only tend to discourage people from speaking out!

> The so-called 'Scandinavian' management style is characterized by flat organizations, open communication, a minimum of paperwork and formality, rapidly going straight to the central problem, actively delegating decisions to the lowest possible level, and getting a large part of the overall organization informed about and involved in the 'change process'.

During their work on this book, the authors have repeatedly discussed the applicability of the Scandinavian management style outside Scandinavia. Per Wejke, who has primarily operated within the highly multinational but largely Scandinavian-based Wallenberg sphere, has tended to believe that Scandinavian management is just 'modern management' and therefore also usually applicable in most non-Scandinavian settings.

The other author, Dr Bo Arpi, who has spent 25 years out of Scandinavia, holds a somewhat different opinion; although the Scandinavian management style works perfectly well in subsidiaries to Scandinavian-based multinationals, it does *not* work particularly well in a French or German environment, for example. This opinion has gained increased weight through the later developments within the Tarkett-Sommer flooring group.

Having just concluded the write-up of the Tarkett case for this book, the following newspaper headlines appeared on 22 October 1998: 'Two Swedish top managers within the Tarkett group have left because of a cultural collision.'

The article (from the Swedish financial daily *Dagens industri*) continued: 'Lars Wisén has had to delicately balance between a French owner, the Tarkett-Sommer group headquarters located in Germany, and several plants located in Sweden, where 2,000 of the Group's 9,000 employees are still located.'

> Further, the same article states:[4] 'Mr Wisén started to get irritated at French bureaucracy and prestige-oriented thinking. To his mind, there was much too much respect shown for the formal 'reporting line'.

When the time was ripe to decide how much of the post-merger rationalization (read: downsizing) should take place in France, Germany and Sweden, differences of opinion became evident. According to Wisén, the French owners simply assumed that most of the unpleasant downsizing activities were to take place in Germany or in Sweden, although (according to LW) the Swedish factories, long since thoroughly rationalized, showed higher productivity than the French factories.

A convenient pretext for letting Lars Wisén and his financial director leave the Tarkett-Sommer group was provided by the international financial turmoil which characterized the autumn of 1998. When the severe financial crisis in Russia blocked Tarkett's very substantial flooring deliveries to this country, much of the surplus tended to end up in Western Europe, presumably pushing the already depressed prices further downwards. On 1 October, when Tarkett-Sommer sent out a warning that 1998 profits might be 20 per cent lower than the previous year, the company's stock fell from DM33 to only DM18. (This might be compared to the situation a few months earlier, during summer 1998, when the Tarkett share was quoted at close to DM70.)

Upon his departure, Wisén made the following comments about the differences in management style.

1. 'Yes, we certainly represent different management styles. My own office door always remains open, while a Frenchman is supposed *to ask for a suitable time to have an appointment with his own boss.*'
2. '*French decision-making is much more formal and much slower* than Scandinavian decision-making. My own style has obviously been a bit too fast for our French owners.'
3. 'As Scandinavians, we are used to *making decisions as soon as possible*, and then *rapidly implementing them*. In French organizations, it seems that they have an unfortunate habit of discussing an issue for at least a month before a decision can be taken. Of course, in the final analysis, *the owners* will always have the last word. They simply *have the right to impose their will and perhaps also their management style.*'

Wisén was rapidly replaced by Marc Assa, CEO of Sommer-Allibert, the majority owner of Tarkett-Sommer. Assa initially refrained from any comments on cultural differences or incompatibilities in management style. However, to the press he stated: 'I intend to speed up certain changes which I hope will contribute to the full realization of the synergy potential. I also intend to reduce Tarkett-Sommer's very heavy debt-burden.' (According to LW, both activities had already been set in motion by the previous management team.)

SUMMARY

When the work on this case started, Tarkett-Sommer was regarded as an excellent example of how well 'Scandinavian management' could also function outside Scandinavia. However, after the developments described above, one is less convinced. Most French, as well as German organizations, are used to more *hierarchical structures*, more *formal decision-making* (that is following the formal 'reporting lines', relying on formal meetings, the issuing of comprehensive memos, and so on), and often preferring *less radical* and more gradual changes in their industrial structures.

What then about American and Scandinavian management styles? After all, the Americans are known to be at least as fast and radical as the Swedes. There are still important differences. For instance, US decision-making is usually more centred on 'the top guy who calls the shots' and who leaves nobody in doubt about what has been decided and by whom. When Swedes honestly believe that a formal decision has been taken, their American subsidiary managers often feel that 'although the meeting atmosphere was good, did we really take any decisions?'

Thus, American managers tend to prefer:

■ to know 'where the buck stops'

■ that decisions are *unequivocally* made, and quite *clearly communicated*. (Consensus around a table is not necessarily enough.)

One irritated US subsidiary manager once said to Bo Arpi: 'We have now been locked up in a retreat by the Swedes for two days. Everybody seems to agree as to what the problem is and what ought to be done about it. But where is the decision? The Scandinavian management style seems to be *management by osmosis*.'

Notes

1. LW is an abbreviation for Lars Wisén, from 1990 to 1998 CEO of the Tarkett group, nowadays called the Tarkett-Sommer group.
2. The reader might like to compare this with the costly 'full-service concept' indiscriminately used by the metal wholesaler discussed in Chapter 8, section 8.5.
3. In the textile carpet business, only a few major players are expected to survive and prosper. Beaulieu (Europe's largest in carpets) has a turnover in the area of DM2,000 million. In spite of such a size, because of constant price and cost pressure, even major textile carpet producers cannot carry any substantial administrative overheads, but thrive on cost-effective hands-on managers. (One such manager was recently seen taking multi-million dollar orders on his GSM phone, while walking down Beaulieu's production line, finally placing the order directly at the relevant workstation.)
4. The text is here slightly condensed.

The Tarkett-Sommer 'Vision' for the new (that is merged) company (released in September 1998):

■ Tarkett-Sommer AG is a flooring company. Our mission is to be a leader in the world of flooring.

■ Our ambition is to understand and satisfy our customers' needs in every respect all over the world.

■ Improving the company's value is the aim of our corporate activities.

■ The pursuit of excellence is the driving force behind all people working at Tarkett-Sommer AG.

■ We strive for excellence and, by using the potential of our two merged companies, Tarkett and Sommer, to create a one-company feeling.

■ Our aim is quality in everything we do. Therefore we understand that ecology and economy are simply two sides of the same coin.

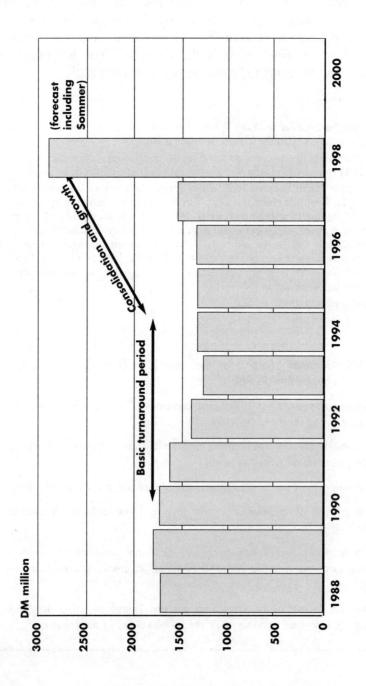

Figure 14.5   Tarkett case: annual sales values
(Company reports)

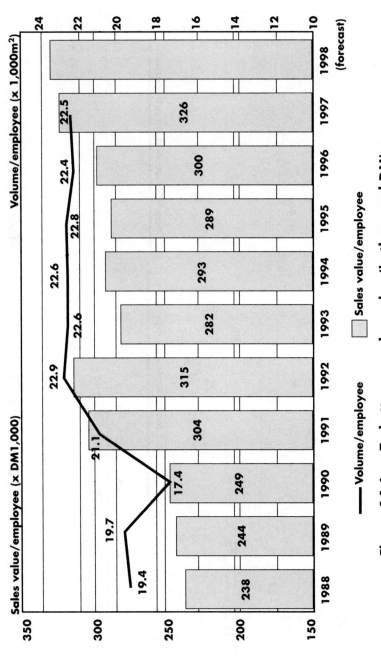

Figure 14.6   Tarkett case: sales value (in thousand DM) per employee and volume (in thousand m²) per employee

(Company reports)

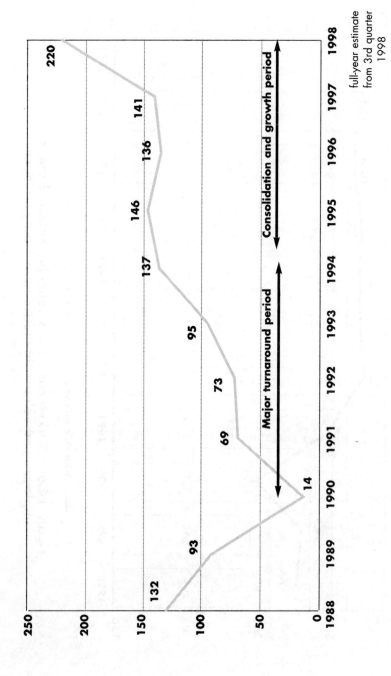

Figure 14.7 Development of EBIT (earnings before interest and tax)

full-year estimate
from 3rd quarter
1998

Index

A

ABB 86
   corporate headquarters 164
   creation of 163–4
   example of cross-border merger 160
   need for high cost-effectiveness 136
   post-merger turnaround 158
   summary of merger 288
ABC *see* activity-based costing
ABV 37, 89
acid test 104
acquisitions 6–7
   ESAB Group 268
   in relation to turnaround 7
   Tarkett 336
activity-based costing 68, 77
   advantages of using 220–2
   an analytical model 213–20
   application in turnaround situations 221–2
   capacity demands on the company 211–13
   characteristics of 220–1
   combined economic result 214
   complete computer simulation 233–4
   computer-simulated 218–19
   concept of capacity demand 213–14
   conceptual starting point 211
   in conflict resolution 238
   as a consulting fad 212–13
   cost allocation keys 223
   cost driver logic 223
   cost drivers 215
   costs in the sales function 217
   definition 212–13
   definition of capacity demands 212
   derivation of cost formulas 213, 215, 217–18
   deriving monetary values 215
   in downsizing 227
   economic realities 230
   as educational tool 234
   evaluation of managerial performance 225–7
   exemplified in the Business Mission Statement 211
   importance of understanding consumption of company resources 211
   managerial responsibility 226
   non-standard tools in turnaround 238
   order lines 217, 224
   organizational tension 229–33
   profit contribution levels 218
   profitability findings 218–19
   promoter of managerial action 238
   reasons for use 233–4
   results 222, 239
   summary of advantages 237
   test of techniques 239
   time pressures on 240–1
   in turnaround situations 211–44
   useful tool in the turnaround situation 214–15
   value of 238–40
   versus cost allocation schemes 220
   vertical distribution chain 227
   see also self-administered frequency study
AEG 85
Alcatel/DSC Communications 10
Allgon 14, 74, 246–64
   Business Mission 247, 262
   changes in organizational structure 258–60
   company development 248–9
   company growth 247
   competence 248, 253, 262
   equity 251
   and Ericsson 249
   financial controls 253
   foreign sales and production companies 253
   functional analysis 252–5

German market 250–1
increase in shareholder value 247
location a strategic advantage 248
market capitalization 247
market focus 248
market opportunities 248, 253–4
marketing competence 251, 260
Orbitel debacle 249–50, 254
risk 248
share prices 247
strategic decisions and moves 252,
   257–8
transfer of technology 250
troublesome situation in 1991 249–51
turnaround 251
US subsidiary debacle 250, 259
'wave propagation' products 247
Alloy Rods 277
Almex 327–34
acquisition by Incentive 329
analysis 332
benchmarking 329, 332
budgets 331
central sales organization 329–30
cost levels 329–30
cost-consciousness 329
introduction 328
key elements of action plan 330–2
management team 329
market share 328
monitoring 331
pricing policy 330–2
product development 328
profitability 328–30
results 332–4
sales growth 328
summary of key problems and actions
   331
technological excellence 328
world market leader 328
Amazon 196
website 196
America Online/Netscape 11
analytical framework 282
Ansoff, Igor 269–70
diagonal growth vectors 282
examination of the matrix 285–8

growth vector matrix 269
market development 286
Arcos 278
Armstrong 347
key competitor to Tarkett 344
Asea 86
announcement of merger 163
ESAB shareholder 288
post-merger turnaround 158
Assa, Marc 357
CEO of Sommer-Allibert 357–8
on management style 358
Assidomän 90
Astra/Britannica Zeneca 10
AT&T 150
change in corporate culture 150
credibility problem 153
example of cross-border merger 160
Atlas Copco MCT 14, 17, 53, 61,
   313–26
accounting principles 317
actions taken 317–26
analyses 320
benchmarking 316
Business Mission Statement 323
causes 316
Cleveland tunnel boring project 316,
   320
cost allocation 316, 323
customer satisfaction research 321
decentralization 318
economic thinking 317
internally developed robot rig project
   317, 319–20
managerial situation in 1984 315
MCT division 315
motivation 315
performance 314
PIMS database 316
political concerns 320
pre-turnaround 314
profitability 314
rationalization 319
service enhancement 321
strategic focus 315
summary of actions and results 323
value benchmarking 131

world leader in drilling equipment 314, 321, 323
Atlas Copco Tools 295–312
  actions taken 301–12
  Blueprint for the Future Company 308
  Business Mission Statement 113–14, 296, 302
  business opportunities 299
  causes of divisional problems 300–1
  corporate culture 305–6
  cost allocation 298
  cost levels 299–300
  definition of Business Mission 303–4
  divisional business concept 299
  future business concept 302–5
  identity 304
  improving cost efficiency 305–6
  international sales organization 298
  morale and motivation 298–9
  pre-turnaround 297–301
  product range 296
  profitability 296, 307–8
  radical turnaround programme 302
  rationalization 307
  strategic focus 298
  strategic plan 1982 303–4
  tools division 297
  viability 297–8, 300
Audi 51, 139
  see also Volkswagen
automotive aftermarket example 227–33
  active field selling 230
  activity-based aftersales studies 230
  advantages of using ABC 228
  application of activity-based costing techniques 227–8
  combination of information 229
  compensation 232
  cost/revenue model, use of 232
  fragmented cost/revenue situation 228–9
  gross margins 232
  identification and analysis 228
  incremental costs 230
  managerial responsibilities 229
  organizational tension 229–33

  profit margin 230, 232
  tension-reducing measures 232
  trade discount 232
  vertical distribution chain 227
Avis Rent-a-Car 89
AXA 92

B

balance sheet see cash
bankruptcy 22
Banque Bruxelles Lambert 92
Barnevik, Percy 164
BCG see Boston Consulting Group
  see also portfolio
Beatrice Food 7, 83, 89
  and mergers 89
Beaulieu 359
benchmark see benchmarking
benchmarking 34, 76
  against competition 118
  Almex 329
  benefits for international companies 132–3
  comparison with asset utilization ratios 104–5
  cross-border value benchmarking 131–3
  establishing numerical benchmarks 60
  externally derived 168
  productivity and value benchmarking 121–31
  profitability benchmarks 126
  purposes of 60, 116–17
  and reality checks 115, 175
  source of data for the Blueprint 167–8
  and strategic choice 108–42
  studies by Atlas Copco MCT 316
  and subsequent implementation 141–2
  value added 105
  verification of targets 98
Blockbuster 171
  creative accounting 171
'blood, sweat and tears' 65
'blue skies strategies' 17, 97
  value system within the company 176

Blueprint for the Future Company 4, 19, 76
action assignment list 113
and activity-based costing 211
compared to Business Mission 111–15
contents 69, 135–7
defining 68–70
establishment of 30
goals and strategy 114–15
implementation during turnaround 26–7, 71–3, 151
internal and external inertia 118–19
meaning and function 109–10
and the new management team 151
non-urgency of detailed implementation 37–8
not fitting the plan 89
openness about 159
post-merger situation 162
preparing and selling 39, 71
quantitative benchmarks and strategic choice 108–42
reality checks 118–20
and the revised Business Mission Statement 39, 151
summary 70
to save the company 109
see also turnaround plan
BMW 93
Mission change 138
purchase of Leyland 138
right to Rolls-Royce brand name 138
BOC 274
Boeing 120
Boston Consulting Group 281
brand names 278
access to established 338
Electrolux and experience of multiple 288
matching to other factors 281
Breuer, Rolf-Ernst 160
Brown Boveri 86
announcement of merger 163
post-merger turnaround 158
Business International 59

Business Mission Statement 4–5, 20–1
and activity-based costing 211
Allgon 247, 262
Atlas Copco MCT 323
Atlas Copco Tools 285
benchmarking 109
defining 68–70
formulation of during turnaround 23
formulation as grand vision 69
purpose of 6
revised under the Blueprint for the Future Company 39
revision of 26
summary 112
Tarkett 345
business process re-engineering 68, 123
Business Week 58

C
capacity demands 211–12
definition of 212
capital rationalization 96
Carlzon, Jan 64
turnaround of SAS 156
Case Studies
Allgon 246–64
Almex 327–34
Atlas Copco Mining and Construction 313–26
Atlas Copco Tools 295–312
ESAB Group 265–94
Tarkett 335–62
cash 30, 79–107
balance sheets 127
cash-flow situation in turnaround 35, 168
debt ratio 106
first concern in turnaround 60, 79–82
inventories and freeing up cash 96–8
inventory turns of finished goods and freeing up cash 97–8
liquidifying balance sheet 67–8
positive spin-offs from lowering inventory levels 98
quantifying cash needs and urgency 101–6
receivables and freeing up cash 93–6

renegotiation of loans and repayment
    schemes 100–1
  summary 81, 101, 104, 107
cash cows 281, 346
cash crisis 34–8
cash-flow
  analysis 102
  calculation 60–2
  projections 36, 60–2
  situation in turnaround 35
Central Statistical Office 127
'Chainsaw Al' *see* Dunlap, Albert J.
change management *see* turnaround
    management
Chrysler Corporation 71, 89
  attempted rescue 99
  cash extension to 82
  major divestments in turnaround 88
  second turnaround of 241
  see also Daimler/Chrysler
co-determination law 49
  explanation of Swedish legislation
    306
  and firing personnel 147
  participative management 49
  use by unions in Sweden 300
Cockerill Sambre 92
commercial press 58
compromise 241
conflict resolution 238
corporate culture 305, 351
corporate strategy 3, 23
corrective management action 255
  signs of need for 282
cost and profit techniques *see* activity-
    based costing
cost cutting
  alternative to 133–5
  and downsizing versus volume-
    improving solutions 40–5
costs 65–7
  austerity measures 65
  cost savings and efficiency
    improvements 68
  purpose of cost controls 65
  summary of controls 66
creative accounting 171–3

crisis management 4
  Allgon 253
  cash crisis 34–8
  cash-flow situation in turnaround 35
  definition of 31
  importance of Business Mission
    Statement 299
  as a key parameter of turnaround 32,
    174
  options 84
cross-border transparency 9–10
CSFB 344
'cultural shock, cross-border' 8, 339,
    354–62
  cultural collision 356
  key reason for collision 51
  Scandinavian management philosophy
    and style 354
  within Brown Boveri 164
current liabilities 104
customer interface 260

D
Daimler 138
Daimler/Chrysler 9–10
  ambiguous cross-cultural actions 138
Dalsbruck *see* Fundia
Data Saab 85
data service provider 58
database 127
  advantages 200
  important source of information
    during turnaround 200
  PIMS database at Atlas Copco MCT
    316
  search results 198–9
  types of information provided 201
  under-utilization by turnaround
    managers 198
de Benedetti, Carlo 86–7
  and cross-border takeovers 92
  selling SGB 90–3
  summary of SGB sale 91
debt ratio 106
decision-making 261–2
  speed 261

delegation 252
  need for systematic 342
  need for within Allgon 256
  see also Allgon
Delta Airlines 92
departmental myopia 25, 73
  activity-based costing as tool to
    overcome 234
  replacement for overview 234
Deutsche Bank
  acquisition of Morgan Grenfell 160
  rapid integration following acquisition
    160
Deutsche Bank/Bankers Trust 9, 11
  example of cross-border merger 160
Digital Equipment 151
  example of cross-border merger 160
dirigisme 52
discussion 55–7
  root causes of need for turnaround 55
distribution chains 228
  ABC-based profit information 232
  cost/revenue model 232
  organizational tension within 229–33
  and time pressures of ABC 240
  vertical 229
DLW 347
  key competitor to Tarkett 344
domestic turnaround
  versus international turnaround 7–12
double management 340
Doughty Hanson 348
downsizing 3–4, 79
  austerity measure of turnaround
    manager 109
  and computer-assisted ABC
    simulations 227
  cost cutting and 40–5, 79–82
  one purpose of turnaround 148
  post-merger rationalization 357
  selling an SBU rather than 81
  unions in Sweden non-acceptance of
    306
Dun & Bradstreet 59, 102
  financial ratios 102–3
  provision of on-line financial reports
    201

Dunlap, Albert J. 241
  management by walking about 242
  turnaround approach 242
dynamics 155
  evaluation of 181–2
  turnaround manager's influence on 181

E
early warning signals 24–5
  intra-company sensors of 186
Economist Intelligence Unit 191
ego
  living happily without consultants
    241–4
  and the turnaround manager 241
Electrolux Group 85, 106–7, 272
  multiple brand names 288
  specialization 272
Engellau, Gunnar 64
enlightened dictatorship 23–4, 354
  acceptance of 155
  purpose of 24
Ericsson 85
  and Allgon 249
  Ericsson Information Systems 85
  Orbitel debacle 249–51
  problem awareness 255
ESAB Group 31, 44, 74, 265–94
  acquisitions 268, 286
  brand utilization 278
  capital utilization 272
  cost advantage 273, 280
  demand 271
  expansion 287–8
  forecasts 271
  growth vector components 269
  market development 286
  market penetration 270, 285
  market research 276
  misunderstanding of current trends
    115–16
  organizing for change 282–3
  overcapacity 268–9, 274–5
  phases of the turnaround 269–78
  policy statement 273–4
  product portfolio/market share matrix
    278, 283

production structure 272–3
rationalization 275–6
regional warehouses 97
restructuring the European welding
    industry 265–94
revision of pricing strategy 279
risk-taking 288
'stocking subsidy' 267
strategic position 283
strategy 270–85
unprofitability of 267
Eskilsson, Bengt 274
    ESAB formula 275
    high-level strategy 288
    management team 288
    reasoning 275
    restructuring of the European welding
        industry 289
    risk-taking 288
Esmark Inc. 83, 89
Euro currency 9, 11
Euro-Disney 53
    Disney 171
Eurocompany 132, 244
Euromonitor 194–5
    turnaround information on CD-ROM
        203–5
    use of intuitive search engines 196
    website 210
    world market forecasts 202
European Union 9
    cross-border deals 161
    cross-border turnaround 49
    differences in turnaround within 53
    distinctiveness, need for 133
    EU law 49
    frontierless Europe 1992 87, 90, 131
    importance of country in which
        turnaround occurs 49–53, 168
    search engines and CDs 203
    types of cross-border takeover 87
ex post facto audit 175
executive myopia 23
executives, classification of 145–6
Exxon/Mobile 11

F
FAG Kugelfischer 44
Fagertun
    brand name 338
    purchase by Tarkett 338
    see also Tarkett
Feldmühle 344
Fellman, Renee 5, 100
Fiat 138–9
Filarc 277
Financial Times 58
    FT Profile service 191
    on-line information source 191
fire fighting 39
fire sale 82–4, 98
    as cash-flow booster 98
firing 146–8
    the controller 172–3
    discreet reversed executive search 147
    outplacement services 147
    summary 148
Forbo 347
    key competitor to Tarkett 34
force majeure 4
Ford 52, 138
    Alex Grotman's forecast for 139
Fortis 92
Frankfurter Allgemeine 58
Frost and Sullivan 59
    market research studies 192
full-service concept 359
Fundia 279

G
GAF
    purchase by Tarkett 338
    see also Tarkett
Geneen, Harold S. 31, 77
    3-dimensional management
        perspective 162
General Motors 89, 138
    Delphi 88
    major divestments in turnaround 88
    and SAAB Automobile 122
Générale de Banque 92
Gerfloor 347
GKN 274

global player 348, 351
globalization 10
'golden shares'
    state-owned 9–10
    French state insistence on 52
Goldman Sachs 348
government bailout 14
Grotman, Alex 139

H
Harris 351
    acquisition by Tarkett 339
    misconception of purpose of
        acquisition 339, 351–2
    see also Tarkett
Hoechst/Rhône-Poulenc 10–11

I
Iacocca, Lee 71, 78
    and cash extension to Chrysler 82
    major divestments in turnaround 88
    negotiation 99
IBH 89
Incentive 288
    acquisition of Almex 329
    holding company in Wallenberg
        sphere 288
intercontinental mega-mergers 10
international headquarters
    and expectations in turnaround
        managers 38–9
international turnaround management
    causes 3–4
    changes indicated by symptoms 23–7
    definition 3–6, 8
    domestic versus international
        turnaround 7–13
    early warning signals 24–5
    purpose 3–31
    symptoms 5, 16–21
    trends 3–31
    turnaround-like activities 6–7
    variables 33
Internet 77
    availability of pertinent information
        191–2
    information from the source 199

search engines 191
    use as information source 191–206
inventories 96–8
    purchased goods and freeing up cash
        96–7
ITT 77
    3-dimensional management
        perspective 162
    action assignment lists 303
    splitting the local legal entity 162

J
J. R. Nabisco 7
JCC 37, 89
Johannesson, Tuve 139
    Volvo's Business Mission 139
Johnson Construction Company *see* JCC
Johnson Group 37
just-in-time 96, 98, 107

K
kanban systems 96
key performance ratios 34
    example of 170
Kübel Group 38

L
L-Tec (Linde Technology) 286
Lackawanna 83, 89
leadership difference 45–9
Leyland *see* BMW
liquidation 14
    liquidation balance sheet 99
    stretching vendor credits 99–100
location
    strategic advantage 248
    strategic disadvantage 278
Luxor 85

M
Magnusson, Bert 37
management buyouts 7, 80, 83
    asset stripping following 90
management by osmosis 8
    Scandinavian style of management 359
management by walking about 62, 149
    Albert J. Dunlap at Chysler 242

cross-functional trail-blazer 176–7
source of in-house data for Blueprint
170
management philosophy 337, 339
management style 62–5, 288–92
American 358–9
and consequent cross-border cultural
shock 354
contrasting practices 161
in fully fledged turnaround situation
302
and importance of ESB board 288–92
key traits of Scandinavian 355–6
Lars Wisén comments on 357
and organization in Allgon 252–3
Scandinavian 354, 358
sending signals with symbolic value 62
symbolic actions 63, 148–50
management-for-hire assignment 74–6
satisfaction with achievement 165–6
managerial responsibilities 40
in turnaround ABC 226
manpower headcount 206
marine satellite communication example
235–6
capacity demands 235
conclusions based on ABC 235–6
external development of systems 236
key decisions 236
moratorium 235
price increases 236
SAS 'Annual Export Award' winner
236
SATCOM activities 235
system-identification 236
market research 189–97
undertaken for Atlas Copco Mining
and Construction 313
undertaken for ESAB Group 276
marketing myopia syndrome 149
Massey Ferguson 89
major divestments in turnaround 88–9
MBL see co-determination law
MBOs see management buyouts
MBWA see management by walking
about
mental exhaustion 344
Mercedes 138

mergers 6–7
between US companies 51
cross-border mergers, need for 136
motivational problems following
158–60
post-merger advice 158–60
post-merger, cross-border turnaround
164
problems with 160
in relation to turnaround 7
Merita Bank/Nordbanken 10–11
Mitbestimmung see co-determination law
Mölnlycke Group 289
monitoring 26
Morgan Grenfell 160
MTV Networks 171
multinationals 14
Murex 278
brand reduction 277

N
Nabisco 90
NCC 37, 89
Nissan 96
Nokia Group 86
Nordbanken 10–11, 82
Nordstjernan 37, 89
Norton Simon 83, 89

O
OCM *see* operating cash management
Olsen, Ken 151
One Step Up 41–3
website 142
operating cash management 93–6
receivables and freeing up cash 93, 95
summary 95
Orbitel 249–50, 254
cleaning up after 257
Orbitel debacle 249–50
see also Allgon
organic growth 337

P
parallel sales force rule 280
paralysis through analysis 62
in the Allgon case 259–60
Paramount 171

Pegulan 164, 339
  acquisition by Tarkett 339
  backbone of German flooring industry 343
  introduction of matrix organization 340
  loss-making carpet operation 344
  main reasons for acquisition 340
  product mix 339
  purchase as a correct strategic move 343
  retrenchment phase 346
  staff turnover since turnaround 342
  strong market position 340
performance-driven company 121–2
  avoidance of mediocrity 137–40
  cost-effectiveness 243
  criteria for 121
  Eurocompany 132, 244
  excellence 243
  from a turnaround perspective 243
  perceived customer value 243
  value benchmarking 124
perspective
  dynamic 282
  market-orientated 284
Petrofina 92
Philips 274
  specialised market segment 287
  see also Filarc
PIMS database 316
Pischetsreider, Bernd 93
Porsche 125–6
  threat of bankruptcy 125
portfolio 277
  Bo Sandqvist and product portfolio models 289
  Boston Consulting Group 281
  product portfolio 278
  product portfolio/market share matrix 278, 280
price umbrella 279
privatizations 6–7
  in relation to turnaround 7
problem analysis 26
  awareness within the organization 255–6

see also Allgon
Procter & Gamble 89
product programme evaluation
  Allgon 254–5, 261–2
  Orbitel 254

Q
quartile values 103
  establishing and checking 116
  manifest turnaround candidates 244
  repositioning by turnaround manager 244
  of a truly performance-driven company 121, 244
  upper quartile 77, 103, 107

R
red flag item 104
Redstone, Sumner M. 171
Renault 52
  and the golden share 51–2
  and plant closures 93
Renault-Volvo 51
  and respective profitability 52
retrenchment 5
  and recovery 26
  at Tarkett 345
Rolls-Royce *see* BMW
Rover 93
Royale Belge 92

S
SAAB 122
  benchmarking 122
Sabena 92
Sandqvist, Bo 289
  conceptual framework for turnaround 289
  marketing thinking 289
SAS *see* Scandinavian Airlines Systems
SBUs *see* strategic business units
Scandinavian Airlines Systems 64
  'Annual Export Award' 236
  turnaround 156
Scania 140

search engine 191, 196
   sophistication of 205
self-administered frequency study
   206–10, 237
   capacity demand 237
   company function 237
   cost drivers 237
   layers of vertical distribution system
      237
   leading to discussion 208
   limitations compared to ABC 240
   pitfalls 208–9
   protection of personal integrity 210
   purpose of 210
   supplementary analysis 208
   see also activity-based costing
SGB see Société Générale de Belgique
SIAB 37, 89
SIC code see standard industry
   classification code
Siemens 136
Simon & Schuster 171
SKF 44–5
   Blueprint for the Future 45
   regional warehouses 97
sleep-walking 234
Société Générale de Belgique 87
   selling 90–3
Sommer 347
   key competitor to Tarkett 344
Sommer-Allibert 339
   merger with Tarkett 339
   see also Tarkett
spin-off activities 88–90
standard industry classification code 192
   identification by turnaround manager
      192
   provision of pertinent information
      198–9
Stanford Research Institute 59
starting point for turnaround 115–18
state-owned companies
   turnaround of European state-owned
      companies 14
steel consumption 268
'Steelworks 1980' 268
steps
   actions to be taken 55

activity-based costing as an important
   tool 211–44
   discussions 55–7
   elements and chronology 54
   homework 57–9
   involved in turnaround 54–78
'stocking subsidy' 267
Stora
   acquisition of Feldmühle 344
   acquisition of Swedish Match 343
   also known as Stora Kopparberg
      343
   and cash-flow from Tarkett 346
   need for cash 344
   rejection of acquisition offer 344
   see also Swedish Match; Tarkett
strategic business units 22
   analysis of 57
   classic US cases 37
   key factors in selling a complete 84–7
   raising cash by selling 36–7
   sell or swap 73
   selling versus downsizing 81
'streaming techniques' 188
subsidiary, unprofitable 38–40
'sudden death' 29
   actions of turnaround manager 82–3
   and crisis management 34–8
   manager's emphasis under sudden
      death circumstances 38
   reaction of turnaround manager 148
survival management 15
Swedish Match Group 38
   and the loss-making Kübel Group 38
   Tarkett Group as part of 343
SWOT analysis 185–6
   definition 210
synthetic costing 222

T
Tarkett 17, 31, 73, 335–62
   access to established brand names
      338
   acquisition of Pegulan 339
   acquisitions 336, 338
   benchmarking 131
   Blueprint for the Future Company
      343

change in ownership structure 337, 347
competitive edge 130–1
export activities 337
future core business 344
history 338
internationalization 337, 351
introduction of matrix organization 340
key competitors 344
key developments 1900–1987 337–9
Lars Wisén 336
management principles 352–4
merger with Sommer-Allibert 339, 347–50
and One Step Up 41
organic growth 337
reasons for acquisition of Pegulan 340
restructuring 344–5
sales growth 337
strategic focus 345–6
strategic keys to success 351–2
strategy 337
successful turnaround 51
summary 349, 358
years of ownership change 343–4
see also Tarkett-Sommer
Tarkett-Sommer
Blueprint for the Future Company 359
cultural collision 356
financial turmoil within 357
profits down 357
and resignation of Lars Wisén 357
Scandinavian management style 356, 358
success of 337
see also Tarkett
teams
aspects of change 151
and the Blueprint for the Future Company 151
building the new management team 150–3
changing group dynamics 182
evaluation 156
improving group dynamics 155

issues related to rebuilding 143–5
motivation 153–6
qualities for turnaround 157
rebuilding the new management team 143–66
replacement of dead wood 258
as second in command 329
turnaround manager's responsibility to 158
time quality management 123
time-frame
establishing chronology of actions 73–6
pressures on activity-based costing 240–1
turnaround exercise and ABC 240
typical for turnaround 74
Time-Warner 188
Timken 44
transfer product 280
Trelleborg 106–7
Trends 58
troubleshooting 40
turnaround management 3–4
activity-based costing a useful tool in 211–44
change management under pressure 108
company size and strategic emphasis 140–1
definition 4
different kinds of turnaround situation 32–53
domestic versus international turnaround 7–13
implementation planning 141–2
key parameters 32
steps involved in 29, 32–53
success of 143–5
typical scenarios 90
turnaround manager 4
actions and reactions 82–4, 148
activity-based costing 211–44
advice for 161–4
aims and objectives 39
backing by the board 35
capabilities 243

and creative accounting 172
documents used by 58
duties 35–6, 71, 79–80
ego 241
evaluation of interim management
    team 156–7
as fire fighter 39
gaining acceptance of turnaround plan
    70–1
homework 34–5, 57–9
identification of core business areas 44
implementation phase 72
and international headquarters 38–9
key performance ratios 34
and the law 147
as maintenance manager 184
manager-for-hire achievement 165–6
motivation of management team 153–6
personality 54, 156
power base 35
qualities 72–3
reaction to 53
responsibilities of 4–5, 40, 143, 152,
    157
self-administered frequency study 210
as troubleshooter 40
and the turnaround plan 112
use of sophisticated information bases
    241
who to fire 146–8
see also Allgon; management style
turnaround plan
    business plan and other strategic
        documents 174–6
    employees as key sources 177–87
    external information sources 187–206
    group assignment 185–6
    group discussions 181–4
    in-house sources of data 169–77
    individual assignment 184–5
    internal accounting 170–2
    learning from management by walking
        around 186–7
    market research 189–97
    one-on-one interviews 177–81
    other data-gathering sources 205–8

outside sources 186
self-administered frequency study
    205–9
sources of data 167
strong impetus for change 207
use of benchmarks 167–8
where to get input data 167–210
see also Blueprint for the Future
    Company

U
unions
    opposition by 343
    see also co-determination law
Usinor 92

V
Valmet 73, 198
value added 105
Varity-Perkins 96–7
    acquisition by Caterpillar 7
vendor credits 81
    stretching 99–100
Viacom 171
    creative accounting 171
    and Disney 171
Volkswagen 138
    acquisition of Audi 139
voluntary liquidation 22
Volvo 42, 45
    acquisition of share of Scania 139
    benchmarking 130
    CEO Gunnar Engellau 64
    French block on 52
    future of 139
    Mission change 138
    non-international sales 337
    president Tuve Johannesson 139
    staying within Business Mission 139
    see also Renault-Volvo

W
W. T. Grant 99
Wallenberg sphere 59, 140, 288
    and Scandinavian management style
        356

see also Incentive
Walter, John R. 150
  change in AT&T corporate culture
    150
warehouse operator example 222–5
  activity-based costing example 222–5
  cost allocation keys 223
  cost driver logic 223
  cost formulas used 222
  evaluation of managerial performance
    225–7
  maintenance managers 223–4
  managerial responsibility 226
  successful turnaround using ABC 227
Wertselä 73
Wesson Oils 89
Whitney, John 41, 77
  and market-orientated solutions 41
Wiedeking, Wendelin 125
  rescue of Porsche 125–6
Wisén, Lars 130, 359
  Blueprint for the Future of the Tarkett
    Group 343

introduction of matrix organization
  341
management philosophy of 337, 339
management principles 352–4
on much-expanded Tarkett group 342
need for enlightened dictatorship 354
One Step Up 142
policy 347
and purchase of Pegulan 344
responsibilities after acquisition of
  Pegulan 341
responsibility for success of Tarkett
  337
Sommer-Allibert and Tarkett-Sommer
  348
Stora's need to sell Tarkett 344
Tarkett-Sommer president 336
and the turnaround plan 343
see also Tarkett
work in progress 96, 98
World cup 1998 53

Z
Zunis 85